"Everything about *They Bled Blue* is completely delightful: The story's delightful. The writing's delightful. The footnotes are a total treat. But Turbow's book isn't just for Dodgers fans — it's for fans of the game, the underdog, and just plain good writing . . . These are true characters who also happen to be Major League Baseball players. Turbow's wrangled them in all their *Bad-News-Bears*-meets-*Field-of-Dreams* glory and recorded them with the most finger-lickin' good sports writing I've read in a while."   *— Deseret News*

"A perfect summary to the wart of an imperfect 1981 mess of a season . . . A World Series trophy hoist worthy of any in the collection of Dodgers' literary history."   — Tom Hoffarth, *Los Angeles Times*

"Riveting . . . With a heady mix of reportage, biography, and classic play-by-play coverage, Turbow meticulously traces the arc of the team's rise . . . Fluidly written and expertly paced, this exciting look at a turbulent team will thrill baseball enthusiasts of all stripes."
                                      — Publishers Weekly, starred review

"The names are larger than life, the games are some of the greatest in major league history. But what makes *They Bled Blue* a fantastic baseball book is the passion. Love the Dodgers or hate the Dodgers, this return trip to 1981 will leave you pining for Fernandomania and wishing you were a kid again, sitting in front of your TV with two outs in the bottom of the ninth, Ron Cey at the plate, and Goose Gossage throwing smoke. Bravo, Jason Turbow. This is epic."
                        — Jeff Pearlman, *New York Times* best-selling author

THEY BLED BLUE

THEY BLED BLUE

FERNANDOMANIA, STRIKE-SEASON MAYHEM, AND THE WEIRDEST CHAMPIONSHIP BASEBALL HAD EVER SEEN

THE 1981 LOS ANGELES DODGERS

Jason Turbow

Mariner Books
Houghton Mifflin Harcourt
Boston   New York

First Mariner Books edition 2020
Copyright © 2019 by Jason Turbow

For information about permission to reproduce selections from this book,
write to trade.permissions@hmhco.com or to Permissions,
Houghton Mifflin Harcourt Publishing Company,
3 Park Avenue, 19th Floor, New York, New York 10016.

hmhbooks.com

Library of Congress Cataloging-in-Publication Data
Names: Turbow, Jason, author.
Title: They bled blue : Fernandomania, strike-season mayhem,
and the weirdest championship baseball had ever seen: the 1981
Los Angeles Dodgers / Jason Turbow.
Description: Boston : Houghton Mifflin Harcourt, [2019] | Includes
bibliographical references and index.
Identifiers: LCCN 2018043599 (print) | LCCN 2018051094 (ebook) | ISBN
9781328715579 (ebook) | ISBN 9781328715531 (hardback) |
ISBN 9780358358930 (pbk.)
Subjects: LCSH: Los Angeles Dodgers (Baseball team)—History—20th century. |
Valenzuela, Fernando, 1960– | Pitchers (Baseball)—Mexico—Biography. |
Lasorda, Tommy. | Baseball managers—United States—Biography. | World
Series (Baseball) (1981) | BISAC: SPORTS & RECREATION / Baseball /
History. | SPORTS & RECREATION / Baseball / General. | SPORTS &
RECREATION / Baseball / Essays & Writings. | HISTORY / United States /
State & Local / West (AK, CA, CO, HI, ID, MT, NV, UT, WY). | HISTORY /
United States / 21st Century.
Classification: LCC GV875.L6 (ebook) | LCC GV875.L6 T87 2019 (print) | DDC
796.357/640979494—dc23
LC record available at https://lccn.loc.gov/2018043599

Book design by Chloe Foster
Front endpapers from Focus on Sport/Getty Images
Back endpapers from Wally Fong/AP/Shutterstock

Printed in the United States of America
DOC 10 9 8 7 6 5 4 3 2 1

To the girl who came up with the title

Contents

Prologue

THEY HAD THE 1978 World Series all but wrapped up there in New York, the Dodgers did, their best team since the Boys of Summer standing poised to snatch a three-games-to-one lead over the vaunted and long-despised Yankees. Decades on, LA players would continue to insist that the title was as good as theirs, right up to the moment when Reggie Jackson literally hip-checked their destiny into foul territory down the first-base line.

The moment in question arrived in the sixth inning of Game 4, with the Dodgers leading the Series, two games to one, and the game, 3–0, on a home run by their own Reggie, outfielder Reggie Smith. Then Dodgers starter Tommy John put runners on first and second with one out, courtesy of a soft four-hopper just beyond the reach of shortstop Bill Russell, and a walk. The Yankees had barely even hit the ball but suddenly were cooking — most of all because this brought Jackson, Mr. October, to the plate as the tying run. Reggie bore an unmistakable swagger, his top two jersey buttons undone, the sleeves of his black undershirt meeting white sweatbands at his wrists, those trademark wire-rimmed glasses perched atop his nose. Had wire-rimmed glasses ever been so intimidating? A year earlier, Jackson had cemented his postseason-hero status with an all-time epic World Series performance, also against LA, with three homers over the span of three pitches in the deciding Game 6, spurring his team on to victory and himself onto a candy wrapper.

Even and still, Jackson or no, the 1978 Dodgers were in terrific position to handle whatever an unloving world might throw their way. Their pitchers led the National League in victories and ERA, finished second in complete games and WHIP, third in shutouts, and fourth in saves. Their hitters led the league in batting average, home runs, runs scored, on-base percentage, and slugging average, had stolen more bases than the league average, and were caught less. The Dodgers had placed six players in the All-Star Game, which the National League subsequently won. It was a better collection of talent, said many members of the team, than either of LA's 1974 or 1977 World Series clubs. Now the Dodgers led Game 4 by a trio of runs, and the primary thing standing between themselves and a short route to a championship parade was the guy they least wanted to see. Jackson stood in the left-handed batter's box, glaring at the pitcher. This was prime-time baseball, Reggie's favorite time.

Even superstars can't homer every at-bat, of course. This time Jackson came through by merely singling in New York's first run, a feat producing less overt drama than his homer barrage of 1977, but, starting only moments later, more enduring agita for those in the opposing dugout. Reggie's hit advanced Thurman Munson to second and, having closed New York's deficit to 3–1, brought Lou Piniella to the plate.

The right fielder promptly tapped a humpbacked liner up the middle, which Russell, moving to his left, reached in plenty of time for the putout. The shortstop, however — whose nervous glove had long belied his supreme athleticism — was coming off a season in which he'd finished third in the National League in errors. He nearly made another one here, the ball clanking off his mitt, a miscue that looked inconsequential when it rolled directly toward second base, allowing Russell to snatch it up three steps from the bag and race over to force

Jackson for the inning's second out . . . which is where things got interesting.

With Russell having been in position to catch the ball on the fly, both runners had retreated to their bases of origin. Munson, in fact, made such a belated start toward third that had the shortstop thought to reach to his right upon gathering in the loose baseball, he might well have been able to tag him then and there. Russell didn't, of course, because there was no need: an accurate relay to first base — which the shortstop provided, firing a bullet to Steve Garvey in plenty of time to retire Piniella — would complete an inning-ending double-play. There was, however, an impediment: Jackson, having backtracked, was rooted in the baseline only steps away from first. As the throw rocketed toward its intended target, Reggie did the only thing he could to extend the inning — he leaned ever so slightly toward right field, his hip jutting out just far enough to deflect the throw, which bounced off him and toward the grandstand alongside the Yankees dugout, allowing Munson to score.

The Dodgers screamed interference. Manager Tommy Lasorda speed-waddled onto the field, tobacco juice dribbling onto his chin as he argued at top volume with umpires Frank Pulli and Joe Brinkman. Pulli, stationed at first, later admitted that his view of the base runner had been obstructed and that he had little idea whether Jackson might have intentionally interfered with the ball. Brinkman said that he'd been looking at second base to call the force-out when the ball hit Reggie . . . or, depending on your rooting interests, when Reggie hit the ball.

The play might have been dirty, but there's no denying that it was smart. Had Jackson done nothing, the inning would have been over. The frame would similarly have ended had Reggie been called for interference, as he should have been. As it was, though, he got away with it, allowing Munson to close New York's deficit to 3–2, *The Sporting News* later calling it "one of the shrewdest and most significant plays" in World Series history. Had Jackson not done what he did, pitcher

Tommy John — whose previous two starts were a four-hit shutout over Philadelphia in the National League Championship Series and LA's victory over the Yankees in the first game of the World Series — would have been in the middle of another four-hitter, trying to protect a two-run lead in the late innings. Instead, with the Dodgers clinging to a one-run advantage, Lasorda pulled the left-hander after Paul Blair's leadoff single in the eighth. Two batters later, reliever Terry Forster allowed a game-tying double to Munson, and the game went to extra innings. New York won it in the 10th, and the Dodgers, instead of being one win from a Series victory, found things knotted at two games apiece. It wrecked them.

"The problem," explained third baseman Ron Cey, looking back, "is that we had an afternoon start the next day, so we went from 2 a.m. in an extra-inning game to 12 o'clock in a heartbeat. If Game 5 had been a night game, we might've been okay, but the early start swung the pendulum heavily in favor of the Yankees. They had hope and we were down. We didn't digest it very well. If the thing would've been reversed, *we* would have been energized to put the nail in the coffin with an early start, and *they* would've had a tough time getting through it."

"We made one mistake," said an angry Davey Lopes in the aftermath. "The ball should have been thrown at Jackson's face. Then we would have seen how smart he was."

Gone was the previous high of winning the Series' first two games. Erased was what had appeared to be a signature moment — Bob Welch's Game 2–ending strikeout of Jackson, who'd driven in all of New York's runs to that point, in an epic nine-pitch showdown. The Dodgers had been giddy after that victory. It was the last game they'd win until April.

From the moment of Reggie's hip-check, the Yankees outscored LA 21–4, winning four straight after dropping the first two. "Unfortunately," said Tommy John, "we'll be remembered for the last six games and not for the first 166."

He was right, at least in the short term. The hangover from '78 would haunt a lost 1979 campaign that saw Los Angeles in last place at the All-Star break and 11½ games off the pace at season's end. A rebound in 1980 fell short with a dramatic playoff loss to Houston, after which the Dodgers spent the winter, like the winter of '78, thinking about what, exactly, had gone wrong.

Whatever it was — and there was plenty to process — proved instrumental in propelling LA to a long-evasive championship in 1981. It was a last-gasp stab at immortality, that '81 campaign, for a tenacious lineup that, with rosters far more talented than the 1981 version, had yet to be the final team standing. Compounded failures — World Series defeats in 1974, 1977, and 1978; the loss to Houston six months earlier — served to inform that 1981 squad. The players knew that odds were against them, but they also knew enough to minimize such negativity. With a big assist from the quirks of a schedule interrupted, the Dodgers spent the ensuing months putting theory to test. Questions abounded about their age, their health, their motivation, their payroll, and their leadership, but the core of the team was essentially the same as it had been two years earlier, back when they considered themselves to be of championship caliber. Their primary concern was time; with a starting lineup where the average age was above 30, it was running out. If these Dodgers — in their current iteration, anyway — were going to win a title, they'd have to do it soon.

By the time the 1981 season concluded, the Dodgers' lineup boasted nearly as many heroes as there were positions on the field, guys like Dusty Baker and Steve Garvey and Rick Monday, without whose timely feats the team would almost certainly have failed to advance through the postseason. Guys like Burt Hooton and Jerry Reuss and an unknown rookie named Valenzuela, upon whose arms the roster relied for enduring stretches. Those players — composing a roster with 66 combined All-Star appearances but not a single Hall of Fame plaque — pushed this team to its eventual heights, lending greatness to a roster projected to top out at something less than it eventually

became. It is their stories that make this ballclub, which has been relatively lost amid the shuffle of champions that remain fresher in our
collective consciousness — including the 1988 Dodgers, seven years
later — so compelling. It was the end of one era and the beginning of
another, the first chance for some and a last chance for others. Ultimately, chances are what we make of them.

The catch with this team is that the 1981 Dodgers did not do particularly well in this regard. They were presented opportunity after
opportunity, throughout the season and into the playoffs, and managed to grab on to startlingly few of them — right up until the players looked around and realized that last-chance options are options
nonetheless, and could be used to great effect.

That, though, would come later. First, there was a season to play,
and everything began with the manager.

1

The Manager

TOMMY LASORDA WAS always a shill. Long before he became a fount of managerial enthusiasm and brand fealty, he was a shill. Back when he was a career minor league pitcher, and then a scout, and then off to manage in remote minor league outposts like Pocatello and Ogden, in the employ of the Dodgers nearly every step of the way, even then he was a shill. The guy loved his team and wasn't shy about letting the world know it.

Stories abound about the point at which Lasorda became relevant to his superiors in the Dodgers organization. It might have been a bus trip in 1950 during the then-22-year-old's fourth professional season, with the franchise's Triple-A club in Montreal. A rookie scout named Al Campanis plopped down alongside the left-hander, full of compliments for his passion, and intoned that Lasorda was the type of guy with whom Campanis would someday staff his own front office. The pitcher couldn't have cared less; at that point, Campanis was a nobody. Sure enough, though, the scout eventually became a key executive, and 23 years later brought Lasorda to Los Angeles, first as a coach, then as manager.

The personality traits that appealed to Campanis were enumerated in 1958 by *The Sporting News*, when Lasorda was a 12-year veteran, still toiling in Montreal. "When not pitching, Lasorda does the coaching at first base," the article reported. "He runs the pitching staff for manager [Clay] Bryant, aside from assignments. He runs the pitchers in the outfield when they're not scheduled to work. He runs with them. He bats for the fielding warm-ups. When the team is on the road, Lasorda handles train and plane transportation, books the players into hotels, ladles out the meal money, looks after injuries and, when necessary, hospitalization. Sometimes he sleeps!" Lasorda had by that point enjoyed two major league cups of coffee with Brooklyn, and one with the Kansas City Athletics. He was 30 years old and likely out of chances for another, so he made his mark however he could.

Lasorda joined the Dodgers organization at age 21 in November 1948, drafted off the roster of his hometown Phillies, for whom he had played two minor league seasons. He was immediately struck by the unparalleled scope of Brooklyn's minor league operation, starting with his first day at training camp in Vero Beach, Florida. It was the second year of existence for the facility known as Dodgertown, and Lasorda watched in awe as nearly 700 players milled about in color-coded uniforms, shifting from field to field, drill to drill, coaches referring to them strictly by uniform color and number. As a guy intent on making a name for himself, Lasorda found the anonymity distressing.

His former team in Philadelphia had just finished 22 games under .500, its 16th straight second-division run, but there was little question that the Phillies gave Lasorda a better chance to reach the big leagues than pitching-rich Brooklyn. Hell, at least people in Philly knew his name. This is how the farmhand, not even 24 hours into his Dodgers tenure, came to seek out minor league director Fresco Thompson and request a trade. Thompson laughed out loud at the audacity. "Son, you've been here one day," he offered. "Stick around."

Sticking around was something at which Lasorda proved enduringly capable. He all but defined the concept of the Four-A player — somebody better than most minor leaguers, but not quite good enough for the Show. Left-handedness and tenacity allowed him to spend most of 11 years in Triple-A, primarily with the Montreal Royals, plus those brief stints with Brooklyn (13 innings across two years) and half a season in Kansas City, where he put up a 6.07 ERA for base-ball's worst team.*

The difference between the pitcher and most of his teammates was that Lasorda played angry. The trait was integral to whatever success he enjoyed—he was a key cog on four International League champions in Montreal—but could be so pronounced that Dodgers brass came to view it as a flaw, detrimental to his long-term success. Examples are legion. Lasorda fought with Billy Martin in the big leagues and Norm Laker in the minors, both scraps spurred by one too many inside pitches. During a winter league game in Cuba, he buzzed an opponent, Lorenzo Cabrera, then, after the guy had the temerity to complain about it, drilled him in the ribs. Lasorda told the story of throwing three straight balls to Phillies third baseman Willie Jones before drilling him, admitting later to Dodgers GM Buzzie Bavasi that "I knew I couldn't throw him three straight strikes."†

---

* Lasorda's best chance at a regular big league job ended before it even began. In February 1953, the Dodgers, loaded with pitching, sold Lasorda and short-stop Billy Hunter to the St. Louis Browns for a combined $140,000. Lasorda responded with a spring training in San Bernardino, California, good enough for pitching coach Harry Brecheen to inform him, on the ride home to open the season, that he'd earned a spot in the starting rotation. The position lasted until the train reached Phoenix, when Browns owner Bill Veeck boarded and informed Lasorda that because the American League had rejected the Browns' proposed move to Baltimore, the team could no longer afford to keep both Lasorda *and* Hunter, and that the pitcher was reluctantly being returned to the Dodgers. Having missed spring training with Brooklyn, Lasorda went to Montreal for the fourth straight season.

† Lasorda's willingness to brawl was so pronounced that his managers occasionally used it to their advantage. In 1956, Denver Bears skipper Ralph Houk, upset over the fact that his team had allowed 32 runs over the first two games of a playoff series against Omaha, asked Lasorda if he could shake things up in the third game by starting a fight. Lasorda wasn't even scheduled to pitch, but his answer—"What inning?"—was as concise as his response was thorough. Stationed in the first-base coach's box—a typical assignment on his off-days—Lasorda fielded a foul bunt and returned it to the mound by firing it as hard as he could at the pitcher's legs, leading to a donnybrook in the middle of the

If the story is true, it happened in spring training, because Lasorda never faced Jones during the regular season. In fact, he hit only one batter during his brief stint in Brooklyn — Gene Freese of the Pirates — in an at-bat that was entirely representative of the left-hander's approach. It occurred in Lasorda's second appearance after being called up in early May, as the Dodgers' fifth pitcher in a blowout game. Things did not go well: the five batters in front of Freese touched the pitcher for, in order, a walk, a single, another single, a home run, and another walk. Before anybody knew what was happening, the Dodgers were at the wrong end of a 15–1 laugher, and Lasorda's ERA had doubled, from 9.00 to 18.00.* It'd be easy to think that he hit the next batter, Freese, out of sheer frustration, but there was more to the story. The previous winter, while pitching in the Dominican League, Lasorda got into a fistfight with one of his own teammates over an opposing batter he'd drilled. The batter in question was the selfsame Gene Freese, and the teammate with whom he brawled was Gene's brother, George. This was simply payback.

"I'd fight just for the fun of it," Lasorda recalled after his career was over. "I was in training to become a professional fighter when I signed my first pro contract. I'm positive I'd have become a champion. I used to love to throw at a hitter and see him lying there, looking up at the big Dodger in the sky."

The brawls sparked by Lasorda's relentless hail of knockdown

---

diamond. It satisfied Houk's intent — Denver took four straight to win the series — but Lasorda later received a telegram from league president Ed Doherty that read: "Dear Tom, the exhibition you put on last night was a disgrace to baseball. You're hereby fined $100 and, furthermore, my advice to you is, if you want to fight, join the International Boxing Congress."

* Lasorda would pitch one more inning for Brooklyn before being returned to the minors. When he protested the decision, Bavasi calmly asked whom he should cut to maintain a roster spot for the pitcher. In what would become one of the manager's favorite stories, Lasorda named a fellow rookie. "If I was in charge," he proclaimed, "I'd cut that Sandy Koufax kid."

pitches raised such cumulative furor within the Dodgers organization that in 1960 Bavasi effectively excommunicated the pitcher, kicking him off the Montreal roster with instructions to never return. Lasorda was devastated. Entirely unprepared to do anything else with his life, he pled for another chance. He could reform, he said. He would pitch nicely, toe the company line, do whatever it took. It wasn't enough. When Bavasi refuted his entreaties cold, the almost-ex-pitcher fired the lone arrow remaining in his quiver and urged his boss to read a letter he'd sent to Campanis years earlier in which he proclaimed undying loyalty to the organization, long before such loyalty was a prerequisite for sustained employment. The GM may have been exasperated, but he knew a good thing when he saw it. Bavasi still wasn't prepared to tolerate any more of Lasorda's shenanigans as a pitcher, but he was sufficiently swayed to hire him on as a scout. At age 33, Lasorda's pitching career was finished.

Having brushed close enough to unemployment to be scared by it, Lasorda set about making a lasting impression. He was still five years away from his first minor league managerial post, but when a temporary spot cropped up during spring training to pilot the team's Single-A Greenville affiliate, Lasorda grabbed it and ran, taking over just in time for an intrasquad scrimmage against the much more seasoned Triple-A franchise from Spokane. It was an unimportant contest, but it goes a long way toward illustrating the type of manager he would one day become.

Just before the first pitch, Lasorda assembled the Greenville team in the dugout and began to pace. As he paced, he talked. "Look at that manager over there," he said, pointing across the field at Spokane skipper Preston Gómez. "This is really ridiculous. This is really sickening." At that point, Lasorda relayed a conversation he'd overheard between Gómez and Fresco Thompson during which Gómez openly questioned the decision to schedule his team against so lowly an opponent as Greenville. So lowly an opponent? Never mind that Lasorda had only just met the Greenville players — the interim manager was

having none of it. "That's a disgrace!" he spat. Lasorda openly positioned it as a challenge, proclaiming that were he on the mound, he
would knock down every member of the Spokane lineup. Were he
pitching, by God, those Spokane guys would know they'd been in a
ballgame. If he was running the bases, he shouted, he'd barrel into
infielders like they were bowling pins. He'd swing the bat as if his dignity depended on it. Then he got serious. "The worst thing you could
possibly do to that man" — Lasorda again pointed at Gómez — "is to
beat his team today. I mean, it's probably impossible. Those guys are
just one step from the major leagues. But do you have any idea what a
feather in your caps it would be if you went out there and beat them?"

It was a bald-faced ploy, a transparent effort to artificially extract
an extra ounce of effort from his players. And it worked in every way.
Lasorda's team, kids in their early twenties, jumped up hollering, passion flowing from their pores. The game wasn't even halfway finished
when Gómez approached Lasorda to ask what the hell was going
on. He was trying only to get in some work for his players in an intrasquad exhibition, and Greenville was playing like a pennant was
on the line . . . and also, for some reason, relentlessly cursing out the
opposing manager.*

Lasorda, of course, had completely fabricated the reason for his in-
dignation: the conversation for which Gómez had been so roundly
condemned never occurred. It didn't matter. The Spinners beat Spokane. For their short time with Lasorda at the helm, the Spinners beat
darn near everybody.† For Lasorda, it was only a start. One morning
shortly after that epic first victory, the interim manager gave his interim players a plan for further psychological warfare against their
intramural opponents, informing the team that toward the end of

---

* When Lasorda took over the Dodgers in 1977, Gómez became his third-base
coach.

† As with many of Lasorda's stories, the details are difficult to verify, their exclusive source being Lasorda himself.

lunch one day he would shout the words "Greenville ballclub" across the Dodgertown cafeteria. "No matter what you guys are doing," he ordered, "drop everything and scream, 'Yes, sir!'" Then, he said, the entire club was to race from the room together.

For Lasorda, the plan had less to do with the players than with the witnesses. He made sure to eat with Thompson and Campanis that day, and as they were finishing he announced to his tablemates that he had something to show them. Standing up, he hollered, "Greenville ballclub!"

From across the dining hall came the enthusiastic reply: "Yes, sir!"

Lasorda screamed "Let's go get them!" and charged from the room, fist raised, his players whooping loudly at his tail. He'd barely taken temporary control over the club, yet virtually overnight had instilled a sense of camaraderie and confidence in his charges. More importantly, he'd shown the men who mattered, Thompson and Campanis, just what he could do. Before long, Lasorda was coaching in the Rookie-level Pioneer League at Pocatello, and then at Ogden, where he won three straight championships. He was promoted to Triple-A Spokane and won another title. When the club transferred headquarters to Albuquerque, Lasorda went along too — and won again.

As Lasorda's managerial skills developed, so too did his shtick. One act had players responding to his shout of *Tell me something* — no matter the situation, at or away from the ballpark — with a response of "I believe!" This begat a full call-and-response routine: *Who do you love?* "I love the Dodgers!" *Where are you going to get your mail?* "Dodger Stadium!" *Who's going to sign your paycheck?* "Mr. O'Malley!"* Lasorda pulled the trick in the clubhouse, on the field, in restaurants, and on buses, in front of executives, fans, and strangers.

"Tommy believed," said Dodgers trainer Herb Vike, who worked with Lasorda in Spokane and Albuquerque before joining him in Los Angeles. "He believed all the time. He went around the clubhouse

---

* Dodgers owner Walter O'Malley, of course.

and all over the field, saying, 'I believe, and *you* gotta believe.' Everything was Dodger blue. He said his blood was Dodger blue. He would
preach to the ballplayers and he would preach to the crowd. He had
everybody believing in the Dodgers."

Lasorda had his players write letters to their major league counterparts — the men who played their positions at Dodger Stadium — informing them that their jobs were soon to be taken away. He hugged
his players when they performed well, a practice he kept up in the
major leagues despite vociferous complaints from members of the
old school. "Lasorda's [Ogden] Dodgers are the talk of the league . . ."
reported *The Sporting News* in 1967. "Never have the fans seen such
spirit on the field." *I love the Dodgers!* became the dugout password.
Lasorda talked to his players about bleeding Dodger blue and rever-
ing "the big Dodger in the sky." He was called "a walking pledge of allegiance," with reporter Thomas Boswell writing that the manager's
"Dodger blue monologues make *The Power of Positive Thinking* sound
like a suicide note."*

Along the way, Lasorda indoctrinated many of the men who would
one day prove instrumental to his big league success. Ogden was
where he first preached to Bill Russell (in 1966), Steve Yeager (for
one game in '67), and Steve Garvey (in '68). Lasorda coached Davey
Lopes in Spokane in 1970,† and a year later welcomed Ron Cey to the

---

* There really was no end to the shtick. Lasorda taught Bill Russell's infant
daughter Amy her first word: "Dodgers." After a physical examination, Lasorda
mentioned that doctors thought they found a spot on his heart, but soon realized it was actually a Dodgers logo. Sample ramble from the manager: "You've
heard about the 'Blue Fever,' 'Great Dodger in the Sky,' 'Dodger Blue,' and how
Dodger Stadium is Blue Heaven? Well, when nine people died in LA last year,
their last words were, 'Did the Dodgers win?'" Lasorda then labeled the fact that
the Dodgers had in fact won "a great Blue coincidence."
† That 1970 Spokane Indians team was one for the ages. In addition to Lopes
it boasted Steve Garvey, Bill Russell, and future big league stars Bill Buckner,
Bobby Valentine, Tom Paciorek, Charlie Hough, and Doyle Alexander. The Indians went 94-52, batted .299 as a team, scored 200 more runs than they allowed,

club.* When Garvey first arrived in Ogden, he introduced himself to Lasorda at the Ben Lomond Hotel on Main Street. "This must be the Garv!" proclaimed the manager, sticking out his hand. "I'm Tom Lasorda, son. Your life has changed forever."

Tall tales became a tangible commodity for the guy. In Ogden, Lasorda issued formal invitations for fans to visit the stadium club and judiciously distributed parking passes for the exclusive A Lot to reward loyal patronage. (There was no stadium club in Ogden, and only one parking lot.) In Spokane, he called in the team's spring training scores to the local newspaper, leaving area residents awed by the fact that the Indians won every game. (They hadn't. Lasorda lied.) "It was all about dreaming big," he reflected. "I wanted everyone around me to dream big, to act like we were Dodgers at Dodger Stadium, who believe they could do anything."

Many of Lasorda's motivational ploys involved considerably less tact. If anybody in baseball cursed more than he — whether adding emphasis to a point or discussing brunch options — his players couldn't imagine what it sounded like. Using a pitch counter to keep track of the expletives during one of Lasorda's clubhouse diatribes in Los Angeles, someone once tallied 110 "fucks"† over the course of 10 minutes. The catch, Lasorda intoned, was that he was squeaky clean away from the ballpark, insisting until the end that he had never once cursed in front of his wife, Jo.‡

---

won the division by 26 games, and outscored Hawaii 38–9 in a championship series sweep. Lasorda was named Minor League Manager of the Year.

* Technically he met Cey in 1969, at the short-season Arizona Instructional League. Bill Russell was also on that team.

† The count included derivative terms like "motherfucker."

‡ The manager went so far as to cut deals with the reporters who covered his team. "Listen, guys, my wife hates the fact that I cuss, and she doesn't want people to know about it," he told one group at the beginning of a season. "I will cooperate with anything you do, whatever you want from me, as long as you don't put those expletives in there." Reporters couldn't print curse words in their news-

"I'd never heard anybody cuss and scream that way," recalled Russell. "I called my mother and said, 'Get me out of here . . . this guy's nuts.' He scared me to death."

Maybe the manager's stories were effective because of their moral clarity, or maybe it was the vigor with which he told them. Ultimately, it didn't matter. Lasorda kept right on spinning, and his teams kept right on winning.

As a minor league skipper, Tommy Lasorda went 542-412 (.560), captured five pennants in eight seasons, and drew coaching offers from multiple major league clubs willing to as much as triple his salary. He turned them all down. The only gig he wanted was in Los Angeles.

From the beginning, Lasorda was seen as a possible successor to Walter Alston, who had been on the job since 1954. Also from the beginning, the same bugaboo that nearly got Lasorda bounced from the organization as a player served to prevent his more rapid ascent as a manager. The guy just couldn't seem to keep from scrapping. Before Lasorda's very first game at the helm of a minor league team, in Pocatello, Idaho, in 1965, Buzzie Bavasi tried to mitigate this very possibility by pulling him aside and issuing a strict order: *No more fights.* Lasorda lasted 13 games before he threw a punch at Idaho Falls manager Fred Koenig over some trivial exchange. A full-fledged riot ensued, featuring all 60 players and taking multiple police officers half an hour to break up. Afterward, authorities were compelled to escort Pocatello's bus to the city limits for the team's own safety.

The brawl was indicative. Lasorda's brashness was so overt that the following season, Dodgers executive vice president Peter O'Malley—son of team owner Walter O'Malley—took a trip to Ogden to interrogate players not only about the preponderance of their fights but also about Lasorda's response when he saw a brawl brewing. "Oh," said

---

papers anyway, of course, but those who so much as intimated that Lasorda possessed a salty tongue would invariably hear about it later.

one of them, "he tells us to stop." Okay, O'Malley replied, then why does your team get into so many fights? "Because," said the player, "Mr. Lasorda said that was a signal to keep on fighting."

"Usually, when a baseball player leaves for the ballpark, his wife wishes him good luck," Lasorda once said. "Jo never did that. Instead, whenever I was pitching, she would kiss me goodbye and ask, 'Please, Tommy, don't start any fights.'"

The manager even harangued umpires in the Arizona Instructional League, where drama should have been minimized given the emphasis on development, not victories. (In 1969, Lasorda became the first manager in league history to get ejected from a game.) So frequently was he tossed that players took to gambling not on whether he'd be run, but in which inning.*

This did not inspire confidence in O'Malley, but it also did not prevent the executive, in 1973, from making Lasorda Alston's third-base coach, the major league opportunity for which he'd long been waiting. Lasorda had played four seasons under Alston in Montreal in the 1950s and immediately felt at home at Dodger Stadium — not much of a surprise, given that 17 members of the team's 25-man roster played for him in the minors at one time or another.

Before making it official, O'Malley sat Lasorda down for a conversation about the importance of refraining from fights while under the big league spotlight. If Lasorda wasn't able to restrain his temper as a third-base coach, the executive said, it would cripple his chances to eventually ascend to the manager's office. Hell, only months earlier at Albuquerque, Lasorda had gone after an opposing pitcher, Hawaii's Dennis Ribant, himself. O'Malley was right, and Lasorda knew it.

The coach, who once said he fought "just for the fun of it," prom-

---

* Once, scout Bert Wells arrived late to the ballpark, by which point every inning for that day's Lasorda ejection contest was already spoken for. "That's fine," he said. "I want the chance that says he'll be ejected walking up to the plate with the lineup card."

ised restraint. That lasted until August, when Lasorda came to blows with San Francisco manager Charlie Fox near the pregame batting cage at Candlestick Park—the culmination of Lasorda's verbal harassment of Giants pitcher Elias Sosa a day earlier,* which was itself in response to a Dominican League game the previous winter in which Sosa threw at two of Lasorda's players.

Lasorda got away with it, mainly because he was by that point a clear asset to the organization, his overt enthusiasm a perfect counter to the detached Alston. That he was not yet the face of the franchise afforded significant leeway to his patented displays of enthusiasm. Lasorda paraded around his third-base coach's box, imploring his players at top volume. He spun his arms and endlessly shimmied in what to an uninformed spectator might as well have been performance art.

Once Lasorda identified the limits of Alston's authority, he set to pressing right up against them, seizing every leadership opportunity that passed his orbit. During his first spring training with the major league team, he initiated something he called the "111 Percent Club," which focused entirely on breeding success among nonroster players (using as leverage rewards such as use of Lasorda's space heater and the opportunity to pick up Don Drysdale from the airport).† The coach delivered pregame speeches and threw batting practice and taunted players about not being able to hit him. Any thoughts that O'Malley or Campanis might have had about the newcomer toning things down were quickly abandoned. Before long, *The Sporting News* proclaimed that "Tommy Lasorda is the most publicized third base coach in baseball. He is colorful, loud, a showman and a lousy loser.

---

* Sosa would join the Dodgers in 1976 and be a key component in their 1977 World Series bullpen.
† The name was a response to Rams coach George Allen, who had recently said that his players gave 110 percent. Lasorda wanted to do him one better.

He is also the next manager of the Dodgers." Which was the other part of the equation.

As soon as Lasorda was brought aboard as a major league coach, questions arose about Alston's shelf life and whether Lasorda would be the one to replace him. There was no forcing Alston from his position; he'd been with the Dodgers for 20 years, since back in Brooklyn, and had won the only four championships in club history. The guy was an institution. Still, as early as 1968, UPI's Milton Richman called Lasorda — who at that point hadn't managed anyplace higher than the Rookie-level Pioneer League — the "heir apparent" to Alston's seat.

Of course, things are never that easy. Lasorda drew outsized attention as the most colorful coach in the game, and before long he was fielding managerial offers from places like Atlanta, Pittsburgh, Minnesota, and Kansas City. In 1975, when he earned $17,000 a year to coach third base for the Dodgers and lived in a small ranch house in the working-class suburb of Fullerton, the Montreal Expos offered Lasorda multiple years and $250,000 to be their manager. He knew the city well, having pitched there for nine seasons. It was about as tempting as a proposal could get.

As it turned out, Lasorda had been sincere in those expositions about the Big Dodger in the Sky. He wanted to manage nowhere but Los Angeles and was happy to proclaim as much to whoever would listen, always with the same caveat: *Whenever Walt is ready to step down*. Still, Lasorda knew that he couldn't wait forever. At some point, outside offers would stop coming.

Peter O'Malley urged patience. He made no promises that the job would ever be offered, but assured Lasorda that he would be a front-runner when it became available. Which, by the time of Montreal's managerial offer, might not be far off. Alston was clearly slipping: the Dodgers had finished a disappointing 1975 season with only 88 wins, and by mid-September '76 were 12 games behind Cincinnati. Media members suggested in ever-louder tones that it might be time for old Smokey to take a seat. The manager was 64 years old and in his 23rd season at the helm. His communication with the clubhouse had deteriorated, his once-keen strategizing had become passive, and an increasing array of fundamental mistakes were going uncorrected.

So Lasorda turned the Expos down.* He turned them all down, every offer. And on September 27, 1976, toward the end of Lasorda's fourth season as third-base coach, Alston formally announced his plans to retire. The following day, O'Malley offered Lasorda the job.†

"This is the greatest day of my life," the new manager said at his introductory press conference. He signed a one-year pact for a reported $50,000, then publicly told O'Malley that the Dodgers had botched their negotiations. "If you'd have waited just a little longer," he said, "*I* would have paid *you* to let me manage."

Lasorda approached his new gig in 1977 with a decided lack of trepidation. When somebody asked whether he felt pressure replacing a legend like Alston, he replied, "No, I'm worried about the guy who is going to replace me." It was sheer chutzpah, and entirely Lasorda. He might even have meant it.

The Dodgers had gone 5-13 against Cincinnati in 1976 and dropped back-to-back division titles to the Reds (who went on to win the World Series both years) by an unacceptable total of 30 games. Thus, not only did Lasorda publicly ban the color red from the LA clubhouse, he expressly forbade players from wearing crimson clothing into or out of the ballpark. Only grudgingly did he allow Red Man chewing tobacco. He even tried to change the nickname of his pitching coach, Red Adams, to Blue.‡

That was the showman part of Lasorda's personality. Privately, to

---

* "I just couldn't see myself telling people about the big Expo in the sky," he said later.

† At which point someone noted that Lasorda had already received more ink than Alston had in 23 years on the job.

‡ Facetiously. Probably.

make sure his players knew precisely where he stood, he wrote each of them a letter explaining the privilege he felt in having a team like the Dodgers under his direction. The players had never seen anything like it. Lasorda followed the letters with phone calls to discuss his expectations for the season. He spoke to Bill Russell about stealing more bases. He told Garvey that he wanted to see more power. He suggested to Davey Lopes that an uptick in walks could make him the game's best leadoff hitter. He informed Dusty Baker that a poor 1976 season — Baker's first with the Dodgers, in which, hampered by a knee injury, he batted only .242 with four homers — had no bearing on 1977 and that the left field job would be his for the duration. He even telephoned reserve players, reminding them that any club with championship aspirations needed contributions from across the roster and that players without starting roles had to become the best backups they could be. The guy long known for surface enthusiasm showed just how deep he could run. Lasorda wanted to reach his players at gut level, and this was an effective first step.

Come spring training, he grouped his starters together and kept them that way. Lasorda was already aware of the discrepancies in their personalities and understood that, with so disparate a group, cohesion would have more to do with professionalism than personal affinity. The starters worked out together on a private field at Dodgertown. They traveled together and ate together. When intrasquad scrimmages began, they were in the lineup together. When they rested, they rested together.

So as to avoid neglecting his reserves, the manager initiated something he called "Lasorda University" — extracurricular practice for young players, featuring off-hours drilling on the finer points of baseball strategy and execution. "Lasorda was the biggest bullshitter in the world," said Dodgers scout Mike Brito. "Even if you were a bad player, he told you that you were a good player, and don't let anyone tell you different. He got into your brain. That's what made him so special — he knew how to get the best out of his guys."

"When Tommy held his first clubhouse meeting in the spring in Vero Beach, he was telling us we *would* win," recalled outfielder Reggie Smith. "I'd never heard any manager anywhere say it so positively. There was never an 'if' or 'maybe we can' or 'if we don't have any injuries,' or anything like that." Such was the new order.

When the team returned to Los Angeles to open the season, Lasorda wasted no time changing things around. Alston's clubhouse office was tiny, so the new skipper took over a much larger room being used by the training staff. Soon it would come to include wood paneling, thick blue carpet, a sofa, 11 chairs, a TV, two telephones, two refrigerators, a beer tap, and a liquor cabinet. The walls were covered to capacity with photos of celebrities, athletes, and the pope. Lasorda had food brought in after games to ensure that players spent at least some time with him away from the field. "It reminded me of my Italian grandmother, Nonna," said second baseman Steve Sax. "We'd go to her house and there was food everywhere — on the staircase, in the kitchen, in the front room. That's what my family was like, and that's how Tommy ran things."* (To procure the spread, Lasorda made everybody on the team sign dozens of baseballs a day, which he used for barter at various establishments around town. "Everybody was a Dodger fan," recalled Reuss. "If you signed the balls, you got to eat."†)

Lasorda dismissed those who felt that his rah-rah attitude as a coach would not play as manager, refusing to put emotional distance

---

* Less enamored with the change were the beat writers assigned to the team. "It can be agonizing going into his office on deadline," said Gordon Verrell of the *Long Beach Press Telegram*. "He's got the whole damn team in there in a buffet line, and you've got to ask something about a guy standing three feet away. Or he's got his pals in there like they're part of the woodwork, and you can't get a straight answer out of him."

† Once, after Lasorda was particularly insistent — pacing the clubhouse, intoning "Sign the balls, sign the balls," just before a game was to start — a couple of veteran players grabbed him, peeled his pants down, and, with a marker, literally signed the giggling manager's testicles.

between himself and his team for the sake of somebody else's conception of how things should work. Which isn't to say that he was unclear about the magnitude of his new job. Lasorda finally took to heart Bavasi's order to stop fighting, controlling his temper to the point that he earned but a single ejection during his first season at the helm, and even that was only because one of his pitchers received two warnings for throwing inside.

"When I said I bled Dodger blue, a lot of cynics laughed and said the act would go sour by June," said Lasorda, looking back. (The comment was merely a setup to the proclamation that "I bled Dodger Blue all year.") The 1977 Dodgers won 24 of their first 30 games, became the first team ever to boast four players with 30 or more homers, and romped to the National League pennant as Lasorda won the UPI and AP Manager of the Year awards. The following season, Los Angeles won the pennant again, making Lasorda only the second manager in National League history to reach the World Series in each of his first two seasons. "I thought he was crazy at the time," reflected trainer Herb Vike, "but it worked out pretty good for him."

2

Snatched

"COCONUT SNATCHING" IS what Branch Rickey called it back in the day, his description for a process institutionalized back in Brooklyn that involved taking dramatic liberty in shifting ballplayers all over the diamond with little regard to the positions they'd been trained to play. Rickey picked up the phrase in the tropics after watching a man scale a palm tree, wrap his legs around the upper trunk, and stretch with both hands for every coconut within reach, dropping them to a partner below. When the snatcher's legs grew fatigued, he returned to earth and the catcher climbed skyward to take over. "You move players from one position to another to fill your needs," explained Al Campanis — Rickey's protégé since his own playing days in the organization — in his 1954 guide *The Dodgers' Way to Play Baseball*.

As general manager, Campanis perpetuated Rickey's theories long after his mentor's departure, not only moving players around like chess pieces but continuing to refer to the process by its equatorially inspired handle. The idea proved instrumental in the construction of the Dodgers' 1981 squad.

On opening day of the 1973 season, LA's infield featured Bill Buckner at first base, Lee Lacy at second base, Ken McMullen at third base, and a prime coconut-snatcher, Bill Russell, at shortstop. Russell had been drafted as a center fielder, played primarily in right during his first two big league campaigns, moved to second base in 1971, and finally, upon the retirement of Maury Wills in 1972, took over the position for which he would come to be known. The transition was far from seamless. Russell made 104 errors over his first three seasons as a shortstop, twice leading all of baseball in the category. It didn't help that he refused to dive after grounders, explaining that he seemed to get injured every time he did. It further didn't help when he copped to being afraid of the ball. Even a decade into his tenure, Russell remained an uncertain fielder. "I'm still rough around the edges," he admitted in 1981. "I'm not a smooth shortstop."

Hailing from Pittsburg, Kansas, a town of just under 20,000 on the Missouri state line, with a high school that didn't even field a baseball team, Russell's acclaim was derived largely from all-state recognition in basketball. Upon encountering Lasorda at his very first professional stop, at Rookie-level Ogden in 1966, Russell was struck dumb when the manager informed him that for all his athletic feats, he "wouldn't be all-streetcorner in LA." Stay humble, young man.

Russell was among the fastest players in the organization, a perfect skill for his position of choice, center field. That's where he played in American Legion, and where he fully expected to play as a pro. The problem for Russell and the Dodgers both was that, after Maury Wills, the organizational depth chart at shortstop was unsettlingly thin. Russell's athleticism made him a perfect candidate to snatch that particular coconut.

Watching Russell's transition from the bench was Davey Lopes, also an outfielder by training, who as a 27-year-old rookie in 1973 found himself filling in, despite his better intentions, at second base. Lopes was the classic Rhode Island success story, the fourth of 10 kids raised in the South Side projects of Providence, with a mixed-up Irish, Portuguese, Cape Verdean, and African American lineage that many mistook for Hispanic. (Not only did Lopes speak no Spanish, but until he left home he'd never even tried Mexican food.) Lopes described his childhood home as "the usual ghetto thing, the typical environment — roaches, rats, poor living conditions, drugs as prevalent as candy, tenement houses with six to a room, welfare, food stamps."* His mother was a housekeeper, his father absent.

Basketball provided Lopes's initial escape; a scholarship to Washburn College in Topeka, Kansas, allowed him to major in education and play a little baseball on the side. Because he refused to go pro until completing his degree, he was already 23 years old upon joining the Dodgers in 1968, making him nearly the oldest player in the Single-A Florida State League, and the only one his age to go on to anything of note in the majors.

Lopes's seniority followed him up the ladder. In 1970, he was among the oldest players at Triple-A Spokane, yet found himself unexpectedly asked by manager Tommy Lasorda to switch positions, from outfield to infield, where the Dodgers had more pressing needs.† The 25-year-old had little interest in a career reboot and threatened to return home to Rhode Island rather than make the move. Lasorda would have none of it. "Maybe they'll let you play outfield on the thread factory team," he spat, calling Lopes's bluff. Chastened, Lopes began infield lessons with defensive guru Monty Basgall, the same man who'd tutored Russell. The process of coconut snatching would not be subverted.

The shift to middle infield was not easy for Lopes. "Davey had terrible hands — terrible — and he couldn't make the double play," recalled Basgall. "But right from the beginning he had tremendous range and

---

* Crime was prevalent in Lopes's neighborhood, and Davey was no exception when it came to perpetrators. Still, he tried to limit his larceny to items for which he had actual need, which meant mostly baseball gear. The bases he would come to steal as an adult ended up going down on his permanent record, but in a good way.

† Lasorda tells the story of watching Lopes, then an unknown Rookie Leaguer at Vero Beach in 1970, hustling a triple out of what should have been a gap double. With no idea who the kid was, the manager insisted that Lopes be promoted to Spokane. "He had literally run into my life," Lasorda said later.

a very strong arm. All I had to do was make him believe he could play second base, make him believe that we really wanted him to play second base. I had to spend as much time talking to him as showing him. Once he decided he really wanted to be a second baseman, he learned fast."

Base thievery presented a quicker learning curve, especially since the lessons came from the best. The first time Maury Wills addressed Lopes on the subject was as part of a group session during spring training, but unlike many of his less-motivated teammates, he was smart enough to pay attention.* "One hundred [Dodgers minor leaguers] were sleeping, but I figured any guy who stole a million dollars with his feet was worth staying awake for," Lopes said, looking back. Soon he would possess the most practiced eye in the sport, stealing bases less with blinding speed than with outstanding acceleration and an innate ability, refined by endless repetition, to read a pitcher's move to the plate. "They're doing me a favor," Lopes said about pitchers obsessed with holding him close to first via endless pickoff attempts. "Every time they throw over there I get to see their move. Every time."† He described baserunning as "psychological warfare" and treated it as such. Soon it would become his most potent weapon. "Davey Lopes," said Chris Mortensen, who covered the Dodgers for the *South Bay Daily Breeze* before moving on to ESPN, "was the most serious player I've ever covered in any sport."

---

* One other detail about Wills that Lopes found appealing: both were 26 upon reaching the major leagues. Wills ended up stealing 92 bases over his first three seasons; Lopes swiped 99.
† Lopes explained it like this: "With a righthanded pitcher, the shoulder is open when he comes to first base, and closed—squared off—when he goes to the plate. Otherwise, he won't get any power when he pitches. Some righthanders have the tendency to lean toward the plate when they're going to deliver a pitch. If that's not working for me—if I can't tell from the shoulder or from the way he's leaning—then I'll go to the back of his left knee. If it's in a stiff position, he's coming to first base; if it's bent, he's going home."

• • •

In 1973, third base for the Los Angeles Dodgers was widely seen as the least stable position in all of baseball. Ken McMullen got the opening day start there that season, a detail noteworthy primarily for how unnoteworthy it was. Forty-two men had manned third for the Dodgers in the 15 years since they moved to Los Angeles, producing such methodical turnover that it had become a running joke around the league. The Dodgers themselves featured a press-guide rundown of their third-base legionnaires, starting with Billy Cox of Brooklyn's Boys of Summer and cascading downward, name by painful name.*

In the sixth game of the season, McMullen was superseded by a youngster named Ron Cey, who to that point had appeared in 13 big league contests across two brief call-ups. Like other members of the infield, Cey played other positions in the minors — second base and outfield, primarily in the Arizona Instructional League — with so dramatic a potential for coconut snatching that the Dodgers even considered switching him to catcher. (They asked. He declined.) Unlike his infield mates, however, Cey *wanted* to be at the position where he ended up. He was so desperate to make it as a third baseman, in fact, that he grew terrified every time a minor league manager stuck him in the outfield, less because of potential difficulty than fear that success might lead to a permanent role there. Once, as a left fielder, Cey

---

* In roughly chronological order they were: Dick Gray, Jim Gilliam, Pee Wee Reese, Randy Jackson, Gil Hodges, Don Zimmer, Earl Robinson, Jim Baxes, Charley Smith, Bob Lillis, Bob Aspromonte, Tommy Davis, John Roseboro, Daryl Spencer, Andy Carey, Lee Walls, Ken McMullen (who came up with the Dodgers, was traded to Washington, and later was reacquired to collect the opening day start in '73), Maury Wills, Marv Breeding, Bill Skowron, Derrell Griffith, Johnny Werhas, Dick Tracewski, Bart Shirley, John Kennedy, Don LeJohn, Jim Lefebvre, Dick Schofield, Nate Oliver, Bob Bailey, Ron Hunt, Jim Hickman, Ken Boyer, Bill Sudakis, Luis Alcaraz, Paul Popovich, Billy Grabarkewitz, John Miller, Steve Garvey, Manny Mota, Dick Allen, Bobby Valentine, and Ron Cey, who played 11 games there in 1972 as a September call-up.

chased a ball into the corner and threw out the runner with a bullet to second base, then wondered whether he'd done the right thing. "I'm walking back to my position and I'm saying, 'You're an idiot,'" he recalled. "They're actually going to think you can play left field if you do that."

Cey was a physical oddity, five-foot-nine, with most of his 180 pounds packed between belt and knees. His legs, like his arms, were short for a pro athlete, and he tended to waddle like a duck ... or a penguin — the nickname foisted upon him by his coach at Washington State University, Chuck Brayton.* (Cey figured that he'd ditched his nickname in Pullman, right up until he met his coach in the 1969 Arizona Instructional League — a guy named Lasorda. "When I left Washington State, no one called me Penguin," he said, "but Tom Lasorda took one look at me and, well, I was the Penguin again."†) Cey's stature did not impede collegiate success, but it made talent evaluators wary. The Giants sent three scouts to assess the third baseman, and all came away unimpressed. San Francisco's farm director offered the simple explanation that Cey was "a dumpy little fellow."

Dumpy or not, he played a mean third base, and the Dodgers snapped him up in the third round of their historically fertile 1968 draft, which, over the course of four phases (two in January and two in June), also netted Lopes (26th overall, January secondary), Geoff Zahn (86th, January secondary), Bobby Valentine (fifth overall, June), Bill Buckner (25th overall, June), Tom Paciorek (89th, June), Joe Fer-

---

* Cey's anatomy was never more apparent than on a team bus in Cincinnati, which had benches set sideways against the wall. After everyone was seated, Bill Russell looked at Cey and started to laugh. Soon enough, so did everyone else. The Penguin's feet were sticking straight out, his thighs too short to reach the seat edge.

† "I don't even know his first name," agreed the manager. "He's the Penguin. That's all I've ever called him." Soon Lasorda would coin phrases like "Walks like a duck, hits like a truck," to describe his newest protégé.

guson (151st, June), Doyle Alexander (185th, June), and Steve Garvey (13th overall, June secondary).*

One thing working in Cey's favor when it came to playing third base was Lasorda's willingness to work him out tirelessly at the position. Among the manager's favorite tactics was positioning himself up the line to smash balls at Cey from a distance of about 40 feet, which he insisted be fielded cleanly upon penalty of running a lap. "I motherfucked him all the time," reflected Cey. "Honestly, how do you hit me a bullet that almost takes my face off, and then tell me to go run because I miss it?"

Cey wasn't humorless, exactly, but was so focused on playing baseball that he could come off that way. It made him a natural target. Teammate Jay Johnstone once used spare lumber to construct a three-foot-high mini-locker inside the third baseman's actual locker, complete with hanging rod, shoe platform, and a baby stool on which to sit — more suitable for someone of Cey's stature, the outfielder said, than what had been there previously. Part of the appeal was the fact that Cey was among the least likely men on the team to appreciate it. "Penguin," said reporter Chris Mortensen, "was a little bit of a grouchy Penguin."†

Eleven days after Cey's arrival, Lopes got the start over Lee Lacy at second base and proceeded to bat .385 with 13 stolen bases over his first month on the job. He never relinquished the role, and three-quarters of the infield-of-the-future was set.

The last piece was put into place on June 13, 1973, when, with LA trailing the Phillies 12–2 in the fourth inning, Walter Alston inserted

---

* Those who didn't end up starring for the Dodgers were used as leverage in deals to strengthen the franchise elsewhere. Valentine was part of the trade for Cy Young candidate Andy Messersmith. Buckner was sent to the Cubs for Rick Monday. Paciorek was instrumental in the Dusty Baker deal. Ferguson was traded to the Cardinals for Reggie Smith in 1976, then reacquired two years later.
† When asked what Cey brought to the team from a personality standpoint, Steve Yeager answered succinctly: "Charm."

Steve Garvey at first base. The move was telling for a number of reasons, primary among them being that Garvey was to that point little more than another in the litany of players to pass through LA's revolving door at third base. His primary issue was a shoulder injury suffered in college while playing defensive back for Michigan State, which would hamper his throwing throughout his career. This was an important detail. A scattershot arm was not only the primary weak link in Garvey's skill set but very nearly a career-killer. He was promoted through the minor leagues on the basis of a thunderous bat, which proved potent enough to earn him the nod as LA's opening day starter at third base in back-to-back seasons — 1970, after which he went 1-for-21 and was returned to the minors, and 1971, when he maintained a tenuous hold on the position until breaking the hamate bone in his right hand in late May. (He would start only sporadically after returning.) In 1972, Garvey's 85 games at third were enough to lead the Dodgers — and his 28 errors, the vast majority of them throwing, were enough to lead all major leaguers at the position.*

When Alston finally shifted him to first base, the move dripped with logic. Garvey's arm may have been untenable, but his fielding mechanics were fine. That he was right-handed and short could be worked around, though at five-foot-ten, he didn't have nearly the reach of a typical first baseman (a not-insignificant detail when it came to an infield known for off-target throws). Garvey handled all five of his chances in his first game at the new position . . . and then waited ten days for his next opportunity. It came thanks in part to Garvey's wife, Cyndy, who called the clubhouse to check up on her

---

* Combined with Bill Russell's 34 errors at shortstop, the most for any big leaguer at any position, LA's left-side defense was unforgivably porous. Dodgers fans did not react well. Garvey's phone number was listed, and people took to calling at all hours, heaping the majority of their invective on Garvey's wife, Cyndy, who was home far more frequently than her husband. On the occasions that Steve would answer, he'd sit and listen patiently — his way, Cyndy theorized, of punishing himself for his miscues.

husband between games of a doubleheader against Cincinnati and ended up, to her surprise, speaking directly with Alston. She was more surprised still when she found herself suggesting that first base seemed to have worked out once for Steve, so why not try it again?

Garvey was aghast upon learning that his wife had advised his manager on matters of strategy, but there he was in the nightcap, starting at first against Reds left-hander Tom Hall, and collecting two hits while playing error-free defense. The Dodgers won, 5–1. The next night, again at first base, Garvey banged out two more hits, including a homer. Again the Dodgers won. Within a week, he'd started six games at the position and raised his batting average 57 points, to .298. Garvey hit .412 that June, .320 in July, and .301 in August. There was no longer any question about who would play first base in Chavez Ravine.*

In 1974, Garvey batted .312 with 31 homers and 111 RBIs, taking home National League MVP honors while leading the Dodgers to their first World Series since Sandy Koufax retired.† Pertinently, he also won a Gold Glove for his fielding at first base. The guy still had throwing issues — his difficulty in starting double-plays frustrated teammates no end, as a string of wild tosses eventually led Garvey to take grounders to first base himself rather than attempting to retire the lead runner at second — but his .995 fielding percentage ranked second among National League regulars, and his ability to pick throws from the dirt was among the best in the sport. This was especially

---

* To accommodate Garvey's shift, incumbent first-sacker Bill Buckner was sent to left field. The team wasn't just snatching coconuts at this point, it was actively juggling them.

† Somehow Garvey was not even listed on the All-Star ballot that year. A fan initiative to deliver write-in votes soon gained national attention, and powered by his bases in Florida, Michigan, and Southern California, Garvey managed to overtake Tony Pérez for the starting job. He became the only National Leaguer to play the entire contest, despite a case of mumps-like symptoms, and won the MVP Award.

important given the ground-ball tendencies of the Dodgers pitching staff. Garvey consistently led the league in chances by a wide margin.

By 1981, the infield had been together for nine seasons, by far the longest such stretch in big league history, outlasting even the Chicago Cubs' famed Tinker-to-Evers-to-Chance combination that ran from 1906 to 1910.* To that point, LA's foursome had collectively made 19 All-Star appearances (seven for Garvey, six for Cey, and three each for Russell and Lopes). Cey's 191 career homers were the most in the team's Los Angeles era, and fifth-most all-time. Garvey was right behind him with 185. Lopes had stolen more bases, 398, than anyone in franchise history save Wills. Each man was among the game's best players at his position, yet their primary success had come as a unit. "You can't mention anyone from that infield without mentioning us collectively," said Lopes, looking back.

That didn't mean that they behaved as a collective anyplace but the ballpark. "That infield was tight on the field, but not anywhere else," reflected reporter Peter Schmuck. "They were all very different personalities. Bill Russell was such a mild-mannered guy. Cey was outgoing but intense. Davey was Davey—tough as nails and in your face. And then Garv, for lack of a better term, was practiced. Totally practiced. He was the image incarnate. They were all so dissimilar, it's no wonder that they went their own ways once the game ended."

The Dodgers did not react well to dropping World Series to the Yankees in 1977 and '78. The devastation following the latter defeat carried inexorably into 1979, weighing them down and hindering any chance at a fresh start. LA lost to the Padres in the season opener, with reliever Lance Rautzhan—a left-hander of limited ability thrown into the closer's role because Terry Forster was injured and Lasorda saw no better options in the bullpen—allowing two runs in the ninth in a

---

* That infield also included third baseman Harry Steinfeldt, the only member of the foursome to not make the Hall of Fame.

4–3 loss. (The 26-year-old gave up 21 base runners over his first 9.2 innings, posting a 7.45 ERA, and was promptly sold to Milwaukee.) The Dodgers lost their second series of the season to a very good Houston team. They lost their third series of the season to a very bad Atlanta team. By the end of April, the defending National League champions were 10-14 and in third place. Then things got ugly.

A 7-20 record in June dropped LA's record to 33-46. In July, the Dodgers lost 11 of 14 before the All-Star break, falling 21 games under .500 and as much as 18½ games behind the league-leading Astros. The infield, long a stabilizing factor, was aging to the point that *Sports Illustrated* ran a story headlined "Dodger Blue Is Turning Gray." The real problem, however, was the pitching.

Tommy John had recently departed to the Yankees as a free agent, and the rest of the staff crumbled in his absence. Newly acquired Jerry Reuss was 2-9 with a 5.59 ERA at the break. Don Sutton went 7-12 over his first 21 starts, with a 4.53 ERA. Andy Messersmith, back in Los Angeles after a high-profile free-agent departure from the club in 1976, went 2-4 with an ERA near 5.00, injured his arm, and retired after 11 starts. As evidenced by Lasorda's choice of closer on opening day, the relief pitching was even worse, with Charlie Hough's ERA topping out at 6.51 in mid-June. (He would join the rotation for the season's second half.) Things got so bad that in May the Dodgers traded for reliever Lerrin LaGrow, whose ERA was 9.17. They traded for reliever Ken Brett, who promptly gave up five runs across his first three outings with the team, raising his own ERA to 6.75. Bob Welch battled arm problems and alcoholism, and was disabled in the middle of July having gone 0-5 with a 6.55 ERA since June 1. That winter he was shipped to in-patient treatment in Arizona.

"I've never had this kind of year," moaned Lasorda in the postgame clubhouse following another loss, a glass of vodka sitting untouched in front of him. "I ask myself if God wants me to lose, if he wants to see how I react to adversity. I go to sleep feeling bad and I wake up feeling the same way."

As if to make things even more difficult, Walter O'Malley — the team's patriarch and chairman of the board — passed away in August.

As the schedule wound down, local newspapers ran polls asking whether Lasorda — who had led the Dodgers to National League pennants in his only two seasons at the helm to that point — deserved to keep his job. Various issues over recent campaigns — a fistfight between Steve Garvey and Don Sutton; Lasorda's profanity-laden riff for the media after Chicago Cubs outfielder Dave Kingman hit three homers against LA*; an incident in which the skipper angrily banished Steve Yeager from the bench midgame; increasing acrimony with the press — were dredged up and examined in granular detail to see whether they might bear signs of deeper discord. These were the kinds of things that winning ballclubs did not have to deal with, at least not in so public a fashion.

Lasorda's relative weakness as a baseball strategist became a topic of earnest discussion, as did his intolerance for being questioned about it. "He didn't like being second-guessed," reflected reporter Chris Mortensen. "It didn't even have to be second-guessing. You could ask a question like, why did you pinch-hit that guy? Or, why didn't you double-switch there? Things that would be considered essential baseball questions, he never liked being pressed on. Often, he countered them by raising his voice and trying to challenge you."

During the 1978 season, in fact, *Los Angeles Herald Examiner* writer Lyle Spencer wrote a glowing feature about Lasorda in which the only real criticism concerned the manager's inability to tolerate criticism. The story was published while the team was in Pittsburgh, but Lasorda found out about it and cornered the reporter in the dugout before that day's game. "He started teeing off on me about writing that he can't handle criticism," Spencer recalled. There was, however, an obvious retort. "Tommy," Spencer smiled to the manager, "you just made my point."

---

* Google it.

Still, those with clear eyes could see that Lasorda's two pennants in as many years provided more cover than some around the club might have wanted to believe. The Dodgers surged to a 34-22 mark over the final two months of the 1979 campaign, a .607 winning percentage that would have been good enough to win the division if sustained for an entire season, but which only served to bring LA's overall record to 79-83, good for third place, 11½ games behind the Reds.

Despite a Rookie of the Year season from Rick Sutcliffe, without Tommy John the team's pitching had been utterly mediocre, finishing in the National League's bottom half in nearly every statistical category. The Dodgers reacted that off-season with their first two big-money free-agent acquisitions, both of them pitchers. Into the rotation stepped Dave Goltz, lured away from the Twins for $3 million over six years. And to bolster a bullpen that blew almost half as many leads (16) as it protected (34), and where nobody saved more than seven games, the team signed Orioles closer Don Stanhouse for $2.1 million over five years. Both arrived for 1980 with question marks. Goltz had averaged 14 wins as a full-time starter during eight seasons in Minnesota, but was coming off a campaign in which he led the league in hits allowed for the second time in three years. Stanhouse had played for three teams in eight seasons before becoming the Orioles' closer in 1978, and was given the nickname "Full Pack" by manager Earl Weaver because his shaky outings inspired the manager to work his way through an entire container of cigarettes by the time they were over.

The experiment did not work as planned. Stanhouse gave up four runs in his first inning as a Dodger, and six over his first six, before being sidelined for nearly three and a half months with injuries to his shoulder and lower back. He finished the season with a 5.04 ERA and ceded the closer's role to rookie Steve Howe. Goltz, meanwhile, admitted that pressure from the contract got to him, leading him to feel like "I had to pitch a shutout in every game, strike out every batter and never make a bad pitch." The right-hander was further troubled by the transition from a four-man rotation in Minnesota to a five-man in LA, which did no favors for his sinker. "To throw that pitch well, your arm has to be a little bit tired," he reflected. "With that extra day of rest I was way too strong, and the pitch didn't move as much as it had with the Twins." Goltz sank to number five in the rotation, where he went 7-11 with a 4.31 ERA.

Despite all of that, the Great Pitcher Experiment was pretty much the only thing that went wrong through much of the 1980 campaign. The Dodgers sent six players to the All-Star Game. Steve Howe was the National League Rookie of the Year, Don Sutton won the league's ERA title, and Dusty Baker took home a Silver Slugger Award. The Dodgers and Astros swapped spots atop the National League West throughout the summer before Houston finally built a three-game lead with three games left to play. The teams closed the season with a trio of contests at Dodger Stadium, each of them must-win for Los Angeles. Nineteen-year-old Fernando Valenzuela, called up less than a month earlier, closed out the opener with two innings of shutout ball, earning the victory after LA scored in the bottom of the 10th to win, 3–2. Now the deficit was two.

In the second game, Jerry Reuss outdueled Nolan Ryan, tossing a complete-game seven-hitter in a 2–1 victory. Now the Dodgers were one game off the pace.

On the schedule's final day, Los Angeles trailed 3–1 in the sixth when Lasorda again called on Valenzuela, who tossed two more hitless frames, allowing Ron Cey to win it, 4–3, with a two-run homer in the eighth. Improbably, the Dodgers had managed to pull into a divisional tie as time ran out.

For the resulting do-or-die playoff, Lasorda had one primary decision to make: who to start. His team's late surge had cost him the services of his top three starters — Sutton, Reuss, and Hooton, leaving him with two options, each with obvious flaws. There was Valenzuela, a September call-up who over $15\frac{2}{3}$ innings across nine relief appearances had won two games and saved another while allowing only seven hits, striking out 15, and failing to yield an earned run. Still, he was only 19 years old, three weeks earlier he had been pitching in Double-A San Antonio, he had pitched two innings the previous day, and he had yet to make a big league start. It was a hell of a spot for a youngster to earn his stripes.

The pitcher upon whom Lasorda settled, Dave Goltz, made sense on multiple levels. He was 31 years old and a nine-year vet, not to mention the highest-paid player on the team. Beyond that, though, the rationale grew thin. In early July, with his ERA sitting at 5.68, Goltz had been yanked from the rotation and didn't return for nearly two months. His .389 winning percentage ranked fifth from the bottom of all qualified National League starters. Still, the right-hander had put up a 3.02 ERA in eight outings after being reinstated in a starting role, and Lasorda hoped that he could at least keep things close against Houston.

He could not keep things close. The Astros battered Goltz for eight hits and four runs over three innings, setting up a 7–1 victory that ended the Dodgers' season in dispiriting fashion. The decision about who should have started lingered all winter, corroding the intestines of anyone who held a vested interest in Dodgers baseball. (The blame was hardly Goltz's alone, of course. Davey Lopes booted the first ball the Astros put into play. Catcher Joe Ferguson dropped a throw that allowed Houston its opening run. Astros knuckleballer Joe Niekro pitched a complete-game six-hitter, and that was pretty much that.)

"We begged Lasorda to go with Fernando," recalled Dusty Baker. "We wanted to go with the talent, but Goltz was the safe answer. Nobody would second-guess that decision."*

---

* Baker later said that Lasorda's decision not to use Valenzuela is what prompted him, once he himself became manager of the San Francisco Giants, to tab rookie Salomón Torres in a do-or-die game against the Dodgers on the final day of the 1993 schedule instead of a more proven veteran like Jim Deshaies or Scott Sanderson. Torres got knocked out in the fourth inning, and Los Angeles won, 12–1, preventing a 103-win Giants team from reaching the playoffs.

Any inclination the manager may have had toward Valenzuela was overruled by a phone call he received at home the morning of the fateful game. It was Al Campanis, who issued a direct order to pitch the veteran. The Dodgers had too much money tied up in the right-hander to take the PR hit should Valenzuela end up battered. Baker was right.

Still, according to nearly all involved, it was the most exciting conclusion to a season in recent memory. There were plenty of questions to answer before 1981 began, but they could wait for a while. First, everybody needed to sit back and absorb what had just happened. Next year would come soon enough, and lessons from this one seemed like they might prove useful someplace down the line.

3

Eighty-One

THE DODGERS WERE barely into processing their 1980 playoff failure when Houston doubled back to deliver what some saw as an even more devastating blow. For 15 years, Don Sutton had been the stalwart of the Dodgers pitching staff, coming up during Koufax's final season and taking over a rotation that badly needed taking over. By 1980, he was the winningest pitcher in the team's 97-year history — it wasn't even close — having racked up a Hall-of-Fame CV that included a five-year stretch, from 1972 to 1976, when he finished among the NL's top five in Cy Young balloting every season.*

When the Astros snatched Sutton up from free agency six weeks

---

* Sutton's long-standing reputation for scuffing pitches led to inevitable speculation about how the Dodgers — who knew all his secrets — would respond now that he no longer pitched for them. The right-hander's response was concise: "What would [Lasorda] say? Those other years I lied?" The manager ultimately opted against having Sutton inspected on the mound, more to protect his own pitchers from retaliatory searches than anything else. During the 1981 season, Sutton agreed to secretly film an instructional video for NBC-TV about how to cheat in baseball, wearing a ski mask to protect his identity, with the film reversed to make him look like a southpaw. (He ended up scrapping the project when a newspaper reporter and photographer showed up at the shoot.) "I keep telling you guys, I don't use sandpaper," he informed reporters before the season opener in Los Angeles. "Sandpaper gets wet and crumbles. [I use a] sanding wheel. I already checked to see if there was an outlet there on the mound, but they removed it." Once, when an umpire searched Sutton for abrasive surfaces, he instead found a note reading, "It's not here, but you're getting warm."

into the off-season with a four-year, $3.1 million offer, it was impossible for Lasorda not to take it personally. The right-hander had been an Alston man, publicly lobbying for coach Jeff Torborg to replace the storied manager in 1976, even when Lasorda was all but a lock for the position. "I just don't believe that I could play for a manager who's a headline grabber, who isn't honest," Sutton said at the time, later refusing to become "one of [Lasorda's] bobos."* Things grew so heated that Lasorda challenged Sutton to settle their differences with fists. The pitcher declined. Their differences remained.

Sure enough, in four years under Lasorda, Sutton never earned so much as a single Cy Young vote. He couldn't leave town quickly enough.

Stripped of Sutton and Tommy John, the two best pitchers from their most recent World Series run, the Dodgers took to considering what remained of their pitching staff. There was left-hander Jerry Reuss, who, after nine years in St. Louis, Houston, and Pittsburgh that ranged from adequate to excellent, had truly blossomed after arriving in Los Angeles in 1979, his 18-6 record and 2.51 ERA in 1980 good for a second-place Cy Young finish and the National League Comeback Player of the Year Award. There was Burt Hooton, a capable

---

* Sutton once told a reporter who was furiously scribbling to keep up with one of Lasorda's Great Dodger in the Sky monologues: "You know what you can do with those notes you're making? Shred 'em and put 'em around your shrubbery at home and watch it grow." The pitcher may have foreshadowed his departure from Los Angeles when, on the final day of the 1980 regular season, with the Dodgers trailing Houston 3–0, he decamped in the fifth inning to watch a football game on TV in the clubhouse. When Sutton reemerged an inning later having already removed his cleats, undershirt, and jock, Lasorda ordered him to the bullpen to prepare for emergency use. "Aw, c'mon, Tommy," the pitcher grumbled. It took Sutton nearly three full innings — until the top of the ninth — to get dressed. Moments later, with the Dodgers clinging to a 4–3 lead, the right-hander was inserted into the game with runners at the corners and two outs. It took him two pitches to induce Denny Walling into an easy ground ball to end the game.

innings-eater who, like Reuss, had found his form since coming to LA via trade in 1975. Beyond that was . . . well, beyond that was hope that things would work themselves out.

As the team prepared for training camp in Vero Beach, concerns burst well beyond the realm of pitchers. There was the index finger on Bill Russell's throwing hand, crushed by a pitch the previous September. The team doctor told Russell it was the worst such injury he'd ever seen, and the Dodgers could only hope that five pins and a winter of rest would be enough.

There was Reggie Smith, who'd been hitting at an MVP pace — a .323 batting average with 15 homers and 55 RBIs through 97 games the previous July — when he tore the capsule in his right shoulder. It had been surgically reconstructed in September, and a winter-long rehab program continued into spring training with no assurances of success.*

There was also Davey Lopes's sore back, Terry Forster's recovery from elbow surgery, and Don Stanhouse's balky back and shoulder. The maladies piled so high that Lasorda dubbed 1981 spring training "Camp If." As in, the Dodgers would be formidable *if* they found a replacement for Sutton, and *if* their injured players returned to form, and *if* third-year outfielder Pedro Guerrero was up for a full-time job, and *if* one of the three catchers on the roster could seize the starting role, and *if* . . .

Beyond all that was the increasingly acrimonious labor discord between the owners and the players union, which even before spring training led to talk of a potential strike down the road.

---

* So dire were the doubts about Smith's health that Al Campanis spent much of the winter attempting to trade for Boston outfielder Fred Lynn, who appeared to be a natural fit given that he grew up 20 miles from Dodger Stadium and played college ball at USC. Campanis and Red Sox GM Haywood Sullivan agreed on terms — relievers Steve Howe and Joe Beckwith, plus a minor leaguer — but when Lynn, an impending free agent, refused to sign for more than one season, talks collapsed.

At least the Dodgers had Derrel Thomas to lend a distraction. In late February, just before spring training, the team's 30-year-old super utility player found himself piloting what was effectively a stolen yacht, apprehended in the San Diego harbor when the 34-foot cabin cruiser ran out of gas. The boat belonged to one of his friends, boxing promoter Harold J. Smith, but had been seized by authorities when Smith became embroiled in a $21 million embezzlement case involving Wells Fargo bank, for which he would eventually spend nearly six years in prison. Smith was not aboard, but Thomas, having been given the keys several weeks earlier with no idea that malfeasance was afoot, was having himself a time. Beyond endless ribbing from his teammates, Thomas didn't get into much trouble for the caper, but Smith subsequently made claims about being hunted by the Japanese mafia, insisted that he'd be totally exonerated, and promptly went into hiding. Thomas, to the contrary, was all too easy to find. After being questioned about his misadventure by the FBI, he went to Vero Beach for spring training. "I'm not in the habit of stealing boats," Thomas said shortly before departing for Florida. "If anything, I steal bases."

If it seemed like every position player on the Dodgers had been around forever, that's only because it was true. Almost. One position of relative youth was catcher, where at age 22 Mike Scioscia was one of only two LA regulars on the right side of 30. Steve Yeager had been the putative starter since 1973, his .208 batting average over the previous three seasons mitigated by his standing as one of the finest defenders in all the sport. Early in his career Yeager had battled Joe Ferguson — poor on defense but a markedly better hitter, not to mention a longtime favorite of Tommy Lasorda — for the starting job, creating a logjam for playing time.* In 1980, Scioscia, then a rookie, was

---

* The competition took a two-year hiatus after Ferguson was traded to St. Louis in 1976 in the deal that netted Reggie Smith, and resumed when he was reac-

added to the mix. Ferguson was 34, Yeager 32, and both found their territory encroached upon by a wunderkind defender with a higher batting average than either of them. The Dodgers won Scioscia's first seven starts.

The catcher grew up as "the little fat kid from Delco,"* according to his uncle Lou, amid six houses owned by family members within a two-block radius, giving Scioscia perpetually open doors through which to find food. The extra bulk would come to serve him well, because even as a kid, Scioscia bore the reputation that would come to define him as a big leaguer: a thorough willingness to protect the plate against base-runner encroachment, no matter the circumstance or size of the encroacher. "I was taught that it was a badge of honor to make plays there," Scioscia said later. "It's your last chance to save a run. That was instilled in me from the time I was eight or nine years old." By the time he reached Triple-A Albuquerque, Scioscia's manager, Del Crandall — himself a big league catcher for 16 seasons — was calling him the best plate blocker he'd ever encountered.

In 1981, *The Sporting News* devoted a feature story to his toughness, focusing on a game that May in which Scioscia was bowled over by Montreal's Warren Cromartie, held the ball for the putout, then caught Chris Speier in a rundown between first and second — at which point Rowland Office tried to score, flattening Scioscia for the second time in the same play. For good measure, Andre Dawson steamrolled the catcher again later in the game (again, Scioscia held the ball for the putout), making a cumulative 540 pounds of Expo barreling into the guy over the course of five innings. Ultimately, the resulting traumatization didn't belong to Scioscia but the entire Expos

---

quired in 1978. Yeager said that thereafter, the starting assignment on any given day was effectively a coin flip. "I'd ask [Ferguson], 'What is it today, heads or tails?'" he said. "He'd say, 'They haven't flipped yet.'"

* Delco = Delaware County, Pennsylvania.

organization, who complained to the National League office about an approach so thorough that they figured it had to be illegal.*

"I really believe Mike could have been a lifetime .300 hitter," reflected future teammate Mickey Hatcher, "but the beatings he took for the team behind home plate took their toll."

The fact that Scioscia grew up in Morton, Pennsylvania, about a half-hour from Lasorda's childhood home in Norristown, did not hurt his prospects with the Dodgers. In fact, as a 17-year-old prep phenom in 1976, Scioscia — about a month after having been selected by LA with its first-round draft pick (number 19 overall) — received a phone call from Lasorda, informing the surprised teenager that the manager would be arriving at the family home in a matter of minutes. The Dodgers were in town to play the Phillies, and Lasorda wanted the kid to work out with the team at Veterans Stadium. So Scioscia, still not sure whether he was being set up for a practical joke, left his parents a note, hopped into Lasorda's car,† and sped off to meet his future.

It was no joke. As they drove, the manager built Scioscia up, inflating the kid's ego with his standard spiel about the life-affirming import of being a Dodger. Upon arrival at the ballpark, however, Lasorda directed the kid to the batting cage and pitched to him personally, delivering an array of curveballs and cutters the likes of which Scioscia hadn't seen in the high school ranks. (Lasorda was 52 years old at that point and could still bring it when necessary.) Scioscia felt like he'd all but forgotten how to hit. "After the workout I probably would have paid them to sign me," he admitted later.

Scioscia's mother, Florence, a teacher, held dreams of her son attending Clemson, where he'd been offered a baseball scholarship,

---

* Scioscia was quick to dismiss the criticism. "Blocking the plate is when you're standing on it without the ball," he said in response to Montreal's complaints. "So tell me how I can get knocked over each time at the plate and come up with the ball. What, am I catching it after I get knocked over?"
† Technically it was Lasorda's brother's car, as the then-coach's own vehicle was back home in Fullerton.

and fell into tears when he returned home and informed her that he wanted to go pro immediately. He shipped out to the team's Single-A club in Bellingham, Washington, the very next day. Lasorda, however, in a key part of the story, didn't let things end there.

Shortly after her son departed, Florence Scioscia received a letter elucidating the gravity of his decision and informing her that the entire Dodgers organization would focus on putting Mike in the best position possible to achieve his goals. It was from Lasorda, and it meant the world to the lady who meant the world to the team's catcher of the future.

"People say I like him because he's Italian," Lasorda said shortly after Scioscia reached the big leagues. "They're wrong. I like him because *I'm* Italian."

Yeager was not exactly bitter about Scioscia's arrival in Los Angeles, but neither was he thrilled. His career had been running on borrowed time since before Scioscia arrived, and now that the dreaded two-headed monster of Yeager and Ferguson had grown a third noggin, the aging veteran feared being glued to the bench . . . or worse. With Scioscia's defense comparable to his own, the one thing working in Yeager's favor was the fact that his young counterpart hit lefty, providing a platoon opportunity. The trouble was, the Dodgers would face only 14 left-handed starters all season in 1981. Yeager couldn't know it at the time, but he would start only 23 games all year.‡

---

‡ By midsummer, Yeager was so discouraged by his abundant bench time that Burt Hooton felt the need to intervene. The Dodgers were in Chicago, and Hooton, with Yeager as his catcher, had just shut out the Cubs. The problem, as Hooton saw it, was that Yeager had all but vanished from the box score, his 0-for-4 including two strikeouts, a popup, and grounding into a double-play. "The way you give yourself up at the plate, I wish *I* was pitching against you," the pitcher told him by way of a postgame pep talk. Yeager could only mutter, "I can't hit playing once a week." Including the just-completed contest, he'd collected nine at-bats over the previous nine games. With that, Hooton officially requested that Yeager become his personal catcher, if only to guarantee his pal a start at least every five days.

The specifics might have been TBD, but the framework was all too apparent. During spring training, rumors arose that Yeager would be traded to Boston—a notion the catcher actively encouraged, up to the point of agreeing to waive his no-trade clause (albeit in exchange for the Red Sox replacing the three years and $775,000 remaining on his contract with five years and $2 million). Yeager's appreciation of the Southern California lifestyle—he embraced the confluence of big league fame and LA's celebrity-driven culture as overtly as anyone on the team— was factored into his price. "LA is probably the greatest place to play," the catcher lamented as he considered his departure. "You'd have to be crazy to think of leaving. The guys who do leave all seem to say they'd rather be back." When Boston refused to meet Yeager's terms, talks fell through, and the catcher steeled himself for a long season on the bench.

Were a team looking for someplace to launch a winning campaign, it'd be hard-pressed to find a location more suitable than Dodgertown. The franchise's longtime training camp in Vero Beach, Florida, all but exuded the aura of success. The historical figures who'd trod those grounds were so significant as to be known simply by their first names: Jackie, Pee Wee, Duke, Sandy. If nothing else, Dodgertown offered tactile affirmation of organizational stability and long-standing success.

The place had been an abandoned naval air station when then–general manager Branch Rickey first leased it in 1948.* Until that point, training camp locations had been short-term rentals, strictly temporary affairs, but Dodgertown was a giant, self-contained machine,

---

* Rickey had sought a location suitable not only for the Dodgers but for all 26 of the organization's minor league teams. Just as importantly, he wanted a Southern site free of restrictions against Jackie Robinson's skin color. Two springs previous, weeks before Robinson was to break baseball's color barrier, the Dodgers had trained in Havana, Cuba, to avoid drawing undue attention to their hot-button player.

with housing—the 80 barracks on the base once sheltered nearly 3,000 military personnel—commissary, laundry facilities, entertainment, and, of course, plenty of space for ballfields. The on-site airstrip was only steps away from team offices. The best part was that, after being stuck with upkeep costs for an unused facility, the municipality of Vero Beach gladly offered a five-year pact at $1 per year. Rickey was overjoyed.

When it opened, Dodgertown was less school than factory, grouping some 660 players into the color-coded uniforms that would drive a young Tommy Lasorda batty a season later. Players rotated from field to field, station to station, running through exercises and drills. The lessons they learned would compose something that came to be known as "The Dodger Way," a phrase referenced repeatedly by Lasorda in years to come. By 1981, the place was the class of baseball, its barracks replaced with bungalows, the camp now featuring a swimming pool, courts for basketball and tennis, three well-seeded fishing ponds, two golf courses, and a hospital. First-run films played in the on-site movie theater.

When it came to baseball, things were even better. Dodgertown featured six full practice fields, two half-diamonds, and, starting in 1953, Holman Stadium, where the team hosted games. Reported *The Sporting News* in 1978: "They hire two guys just to pick up the balls off the ground in the eight batting cages. That's right, eight. The Tigers have one and think it's nuts. Here they've got six equipped with pitching machines, and two others which feature live arms."

By that point, Lasorda had been a Vero Beach fixture for more than three decades as player, coach, and manager, the long-standing resident of Room 112. Attendance counted for something, but when it came to the embodiment of Dodgers spring training in Florida, it wasn't the manager to whom the honor fell, but the team's most decorated player.

At age 32, Steve Garvey had batted .300 seven times over the previous eight seasons, banged out 200 hits in six of the last seven, topped

100 RBIs four years in a row, been named to six All-Star teams, and won the 1974 National League MVP Award. His first camp in Vero Beach as a player was in 1969, but that was hardly the first time he'd roamed those halls.

When Garvey was growing up in Tampa, his father, Joseph, drove buses for Greyhound — a job that each March included ferrying baseball teams from airport to ballpark and back. Joe Garvey grew up in Brooklyn, the son of a cop whose beat included Ebbets Field, and would pass down his love of the Dodgers like an inheritance. As a kid, Steve would whack a broomstick at grapefruits fallen from a backyard tree while pretending to be the entire Brooklyn lineup, one hitter at a time.

When Steve turned six, Joe brought him along on one of his team pickups. The boy could do little but gape as players decamped their plane for his father's bus, breathing in baseball up close as the players brushed past. Many of their faces were already familiar: Robinson, Reese, Roy Campanella, Gil Hodges. Things got even better when they arrived at the ballpark and the lad was enlisted as a batboy.

Over the years, young Steve became something of a regular around Dodgers camp, growing so familiar after three or four visits each spring for seven years running that he eventually took to warming up with players before games.* Upon joining the Dodgers himself, the fable of being the bus driver's kid helped cement Garvey's status as the most Dodger-y of them all.

Still, he'd never won a ring. Together, the fabled infield — Garvey, Lopes, Russell, Cey — had produced three first-place finishes, three second-place finishes, and three World Series appearances, and not a one of them was satisfied. Moreover, each player's increasingly veteran status made time a precious commodity. By 1981, Lopes was 36,

---

* Steve was so polished by age 12 that Frank Howard took to humming throws at him full bore, leading coach Pete Reiser to scream, "What're you doing? He's just a little kid!'"

Cey 33, Garvey and Russell 32. They were breaking down more frequently (save, of course, for Garvey, whose consecutive-games-played streak would become the longest in National League history in 1983), and each one had seen an offensive decline between 1979 and 1980. Talk grew pronounced that their longevity as a unit was by that point primarily a function of no-trade clauses, and talk swirled throughout the winter about the Dodgers trying to acquire Toronto second baseman Dámaso García to replace Lopes.* "We don't know how much longer we'll all be together," said Russell at the time. "It's in the back of our minds. We've been denied a championship three times. The Dodgers are run like a business. You've got to produce or you're gone."†

As the players ran through drills in Vero Beach that spring, the pressure — not even to succeed so much as to simply perform capably — was unlike anything the veteran infielders had experienced. Never mind their status; the Dodgers' minor league system was loaded, and the organization was actively seeking to make the lineup younger. Garvey had seen this story before. Those Brooklyn Dodgers for whom he'd grown up cheering, great as they were, had been unceremoniously dismantled, one disgruntled player at a time. Hodges was made available to the Mets in the 1961 expansion draft. Jackie Robinson was effectively forced into retirement rather than accept a trade to the Giants. Carl Furillo was released just a few months short of qualifying for a full pension, leading to a lawsuit against the team. Personal statistics and past championships mattered little. When one's time was up with the Dodgers, there was little to offer by way of response.

---

* Even the team's hometown newspaper, the *Los Angeles Times*, ranked the Dodgers infield as no better than the fourth-best unit in the National League in '81, behind Philadelphia (Rose-Trillo-Bowa-Schmidt), Cincinnati (Driessen-Oester-Concepción-Knight) and St. Louis (Hernandez-Herr-Templeton-Oberkfell).
† When Garvey discussed the possibility of winning a World Series with his infield mates, he was compelled to add that it would be "for sentimental reasons, if nothing else."

The undercurrent of inevitability swirling through Vero Beach that spring was impossible to miss. The end was near, and everybody knew it. The only question was how much more time the infield — *The Infield* — would be granted.

In March, in a hedge against Reggie Smith's questionable return from shoulder surgery, Campanis agreed to send minor league infielder Mickey Hatcher and pitcher Joe Beckwith to the Cubs in exchange for former Dodger Bill Buckner, the defending National League batting champion.* Then Beckwith damaged the optic nerve in his left eye during training camp (while avoiding a line drive, of all things), leaving him with double vision that ended up costing him the season. "Well," responded Chicago GM Bob Kennedy in killing the deal, "that's that."

So instead of sending Hatcher to Chicago, LA shipped him, along with two minor leaguers, to Minnesota in exchange for Ken Landreaux. The outfielder may not have been Campanis's first choice, but this was no minor haul. Landreaux, 26, was the sixth overall pick in the 1976 draft, batted .305 with 15 homers for Minnesota in 1979, and was an American League All-Star in 1980, when his 31-game hitting streak was the league's longest since 1949. As the 1977 Minor League Player of the Year, Landreaux had been the key cog in the trade that brought Rod Carew to Anaheim two seasons earlier.†

There was the added bonus that Landreaux was a local kid, having grown up about 20 miles south of Dodger Stadium, in Compton. As a toddler, he'd attended games at the LA Coliseum prior to the opening

---

* Hatcher's youthful upside made him attractive to Chicago. So did the fact that he was not among the 15 Dodgers with no-trade clauses.

† The move effectively erased the possibility of 24-year-old Rudy Law, who'd stolen 40 bases for the Dodgers in limited playing time in 1980, taking over a bigger role. Because Law had minor league options, he was shuttled back to Albuquerque. Because veteran outfielders Rick Monday and Jay Johnstone did not, they stuck around.

of Dodger Stadium, sitting in the upper reaches of the vast bowl, so high that binoculars were necessary to make out the action far below. In high school, Landreaux skipped lunch to save his money for Dodgers tickets — $1.50 per seat, plus 75 cents for parking.* He attended team-sponsored clinics at Roy Campanella Park, near his home, that featured players like Johnny Roseboro, Maury Wills, and Willie Davis. One even boasted Steve Garvey, a detail that Landreaux pointed out to the first baseman upon joining the team. "Man, I'm not *that* old," Garvey replied. (He was that old. Landreaux, six years Garvey's junior to the day, had been in high school at the time.)

Landreaux's distinctly SoCal flair didn't stir much drama during his time with the Angels, but in Minnesota it stood in stark contrast to the authoritarian structure built by manager Gene Mauch. The outfielder's attitude was quickly branded as problematic, and by 1980 the Twins were fining him for minor infractions like wearing the cuffs of his pants low enough to cover the logo on his socks. The team failed to recognize in any way Landreaux's hit streak that season and by the time of the 1981 winter meetings was actively shopping him. Once the deal for Fred Lynn fell through, the Dodgers moved quickly, giving up relatively little, thanks in part to the fervor with which Minnesota was trying to unload the outfielder.†

Landreaux immediately made a splash at Dodgertown by taking

---

* One of Landreaux's heroes, outfielder Tommy Davis, also lived in Compton; whenever Davis hit a home run at Dodger Stadium, the team would donate bats to the Compton Little League. "There were times that we'd be low on bats," recalled Landreaux. "We were like, we've got to go to the game and say, 'Come on, Tommy, hit a home run.'" Davis didn't know a thing about it until after his career, when Landreaux, by then a pro himself, informed him.

† Having no place to stay upon being traded to the Dodgers, Landreaux moved in with his parents — into his old bedroom no less, which he originally shared with his two brothers but now shared with his wife. Clissy Landreaux was more than willing to tolerate it. "If you'd stayed in Minnesota, I'd have divorced you," she told him. The arrangement lasted several months, until Landreaux secured housing of his own.

a limousine the two hours from Twins camp in Orlando. It mattered little that the limo company was owned by a friend of his; the impression was made: Ken Landreaux traveled in style. The arrival of the new center fielder allowed 24-year-old Pedro Guerrero — who'd racked up a .322 batting average and seven home runs in limited playing time in 1980 — to shift to Reggie Smith's spot in right. Which was itself a story.

By the end of training camp, Smith's surgically repaired shoulder was still in no shape to throw a baseball, despite twice-daily stretching exercises to tear built-up adhesions, a regimen aimed at muscle growth. When the temperature dropped, the shoulder seized, forcing Smith to dial back his program. By the end of March, Smith, once in possession of among the strongest outfield arms in the sport, was hoping merely to regain 80 percent of what he'd once had. He even envisioned a scenario in which Davey Lopes would race toward right field from second base to handle his truncated tosses.

If anything, Smith's infirmity exacerbated his long-standing surliness, a detail best exhibited during the final Florida exhibition game, just a few hours before the team packed out of Vero for its flight to Los Angeles. Smith had been trying to get his arm loose on the sidelines near the press room when three young men, several beers into their morning, began to ride him. As reporters watched through an open window, one of the men called Smith a sissy and began blowing him kisses. Sandy Koufax, in camp as a pitching instructor, attempted to intercede, and PR man Steve Brener raced off to find a security guard. He never stood a chance. Smith brushed off Koufax, hurdled a rope barrier, and split the heckler's lip with a punch.

No charges were filed, but the incident served to illustrate two things: Reggie Smith was serious about returning to baseball, and was frustrated no end by his lack of rehab progress. It also reminded Smith's teammates how much intensity the guy brought to the ballpark, and what the team would miss so long as he remained absent. "When it comes to Reggie Smith, I don't believe in saying he can never do anything," said Dusty Baker. "There's a certain thing called ability, a certain thing called pride, a certain thing called desire, a certain thing called need. And we *need* Reggie."

Instead, they had Pedro Guerrero and Ken Landreaux. It would have to suffice.

A return home did little to staunch the team's drama. After closing out the exhibition schedule with three games against the Angels in Southern California's annual Freeway Series, the front office had to make some painful roster decisions—none more difficult than the final spot on the pitching staff. After considerable discussion, they decided to ship out rookie right-hander Dave Stewart, who after six minor league seasons had conclusively proved his ability to handle Triple-A hitters. That the right-hander had been solid in spring training made his demotion to Albuquerque something of a shock, to nobody more than Stewart himself. Further muddling the decision was that the pitcher was out of options; to be successfully relegated he'd first have to clear waivers, an unlikely eventuality for a player of his caliber. After so many years with the organization, and now finally on the cusp of winning a big league roster spot, Stewart was instead called into Lasorda's Dodger Stadium office following the Freeway Series closer and informed that he was the team's final cut.

His response was concise. "I won't go," he said simply.

The manager was surprised by this answer. Lasorda didn't expect the news to be greeted with joy, but he hardly anticipated outright refusal. Before he could formulate a retort, Stewart continued.

"I have nothing left to prove in Albuquerque," the pitcher said. "It's not my business what you guys do, but I'm not going back there. So I'll go pack my stuff." Stewart had just won 15 games for the Dukes, with a 3.70 ERA in a hitter-friendly league where the average was 4.47. He'd thrown 200 innings and tossed 11 complete games. He was right—he had nothing left to prove. "You guys let me know what your plan is once I get back to Sacramento," he told the manager.

Lasorda attempted to mollify the pitcher, but Stewart was too upset to process the manager's words of encouragement. He emerged from the office, pounded a fist upon a concrete hallway wall, and stalked back to his locker. Given a moment to absorb the implications of the decisions—his and the team's alike—he slumped in his chair and broke into tears. The pitcher was angrily slamming his gear into a duffel bag when reliever Don Stanhouse sidled up to offer consolation. "Sometimes there's no justice, Stew," he said softly. It wasn't much, but what else, really, could be said?

Stewart left the ballpark for his room downtown at the Biltmore Hotel, the early-season home to players who had yet to establish housing in Los Angeles. With nowhere to be and evening approaching, he ordered room service and turned on the TV. Driving to Sacramento could wait until tomorrow.

At about 9:00 p.m., some six hours after being informed of his demotion, Stewart's phone rang. It was traveling secretary Billy DeLury with a simple message: *Not so fast.* Come on back to the stadium, DeLury said. We have to talk.

When Stewart arrived at the team offices, he gave a nod to Stanhouse, heading in the opposite direction. The pitcher didn't give it much thought as he was led to Al Campanis's office. When he arrived, he found the GM and Lasorda both. Campanis did the talking.

"We have made a decision," he said. "We are going to eat the contract of Don Stanhouse in order to clear roster space. Welcome to the team." Campanis did his best to spin the revelation in terms of gratitude—Stewart's, toward the Dodgers, for electing to keep him around. Angry as the pitcher was, he realized that Campanis was right. "He tried to make it seem special—which it *was* special," said Stewart, looking back. "It was a big deal to sign Stanhouse the year before, and a bigger deal to release that kind of money. Those dollars were *big* dollars."

Stanhouse was only one season into a five-year, $2.1 million contract signed during the Dodgers' free-agent acquisition spree of 1980, but had been dealing with health issues almost since he arrived. The right-hander had pitched only 25 innings the previous season, with a 5.04 ERA and five strikeouts against 16 walks. Even worse, he had only just complained of a new round of back spasms. The Dodgers initially planned on disabling Stanhouse to start the season, but belatedly realized that such a minor malady did not qualify for the DL. The team needed arms, and so went with the young, cheap pitcher who could help in the short term over the old, expensive one who could not. LA absorbed the $1.36 million remaining on Stanhouse's contract—the largest such buyout in baseball history. Stanhouse, bewildered, called it a "complete puzzlement."

It served to make for some exceptional drama, which would have been better remembered had Fernando Valenzuela not shown up the following day and set the world aflame.

4

Mania

THE GUY STANDING on the mound at Dodger Stadium on opening day was not the guy the Dodgers wanted standing on the mound at Dodger Stadium on opening day. The home team faced pressure aplenty without having to consider an emergency starter in the very first game of the 1981 season, let alone it being a 20-year-old with all of 17 innings of big league experience under his belt, every one of them out of the bullpen.

At that point, LA's pitching concerns were more akin to triage than anything resembling strategy. This was the *Dodgers*, for crying out loud, the closest thing to a pitching factory that baseball had known since way back in the Brooklyn days of Drysdale and Newcombe and Sandy Freaking Koufax. One might assume immunity to this sort of dilemma. Nope. Their previous game — the one-and-out playoff against Houston that closed the 1980 campaign — had hinged on just this kind of drama. Hell, it even included the same opponent currently in town to christen the new season, almost as if baseball's schedulers wanted to help Los Angelinos clear their palates as expediently as possible. Whether that was achievable remained to be seen.

The Dodgers were already without Don Sutton, now pitching for Houston.* Left-hander Jerry Reuss, coming off an All-Star campaign,

---

* Sutton showed up for the opening series at Dodger Stadium wearing a T-shirt that read, in blue script, I LUV DODGERS — with DODGERS crossed out and

was ready to slide into Sutton's slot atop the rotation, but in the final workout before opening day pulled a calf muscle so severely that he ended up sidelined for the first 10 games of the season.

Lasorda would have bumped up the next guy, but Burt Hooton, thinking he had an additional day to recover, had undergone a procedure to remove an ingrown toenail and was forced to sit. Number 3 starter Bob Welch was tending a bone spur in his elbow that would cost him three games. Dave Goltz and third-year pitcher Rick Sutcliffe had just closed the exhibition schedule with Freeway Series starts against the Angels.

This is how Fernando Valenzuela came to be pulled aside by team brass shortly after reaching the ballpark and told that he was about to become the first rookie pitcher to start on opening day in the 98-year history of the franchise.

Valenzuela's ascent the previous autumn had been the main reason Lasorda's decision about who to start in the playoff against the Astros was anything but pro forma. The left-hander had debuted only three weeks earlier, on September 15, jumping from Double-A straight to the majors, and failed to yield an earned run over 17⅔ innings of relief work covering 10 appearances. It was impressive, but the kid was fresh out of Mexico and still a teenager, for crying out loud. More importantly, the last time he started a game the opponent had been the Amarillo Gold Sox. An elimination contest against the class of the National League would be a hell of a spot for Valenzuela's premiere. So Goltz was tabbed, it ended badly, and now Lasorda had a chance to see what he'd missed out on six months earlier.

Valenzuela was a physical curiosity, with chubby cheeks and rotund belly, his Mayo features accentuated by bushy black hair spilling straight down from his cap. Wrote Jim Murray in the following day's *Los Angeles Times*: "He is, how shall we say it — he is — well, he's

---

ASTROS written beneath it in orange. Sutton's son Daron, joining him at the ballpark, wore a miniature version.

fat, is what he is."* Fernando did not disappoint. The guy who ended the 1980 campaign without ceding an earned run over his final 52⅔ innings, majors and minors combined, began 1981 precisely the same way. In a performance that belied his carriage, the left-hander tantalized Houston's roster inning after inning, giving up assorted singles and not much else. By the time he struck out Dave Roberts in the ninth — with a *screwball* of all things — Valenzuela had thrown 106 pitches, and also a complete-game, five-hit, 2–0 shutout. The 50,511 fans crowding Dodger Stadium could hardly believe what they'd seen. A day earlier the pitcher had been so in the dark about the possibility of drawing this assignment that he threw batting practice. Now he spun gold. Fernando, too young to legally buy a beer, was seemingly beyond distraction.

"We don't know what's going on inside him," marveled Dodgers second baseman Davey Lopes after the game, an understandable sentiment given his new teammate's language barrier. "All he does is smile."

"He wasn't one bit nervous," catcher Mike Scioscia informed the press. "He's so cool out there, I don't think he even broke a sweat."

The thing about Valenzuela wasn't that he was an unknown pitcher making his first major league start on the early season's biggest stage. It wasn't that he spoke virtually no English, necessitating Spanish-language broadcaster Jaime Jarrín to translate for him at nearly every turn. It wasn't that as a kid from the dusty plains of Mexico he had not yet adapted to life in Los Angeles. It was not his pudgy cheeks, or his stomach bulging over his belt, or the unique hitch in his delivery in which, with his lead leg lifted, he gazed skyward while clasping his hands above his head. It was not his habit of constantly blowing chewing-gum bubbles, sometimes in the middle of his windup. It was

---

* "All I'm worried about," said Red Adams, the Dodgers pitching coach in 1980, "is that someone will make him lose 25 pounds and he'll be the most physically fit pitcher in Lodi."

not that he was a 20-year-old who looked to be in his middle thirties. It was not even that he was left-handed, or that his out-pitch was a flippin' screwball.

It was all of it together, a full package containing mystery (*The guy barely talks!*), comedy (*That belly! That haircut! That form!*) and straight-up befuddlement (*How does he do nothing but win?*). Baseball had seen its share of flashing mound talent over recent years — Mark Fidrych in 1976, Vida Blue in '71 — but nobody quite captured the collective imagination like Fernando. The guy had been so anonymous that in a baseball card industry recently flush with competition, only Fleer saw fit to include him in its 1981 set . . . and misspelled his name.

Valenzuela seemed imperturbable — *Pedazo de pastel*, he said when asked how he felt about starting the season opener, Piece of cake — so composed through what should have been a fraught-filled start that the *Los Angeles Times* was compelled to report that "if he had been 100 years old and in the majors for 90 of them, he couldn't have looked more in control."

As if limiting Houston to five hits in a 2–0 opening day victory wasn't enough, two of those hits came off of broken bats, and a third didn't breach the infield. Said Fernando with such unassuming ease that it was impossible to confuse the sentiment for bravado: "When I get on the mound I don't know what afraid is."

"Hell," shrugged outfielder Jay Johnstone, looking back, "you've got to break him in somewhere."

To that point, Dodgers players didn't know what to make of the youngster. They'd spent most of spring training watching Valenzuela get knocked around by their own hitters during batting practice at Vero Beach, but in retrospect it became clear what he'd been trying to do. "Fernando threw the best BP," reflected Derrel Thomas. "He could make a bad hitter look good, that's how great a batting practice he threw. It was *right there*, all the time." So hard was the left-hander getting hammered that some of the team's Latino hitters began teasing him about the distance of the shots he was giving up. "No," Valenzuela responded in Spanish from the mound, "I *let* you do that." Challenge accepted. Lasorda, who'd been listening in, immediately gathered three of his top-line guys — Reggie Smith, Dusty Baker, and Pedro Guerrero — to do their damnedest in the batting cage, then ordered Valenzuela to let loose. Three pitches and Smith was done. Three more pitches, and so was Baker. Likewise, Guerrero. Heads immediately swiveled toward Lasorda. "Okay," he shrugged. Point proved.

By the time Valenzuela's second regular-season start came around, the Dodgers were 4-0, having swept Houston and taken the opener of a three-game set in San Francisco. It would be, pundits suggested, a different kind of test for the rookie. Fernando would be leaving balmy Los Angeles for windy, frigid Candlestick Park, while pitching in front of the most fervently anti-Dodger crowd in the big leagues. The day before the game the ballpark wind chill dropped to near 40 degrees, with gusts so strong that the grounds crew had to secure the center-field fence lest it blow over.

Valenzuela tossed a four-hitter with 10 strikeouts. He did give up a run in the eighth inning — not only the first of his big league career but dating back through his final 35 frames at San Antonio as well — leading to his first on-the-record admission ("The cold weather, it made me a little stiff toward the end") that he might be human after all. Yeager said afterward that Valenzuela could have gone another nine had he so chosen.

The Dodgers would win again the next day to sweep the series and go 6-0. After an off-day and an extra-innings loss to San Diego, Fernando headed back to the hill in wet weather, on three days' rest for the first time in his career, and delivered his second complete-game, five-hit shutout in three tries, walking no Padres and striking out 10. Gene Richards's leadoff single? No problem. When Ozzie Smith tried to bunt Richards over, Valenzuela coolly fielded the ball and rifled a strike to Russell at second to force the runner. A moment later, the lefty picked Smith off of first. By that point, said GM Campanis, he was "catching hell for not bringing him up earlier."

On Valenzuela's fourth turn, the Dodgers were 9-2 and the country was paying attention.* It was pegged as another hurdle for the young pitcher, the first time a team — the Astros — would get a second look at him. It was one thing to beat the woeful Giants and Padres, but Houston was the defending division champ and would be playing at home, marking Fernando's first appearance indoors, not to mention his second straight start on three days' rest. No phenom could be *this* phenomenal.

Could he?

Another complete-game shutout had even the doubters convinced. Tossing a seven-hitter with 11 strikeouts was one thing, but doing so in a 1–0 victory proved Valenzuela's mettle in new ways. Houston's leadoff hitter, Terry Puhl, opened the game by smacking a double into the right-field corner. When the next batter, Craig Reynolds, tried to bunt Puhl over, Valenzuela, unperturbed, fielded the ball in front of the mound and, upon spying the runner too wide of second, ran him down and tagged him out himself, then instinctively wheeled and threw the ball to first, nearly catching Reynolds off the bag. Moments later, Valenzuela *did* catch Reynolds off the bag, picking him off cleanly, but in the ensuing rundown Steve Garvey hit Reynolds in the back with his throw. Houston eventually put runners on second and third, at which point Valenzuela struck out José Cruz and Mike Ivie to end the inning. There seemed to be no limit to his baseball sense.

As if to answer anybody who wasn't yet ready to acknowledge him as Superman, Fernando also drove in the game's only run as part of a 2-for-3 day that brought his season batting average to .333. "There

---

* LA's record was almost entirely a function of its pitching. Lopes was batting .095, Garvey .208, Scioscia .200, Russell .214, and Landreaux was 0-for-his-last-10.

was no one moment when I realized he was for real," reflected Dave
Stewart about the pitcher's magical start. "With Fernando, it was *every* moment. Every game he would show you something. He could
make the opposition look absolutely useless." Valenzuela was 4-0
with four complete games in four starts, including three shutouts and
36 strikeouts over 36 innings. His ERA was 0.25 (and 0.17 for his career). He led all of baseball in wins, strikeouts, innings pitched, and
shutouts. Wrote the *Los Angeles Times*: "After his first single, he got a
standing ovation, and first-base coach Manny Mota told him to tip his
cap. It was the first thing anyone has had to tell Valenzuela all season."
There was no way things could get any better. And then they did.

Fernando's fifth start, at home against the Giants, was another complete-game shutout, because of course it was, this one a seven-hitter
with what even the pitcher acknowledged was not his best stuff. In
the process, he dropped his ERA to 0.20 while raising his batting average to .438, thanks to a 3-for-4 day at the plate. Los Angeles was
14-3 and led the National League West by four and a half games, a
ridiculous margin so early in the season. By that point people weren't
just paying attention, they were urgently scrambling to board Fernando's contrail. T-shirts and buttons featuring the pitcher's name and
image cropped up across the Southland. Songs of devotion were recorded. Tickets for his future starts, home and road, were snapped
up at premium prices. The *Los Angeles Herald Examiner* ran a contest to find the pitcher a nickname. (The closest one came to sticking
was *El Toro* — The Bull.) *Sports Illustrated* ordered a feature story, as
did *Inside Sports*. Reporters appeared in the clubhouse in such overwhelming numbers that the Dodgers took to staging pregame press
conferences as a means of clearing out some space for the rest of the
roster. Someone even came up with a name for the whole, wild affair:
Fernandomania. Valenzuela was five starts into his big league career.

"He seems to think there's a better league somewhere else," said
Lasorda, "and he's trying to pitch himself out of here."

It was about that time that people began asking in earnest where in the world the kid was from. The answer wasn't exactly *nowhere*, but it was in the neighborhood.

Etchohuaquila is a communal farming village in the state of Sonora, on Mexico's west coast, about 20 miles inland from the Gulf of California. It sits two pockmarked, unpaved miles from Federal Highway 15, its main artery to life in Navojoa to the south and Ciudad Obregon to the north. Following the road north for another 335 miles will lead one to the United States, a place about which Valenzuela gave no serious thought until the Dodgers began courting him in earnest.

The Etchohuaquila of Valenzuela's youth consisted of a few dirt roads, a handful of shacks, 140 or so people, and a whole lot of dust. It is where Fernando was born and raised. If the community there had any interest beyond the underlying farm culture, it was baseball. The town was tiny, but it was rarely difficult to field a team, mostly because for a stretch in the 1970s seven local players were Valenzuela brothers. Rafael and Avelino Jr. pitched. Francisco played second, Daniel shortstop, Gerardo third, and Manuel de Jesus roamed the outfield. As the youngest of the bunch — the seventh son — Fernando was relegated to first base. He was not allowed to pitch until he was 13 years old, and even then only barely. "I was too young," he recalled. Still, it was an eye-opening experience. Fernando was not afraid, he said later, because his brothers were there to protect him.

The boys' parents, Avelino and Emergilda, also raised five girls, the lot of them living in a whitewashed adobe house with no running water that originally belonged to Avelino's father. The roof was made of sticks and mud, standard fare for the area, and covered five rooms — including a kitchen, a bedroom, a hallway, and a porch where people slept. The slate tile on the living room floor was the structure's only reprieve from dirt underfoot. A single bulb dangled from the ceiling, an unusual luxury compared to many homes in the village. The sisters slept in one room, five to a bed, and the brothers in another — all except Fernando, who made a habit of crawling in next to his mother in the middle of the night. He was afraid of the dark.

The family plot was barely big enough to cover half a big league infield. Like the rest of the town, it was unirrigated. During morning hours, the Valenzuelas tended their crops — chickpeas and sunflowers mostly — and in the afternoons the sons hired themselves out as hands on larger farms to earn necessary cash.

Behind the house was a pig pen, the existence of which was noteworthy primarily for what lay alongside it: a thick slab of wood hammered onto a slight rise in the dirt. It was a pitcher's mound, built by Avelino's boys. Their games took place at the community ballfield, which was little more than a dirt clearing without backstop or plate. Logs served as benches.

Being the youngest allowed Fernando to get away with watching his brothers do most of the farm work, which suited him just fine since he spent most of his time playing baseball anyway — even during school hours. Once he was finally allowed to pitch, it didn't take long before Valenzuela (along with everybody else) recognized his strength on a ballfield. Soon he was holding his own against players as much as five years older.

Soon Fernando made a local all-star team, which took him to a tournament in the state capital, Hermosillo. Pitching relief in four of five games, he went 3-1 and was named series MVP. That led to a spot on the state all-star team, which traveled to the national tournament in La Paz, across the gulf to Baja California. There, encountering the same bias he'd been battling for much of his young life — *You're too young*, they told him — Valenzuela barely saw the field.

Still, Etchohuaquila's local team, the Navojoa Mayos, were sufficiently impressed to offer Fernando 5,000 pesos, or $250, for three months' work — not to play for their main club, located only about 30 miles from the Valenzuela homestead, but for a farm team in the mountain town of Tepic, some 550 miles down the coast. It was the first time Fernando had truly left home. "I remember waiting at the bus station with my father and mother," the pitcher recalled. "My mother cried and my father wanted to cry. My father told me only to behave myself and work hard."

From there, it was a whirlwind. Never mind that Fernando, having finished only one year of high school and still years away from needing to shave, was playing with grown men; after a winter in Tepic, he jumped to Puebla of the Mexican Central League, and then to Guanajuato, just north of Mexico City, where, pitching in relief, he led the league in strikeouts, with 91 in 96 innings. Any thoughts of returning to school were subsumed by baseball.

Enter the Dodgers.

Mike Brito was a man with big league dreams, signed out of pre-Castro Cuba as a teenage catcher in 1955 by legendary Washington Senators scout Joe Cambria.* During his later years, he became known as the man in the Panama hat holding a radar gun behind home plate at Dodger Stadium.

In between is where Brito made his mark. He spent five seasons in the minors, advancing as far as Hobbs, New Mexico, in the Class-B Southwestern League. That was where a home-plate collision in 1959 ruined his throwing elbow and relegated him to life as a Mexican League journeyman. Brito eventually moved to Los Angeles, where he founded a semipro league while driving an RC Cola truck for a living.

It wasn't until 1975 that his fortunes turned. Brito's team, the Latin Stars, was playing a game at Evergreen Park, about five miles southeast of Dodger Stadium. He came to bat late in the contest, his club trailing 3–2, with the tying run at third. On the mound for the opposition was

---

* "Cambria signed Tony Oliva, Camilo Pascual, Zoilo Versalles, Pedro Ramos," said Brito, looking back, "but he fucked up when he signed me. All those other guys made it to the big leagues."

a kid out of nearby Lincoln High School who'd recently washed out of the Kansas City Royals system, where he'd been trying to make it as a third baseman, after a single Rookie League season. His name was Bobby "Babo" Castillo, and his five-foot-ten, 170-pound physique seemed better suited to the assembly line on which he worked his day job than whatever big league aspirations he might once have held. The right-hander's fastball possessed so little life that Brito, far out in front on the first pitch, pulled it sharply foul.

Castillo's next offerings, however, were different. A breaking ball that seemed too developed for that level of play sailed almost side-ways across the plate. Brito swung and missed. Castillo followed with another, but this time the hitter was expecting it, and pulled it down the left-field line — foul by inches. Castillo had Brito right where he wanted him. He went to the well once more, offering up his third straight bender, this one even more dastardly than the other two: instead of breaking away from the hitter, it somehow broke *toward* him. Brito missed it by two feet.

He couldn't let it go. After the game, Brito tracked the pitcher down and brought up the offering that had fooled him so badly. "Was it a changeup?" he asked. Nope, said Castillo. Screwball.

"*Cabron*, a screwball?" exclaimed Brito, his mind awhirl. In addition to driving a truck and running a semipro league, he also served as a part-time scout for Reynosa of the Mexican League. Castillo seemed like a perfect fit. Soon thereafter, he called the young ballplayer at home and leveled a proposition. "Hey," he said eagerly, "do you want to play in Mexico?"

That was how Bobby Castillo ended up playing south of the border, so successfully that the Dodgers ended up traveling 1,600 miles to assess, and then sign, a hometown kid.* Campanis figured that, while he was at it, he might as well enlist the guy who discovered the pitcher, and brought Brito on as a part-time scout for $14,000 per year.

---

* Technically, the Dodgers purchased Castillo's contract from Kansas City.

That was the beginning.

The next step occurred on one of Brito's early assignments for the Dodgers during the summer of 1979, in Silao, a city smack in the middle of Mexico, where he went to see a minor league shortstop named Lazaro Usganga. It was Holy Week in the predominantly Catholic country, the final days of Lent, and with both of the city's hotels fully booked, Brito had to spend the night in the bus station, propped across the only four chairs in the place while he tried to approximate sleep. By the time he made it to the ballpark the next day, he was desperate to be impressed, but it turned out that Usganga was not the man for the job. Instead, Brito turned his attention to the left-handed pitcher from visiting Guanajuato, who struck out 12 batters, including the guy Brito had come to see.

It was, of course, Valenzuela. Even then, the lefty had the big leg kick and swinging arms, the ease of delivery and the gaze skyward that threw so many hitters for a loop. For Brito, the main attraction was not even Fernando's stuff, which was admittedly good, but his composure. "Twice, the other team had the bases loaded in that game, and he struck out the side both times," the scout recalled.* Brito tracked Valenzuela down after the game. "Do you feel like you can pitch in the big leagues?" he asked in Spanish.

"*Seguro*," Fernando said. *Sure.* The pitcher's nonchalance left an impression. Confidence was one thing, but this guy was in no way impressed that a big league ballclub knew his name, let alone might have wanted to sign him. "I said, 'I'm Mike Brito from the Los An-

---

* Valenzuela's 2.23 ERA for the Guanajuato Tuzos that season seemed dominant, but the Mexican Center League wasn't exactly known for offense. (Three teams boasted staff ERAs lower than Fernando's.) Still, Valenzuela was such an early sensation that a second scout, Corito Verona, had already alerted the Dodgers to his presence, reporting in 1978 that the teenager was a little wild and had "a chance" to make the big leagues. While noting the pitcher's weight, Verona even pointed out that he wasn't fat all over — his arms and legs were slim. The report failed to put Valenzuela on the team's radar.

geles Dodgers,'" recalled Brito. "He looked at me like I was nothing. He didn't give a shit. When I asked him questions, I had to pull the words out of his mouth. The guy has cold, cold blood." Fernando was 17 years old.

From that point forward, Brito served as Valenzuela's shadow, following him everywhere he pitched. He filed regular reports for the Dodgers and before long started calling Campanis directly to make sure his enthusiasm was properly received. It took the GM some time to come around. Fernando was so juvenile that he couldn't even vote in his home country, and the better part of a year passed before Campanis traveled to Mexico to see for himself what the fuss was all about. By then, Valenzuela was playing in the capital city of Merida, for the Yucatan Leones, after being signed by Puebla for 7,000 pesos — $320 — and put on loan. The Leones weren't good, and Fernando's record was only 10-12, but he struck out 152 in 25 games, including 15 in one contest, and would go on to win Rookie of the Year. Campanis was immediately smitten and quickly agreed to a $60,000 transfer fee to acquire the pitcher.* Everything seemed fine until the GM learned that the man with whom he'd dealt, Vicente Perez Avella, wasn't the team owner, as he'd thought, but the *son* of the team owner, Jaime Perez Avella. And Jaime Perez Avella had just fielded a $100,000 offer from the Yankees for Valenzuela. If Campanis wanted his man, the father informed him, he'd have to top it.

The general manager was outraged. Avella's son had bargained with him as a fully vested representative of the Puebla organization and had given his word. This was simply not how business was done. His trip wasted, Campanis was prepared to storm from the country

---

* It took some time for Campanis to let Brito in on his feelings about Valenzuela. After scouting the teenager in Merida, the GM took Brito to dinner, whereupon he didn't say a thing about the pitcher. It wasn't until they returned to their hotel, as Brito was unlocking the door to his room down the hall from Campanis that the GM piped up. "Mike, you're right," he said from in front of his own door. "This kid is a prospect."

and let men with lower standards conduct their affairs however they saw fit. The only thing keeping him rooted was Brito. "Chief, you're right," the scout pleaded. "You shook his hand. But are you really willing to lose this guy, Valenzuela, over a few thousand dollars?"

"Mike, it's not the money, it's the honor," Campanis responded. "You have to keep your word."

Brito knew how fastidious Campanis was when it came to deal-making, and was entirely unused to challenging his boss, but in this matter he was adamant. Virtue, the scout insisted, wouldn't keep Valenzuela off of somebody else's roster should the Dodgers turn their backs. Integrity wouldn't help a bit should the pitcher benefit some other team's bottom line, never mind the possibility of the Dodgers having to face him in a game. Surprising even himself, Brito began to get angry, less at Campanis than the fact that, for reasons beyond his control, the process was imploding. "We're not going to lose this guy," he shouted. "That will *not* happen." The GM, startled by his employee's fervor, took a moment to consider the sentiment. Recognizing the soundness of Brito's logic, he grudgingly returned to Avella and upped his offer to $120,000. Avella accepted. The sale was finalized on July 6, 1979, with $20,000 of the purchase price going to Fernando himself, as stipulated in Mexican League bylaws.*

The pitcher was given a temporary B-1 visa and sent straightaway to Lodi for the final weeks of the Single-A California League season, where he started three games, averaged eight innings per, struck out 18, and racked up a 1.12 ERA. His sparkling statistics, however, effectively masked the difficulties inherent to such a transition, made especially pronounced by the fact that Valenzuela was still a teenager and had never before crossed a national border. The Lodi club had a handful of Latino players on its roster, but Fernando ended up spend-

---

* Avella not only accepted the deal but honored it even after the Yankees tried to re-up the ante to $150,000. It didn't hurt that the Dodgers had faxed their end of the contract to Avella's office just before New York's new figure arrived.

ing most of his free time alone. Rural California, it turns out, has little in common with rural Mexico.*

From the very beginning, the Dodgers were enamored with Valenzuela's poise and command, but underwhelmed by his fastball, especially when he showed no improvement from the 88 miles per hour he'd displayed in Mexico. In a progress report to Campanis, Brito suggested that adding another pitch to the kid's arsenal — a split-fingered fastball, perhaps — might do the trick. A decent thought, responded Campanis, but we don't have anyone in the system who knows how to throw one.

Mulling it over, Brito realized that there was more than one direction by which they could reach their desired destination. Splitter tutors may have been scarce around the Dodgers chain, but there was one guy in the organization who possessed a unique and wildly effective breaking pitch: Bobby Castillo, the third baseman–turned–pitcher whose screwball had struck out Brito in a semipro game four years earlier, whose discovery had landed Brito a scouting gig with the Dodgers in the first place.† Castillo had by that point spent parts of three seasons in the big leagues. That October, Campanis sent Castillo and Valenzuela to the Arizona Instructional League to work things out.

"If that foul ball I hit had landed fair, I never would have signed Bobby Castillo, and Fernando never would have learned the screw-

---

* "He was this guy with a long Indian hairdo, this long strand of hair, and his baseball glove was like a tortilla, so wobbly and used up," said Paul Padilla, a trainer with Triple-A Albuquerque who, while passing through Lodi in 1979, saw Valenzuela shortly after the pitcher arrived in the country. Padilla was promoted to Los Angeles along with Valenzuela in '81, in part because, unlike anybody else on the big league training staff, he spoke Spanish and could communicate with the pitcher.

† An alternative narrative to Brito's story has Castillo learning the pitch *after* he got to the Mexican League, by watching an opponent named Enrique Romo throw one for Puerto Mexico. Romo went on to a six-year big league career.

ball," said Brito years later, describing his fateful at-bat against Castillo. "If that had been a fair ball I hit, who fucking cares about Bobby Castillo because I'd have tied the game. But he struck me out with a screwball, so I wanted to learn more about him. It was a difference for Fernando, for Babo, for me, for everybody. You see how destiny is."

The screwball looms large in baseball lore, in part because of its rarity and in part because of its daffy name. In simple terms, a screwball is a reverse curve. Whereas a typical breaking ball thrown by a lefty will bend in toward a right-handed hitter, a screwball bends away.* The benefit to the pitch, apart from its unusual break, is that when it's thrown properly, the pitcher's arm motion is indistinguishable from that of his fastball delivery. This means that hitters have to protect against the possibility of a fastball, even for screwgies that arrive a dozen miles per hour slower — never mind their bend — a difference in timing that is difficult to overcome. The pitch isn't more widely adopted because it can put unusual strain on the arm and is notoriously difficult to control. Where a regular curve is the result of a natural wrist snap in which the hand rotates outward, thumb to the sky, the screwball necessitates the opposite motion, effectively sending the ball out the back of the hand instead of the front. There's a reason that Castillo was the only pitcher in the organization who knew how to throw one.

Luckily for the Dodgers, he was a good teacher. Somehow, the US native with limited Spanish and the immigrant who'd barely adapted to his new country were immediately compatible.

Fernando's early screwball efforts crossed the plate flat and hit-

---

* It's not a perfect comparison, said catcher Mike Scioscia, intoning that Fernando's screwball was actually more like a right-hander's slider. The trick in catching it, he pointed out, was not in receiving the pitch but in blocking it when it hit the dirt. "It has different spin that'll stay down instead of coming up," he said, "so where a curveball will pop up a little bit, the screwball wouldn't."

table, which came as no surprise to Castillo, given his own steep learning curve. The greatest screwballer in baseball history was New York Giants Hall of Famer Carl Hubbell, who during the 1934 All-Star Game famously used the pitch to strike out, in order, Babe Ruth, Lou Gehrig, Jimmie Foxx, Al Simmons, and Joe Cronin, future Hall of Famers all. Hubbell, who was self-taught, said that it took him six years to master the pitch.*

Fernando wasn't much for waiting. A week into his lessons, his screwballs were no longer flat. When the season started, Castillo returned to Los Angeles, and Valenzuela was assigned to Double-A San Antonio, where he continued to refine the pitch with roving minor league instructor Ron Perranoski. Because right-handed hitters were able to lean in for screwballs that broke away from them, the coach tutored Fernando about how to back opponents off the plate with inside fastballs. The lefty made up for a lack of velocity with outstanding control, and took naturally to the instruction.

At first, Valenzuela used his screwball primarily in place of a changeup. By mid-June, he was throwing it not only more frequently but at different speeds. Soon he could augment his primary 77-mile-per-hour screwgie with a second offering that lolled in at 70 miles per hour, a 20-mile-per-hour difference from a fastball that suddenly bordered on being unfair to hitters. Prior to Perranoski's repertoire revamp, Valenzuela's record with San Antonio had been 6-9. In the eight games that followed, the left-hander went 7-0, with an ERA of 0.87. By their final session together, said Perranoski, "it was like watching a great horse in his last workout before the Kentucky Derby."

By season's end, Fernando led the Texas League in strikeouts and finished tied for fourth in victories, all while being the league's young-

---

* Hubbell, who named the screwball (its spin reminded him of a screw being driven into a board), came up with some indelible imagery in describing the difficulty of throwing it. "Nature never intended a man to turn his hand over that way throwing rocks at a bear," he offered in one such bromide.

est player and one of only two teenagers. As a lefty employed by the Dodgers, comparisons to Sandy Koufax were inevitable . . . although they were lost entirely on Valenzuela, who had never heard of the Hall of Famer.

Valenzuela's increasing comfort was not limited to pitching. The preponderance of Mexican culture in San Antonio, not to mention that familiar heat, offered soothing reminders of home. Still, he preferred to keep mostly to himself, watching a lot of TV — *The Pink Panther* cartoons were a favorite, given their lack of dialogue — in the hotel room where he stayed.

Valenzuela was unscored upon in 35 straight innings in 1980 when the Dodgers took a clear gamble and bypassed several prospects at Triple-A to bring him to the big leagues that September.* He'd made only 28 starts since leaving Mexico.

Fernando's first appearance as a major leaguer came on September 15, 1980, and presented one of the few times — the only time, really — that Lasorda tried to ease him into competition. The Dodgers were in Atlanta, and the Braves had already teed off against Burt Hooton for seven hits, scoring three runs in the first inning and two more in the third. LA trailed 5–0 in the sixth when the manager called for Valenzuela to be LA's third pitcher of the night. The left-hander allowed one hit over two innings of work, with two unearned runs scoring thanks to a pair of errors and a sacrifice fly. Following the 9–0 loss, Mike Littwin of the *Los Angeles Times* reported that "the only Dodger performance worth noting was by pitcher Fernando Valenzuela, who made his major league debut." It was the lefty's only mention.

Things improved from that point. Three scoreless innings against

---

* The kicker was that Valenzuela didn't even want the promotion. San Antonio was in the playoffs, and the pitcher wanted to see things through. When Fernando's Double-A manager, Ducky LeJohn, gave him the news, Valenzuela responded, "No, I want to finish here, I want to be a champion here." Eventually, and with no small effort, LeJohn convinced the kid to pack his bags.

Cincinnati here, one and a third scoreless against the Giants there. Fernando picked up a save on September 27, and a victory shortly thereafter, tossing shutout frame after shutout frame. Lasorda took to calling him "Carl Hubbellito," a screwball reference that was entirely lost on the youngster.*

Dodgers players exaggerated the culture gap for reporters, tongue almost always in cheek. "The only words with which I'm able to communicate with him are 'beer,' 'light beer,' and 'tacos,'" Scioscia said early on, despite being able to speak some Spanish himself. "So when he gets into trouble in a game, I call time and walk to the mound for a conference. I say to him, 'Beer, light beer and tacos.' He nods. I then call for a screwball, he strikes the man out and we win the game."

Less smooth was Valenzuela's transition to big league life. Upon arriving at the team hotel in Atlanta, he spent an hour in the lobby waiting for his suitcase, until bullpen catcher Mark Cresse informed him about the existence of bellhops, and let him know that his bag had already been delivered to his room. Communication suffered on the field as well, exemplified by the spring training discourse in which Perranoski told the *Los Angeles Times* that the pitcher threw one type of fastball, which catcher Joe Ferguson countered by saying that it was actually three fastballs — a cutter, a sinker, and a four-seamer — before Bobby Castillo countered *that*, clarifying that the sinker in question was actually a screwball. Valenzuela, of course, never weighed in at all, given the language barrier.†

---

* The resurgence of the screwball onto the big league scene got Hubbell's phone ringing like it hadn't in years. Yes, he told those who asked, he'd seen Valenzuela. "He has the right formula exactly for the screwball," said the 78-year-old legend, who called Fernando's screwgie "the best since mine."

† The following spring the team eventually asked Spanish-speaking reporter Lyle Spencer, from the *Los Angeles Herald Examiner*, to try to teach Valenzuela some English. The two ended up walking the Dodgertown grounds after dinner, Spencer drilling vocabulary for the increasingly frustrated pitcher, who said *no mas* after a handful of sessions.

The left-hander's appearances drew increasing amounts of interest, particularly, as concerned the Dodgers' ticket department, from the Los Angeles area's Hispanic population. "I've never seen anything like it," said Rudy Hoyos, a Spanish-language broadcaster who occasionally served as translator for Valenzuela early on. "They love him already." The news was well received by the front office, who'd long been seeking somebody with whom the local Mexican population could fall madly, enduringly, in love. Despite three championships and four additional World Series appearances over 23 years in Los Angeles, despite one of the most charming ballparks in baseball, and despite the fact that the Dodgers consistently led the major leagues in attendance, the team had never reached the one SoCal demographic that seemed most ripe for activation: Mexican expats. As it turned out, there was good reason for that.

Also, as it turned out, things were about to change in that regard.

5

Buried

They never told you about the conflict with the Mexican community in Chavez Ravine?

"No, never. They never spoke about what happened."

— Fernando Valenzuela

Chavez Ravine was once considered such undesirable real estate that for a time in the 1800s the city of Los Angeles used it to isolate smallpox patients. The place was only a mile northeast of downtown, but it might as well have been on the other side of the planet for the lack of interest shown by local developers.

The rugged hills surrounding the area's gorges and gullies kept the land available for generations of Mexican immigrants looking for a place to settle. Their numbers exploded following the revolution in their country in 1910, and again in 1913, when the city chose the spot to relocate about 250 families from the floodplain of the Los Angeles River. The influx led to the emergence of three barrios, called La Loma, Palo Verde, and Bishop, each nestled in its own ravine. A patchwork array of houses, hundreds strong, dotted the hillside, serviced by neither streetlights nor a unified sewage system. Only some of the roads were paved. About a quarter of the homes were built to modern standards, but many were effectively lean-tos, slabs of board or tin propped atop patchwork frames. According to a 1949 survey, one-third of the area's houses had no toilets and a significant percentage were without running water. Nearly 4,000 people lived in those hills.

The canyons, dotted naturally by meadows and wildflowers, came to bear an array of family orchards and gardens. Goats, chickens, and pigs wandered the hills, munching slopeside grass. The Palo Verde Street School provided American-style elementary education for area kids, while the Paducah Street School was geared more toward domestic skills like gardening. The community's center was the Santo Nino Church. For many residents, life in the ravines was as good as they could have hoped. It was both available and affordable. It also wouldn't last.

In late 1949, Los Angeles mayor Fletcher Bowron enlisted federal help to design and build 10,000 units of public housing in Chavez Ravine. That the land was already inhabited bore little consequence to city fathers; much of the extant development failed to meet civic standards (a Department of Health report called it "the worst slum in the city," despite the area possessing little of the blight typical of urban tenements), and besides, new construction would be easier there than in more populated regions of greater LA. So an offer was extended to area homeowners: sell your property to the city housing authority and receive, in addition to fair market value,* first crack at a spot in the soon-to-be-constructed apartment buildings, named Elysium Park Heights, after the surrounding parkland.

The clear-eyed among the residents saw the offer for what it was: an eviction notice with the chance to recoup at least something in exchange. The barrios were bound for demolition, that much was certain, and unsurrendered land would be seized via eminent domain. Cashing in was strictly optional.

---

* The definition of "fair" being entirely subjective, of course.

The planned housing would accommodate up to 17,000 residents, a massive population increase. At the city's instruction, architects Robert Alexander and Richard Neutra designed 13 high-rise towers, a number far exceeding what either man thought appropriate. Amenities in the blueprint included space for preschools and three churches, as well as a shopping center and a 1,500-seat auditorium.

When the housing authority began to purchase property in earnest in December 1950, a number of residents jumped aboard. With many offers failing to reach even five figures, however, sale prices did not come close to enabling the purchase of equivalent property elsewhere in Los Angeles. Some holdout residents were scared into selling by rampant rumors that the city would set fire to unevacuated dwellings, or that the police would arrest those who lingered too long.

As it turned out, those who lingered too long ended up making the most noise. A steadfast band of resisters refused to relinquish their homes, even in the face of increasing governmental pressure — pressure that, in 1953, came to include a new foe. Mayor Bowron was facing a reelection fight against conservative candidate Norris Poulson, whose campaign encouraged the red scare prevailing in American politics at the time. Poulson's platform decried the socialist nature of subsidized housing, a stance buffeted by local real estate developers, who by that point saw the abundance of available acreage so close to downtown as a potential gold mine. They even banded together, with Poulson joining the *Los Angeles Times*, the Chamber of Commerce, and a local home-building coalition to form a group called CASH — Citizens Against Socialist Housing. Spurred by donations from the construction sector, the city council repudiated its earlier authorization for the construction of Elysium Park Heights, mostly under the auspices of a gathering Communist threat. Councilman Harold Harby denounced public housing as a "creeping cancer" that would lead to "social decay."

Bowron vetoed the council's plan, insisting that the specter of returning some $13 million in federal development grants that had already been accepted for the Elysium Park Heights project would put the city at risk. Trying to placate the opposition, he negotiated a reduction in scope, to 7,000 units. Faced with two choices widely seen as unpalatable — condense the plan or scrap it entirely and refund the government's money — the population went for a third option: they voted Bowron out of office, in favor of Poulson. Among the new mayor's first acts was scuttling the proposed development.

That left the city with a bunch of mostly empty acreage and not a lot to do with it. Though the land had been earmarked for public use, the definition of that term changed markedly over time, especially once Walter O'Malley decided to move his baseball team out of Brooklyn and sought someplace in Los Angeles to plant his flag.

The Dodgers were an integral part of Brooklyn's fabric in the middle of the last century, but their 32,000-seat ballpark, Ebbets Field, was tiny even by 1950s standards. The team enjoyed a consistent draw, ranking among the National League's top two in attendance 15 times over 19 seasons through 1957, but Walter O'Malley could not help but consider the revenue lost from people he'd had to turn away. When Los Angeles made 300 acres of Chavez Ravine available for a proposed ballpark, then agreed to spend nearly $3 million on infrastructure improvements to the area, he packed up his ballclub and headed west.* The announcement was made one day after the LA city council approved the deal by a 10–4 vote.

Assorted opposition condemning the excessive public giveaway cropped up throughout Los Angeles, though virtually none of it championed displaced Mexicans as a central cause. That ended when the state supreme court overturned a lower-court injunction against the

---

* O'Malley's part of the bargain included building a 40-acre recreation center in Elysian Park. Even though it was the closest line item resembling something for the "public purpose" mandated in the land-use agreement, the center was never completed.

use of public land for a private ballpark, and the US Supreme Court refused to take up the case.

On March 10, 1959, the few families remaining in Chavez Ravine were informed that failure to vacate their homes would result in forcible removal. It was no bluff. The sheriff's department descended for compulsory evictions, TV crews close on its tail to record people being dragged from houses that in short order would be bulldozed in front of them.*

That was all it took, more or less. Ground was officially broken for the ballpark in September 1959, the woods and meadows bulldozed, and the hilltop flattened. The Santo Nino Church and Palo Verde Street School — not to mention Palo Verde Street itself — soon lay under tons of rubble. In all, more than 8 million yards of earth were displaced by the leveling of the ravines. Construction took three years, after which the main thing standing in Chavez Ravine was a shrine to baseball the likes of which the sport had never seen — a sleek, 56,000-seat treasure that, thanks in part to its proximity to the I-5 and I-10 freeways, would continually be filled to near-capacity.

The Dodgers sold just over a million tickets during their final season in Brooklyn. They about doubled that in each of their first four years in Southern California, and that was *before* Dodger Stadium opened, while the team was temporarily housed at the Los Angeles Coliseum.† Once the club moved into its new home in 1962, it blew at-

---

* The most prominent of these families, the Arechigas, had their door broken down and their belongings tossed to the curb. In an enduring TV image, one of the family's grown daughters, Aurora Vargas, was carried, shouting, down her soon-to-be-former front steps. All but powerless, the Arechigas returned to their property later that night, their house demolished, and set up camp, vowing never to relinquish their rights. They were forced out within a month.

† Constructed in the early 1920s, the Coliseum had been utilized almost exclusively for football, serving as the home field for the NFL's Rams and the University of Southern California football team. While the configuration of the oblong bowl was perfect for a rectangular football field, shoehorning a baseball diamond into it proved somewhat problematic. Home plate sat at the west end

tendance records from the water, setting a new standard with a draw of 2,755,184, and leading the National League in tickets sold for the next five seasons. LA reached the World Series four times during that span, winning three. People could not wait to see the Dodgers play.

All of them, anyway, but area Mexicans, many of whom refused to forgive the city — and by extension, its new baseball team — for its treatment of the former residents of Chavez Ravine.

The Dodgers knew exactly what they were missing. Apart from Mexico City, Los Angeles boasted a higher concentration of Mexicans than anyplace in the world, who by 1981 represented 2 million out of 7.5 million people in LA County. The potential for a Hispanic fan bloc was overwhelming, if only it could be reached. Doing so was not easy.

The Dodgers had been scouting south of the border since 1950, during which time they'd fielded a variety of Mexican players, none of whom inspired the masses. There was Vicente Romo, a pitcher out of Santa Rosalía, snatched from Cleveland's minor league system in the 1967 Rule 5 draft. He pitched one inning for LA before being returned to the Indians.

There was pitcher José Peña, from Chihuahua, acquired in a 1970 trade, who won six games over three seasons and was released. Catcher Sergio Robles was signed out of the Mexican League, went hitless in three at-bats with the Dodgers, and promptly returned home.*

When Mexican nationals failed to turn the trick, the Dodgers

---

of the Coliseum's floor, with the left-field wall only 250 feet away, its chip-shot distance mitigated by a 40-foot-high screen. Right-center jutted out to 440 feet, bounded by a temporary fence. Foul ground along the first-base line was nearly nonexistent, while on the opposite side it was enormous.

* It wasn't like other teams were having better success. Jorge Orta and Aurelio Rodríguez were the most prominent Mexicans to emerge in the big leagues during this time, but after that the ranks grew thin. The problem wasn't lack of talent so much as the fact that Mexican League teams, reluctant to cede their

tabbed players like pinch-hitter extraordinaire Manny Mota, who was Dominican but at least spoke Spanish. The closest they came to their original plan was Bobby Castillo, the guy who taught Valenzuela his screwball. Castillo had Mexican heritage, but grew up in East Los Angeles and spoke only English. Mexican fans continued to stay away.

Not that it hurt the bottom line. The Dodgers consistently led baseball in attendance, in 1978 becoming the first team to draw more than 3 million fans. Still, Al Campanis never stopped ordering his scouts to try to dig up a Mexican Sandy Koufax, somebody to activate Latinos the way that the Hall of Fame left-hander had activated Jews.

By the time Valenzuela's record hit 5-0 in 1981, it was safe to say that Latinos throughout the Southland were activated.* So, for that matter, was everybody else. Vendors began to crop up on the streets leading to Dodger Stadium, hawking all manner of Valenzuela-related fare, from souvenir T-shirts to buttons bearing slogans like I LIVE IN THE ~~SAN~~ FERNANDO VALLEY. The team's switchboard was inundated with ticket requests for the lefty's upcoming starts, and rumors swirled about John Belushi playing him in a biopic.† The pitcher would soon sign a deal to put his image on posters, and by the end of the season he had endorsed everything from flashlights to fruit juice to Mexican banks. "Our base scale for endorsements is $50,000," said

---

stars to the United States, tended to price them beyond the interest of foreign clubs.

* Steve Garvey described Valenzuela's influence in terms of overall attendance. "At Dodger Stadium, Monday nights are filled with season-ticket holders, people who come out and love the game," he said. "Tuesday nights you get a lot of people who are traveling, from out of town. On Wednesdays you get a mixed crowd. Friday nights they come in after work, a late crowd that has a few drinks and gets louder. Saturday's date night, Sunday's family night. LA has its nights, but in 1981 you started to see the emergence of the Hispanic fan — somebody who was engaged. They were there, they were active, they were cheering."

† It's not like reporters couldn't have guessed the answer when they asked the pitcher if he'd ever heard of the actor.

Valenzuela's agent, Antonio De Marco, toward the end of the season, though many of the pitcher's contracts were assumed to be for much more.

"The fan demographics of Dodger Stadium changed in a month," said reporter Peter Schmuck. "It was stunning to pull your car into the parking lot and drive by mariachi bands. Sure, Mexican Americans came to games, but not like *that*. It was so much fun, just a wonderful, unbelievable circus."

"The best part about it is that it was completely spontaneous and real," said Lyle Spencer, who covered the team for the *Los Angeles Herald Examiner*. "There was nothing fabricated about it. Fernandomania wasn't a creation of some PR department — it just happened."

Newspapers and magazines sent waves of reporters to Etchohuaquila for endless features that repeated the same details again and again.* New attention was paid to long-expired stars like Dizzy Dean (the last National League pitcher to win 30 games), Rube Marquard (the guy with the best start to a season in big league history, at 19-0), and Jack Chesbro (the last 40-game winner). Dean turned his trick in 1930, Marquard in 1912, and Chesbro all the way back in 1904. To say that Valenzuela's start was being viewed in anything but historic terms is to sell short the national obsession with the pitcher. Even long-forgotten hurlers like Hooks Wiltse and Atley Donald drew notice, owing to their sharing the rookie record with 12 consecutive wins, for the 1904 Giants and 1939 Yankees, respectively. Writers took to referencing a pitcher named Boo Ferriss, who upon being called up to Boston in 1945 completed his first 11 starts, including four shutouts

---

* Fernando's family, nonplussed by the attention, offered increasingly little information to the horde. So spooked were they by the outsiders that only four of the remaining six Valenzuela brothers agreed to a photo shoot at the local ballfield for the *Los Angeles Times*. Geraldo Valenzuela not only refused but hid inside the house.

and one 14-inning affair, with a relief appearance in between in which he earned the save. After Ferriss's first five starts, he was 5-0 with three shutouts and a 0.60 ERA. After Valenzuela's first five starts, he was 5-0 with three shutouts and a 0.20 ERA. Even better than the best ever, said Los Angelinos unconcerned with hyperbole.

The Dodgers did their best to foster a sense of order within the clubhouse. Rather than subject Fernando to unrelenting pregame attention, they arranged for a one-stop press conference in Houston to slake the media's thirst — and then expanded the policy to each city they visited thereafter. So as to avoid resentment among the rest of the staff, Lasorda offered press conferences to his other starters too. (They rejected the idea outright, unanimous in the opinion that more attention slathered upon Valenzuela meant more freedom from the press for themselves.)

The pitcher built camaraderie in his own low-key way, crafting lariats out of twine, which he'd use to lasso the feet of unsuspecting teammates as they walked past in the dugout. He'd perpetually tap players on the shoulder from behind, then disappear in the opposite direction. He juggled a hacky sack during pregame warm-ups for what seemed like hours on end. "He looked like a man, but he acted like a kid," recalled Dusty Baker, who, given his ability to speak Spanish, was one of Valenzuela's primary conduits to the team.*

Finally, during Fernando's sixth start, things fell apart . . . relatively speaking. Playing in Montreal — north of the US border, rather than the familiar south — Valenzuela had to be removed from a game for the first time as a big leaguer. Still, he pitched a full nine innings (the game went extras) and limited the Expos to one run on five hits with no walks while striking out seven. It took the opposition six innings to get a ball out of the infield. In the process, Fernando ran his record to

---

* The fact that Baker once played winter ball in Ciudad Obregon, just up the highway from Etchohuaquila, didn't hurt.

6-0 when the Dodgers scored five times in the 10th for a 6–1 victory, minutes after the pitcher was removed for a pinch-hitter in the top half of the frame. "We scored a run off him," enthused Expos catcher Gary Carter in the postgame clubhouse, seizing upon whatever positives he could. It was the second run Valenzuela had yielded as a big leaguer, and the first that meant anything. Back home, 59 percent of televisions tuned in to the game.*

The whirlwind got truly whirly at Fernando's next stop, in New York. It was unusual from the start, given that the Dodgers were still in Philadelphia when he arrived, but Valenzuela was scheduled to pitch the series opener at Shea Stadium, so the team sent him ahead a day early to meet the press. Wearing a brown leather jacket and slacks, Fernando uneasily stared down an interview room flooded with some 100 media members, as well as Hall of Famer Monte Irvin, serving as special envoy from the commissioner's office, and Mets catcher Álex Treviño, in the starting lineup for that night's game against the Giants, who, being from Monterrey, Mexico, did not want to miss it.

Valenzuela, a guy who didn't much like speaking even in general terms, found himself fending off increasingly pointed questions for more than an hour, fielding query after query about things like the labor discord that was making a strike look more likely by the day. "New York writers are so mean, and they tried to trap him in something," recalled Valenzuela's translator, broadcaster Jaime Jarrín. "Fernando didn't know anything about the strike. They said, 'How is it that you're so unaware of what's happening?' He said, 'I know how to pitch, that's it.'"

The rest of the Dodgers showed up at Shea Stadium a day later to face the Mets in front of 39,848 fans — not bad for a team that averaged

---

* The Dodgers' postgame show was the highest-rated program in Los Angeles that week, which is saying something in a town filled with screenwriters.

11,300 — plus noted sports artist LeRoy Neiman, who appeared before the game to sketch Valenzuela's portrait. As the pitcher attempted to put on his uniform, he was jostled by two photographers and an ESPN cameraman, part of a media contingent swelled to twice its usual size. When Fernando took the field for batting practice, he was followed down the runway by a bona-fide horde. "I felt like I was following the heavyweight champion, with all the media people and the handlers walking down to the field," recalled reporter Chris Mortensen. Upon returning to his locker after warm-ups, Valenzuela was forced to fend off *five* photographers, enough for Lasorda to chase the entire assemblage out of the clubhouse and lock the door, which was ordinarily open until first pitch.

The attention might have had something to do with the worst start of Fernando's career, the left-hander giving up four hits and four walks over the first three innings — and *still* he threw a complete-game shutout. He did this by getting Dave Kingman to ground into a bases-loaded double-play to end the first, striking out Bob Bailor with the bases loaded to end the second, and inducing a comebacker from Treviño with two men on in the third. The lefty settled down after that, holding the Mets to three harmless singles over the final six frames while whiffing 11 over the course of 142 pitches. He also gave away his inexperience when, with nobody on base in the middle innings, he caught sight of one of the jets that frequently buzzed Shea Stadium when taking off from nearby LaGuardia Airport. Entranced, the pitcher simply dropped his leg, held the ball, and watched in awe as it passed overhead.

At Valenzuela's postgame press conference, somebody asked whether he thought he could go his entire career undefeated. "Es my muy dificil," he said quietly. *It's very difficult.* After a brief pause, he finished the sentence: "Pero no es imposible." *But it's not impossible.* The way Fernando was going, the point had to be considered.

· · ·

It was supposed to be a walk in the park, almost literally. The Dodgers staged this kind of thing dozens of times each season, sending handfuls of players across the city for baseball clinics to build civic goodwill. The events would draw a couple hundred people, kids mostly. Players would sign some autographs, and everyone went home happy. Until Fernando came along.

On May 16, eight days after his start in New York (and two days after his subsequent complete-game victory over the Expos at Dodger Stadium, in which he gave up a career-high two runs while yielding a career-low three hits in running his record to 8-0), Valenzuela, Manny Mota, Bobby Castillo, Pedro Guerrero, and Steve Howe — the latter two being last-minute additions in a futile attempt to help divert the mob's attention from Valenzuela — were ferried in a white sheriff's van to Terrace Park in East Los Angeles. Four of the guys might as well have stayed home. From the moment Fernando stepped out of the vehicle he was overwhelmed by a crowd of more than 2,000 people, mainly adults, all of whom seemed to ask for his autograph at once.* The security detail, a dozen sheriffs and park guards, was entirely overwhelmed. A law enforcement helicopter hovered over the proceedings as if a crime was under way, lending a pastiche of *Escape from New York*, which would be released less than two months later.†

Valenzuela may have been imperturbable atop a baseball mound, but this kind of scene made him queasy. Four times during a five-min-

---

* Mike Brito and Valenzuela's agent, Antonio De Marco, were there, as was Fernando's father, Avelino. The senior Valenzuela, wearing a brown sweater and white shirt, looked on in bewilderment, offering not so much as a word to his son throughout the event. "His father didn't talk too much, and his mother was also very quiet," recalled Brito. "You had to push them just to answer questions. I thought, no wonder Fernando's so quiet."

† The more geographically appropriate follow-up, *Escape from LA*, didn't come out until 1996.

ute talk he said to the crowd, *"Es un placer para mí estar aquí con ust-edes de nuevo."* ("It's a pleasure for me to be here with you again.") As soon as he finished, the mob closed in, cutting off Fernando's primary avenue of escape and forcing the nervous pitcher backward into a women's restroom, where he shut himself in and waited for a police escort to safety.

Even at home, the pressure mounted. At first, Valenzuela lived in a motel in a Hispanic part of town near Dodger Stadium. Eventually, Brito invited the pitcher, along with his girlfriend (and future wife), Linda Burgos, to move into his guest house on Grande Vista Avenue in East Los Angeles. Brito's wife, Maria, cooked meals for them and washed their clothes. Fernando swam in the pool. Teammates like Pepe Frías and Pedro Guerrero visited for cookouts. Life there was fine. But as soon as Valenzuela passed through the front door, there they were, waiting, up to 50 fans at a time. "Fernando!" they screamed. "We love you!"

"Fernando liked his privacy," recalled Brito. "Sometimes he'd come out and sign autographs, but sometimes he wouldn't come out until the next day."

Perhaps it took something out of him. The pitcher's next start, at Dodger Stadium two days after the Terrace Park clinic, was the worst of his career.* That Mike Schmidt touched him for a first-inning ho-mer was one thing, but Philadelphia's rally in the third was more tell-ing. Valenzuela opened the frame with back-to-back walks, followed by back-to-back singles. The Phillies ended up scoring three runs and would add another before Fernando was removed for a pinch-hitter in the seventh — a jarring stat line considering that to that point he'd

---

* Fernando's heat in LA was actively measurable. He'd initially been scheduled to pitch a day later than he did, at which point the game sold out. When it was sub-sequently announced that Valenzuela's start would be bumped up, some 6,000 people exchanged their tickets, leaving the official gate at 43,812.

given up four runs *total* in eight starts and 72 innings. Perhaps the left-hander was preoccupied — his parents were in attendance — but more likely it was because opponents were starting to figure him out. Deadly as Valenzuela's screwball was, teams were recognizing that its primary power lay in its lure, tempting hitters to swing before it dropped wide of the strike zone prior to crossing the plate. Those able to lay off it were rewarded by jumping ahead in the count. That's what the Phillies did, handing Valenzuela his first loss in the ninth start of his career.

Fernando's next start was more of the same. Over eight innings at Cincinnati's Riverfront Stadium, he gave up his most-ever hits (eight), runs (five), and walks (three), while striking out only three. He was also caught looking unexpectedly boneheaded when, with Reds on first and second in the fifth inning, an infield rotation for a pickoff play at second base left nobody manning first.* This wouldn't have been a problem had Valenzuela thrown to the base as planned. Instead, he missed the sign and delivered a pitch, which Mario Soto bunted back to the mound. Fernando fielded it and instinctively threw toward first, then watched as the ball rolled unmolested toward the right-field corner as everybody, even Soto, rounded the bases and scored. Valenzuela didn't take a loss — the Dodgers tied it in the ninth and won it in the 10th — but his ERA, 0.29 only three starts earlier, was

---

* Wherein, with the batter squared to bunt, the corner infielders charge the plate; the shortstop (Russell) breaks for third, and the second baseman, in this case Derrel Thomas, slides in behind the runner at second to field the throw from the mound. It was the first time the Dodgers had used the play with Valenzuela on the mound, which was primarily a function of his barely being in trouble to that point in the season. Before the lefty faced Soto, Mike Scioscia and Ron Cey tried to explain the particulars to him, but were met mostly by the pitcher's laughter at the rudimentary nature of Scioscia's Spanish. "Obviously," said the catcher later, "I didn't get through." Two innings later, Valenzuela, again trying to force a runner at second on an attempted sacrifice, threw wide of the base for his second error of the day.

all the way up to 1.24. Still, Fernando was 8-1 and leading the hottest pitching staff in baseball. Two days later, Hooton won his seventh game without a defeat while dropping his ERA to 1.91. Reuss was 4-1, 1.51.* Most importantly, the Dodgers were 31-12, six and a half games in front of Cincinnati.

It was almost enough to obscure the fact that a strike loomed.

---

* The only pitcher to harbor apparent dissatisfaction was Rick Sutcliffe. The 1979 National League Rookie of the Year had gone from 17 wins in 1979 to three in 1980. He'd enjoyed a solid April in '81 (2-1 with a 2.30 ERA), but after he lasted a combined three and a third innings over his first two May starts, Lasorda dropped him from the rotation. "It just kind of makes me wonder if I wasn't sitting on a time bomb the whole time," said the bewildered pitcher, who wouldn't start another game all season.

6

Struck

By 1981, Major League Baseball had eclipsed the decade mark for its most extended period of tumultuous labor relations. Following nearly a century of copacetic existence — as defined by team owners telling players what to do and players doing it — the working-class members of baseball's hierarchy had gradually become well versed in how to push back.

It started, more or less, in 1969, when Curt Flood — 31 years old and a three-time All-Star for the St. Louis Cardinals — resisted a trade sending him to Philadelphia. After Commissioner Bowie Kuhn refused to honor his petition claiming the right to field offers from other teams before accepting transfer to the Phillies, Flood sued Major League Baseball, claiming antitrust violations — a case that reached the US Supreme Court.

Flood lost, 5–3 — baseball, ruled the majority, was a sport, not a business, and thus outside the scope of antitrust law — but his precedent emboldened others. In 1974, the players grew serious. At the urging of the MLB Players Association, pitchers Andy Messersmith (who'd racked up two top-five Cy Young finishes in his three seasons with the Dodgers) and Dave McNally both played the season without signed contracts — a status, claimed the union, that should qualify them for free agency. Until that point, players had been bound to teams by something called the reserve clause, which effectively kept them under team control until the team decided otherwise. Players could negotiate their contracts, of course, and owners were generally willing to enjoin them in an effort to keep the peace . . . but only up to a point. Should mutually agreeable terms fail to develop, the player had only two options: hold out or acquiesce.

The owners held virtually all the leverage. Under the reserve clause, management had the right, via section 10(a) of the Uniform Player's Contract, to renew a holdout player at the same terms as the previous season. Owners viewed this control as indefinite — invokable season after season. Marvin Miller, executive director of the Players Association, held a different opinion. Under his reading, the language described a one-off deal to be enacted and then discarded, after which the player should be absolved of his contract and thus become available to the highest bidder.

In March 1976, this is exactly how an arbitrator ruled, setting a groundbreaking precedent that would shake baseball's salary structure to its core.* At the end of that season, the first crop of 24 free agents was set loose upon baseball's landscape, with new deals averaging more than $200,000 at a time when baseball's average salary was just over $50,000. Reggie Jackson received a five-year, $3 million pact from the New York Yankees and would be a difference-maker in the next two World Series. Six members of the Oakland A's — Sal Bando, Don Baylor, Bert Campaneris, Rollie Fingers, Joe Rudi, and Gene Tenace — who had collectively earned $366,400 in 1976, signed with four teams, none of them the A's, for a total of almost $9.5 million over a combined 33 years.

By 1980, baseball's average salary had nearly tripled, to $143,756, and Kuhn was referring to free agency as a "time bomb." Financial losses over the next five years, the commissioner warned, would be

---

* In short order, Messersmith signed a three-year, $1 million deal with Atlanta. McNally, who had all but retired, was included in the claim to prevent the Dodgers from short-circuiting the process by offering Messersmith so outrageous a contract that he would withdraw his motion.

ten times greater than the "many millions of dollars" that owners had lost over the previous five.* Never mind that attendance had risen by nearly 50 percent during that span, from 29 million in 1975 to 43 million in 1980, or that the advent of cable TV was spurring a spike in franchise values. Baseball's owners wanted more.

Kuhn had first raised the prospect of change in 1979, when he invited Miller out for a drink at the 21 Club in New York and laid it on the line. Free agency was an experimental system requiring adjustments, he explained, and management was capitulating to the union at far too rapid a clip. "Marvin," he pleaded, "the owners need a victory."

What he had in mind involved expanded compensation for every free agent lost, a check on those who opted to spend too freely. Miller did not buy it. "Bowie," he rejoined, "they'll get compensation over my dead body." Miller meant it figuratively, though a number of owners considered the possibility. Teams that lost free agents were already being recompensed with additional selections in the amateur draft, which seemed paltry given that only three out of 60 such picks to that point had ever reached the majors. Then again, one of those players was Steve Howe, LA's 1980 National League Rookie of the Year, who from nearly the moment he stepped foot in Dodger Stadium had been ensconced as the team's closer.

Owners decided to set their sights higher. Any team losing a top-tier free agent ("Type A" in their parlance) should receive a bona-fide big leaguer in return, they said — not a star necessarily, but somebody roster-worthy. Under their plan, teams could protect between 15 and 18 men, depending on the quality of player they lost.† Everybody else was fair game.

---

* Kuhn was fond of using payroll increases to model uncontrollable salary growth, but failed to account for the natural leveling that was already occurring as owners and players alike settled into the process.

† The owners' qualifications for a "quality" player included finishing in the top

Management's argument hinged on its insistence that only three players would have qualified as Type A the previous season, based on an arcane system in which teams had to "draft" free agents before negotiating with them; Type A players would be those drafted by at least eight potential suitors. (The system, which capped the number of bidding teams at 12, was designed to artificially limit participation.) Miller was too canny to fall for it. He understood that top-tier free agents, no matter how populous their ranks, set the standard for the rest of the field. To diminish their value by tying them to compensatory selections from the major league roster — which would effectively turn every high-end free-agent signing into a straight-up player swap — would roll back numerous union gains. Marvin Miller did not do rollbacks.

Baseball's counterparts in the NFL offered clear evidence in support of Miller's stance. There, Commissioner Pete Rozelle had already established a similar equal-value system to compensate teams losing free agents, which effectively killed the practice. Baseball's proposal, though less stringent than the NFL's, shared the goal of discouraging such signings.

The disagreement left each side fervently guarding its borders. When the owners called for unilateral implementation prior to the 1980 season, the union set a strike deadline of May 22. An arrangement, however, proved elusive. The sides could agree on next to nothing, beginning with the definition of what even constituted a premium free agent. Forget the three guys who owners had bragged would have been the only Type A qualifiers in 1980* — by '81, the rule

---

half of the league in plate appearances (for hitters) or start/relief appearances (for pitchers), but somehow not the statistics therein. Miller immediately labeled the criteria absurd. He suggested benchmarks like rankings in Cy Young and MVP voting, and starting assignments in the All-Star Game. His notion was immediately rejected. Ray Grebey, the owners' chief negotiator, offered to include batting average, RBIs, and ERA, which the union summarily dismissed.
* Dave Winfield, Don Sutton, Darrell Porter.

would have sucked in half of the free-agent class. Said Miller: "They started out giving us Rod Carew and Vida Blue as examples of what they meant by premiere free agents. Now, their eleventh-hour proposal includes hitters with .222 averages and pitchers with earned-run averages above six."

A strike was averted with a compromise four-year agreement that tabled the free-agency issue until February of the following year, 1981, by which point not much had changed. With the owners still ensconced in their original position, the union set a new strike deadline of May 29, a mediator was enlisted, and talks began anew.

One thing that *had* changed was management's activity during the interim, the owners having arranged for $50 million worth of strike insurance in case the players walked.* That type of financial buffer, they figured, would provide significant leverage over the players, who'd been unable to secure a similar policy of their own. "They're trying to ram it down our throats," spat Dodgers player rep Jerry Reuss of the owners' plan. "They've got more money now than last year to combat a strike. I think that's what they've been planning all along."

As the deadline approached, the possibility of a walkout was at the forefront of every baseball discussion. If such an action occurred, it would mark baseball's first labor disruption since players were locked

---

* The full accounting included not only $50 million in insurance — withdrawn in one payment of $10 million and two of $20 million — but an estimated $15 million mutual assistance fund that the owners set up for themselves using 2 percent of their revenues in 1979 and '80. The fund was enacted to bridge the insurance policy's 153-game deductible, which covered the first 13 days of a strike, more or less. The policy itself — handled mostly by Lloyds of London at a cost of some $2 million — covered 500 games, with a payout of $1.8 million per team, which was enough to last more than two months. Insurers had accepted the contract under the impression that a strike was a remote possibility, even though baseball management clearly knew otherwise. It was a terrible deal for the insurers, a great one for the owners.

out for two weeks during spring training in 1976, and the first actual strike since 13 days were wiped off the front end of the 1972 schedule.

Management was all but counting on it.

With players set to lose $600,000 a day in salaries,* the owners — confident that even in the unlikely event of a strike, discord would not last more than a week or two — all but refused to negotiate as D-Day drew closer. The strategy served mostly to show how poorly they understood their employees. Marvin Miller recounted a player who, at the outset of the league's first walkout, in 1972, complained that the two-week strike would cost him $6,000 . . . and then earned back that same amount every one and a half days upon signing his first free-agent deal several seasons later. The union had battled tirelessly for this system, and damned if Miller would sell them out in the name of labor peace.†

Miller also knew that the owners' strike insurance policy was finite — providing $100,000 for each game missed, it would last only about two months. High-revenue teams like the Dodgers, on pace to draw 3.8 million fans, would suffer noteworthy hits to their bottom lines. Midmarket clubs like the Angels would probably break even if the season was canceled midway through the schedule. For teams at the bottom of the attendance barrel, like the Cubs, the Twins, and the Padres, the strike actually stood to be a moneymaker. With payroll and operating costs accounting for as much as 60 percent of their budgets,

---

* The number was provided by ownership's Player Relations Committee and included only straight salaries, not contractual obligations like bonuses or deferred compensation. The figure's total amount was $77.4 million, based on an average salary of $163,000.

† "Marvin had a saying along the lines of, 'Once it's in the pocket, you don't take it out and give it away,'" recalled Rick Monday. "When I came up, I was playing for $7,500. Not a week, and not even a month — for the entire year. In my estimation, Marvin Miller should be in the Hall of Fame."

slashing expenses made the possibility of insurance remuneration more lucrative than actually playing games.

The players pushed the deadline back to June 12 and, in conjunction with the National Labor Relations Board, filed an injunction claiming that the owners were bargaining unfairly. Even before the motion lost in court, the strike was in the foreground of virtually every conversation about baseball.

Whatever worry the Dodgers felt was reflected by their play. Los Angeles, six and a half games up in the standings on May 25, lost seven of their next 10. They dropped two of three to fourth-place Atlanta, then two of three to the last-place Cubs, their lead over Cincinnati shrinking game by inexorable game. By the time the Dodgers traveled from Wrigley Field to St. Louis on June 8, their cushion was down to two and a half games. "You could feel the tenseness in the air," recalled Dave Goltz.

Things were imploding across the roster. Hooton was hammered in his first loss of the season, yielding five runs over five innings in a 9–1 throttling by Cincinnati. In his next start, he didn't make it out of the first against the Braves, dropping his record to 7-2.

Even more worrisome was Valenzuela. After surrendering five runs to the Reds on May 23, the lefty put up his new worst start ever, giving up six hits and seven runs to Atlanta across three and two-thirds innings in a 9–4 loss. Two starts later he was even shoddier, yielding seven runs over three and a third to the Cubs, who at that point had won only 12 of 48 games. Making things even more painful was that the Cubs not only possessed the worst record in the majors and were the National League's lowest-scoring team but were without their two best hitters, Leon Durham and Steve Henderson. There was also the fact that the Dodgers had staked Fernando to his biggest-ever early lead, 4–0, in the second inning. He didn't come close to making it hold up.

Suddenly, the success that had looked so immutable only a week earlier appeared to be strictly temporary. LA's masterful early-season pitching, it turned out, had masked some serious offensive deficiencies. Davey Lopes — 2-for-his-first-35 on the season, including a 25-at-bat hitless streak — was batting only .171 before jamming his ankle against the Mets on May 17, which sidelined him indefinitely.* Bill Russell was hitting .191 with no homers and four doubles when the calendar turned to June. Even Steve Garvey, who'd finished in the league's top 10 in hitting six of the previous seven years, slipped to .218 in the middle of May. "Maybe age had started to show, and guys were thinking about the same thing," reflected Goltz. "They had only a certain amount of time left, and they wanted to do something good with it. Maybe that half-step that they were used to having was starting to go away, and they were realizing that too."

"We've got some key guys not hitting," said a defiant Lasorda in May, "but I'm not taking them out."

In Valenzuela's five starts following his 8-0 skyrocket opening to the season, he went 1-3 with a 6.97 ERA. His screwball wasn't as crisp as it had been early on, and his walk rate doubled to more than four per contest. People started talking about the 14 pounds he'd gained since spring training, and Brito was tasked with implementing a strict diet that eliminated soda and tortillas while restricting the pitcher to two meals per day. For the first time in Fernando's short career, he refused to speak with the press after a game. *No quiero hablar.*†

It didn't stop his freight train, of course. Even as Valenzuela strug-

---

* The injury occurred on a steal of third, with Los Angeles leading 5–0. It was not appreciated by Mets pitcher Dyar Miller, who walked over to Lopes, still writhing on the ground, and told him that he deserved to get hurt for trying such a stupid play. Various Dodgers charged from their dugout in short order, and Reggie Smith had to be restrained from going after the pitcher. The injury was especially painful since Lopes was just starting to heat up, putting together a five-game hitting streak during which he'd scored a dozen runs and raised his average by 28 points.

† That decision came courtesy of Davey Lopes, who, upon espying a distraught Valenzuela fretting about his impending postgame press conference, issued point-blank orders to ice his arm and get the hell back to the hotel.

gled, intrigue about him climbed to the highest ranks of American society, culminating with a call from the White House, which issued an
invitation to join Ronald Reagan and Mexican president José López
Portillo for a state luncheon in Washington, DC, on June 8. Coming
as it did on an off-day, the request was difficult to refuse. The pitcher,
along with translator Jaime Jarrín and agent Antonio De Marco, flew
to Washington with plans to rejoin the Dodgers in St. Louis the following morning.

The US president is usually the most magnetic figure in any room
he enters, especially during state events. In this case there were *two*
presidents present—Reagan and Portillo—but neither could touch
Fernando's star power. As press corps photographers jostled for position, the attending dignitaries—including Vice President George H.
W. Bush, Secretary of State Alexander Haig, and Secretary of Defense
Caspar Weinberger—brushed off usual protocol and took their turns
approaching the pitcher, who looked unusually dapper in a gray pin-
stripe suit. Throwing his arm across Valenzuela's shoulder, Haig said
breezily, "I hear you're a great ballplayer."*

"The most powerful people in the country were in line, waiting for
this kid from Mexico to sign an autograph for them," recalled Jarrín.
"It was unbelievable."†

The trip did little to salve Valenzuela's issues on the field, let alone
those of his teammates. In St. Louis, Hooton picked up his third loss
in as many starts, surrendering five runs over four innings and shoot-
ing his ERA to 2.97, more than a full point higher than it had been at
the start of the run. Two days later, Valenzuela suffered his fourth

---

* It was an easier topic than the other item currently dominating Haig's attention: Israel's recent raid on an atomic reactor in Iraq.
† When Mike Brito asked Valenzuela about it later, he couldn't believe the response. "He didn't give a shit," said the scout, looking back. "I asked how he liked
it, and he said, 'I went to say hello to him.'" *Him*, meaning Reagan. "A young man
like that, coming from a Latin American country, going to see the president of
the United States . . ." said Brito. "You know, he just didn't get that excited."

loss in five decisions, giving up two runs across seven innings in a 2–1 defeat to the Cardinals.

Hooton's loss knocked the Dodgers' lead over Cincinnati down to a game and a half. Valenzuela's shrank it to half a game. Five games' worth of ground had disappeared within the span of a week. "Things got very quiet in that clubhouse," said Rick Monday, looking back. "We had a bunch of veterans who understood that the way to get out of this thing is not by waving rally towels, but by busting our butts and getting to work. And we knew that a work stoppage was probably right around the corner."

If a strike occurred as advertised, it would be just in the nick of time as far as LA's postseason hopes were concerned. The Dodgers' last win — a three-hit, 4–1 victory by Jerry Reuss in the second game of the series, sandwiched between the losses by Hooton and Valenzuela — would effectively clinch the National League West should play fail to resume.*

That was itself something. Reuss was known for his dour disposition on the days he pitched, his usually sunny demeanor shifting into something far darker, a mask that discouraged anybody around him from approaching on game day. Usually this wasn't a problem, but Reuss also served as the Dodgers' union representative and, as such, was the man his teammates — with a potential strike sprawled across their collective doorstep — turned to for updates and information. The pitcher had phoned the Players Association offices for a labor update before coming to the ballpark on the day of his start, and he briefed his teammates upon arrival. He also held an unusual, strike-related press conference to fill in reporters, which ran to within 45 minutes of first pitch. Among the questions he fielded was, "You got anything else to do tonight, Jerry?"

---

* Fittingly, Reuss, a St. Louis native, stayed with his parents — in his childhood bedroom no less — when the Dodgers visited town. The space remained unchanged from his time there as a teenager in the mid-1960s.

As it happened, he did. Reuss tossed an 85-pitch complete game, with stuff even better than he displayed while no-hitting the Giants in 1980, he said later. With the understanding that the season might well collapse in on itself in a matter of hours, the importance of the victory was well understood.

After the game, Jay Johnstone posted a sign above his locker that read, "FOR WHOEVER CARES, I'LL BE IN LAS VEGAS AT THE DUNES HOTEL. JAY." In the manager's office, Tommy Lasorda wanted nothing to do with strike talk, proclaiming bluntly, "There is no strike." When somebody pointed out the abundant potential for one, Lasorda replied, "There's potential for a hurricane, too."

That was Wednesday. By Thursday night, the Player Relations Committee had issued a statement declaring the season "canceled until further notice." Miller set about notifying union leaders. The strike was on.

The Dodgers were scheduled to fly to Pittsburgh immediately following Thursday's game, but instead, with the strike looming, spent the night in St. Louis, with morning travel planned in either one direction (east, to Pennsylvania) or the other (west, back home), depending on how things played out. When word of the walkout came down, management informed players that they would be ferried to the airport and no farther. They were refusing employment by the Dodgers and so were cut off from access to the team plane.

The Kay-O II* was there, of course, parked at gate 22, but the only people getting on were Lasorda, the coaches, trainers, equipment managers, a clubhouse kid, and various management types.† Striking

---

* The Dodgers' aircraft, named after Walter O'Malley's wife, Kay.

† Early in the season the Dodgers began a tradition of settling into every flight with a song made up in honor of bald-headed trainer Paul Padilla. As the jet taxied down the runway, the entire team, led by Terry Forster, would sing (to the tune of "Hooray for Hollywood"): "Mr. Potato Head / Mr. Potato Head / You have

players watched helplessly through terminal windows. "[Refusing entry onto the plane] is not a punitive action," insisted Al Campanis, one of those to board. "These are just the measures accepted in this type of situation. This is part of our overall arrangement with the player relations committee."

Players had a decision to make: return to Los Angeles on a different flight, in case the strike was settled quickly, or head home, wherever that might be. Limbo, thy name is Lambert Field. The situation wasn't pleasant for anybody, but for some members of the roster it was downright terrifying. Dave Stewart, for one, couldn't afford the last-minute airfare and had to borrow money just to make it home.*

Dodgers players lit out across the map. Many of the veterans who lived in Southern California had already made contingency reservations on a 6:15 p.m. flight to Los Angeles. Mike Scioscia rented a car and drove two and a half hours to visit his brother in Bloomington, Illinois, before returning home to Philadelphia. Ken Landreaux ended up at his off-season home in Tucson,† and Dave Goltz traveled to his lake house in western Minnesota. Assistant trainer Paul Padilla, in his first year with the team, made so little money that, upon returning to LA, he couldn't afford to see his wife and three young children in Albuquerque. Enter Dusty Baker, who upon hearing about the trainer's plight, extracted $300 from his wallet, with which Padilla booked a bus ticket.

The issue at hand was straightforward, but the solution was complex. The union proposed a compromise measure wherein clubs draft-

---

more hair on your ass / Than on your head." The return trip to Los Angeles that day marked the first time all season the song was not sung.

* As if to intentionally lend extra surrealism to the situation, about an hour after the team's front-office personnel boarded the jet, they were forced to return to the terminal, their flight delayed by engine trouble.

† It was the first time Landreaux had spent any time in Arizona during the summer, and the heat was sufficiently brutal to inspire him to ditch the place altogether and move back to California full-time.

ing free agents would contribute four players each from their 40-man rosters to a pool from which the teams that lost free agents could fish. This would avoid the one-for-one balance of the owners' proposal and make free agency seem less like a straight-up player swap. The owners said that in order to accept such a plan, teams contributing players had to *sign* free agents, not just draft them, and that 25 players off of each 40-man roster should be eligible, greatly increasing the cost of new signings. Commissioner Kuhn bandied about a term he'd coined — *competitive balance* — to describe what he was seeking.

It was a nonstarter, which the owners knew when they proposed it. Management, in fact, seemed so uninterested in compromise that Marvin Miller didn't even show up during the early talks, feeling that he'd serve mainly as a distraction. Instead, he left matters to MLBPA attorney Donald Fehr and a handful of players.

In the face of the stubbornly cohesive union, management set out to shore up its own ranks. On the strike's very first day, Angels boss Gene Autry telegrammed his ownership peers, urging (or strong-arming, depending on one's perspective) unanimous embrace of management's Player Relations Committee, for which disdain of compromise was old hat. It didn't take long, however, for cracks to appear. Even as hard-liners like Tigers owner John Fetzer and Royals owner Ewing Kauffman threatened to sell their teams should management cave,* several others — Peter O'Malley prominent among them — lobbied for conciliation. As the scion of baseball's most powerful owner and a member of MLB's Executive Committee since his second year as club president, O'Malley's rational pliability was no small matter. Soon reports circulated that even George Steinbrenner, speaking for several of his colleagues, was questioning whether baseball's chief negotiator, Ray Grebey, had more interest in beating Marvin Miller than in

---

* Kauffman did not sell his team. It took Fetzer two years to do so.

crafting a deal that made sense for the sport.* In response, the Player Relations Committee implemented a crackdown on dissent, docking Brewers GM Harry Dalton fifty grand for publicly rooting against what he called "another macho test of wills" and threatening fines of up to half a million dollars for any future insurrections. When it became clear that some labor-friendly owners planned to publicly air their grievances at an upcoming owners' meeting — called long before the strike to discuss broadcast arrangements — the Executive Committee responded by scrapping the meeting altogether. The playing of baseball, it seemed, was a long way off.

Radio and TV stations that had been counting on full broadcast schedules scrambled for replacement programming. On the first Saturday after the strike, NBC showed highlights from Game 6 of the 1975 World Series rather than its previously scheduled game of the week. ESPN, along with radio outlets in places like Cleveland, Baltimore, and Cincinnati, aired minor league baseball.

In Los Angeles, instead of Dodgers broadcasts, KTTV eschewed baseball entirely for what it called "normal, family-oriented programming." The team's radio home, KABC, followed suit.

On June 16, less than a week into the strike, the *Los Angeles Times* reprinted its account of the Dodgers' first game in Los Angeles, a 6–5 win over the Giants. Soon the newspaper would report on games from 1951 (Bobby Thomson's "shot heard 'round the world"), 1956 (Don Larsen's perfect game), 1959 (beating the Braves to clinch the National League pennant), 1961 (the first-ever Angels game), 1962 (the first no-hitter at Dodger Stadium, thrown by Sandy Koufax, and the Giants squeaking by the Dodgers for the National League pennant),

---

* Not helping was Kuhn's refusal to allow Steinbrenner, Rangers owner Eddie Chiles, and Orioles owner Edward Bennett Williams — three of the most pro-settlement owners — to join the negotiating sessions. Chiles responded by waging a protracted behind-the-scenes campaign to oust the commissioner.

1965 (Koufax's perfect game against the Cubs and Juan Marichal going Paul Bunyan on the head of Johnny Roseboro), and 1975 (Nolan Ryan's fourth no-hitter).

Across town, the *Los Angeles Herald Examiner* published something called "Strikeball," a daily feature based on simulated games. (On Father's Day, the newspaper, acquiescing to a request from the father of Red Sox catcher and Southern California native Gary Allenson,* had the player hit a called-shot home run in honor of his dad.) The *Long Beach Press-Telegram* tapped staffers and readers for firsthand accounts of their most memorable sporting moments. Up the coast, the *San Francisco Examiner* went full fiction, printing a fantasy story about Giants free-agent bust Rennie Stennett — at the time hitting a punchless .231 and reduced to backup status in the second season of a five-year, $3.25 million deal — giving up his salary to live life as a beach hermit subsisting on abalone.

The players, most experiencing their first event-free summer in years, endured similarly difficult transitions. Pam Forster, wife of Dodgers pitcher Terry, may as well have been speaking for the majority of her counterparts when she said, "The worst part is the realization that there is nothing else out there that he is trained to do. All Terry was trained for was to be a baseball player from the time he was 15, and even younger. He didn't go to college because he was offered a contract. Everything in the last 15, 20 years has been geared toward baseball. All of a sudden there's nowhere else to go." Players' final paychecks, prorated, arrived on June 15. The money would have to last.†

· · ·

Early on, Dodgers players maintained a semblance of communal activity. On June 18, a week into the strike, eight of them, all living locally, showed up for a workout at USC's Dedeaux Field, where at high noon and in 100-degree swelter they took batting practice against a Trojans assistant while giddy undergrads shagged. "Somehow," recalled Monday, "bats and balls mysteriously appeared for us to use." It didn't take Detective Lieutenant Dan August* to connect Trojans coach Rod Dedeaux with his good friend Tommy Lasorda, who may or may not have possessed a vested interest in making sure his charges stayed sharp.

Most prominent in the day's activities was the fact that a passel of players was suddenly available for on-the-record comment. The media descended, and hard-line rhetoric ensued. "I don't care if we've got to sell our homes, we will hold out," proclaimed Dusty Baker. Added Bill Russell, endorsing his teammate's avowal: "Hell yeah, I would."

Before long, however, the passion waned. Attempts to field regular workouts fizzled, precisely because Baker and his teammates did not have to sell their homes.† With residences spread across the San Fernando Valley to the north and Orange County to the south and seemingly perpetual traffic in between, players were simply too isolated from each other for sustained motivation to gather. Soon, even the effort to meet in some central location seemed a bridge too far. "We were just taking ground balls and fly balls, and running and throwing and hitting," recalled Ron Cey. "After a while it got pretty stale. We were able to stay on top of it when we were hopeful that things would

---

income, especially considering that a 10-game homestand had been scheduled to start only days after the players walked.

* As portrayed by Burt Reynolds in the early-1970s ABC-TV series *Dan August*. Reynolds was a regular in Lasorda's office over the years, at least partly mitigating the obscure reference here.

† Baker, in fact, was building a house in Calabasas, with construction costs that made his $4,444 daily salary loss particularly painful.

get better quickly, but then the strike went on and on, and guys got discouraged."

"We thought at first it would only be a week or two, and then it got depressing, frustrating," said Monday. "After a while, you start to wonder if it's frivolous."

So instead of meeting, they stayed near home. Baker worked out with neighbor and former teammate Lee Lacy, integrating solo activities like swimming into his regimen. He recalled the 1972 strike that began his rookie season with Atlanta, when he ignored Hank Aaron's imploration to stay in shape. Figuring that the discord would last only a few days, Baker assumed he wouldn't play anyway once games resumed, given his low spot on the totem. Then, in the first game back, Orlando Cepeda hurt his knee, Aaron was shifted to first base, and Dusty was asked to cover in the outfield. He hit an RBI single in that game, then went 0-for-his-next-20. "I *told* you to work out," Aaron scolded.*

Now, to keep his eyes sharp, Baker took occasional trips to Buddy's Bat-a-Way in Van Nuys and played wiffle ball with his 11-year-old nephew, Juan. "He killed me at first, but then I got the knack back," recalled Baker. "I figured if I could hit that wiffle ball, I could hit anybody."

Across town, Landreaux spent time in his garage with weights and a speed bag. Johnstone also drilled in a garage, this one at his childhood home in West Covina, where from the driveway he hit tennis balls off a tee into the open doorway. ("My dad's garage was bigger than mine," he reasoned. "Also, I didn't want to damage my own garage.") In LA, Goltz long-tossed with his old pitching coach from the Twins, Don McMahon, and upon returning home to Minnesota pitched to his old youth league catcher. Mike Scioscia took things a step further and practiced with his former Babe Ruth team in Pennsylvania. "I ac-

---

* The kicker: Baker would finish third in the league with a .321 batting average. Minus that hitless stretch, he would have finished first, at .335.

tually played in a couple of games, scrimmages with semipro teams," he said. "I wasn't really supposed to do that, but I was just so bored."

Dave Stewart and Bobby Castillo occasionally drilled together at Cal State Los Angeles. Derrel Thomas worked out at Mar Vista High School in San Diego with whoever happened to be around. Terry Forster threw every couple of days, but most of his time, he said, was spent "getting anxious," "getting old," and "going crazy."

Steve Garvey, for one, was grateful for the break, if only because he had injured his wrist sliding into second base two weeks before the strike. Treatment had not helped, and loathe as the iron man was to taking a day off, that eventuality had been looking more and more likely. When the strike was called, he'd played in 892 consecutive games dating back to September 2, 1975, powering through bouts of flu (1976), a pulled hamstring (1977), and 22 stitches after he caught a pickoff throw from Bob Welch with his face instead of his glove in 1978. His wrist, though, simply wasn't allowing him to perform. "Eventually I realized that if something doesn't get better, it's probably getting worse," said Garvey, looking back. "I was pretty much resolved that this might be it, and that I'd have to take some days off. I said a few Our Fathers and Hail Marys and put it in God's hands . . . and then the call came. The strike was on." Any number of players viewed Marvin Miller as heaven-sent, but Garvey may have been the only one to mean it literally.*

Al Campanis sent letters to Dodgers players requesting restraint from various household activities while away from the team. "He didn't want us to use power tools or to mow our own grass," recalled Yeager, "because he was afraid we'd slip and fall." For some Dodgers, though, inactivity was not an option. With income erased and no union strike fund on which to lean, the lesser-paid among them — mostly younger guys, who'd had neither the time nor the resources

---

* Garvey would go on to play in 1,207 straight games, at the time second only in the modern era to Lou Gehrig.

to build up excess liquidity — were forced to seek work. Other players picked up summertime gigs simply because they had nothing better to do.

Steve Howe became a celebrity salesman at a Chevrolet dealership in East LA. Jerry Reuss endorsed the En'Chante line of women's jeans. Johnstone went to work at his father-in-law's auto parts store, helping with deliveries. He also used his entertainment industry connections to pocket some extra cash with another sort of delivery, ferrying a new rock record to radio stations via limousine. The tie-in: it was called "On Strike," by a band called Union.*

Ron Cey used his Hollywood adjacency to pursue loftier entertainment positions, enlisting to appear alongside David Carradine in a B movie titled *Serpent: The Ultimate Thriller*,† which began filming shortly after the strike hit. "I play an LA-based detective working with David on a series of mysterious murders," said an excited Penguin upon signing on. "He has this theory that a giant snake is killing the people, and I'm skeptical about it." (The snake was actually a resurrected serpent god, partial to using his power of flight to snatch bikini-clad, sunbathing New Yorkers from Manhattan rooftops.) Cey sat alongside Carradine at the promotional press conference in Beverly Hills, which was covered by another Dodger who'd taken part-time work in front of a camera, Rick Monday, there on behalf of ABC-TV's Channel 7 news. Ultimately, Cey's character, Detective Hoberman, didn't appear until 82 minutes into the 92-minute runtime, and then only for a nervous look skyward and a quick burst of gunfire.‡

Still, it was a glamorous way to spend some downtime. As a nine-

---

* Featuring Randy Bachman and Fred Turner from Canadian darlings Bachman-Turner Overdrive, of "Taking Care of Business" fame.

† Later rebranded as *Q: The Winged Serpent*.

‡ It wasn't Cey's first foray into the entertainment industry. In 1976, the third baseman — at the urging of Al Campanis's son, Jim, a community affairs representative for the team — recorded a country-tinged song called "Third Base Bag," backed by the R&B-ish "One Game at a Time." Cey laid the tracks down in one

year veteran, Cey could afford it. At the opposite end of the spectrum was Dave Stewart, whose financial outlook was sufficiently dire for him to take a job with a hardware manufacturer, packaging nuts and bolts (among other duties) for $75 a day. It wasn't Stewart's celebrity that landed him the gig, but concern from a member of the Dodgers' publicity staff, Jo Wetton. "I just knew how the strike was going to affect many of the younger players," she said, looking back. Stewart was, in fact, having trouble squaring indeterminate joblessness with accruing bills for two cars and an apartment on Overland Avenue in West Los Angeles, not to mention responsibility for a wife and a four-year-old son. He'd been pulling in the major league minimum, $32,500, and was in no shape to absorb a financial hit.*

Wetton's son, Scott, a former batboy for the team, worked at a place called Smith Fastener Company, in the industrial LA suburb of Bell, and at his mother's urging spoke to his boss about temporarily bringing an unemployed Dodger into his fold. This is how the company's owner, Brad Jenkins, a man who knew little about baseball, came to hire a ballplayer who knew little about hardware. The pitcher did some warehouse work and was interested in the accounting end of the organization, but his true value was as arm candy to Jenkins — somebody to bring to client meetings.

Stewart ended up spurring a bounty of positive PR for the company, with features in the *Los Angeles Times* and on the local CBS affiliate. "I certainly got name recognition out of it," said Jenkins, looking back. "Whether or not I got sales, who knows?"

After his warehouse shifts wrapped up, Stewart took to joining Castillo for workouts with a semipro team called the Redbirds.

---

sitting on his way to a game in San Diego. He went 0-for-4 in the game, then went hitless in the studio as well. Worth a cringe listen on YouTube.

* "We don't have people in socially anymore," said the pitcher at the time, describing some ways in which he was cutting down on expenses, "but the big thing is that we don't go dancing every weekend like we did."

"Man," said the pitcher in bewilderment, "we didn't have this kind of problem at Albuquerque."

Stewart's dilemma stood in stark contrast to about a dozen players around the league, including Steve Garvey and Derrel Thomas, who, through means that most could not fathom, were getting paid through the strike.

Garvey had filed an official notice of contract default, which, effective or not, the team had 10 days to resolve at risk of the player being declared a free agent. This is more or less what happened eight years earlier when Catfish Hunter was ruled to have played the 1974 season without a valid contract and was subsequently allowed to sell his services to the highest bidder. Peter O'Malley tried to get out in front of the issue, clarifying that "nobody has a clause that says they'd get paid in case of a strike, but in the cases of Garvey and Thomas, they filed default notices and we have to protect ourselves."

This was not entirely accurate. Thomas's contract, at least, had wording that, while not specifically citing a strike, ensured that his paychecks would continue to flow uninterrupted. "The contract guaranteed payment except in cases of things like voluntary retirement and suspension for bad behavior," said Thomas's then-agent, Steve Greenberg, looking back. "Because we specifically enumerated the circumstances under which he would *not* be paid, and a strike was not among of them, he ended up getting paid." Thomas had signed a five-year deal as a free agent in November 1978, only two seasons after baseball's first free-agency class had come to the fore. Such language — anything outside the parameters of the standard player's contract — was new to the sport. "We just got lucky that the Dodgers missed it," said Greenberg years later. "It would be standard operating procedure today for teams to call out that kind of thing."

Garvey said he felt that others would not resent him for being paid because "everybody had an opportunity to negotiate their contract, and had input into the wording." It was a tone-deaf response, an example of the first baseman's inability to read the temperature of a room. His teammates *were* upset, and his proclamations did nothing to assuage them.* Bill Russell called out the maneuver as running counter to the ethos of the strike. Reggie Smith dismissed Garvey's explanation entirely, reading into it a veiled insult toward those players not smart (or ballsy) enough to explore similar options.

As usual, the most outspoken Dodger on the topic was Davey Lopes. He and Garvey had been teammates since Triple-A Spokane in 1970, but a decade on, Lopes had little use for the first baseman's approach. "We all voted to strike, and now what does his vote mean?" he asked. "It means absolutely nothing now. It means absolutely nothing for anybody who accepts money, regardless of their intentions. I think it's very hypocritical. This is one of the reasons players are made to look like jerks. This stuff snowballs." Lopes denied that he'd personally hold grudges once play resumed, but added that "I think you are going to see hostilities . . . especially by some of the players who could have done the same thing but didn't." ("I just try to control the things I can control," responded Garvey. "I respect your opinions, but in this case there was no wrong or right, it was just the power of a smart agent who understood the system.")

For all the intrigue of their collective adventures, the Dodger who stirred up the most strike-time drama was the same guy who'd been stoking LA's engine all season long. Fernando Valenzuela headed back to Mexico (which made sense) to play some baseball (which didn't, seeing as how his contract, like those of his colleagues, expressly forbade him suiting up for anybody but his primary employer). On June 20, he went to Tijuana, home of the Potros of the Mexican League, and a day later traveled to Mexicali, home of the Águilas, for a pair of exhibition games organized by scout Mike Brito.† Joining him were Pedro Guerrero, Pepe Frías, and assorted semipros.

---

* Garvey did say that he'd put salary earned during the strike into a separate bank account, making it easier to return if that were to become necessary.
† The traveling party was slated to include Bobby Castillo, but upon hearing

If appearing for a club other than the Dodgers in the middle of baseball season looked bad, reports that the LA trio were each paid $3,000 to do so looked considerably worse. Unnerved by the unexpected attention, the participants transitioned quickly into spin mode. Brito claimed that the players had merely put on informal exhibitions, an especially disingenuous claim given that they were on a team called the Mike Brito All-Stars and playing in games arranged by Brito himself. Their opponents were the Orange County–based La Fonda All-Stars, sponsored by a restaurant of the same name, which included among its ranks Angels rookie Mike Witt.* Despite initial pronouncements to the contrary, Valenzuela pitched three innings in one contest and played first base in the other.

Valenzuela had never encountered attention like this. His preternatural cool on a ballfield may have allowed for easy adaptation to the major leagues, but in front of reporters, Fernando awkwardly tried to make the entire affair go away as quickly as possible. Not only hadn't he been paid, he insisted, but he hardly even considered what he did to be playing baseball. He said that anything that may have happened south of the border was merely an effort to stay in shape. "My intentions were good," he proclaimed.

When reports of the trip reached the Dodgers front office, Al Campanis was irate. He limited his public statements to, "I just can't be-

---

from Marvin Miller's office that participation would violate the Uniform Player's Contract, the pitcher canceled his plans.

* Witt had been recruited by his older brother, Adrian, already on the La Fonda team, and had no idea that he'd be bumping into baseball luminaries until he took the field. "I was warming up and there was a buzz," the pitcher recalled. "Guys in our dugout started saying, hey, that looks like Pedro Guerrero swinging the bat over there. Sure enough, it *was* Pedro Guerrero. Then the word got out that Fernando was there too." When Angels GM Buzzie Bavasi heard about the excursion, he was less than pleased. Witt's punishment was limited to a chewing-out because, unlike the participants from the Dodgers, he had not been compensated for his time. "They got paid how much?" he asked years later, upon being informed of their moneymaking turn. "Oh man, I got screwed."

lieve it happened," but privately it was a different matter. "I almost got fired," recalled Brito, who'd intentionally kept the GM in the dark about the trip because he knew that it never would have come off otherwise. "Al Campanis was like a father to me, but he was *mad*. He said, 'You really fucked up.' That got my attention."

"The Dodgers insisted that it didn't happen for about four days," said Peter Schmuck, who broke the story for the *Orange County Register*. "They were protecting Fernando's image, but finally they had to concede what had taken place, and sent out a one-sentence press release saying that no further action would be taken." That Campanis didn't fire Brito may have been thanks to Valenzuela. The last thing the GM wanted was to alienate the brightest star that baseball had seen in a decade, so, with the sentiment that "Solomon the Wise was lenient," he more or less let the entire affair fade from memory.*

As the strike dragged on, additional issues worked their way into the mix, not least of which was players' contention that they should be credited for service time — a valuable step toward hotly contested free agency — while striking. Six full seasons were necessary to reach that goal, and removing credit for time served would set everybody back a year, with stars like Reggie Jackson, Ron Guidry, and Bobby Grich, all on expiring deals, bracing to be tethered to their teams longer than they'd originally expected. The demand muddled already murky waters, and collective patience drew thin on both sides of the table. The *New York Daily News* polled 65 players and found only three willing to return to work without a convincing settlement. Bill Russell threatened to quit baseball altogether, saying, "I'm so angry

---

* Valenzuela's Mexican excursion didn't stop with exhibition games. While in the country, he picked up a key to Mexico City and visited president José López Portillo for the second time in a month. This time it was at the official residence, Los Pinos, where Fernando demonstrated his screwball over a state dinner. Later, he threw out the ceremonial first pitch in a game between the Mexico City Red Devils and Campeche for a reported fee of $10,000.

I'd sell everything I have and get another job before I would give in to the owners." Addressing what he felt to be insufficient management proposals, Reggie Smith muttered that "the only time I pay any attention to crap is when I step in it."*

Spurred by the lack of progress 20 days into the strike, Marvin Miller finally disregarded those who insisted that his presence would hinder negotiations and attended his first meeting. The tableau he found was far from hopeful. "The gap between us is so great that it defies my vocabulary to describe it," he said afterward, morosely.

This wasn't just any industry, however, but an institution upon which millions of Americans relied to mark the passage of time. After seeing the century's first Independence Day without major league baseball, the union and owners alike began reflexively to bend, offering a trickle of compromise solutions about how many players from a given team could be made available in exchange for a free-agency signing. Even then, though, the issue of where they would go — into a collective pool or one-for-one compensation — continued to divide the factions. The players demanded two and a half days of training camp prior to the season's resumption for every week lost to the strike. The commissioner, meanwhile, bumped back the date of the All-Star Game from July 14 to July 30, simultaneously providing a reality check and offering hope that resolution might be within reach.†

---

* The labor unrest led people to recall the founding of the MLBPA in 1947. Duke Snider was a rookie with the Brooklyn Dodgers that year, and his roommate, Carl Erskine, the player rep, fed him regular progress updates. "The players would come in with a list," he recalled. "One guy might say the locker room in St. Louis needed a new shower head, that only two were working and they needed three. Somebody else might say they needed a door on the toilet in Philadelphia, or a new water cooler in Pittsburgh. There would be about 15 things, and the owners would just go through them one by one, saying there were some things we could have and some things we couldn't. Maybe we weren't very bright, but we were usually happy with the way things turned out." How times had changed.

† On July 14, the day on which the All-Star Game was originally scheduled, 15,000 people gathered in downtown Cleveland, where the game was supposed

Federal mediator Kenneth E. Moffett laid out a proposal intended to bring the sides together, going to some lengths to acknowledge the necessity for high-level compensation for free-agency losses, while also endorsing the union's idea of a player pool from which teams could fish. It was a nod to everybody at the table: should each team that drafted a free agent contribute rosterable players to a community kitty, Moffett pointed out, those teams losing free agents would have more talent from which to pick as compensation. It directly addressed Kuhn's stated objective of competitive balance.

Despite on-the-record reservations, Miller agreed. However, the owners' chief negotiator, Ray Grebey, rejected the plan out of hand. That his response seemed contrary to the goals of the commissioner served mostly to show how little sway Kuhn actually held, with several owners all but renouncing the commissioner's authority when it came to negotiations. Then again, it had been clear from the outset that competitive balance wasn't the real issue. As the owners saw it, teams willing to spend big on free agency should be harshly punished, diminishing others' motivation to do the same.* Allowing teams to gather compensatory picks from a pool made it possible for high-spending teams—those that signed the most free agents—to skate away unhindered. Which wasn't much of a deterrent at all.

Not every owner took the news of Grebey's rejection well. "Many of us felt this should have been resolved before the strike even began,

---

to have been played, to, as best as anyone could figure, boo. So vigorous were their efforts that the noise reached 130 decibels—the level of a military jet taking off from an aircraft carrier. It was clearly intended as motivation, but when it came to impact on players, fan anger couldn't touch the fact that cancellation of the game would erase more than $2 million worth of revenue earmarked for the players' pension fund.

* Also in play was the idea that in the next basic agreement a new revenue stream —pay TV—would be parsed between owners and players in yet-to-be-determined ways, and owners wanted to make sure the union was sufficiently pliable when those decisions were made.

and it is reasonable to assume that the ranks of people feeling this way is swelling," said Orioles owner Edward Bennett Williams, speaking for those owners seeking compromise, a group that included O'Malley, Steinbrenner, Eddie Chiles of Texas, George Argyros of Seattle, and Wally Haas and Roy Eisenhardt of Oakland.

Among LA players, Lopes was the most outspoken about where he thought things were headed. It was hardly surprising, given that he was the most outspoken Dodger on pretty much every topic. What *was* surprising, given Lopes's nearly silent beginnings with the organization after he was drafted back in '67, was that he could fill this role at all. While playing for Lasorda at Triple-A Spokane, the infielder was so reserved that his manager thought it a detriment to his play. "He kept needling me," Lopes recalled. "He kept saying, 'When are you going to start talking? When are you going to start making some noise?' He'd say, 'You have ability, you have a style, you have a gift, but you just can't become the kind of ballplayer you want to be if you're going to be introverted. You've got to be more cocky if you want to be noticed.' I could see my personality changing. Pretty soon, I knew, I really knew I was going to make it to the major leagues, and I began to blossom. I began to get a little cocky."

Did he ever. Months into the strike, the *South Bay Daily Breeze*** tracked Lopes down for comment on the proceedings, and once he turned on that particular tap he couldn't seem to shut it off. During the course of a rambling conversation, the second baseman targeted Garvey and Thomas, the guys still getting paid. He denounced union leadership as a whole. He called the entire affair "a circus" and blasted the credentials of the player reps involved in negotiations. "Do Doug DeCinces and Bob Boone have legal backgrounds?" he asked about the union's primary player envoys, from the Orioles and Phillies, respectively. (Boone had earned a psychology degree from Stanford University, and DeCinces, involved with the union since the mid-

---

* Out of Torrance, California, at the southern edge of Los Angeles County.

1970s, was as well versed in the issues of the day as anybody at the table.) "I didn't see any postal clerks* going into *their* negotiations," Lopes continued. "As an entity, we have become the laughingstock of the United States. Everybody's laughing at us. We are not to be respected as a union."

We are not to be respected as a union.

The second baseman wasn't finished. "The last thing I want to do is pick up a paper and read Doug DeCinces's synopsis about the players' feelings," he said, "because he is not qualified and he doesn't know what he's talking about." Lopes bashed the lack of communication from the Dodgers' own player liaison, Jerry Reuss, saying, "The only thing I've seen is what I've read in the newspapers. Jerry Reuss? Is he still our player rep?" (Responded an exasperated Reuss: "It's impossible to make 25 telephone calls a day. They know my number and I'm here. It's become so complicated I'm not sure I can explain it to everyone. It would take a lawyer to interpret what's going on right now.")

Toward the end of his discourse, Lopes took aim at the process as a whole, appearing to withdraw whatever support he might once have held for the union. "This forget-the-season attitude really eats at me," he groused. "Before we do that, brother, we better stop and take a vote. We all better stop and think about that before we get so deep in the strike that we can't dig ourselves out. We've got to get back to the field. It's my life, my livelihood."

What Lopes didn't consider prior to his candidness was how such outspoken criticism might affect negotiations. Not long after the interview was published, mediator Ken Moffett called the situation "worse than ever," saying that a deal had appeared imminent . . . and then "it just went, like, boom."

Did Lopes's comments have anything to do with that?

Just before things went, like, boom, management's Player Relations Committee was meeting with the union — Miller, player reps, and law-

---

* Who were also on strike.

yers—for the second consecutive day. It seemed as if a breakthrough
was close, with talks more substantial than any since the walkout began . . . right up to the point that one of Grebey's staffers handed him
a wire-service story bearing Lopes's quotes.* Sensing cracks in the
previously impenetrable union facade, the lawyer quickly called a private meeting with management, after which the emboldened ownership ranks backed away from conciliation and firmed up their stance.
Those owners agitating for compromise lost immediate ground to the
hard-liners in their midst, and players instinctively recoiled. "They
still think they can bring the union to its knees," said a bewildered
Miller afterward.

Only a week earlier there had been a failed attempt to oust the in-
flexible Grebey as the owners' representative. The complaints about
him from his own side of the table included his having offered differing
accounts of his negotiating sessions to different parties, depending on
which facts would curry him the most favor, and that he had withheld
some information entirely in an effort to make the players look less
reasonable than they actually were. Grebey had also been authorized
to adjust management's official stance on various issues as best suited
negotiations, but failed to do so with anything approaching thoroughness. The players union felt similarly. One example of Miller's frustration was Grebey's assertion that the $15.5 million player pension
fund was endowed entirely by the owners, which omitted from the
narrative the fact that players contributed 60 percent of their World
Series TV revenue share.†

---

* To be fair, Lopes was not the only contradictory voice among the player
ranks. Detroit's Champ Summers said, "I don't want to be a martyr and give up
$200,000 so [teammate] Steve Kemp can become a free agent." Red Sox pitcher
Dennis Eckersley said, "Screw the strike. Let's play ball." Those comments came
well ahead of Lopes's, however, when negotiations were still in massive flux.
Things had solidified significantly by the time Lopes spoke out, and it was he
who most roiled the waters.

† The Player Relations Committee hadn't had a leader since Walter O'Malley

Despite the setback, it was impossible to ignore one indisputably salient detail: the owners' insurance money was scheduled to run out less than two weeks hence, on August 6. At that point, many among the union ranks were convinced, a speedy settlement would be imminent.

On July 26, at a meeting in Chicago, player reps from all 26 teams, plus another 30 or so big leaguers who lived in the area, offered Miller unanimous support, effectively granting him carte blanche to dig in his heels however he saw fit. Miller had initially called the meeting in response to complaints from players like Lopes about the way the union had been disseminating information.* Temperatures were hot going in, and as grievances flew over the course of five and a half hours, they only grew hotter. The strike was testing the limits of a significant number of players who wanted not only answers but paychecks. Issue was taken with leadership, and issue was taken with those taking issue with leadership, and issue was taken with the ready abundance of issues. This wasn't how a united front was supposed to act. Just as things seemed about to burst, one player in attendance decided to grab the meeting by the throat and throttle it into submission. Enter Jerry Reuss.

Seizing the floor, the left-hander addressed the Lopes issue directly, intoning how difficult it was to keep everybody informed. He

---

died. In discussions, Peter O'Malley's name came up for the position, but hurting his chances among management hard-liners was that he was seen as being far too conciliatory toward the union. Still, when a group of owners tried to oust Grebey from his position, it was O'Malley's support that ultimately saved the negotiator.

* Lopes, being neither a player rep nor a Chicago resident, did not attend, a detail that Reuss made sure to point out. "If it's information he wants, the telephone is a remarkable instrument," the pitcher said. "You can use it to call in or out. [Lopes] can always get hold of me by dialing 10 or 11 digits. I would think he would want to be here."

called players regularly he said, but was rarely able to reach them, forced instead to leave messages with their housekeepers that were almost never returned. "I don't know where my players stand on the issues," he confessed, "but we have the support of their hired help." The remark was classic Reuss, lending pointed humor to an otherwise dire situation. His speech lightened the mood just enough for Miller to spend the remainder of the session poring over ownership's latest proposals unimpeded, and it opened some space to consider how processes might be improved going forward.

Ultimately, Miller proposed an informational barnstorming tour on which he would meet with players across the country. "About half the players here tonight didn't have the facts," he theorized. "Once the facts were given, the players became convinced of their rightness, and gave us 100-percent support." The next meeting was promptly scheduled for three days later in Los Angeles.

When the time came, it drew about 70 players from across the Southland to the airport Marriott near LAX. Noteworthy among them was Lopes, the source of labor's most recent turmoil. He walked into the meeting unafraid, wanting mainly, he said afterward, "to see what the hell was going on." The infielder was open to being swayed, and swayed he was. The event lasted about two hours, with Miller —barely sleeping over recent weeks, and smoking way too much— sticking to the sidelines, opting instead to let player reps deliver briefings and proposals. When it came time for comments from the room, Reuss, from the podium, drew a steady bead on Lopes. "If someone has an objection," he said, glaring, "dammit, say something."

Someone did say something, but it wasn't Lopes. Before the outspoken second baseman could respond, one of his teammates seized the floor. "Who in this room isn't with the Association?" bellowed Reggie Smith, eschewing the microphone. Back in 1972, Smith had actually voted against striking, but had since come around on the necessity for a united front, having learned lessons that Lopes—whose big league debut came some five months after that settlement — was experiencing for the first time. Smith lit into his teammate about his ill-considered comments, their closeness as friends failing to impede him in any way. "That was like a civil war," reflected Dusty Baker, "brother against brother."

Forced to backpedal, Lopes took the floor. He claimed that his remarks were taken out of context and asserted that his real issue was with players like Garvey, who were getting paid through the strike. When somebody raised the topic of how close the Association had been to reaching a deal before Lopes's comments in the *Daily Breeze* blew things up, temperatures rose further, and Miller had to intervene, calming an increasingly agitated crowd with a plea to stick to the facts while avoiding emotional outbursts. That managed to hold things together until meeting's end, at which point a voice vote affirmed the union's entrenchment. Somehow, players were more solidified than ever. They could see it. More importantly, the owners could see it too.

If Lopes could be accused of speaking his mind without considering the consequences, so too was he quick to admit his errors and accept the resulting fallout. After the meeting, he apologized to DeCinces, and the two shook hands. In speaking with reporters afterward, the second baseman owned up to having been "upset and emotional" when he spoke to the *Daily Breeze*, and clarified that player leadership, the same guys he said had no business participating in negotiations, "are, indeed, an integral part of the team." He also went out of his way to publicly support whatever tactics the union thought best, up to and including a season-long walkout. "If that's what it takes, yes sir," he said. "We've done everything we possibly could. The ball is in the owners' court. If they want baseball to be played again this season, it will be played. If they don't, it won't be played."

The show of unity may have been all that was necessary. The following day, leadership from both sides was scheduled to meet in New

York with mediator Ken Moffett, but Grebey circumvented the agenda by suggesting that he and Miller confer separately.* Miller, having refused similar overtures over what he said were discrepancies in their respective public recollections of their discussions,† accepted, with the caveat that each party bring a second to help verify details later. Grebey tabbed American League president Lee MacPhail (itself a laden decision, given MacPhail's standing as a key proponent of compromise), while Miller brought MLBPA attorney Donald Fehr. They met at the office of National League president Chub Feeney, overlooking Rockefeller Center. With no table in the room at which to sit, the men grabbed chairs, Miller taking a spot on the room's lone couch.

The owners felt newfound pressure on two fronts. The most obvious was that their strike insurance was about to expire. Less visible but more pernicious was the fact that too much more lost time might scuttle the season entirely, an eventuality that held repercussions far greater than lost revenue.‡ Rumors were gaining steam about a new rival league planning to pirate major league free agents, ticket sales for '82 were sure to take a hit, and the likelihood of further scrutiny from the National Labor Relations Board was increasing by the day.

The conversation lasted two and a half hours, after which the

---

* The official meeting had been set for 2:00 p.m. in room 1706 at the Doral Inn — the same location as previous sessions — with Moffett being tipped to the alternative plan only when neither of the principals bothered to show up.

† Laborspeak for "Grebey lies about everything, and he'll lie about this too."

‡ In the aftermath, teams mostly remained mum on how much the strike cost them, but Cleveland's Gabe Paul said that his club would have lost $2 million after strike insurance payouts had the season failed to resume. That was nothing compared to big-market clubs. The Dodgers lost $7.6 million in tickets and concessions alone. The Yankees, who made $9 million for local TV rights and another $1.8 million from national networks, lost $3.6 million in broadcast revenue. Even the worst draw in the majors, the Twins, lost about $1.6 million in tickets and concessions (before insurance payouts). The Astros incurred further losses when, spurred by the Texas attorney general, they refunded $1.1 million in season-ticket sales.

groups split off—Miller and Fehr to the MLBPA offices on Sixth Avenue, Grebey and MacPhail to the National League's legal offices at Citicorp Center—to talk things over with their teams. They returned to Feeney's office at 6:00 p.m., broke again at 9:00, reconvened at midnight, and talked into the wee hours. This is what things looked like when, finally, Grebey made an offer and Miller accepted. At 1:48 a.m. EST on July 31, it was done. The sides stayed up until dawn getting it onto paper.

A press conference was called for 6:00 a.m., by which point news of the settlement had already broken. In the middle of the proceedings, Grebey was handed a late edition of the *New York Daily News* bearing the headline "PLAY BALL!"

Nobody seemed particularly happy about it. In their joint post-settlement comments, Miller—with Grebey looking on—pulled no punches in suggesting that the entire affair had been a failed effort to break the union and called the settlement "a victory for the spirit of the players." So unhappy were the principal negotiators with each other that Miller even refused to pose for a photograph with Grebey, who was so desperate for a hand to shake that he literally chased reluctant Mets outfielder Rusty Staub around a conference table, giving up only when Staub wheeled and yelled, "You're a liar!" At that point, Grebey nearly walked out altogether, mumbling that the entire event had been "a paid commercial for the players."

"You don't see any of us jumping for joy," sighed DeCinces. "This never should have happened."

Ultimately, the owners got what they wanted—compensation for free agents—but it had nothing to do with the players caving. In agreeing to the deal, the union was able to dictate the terms therein: compensation would be indirect, with strict limits on the number of free agents classified as "premier." Ultimately, the settlement looked a lot like the deal the players had proposed back in the spring.*

---

* The details were hardly the stuff of adventure novels: a premier free agent

Lingering questions about the possibility of future work stoppages were partly answered by the remote chances that management would find another insurance company to underwrite a strike-based policy. There was also the not-insignificant detail that the players' stance under withering circumstances—estimates said that they lost a cumulative $30 million in salary—indicated a willingness to do so again should circumstances dictate. By strike's end, the union had never appeared stronger.*

would be defined as ranking in the top 20 percent of statistical data for his position; the number of premier free agents would max out at eight in 1981 and nine in '82 and '83; teams signing such players could protect 24 players from their 40-man rosters, with the remaining 16 entering a collective pool; teams losing non-premier free agents that ranked in the top 30 percent could protect 26 players from their 40-man rosters; teams losing free premier free agents would be able to select from players in the pool; teams losing nonpremier free agents in the top 30 percent would accrue two extra selections in the amateur draft; teams losing players from the pool would be paid $150,000 per player from a central fund to which every team would contribute; and players would accrue service time during the strike, a demand the owners granted in exchange for an extra year being tacked onto the basic agreement, which subsequently ran through 1984.

* The highest-paid player, Dave Winfield, lost about $388,500, or $7,770 per day of the strike. Those making the major league minimum lost $180 per day. The entire affair effectively served to doom the remaining tenure of Bowie Kuhn, who, with an increasing number of owners set against him, resigned in 1983. That, in turn, stripped Peter O'Malley, one of Kuhn's staunchest allies, of much of his sway among ownership ranks.

7

La-La

IT IS IMPOSSIBLE to understand the 1981 Dodgers without understanding 1981 Los Angeles. It was the dawn of New Wave, of hair metal, of an exploding drug scene. The city was a massive, smog-choked urban sprawl covering hundreds of square miles, at its heart the iconic Sunset Strip — which, pointed out *Los Angeles Times* columnist Scott Ostler, "runs approximately parallel with the third base line just a short hop over the ravine." Once home to poinsettia fields and avocado groves, the strip's transformation into after-dark epicenter had to do with its location just outside city limits and the fact that county sheriffs had better uses for their time than cracking down on carousing. Starting in the 1920s, the area developed a reputation for late nights and early mornings, serving up all the revelry the glamour-soaked Hollywood culture could have wanted. It was as integral to its host city as any neighborhood in the country.

Early on, the French-themed Café Trocadero hosted stars like Fred Astaire, Bing Crosby, and Lana Turner. In the back room, movie mogul Samuel Goldwyn played high-stakes poker on Saturday nights. Ciro's opened in 1940 with plush decor that attracted Frank Sinatra and Humphrey Bogart. Gangsters Bugsy Siegel and Mickey Cohen frequented the area, gambling at the Melody Room and, in the case of Cohen, surviving an assassination attempt at Sherry's Restaurant.

It wasn't until the 1960s, however, that things grew truly wild. The Whisky a Go-Go, with its ultra-mod, white-booted go-go girls dressed in miniskirts and shimmying inside cages, opened in 1964 and soon boasted the Doors as its house band. Fewer than 100 yards down the strip was the Villa Nova, where once upon a time Joe DiMaggio met Marilyn Monroe, which in the 1970s was rebranded as the Rainbow Bar and Grill to become a headbanger's heaven, hosting acts like Jimi Hendrix, Led Zeppelin, and the Who. (John Belushi ate his last meal —lentil soup—there in 1982 before overdosing at the Chateau Marmont, a hotel a mile and a half down Sunset Boulevard.) Just across the parking lot, the Roxy helped bring to prominence up-and-comers like Bruce Springsteen.

By the early 1980s, glam rock was spreading throughout West Hollywood. Mötley Crüe debuted at the Starwood, on the corner of Santa Monica and North Crescent Heights (gaining a spot on the bill because bassist Nikki Sixx had a daytime job cleaning the place up). Gazzarri's broke in a teenage Van Halen over the course of several years in the 1970s. The Troubadour was about to give Guns N' Roses their first-ever show.

As it happened, 1981 was the bicentennial of Los Angeles (the Dodgers wore commemorative patches on their jerseys throughout the season), not to mention the tail end of the disco era, which served mainly as a further excuse to party. Many of the Dodgers were family men who tended to stay home when the team was in Southern California, while others made their homes in Orange County, far from the action. Still, opportunities abounded for those who wished to seize them. "As a Dodger, the scene opens up for you," reflected Ken Landreaux. "It's a different world. It's Hollywood, and you've got celebrity status."

The Bonaventure Hotel. The nightclub at Carlos'n Charlie's. Black players gravitated toward Total Experience and Maverick's Flat on Crenshaw. Waiting in lines was unheard of, and drinks were always free. Unexpected venues included the male dance revue at Chippendales, which, said Landreaux, was an unbelievable place to meet women, given the demographics of the crowd. "The dancers weren't our concern," he said, "or our target." Hell, Steve Yeager, the catcher with a penchant for open collars and gold chains, appeared in the pages of *Playgirl* three times. No Dodger better embodied the young-and-swinging ethos than he.

The strongest proponent of Los Angeles, the deepest of divers, the one who more fully acknowledged the extent to which one could be free in such a city at such a time, was connected to the team not as a player or even an employee. It was Tommy Lasorda's son, Tommy Jr., known to all as Spunky. The two were close, Spunky and his dad, the boy being a ballpark regular and occasional companion on road trips. There was, however, a twist. Spunky was flamboyant, and not in the Ken Landreaux wear-your-pants-too-long way. He wore his blond hair past his shoulders and dressed in delicate designer clothing. He smoked cigarettes through slender holders and studied fashion design. Starting in 1980, at age 22, Spunky became a regular on the West Hollywood gay club scene. Obvious as it may have seemed, his father forever insisted that the lad was not homosexual.

Those around the team knew better. Reggie Smith called Spunky "overt." Bill Bean, who played for the Dodgers in 1989 and came out as gay himself a decade later, said that "Tommy [Sr.] was obsessed with the word *faggot*, probably because of his experience with his son." In the 1970s, that experience included Tommy Jr.'s friendship — which may have been more than that — with Dodgers outfielder Glenn Burke, whose orientation was more or less an open secret during his time with the team.*

If it seems like willful ignorance for the father to refrain from admitting that his son was gay, it should be noted that the son himself fit the same description, at least for a time. "I like all people, "Tommy Jr.

---

* When rumors about Burke's sexuality grew too hot to ignore, Campanis stepped in, offering the outfielder $75,000 prior to the 1978 season to get married. "I guess you mean to a woman," Burke snapped, turning him down. That May the Dodgers traded Burke to the Oakland A's in exchange for outfielder Billy North.

said in a 1981 interview when confronted with the idea that his feminine appearance made it easy to leap to conclusions. "I have no label on myself because then I have restrictions."

Spunky Lasorda's personal life is pertinent to this tale mainly because in 1981 Los Angeles was ground zero for a stunning report, released that June by the US Centers for Disease Control and Prevention, detailing a rare lung infection in five previously healthy, local gay men. It was the opening chapter in what would soon become an outright epidemic, AIDS jumping to the fore of national consciousness while terrorizing and devastating communities, gay and otherwise, across the world. A decade later, in 1991, Tommy Jr. would die at age 33 from pneumonia, the most common killer of AIDS patients. Despite his death certificate identifying the cause of his passing as "probable AIDS," Tommy Sr. — while never ceasing to deeply mourn his son — forever insisted that Spunky's demise was unrelated to the stigmatic disease.

The elder Lasorda "really loved his son and was always there for him," said Steve Garvey, shortly after Spunky passed away. "The two loving parents" — Lasorda and his wife Jo — "tried to do as much for [Spunky] as he chose to let them do . . . Junior chose a path in life, and that's his prerogative."

Whatever understanding father and son shared about Spunky's lifestyle, they remained close. Despite his heady embrace of early-'80s Los Angeles, Junior insisted that their biggest arguments came over money, not the boy's romantic interests. "It's hard not to like him," Spunky said about his father in 1981. "He's really quite phenomenal. He's so verbal, so kind and generous, and he gives so much of his time. He really cares for people, and it comes back to him." They were qualities that would serve the elder Lasorda well, especially when it came to his baseball team.

The true nature of Los Angeles, of course, could be found in Hollywood, with the entertainment industry ensconced firmly in the heart of local culture. This worked well for Tommy Lasorda, because if the manager loved anything apart from God, family, baseball, and food, it was the celebrity hob-nob. For a guy from Norristown, Pennsylvania, who spent the bulk of his playing career in Montreal, Southern California suited him just fine. The man with the most outsized personality in the organization, who was happiest when people were paying attention to him, was delighted by his ability to integrate himself into LA's civic fixation with celebrity, and was genuinely tickled when movie stars were as thrilled to meet him as he was to meet them. A-listers from Dean Martin to Jack Lemmon became frequent clubhouse visitors before and after games. The manager dined in the Dodger Stadium Club with Gregory Peck, and Mike Douglas filmed a segment of his talk show in Lasorda's office. "He basically turned the clubhouse into the Friars Club," reflected Dodgers historian Mark Langill.*

It wasn't like Lasorda invented the idea—celebrities had been flocking ever since the Dodgers moved to town. In 1958, the first-ever game in Los Angeles included fans like Nat King Cole, Groucho Marx, Edward G. Robinson, and Jimmy Stewart. It being Hollywood, the river flowed both ways, with Dodgers players like Sandy Koufax, Duke Snider, and Wally Moon showing up across the TV spectrum, frequently portraying cowboys in a spate of western-themed episodics. Lasorda, meanwhile, along with guys like Don Drysdale and Leo Durocher, had star turns portraying themselves in TV shows like *Leave It to Beaver*, *The Brady Bunch*, and *CHiPs*. After failing to beat out Gil Hodges as the team's starting first baseman, Chuck Connors turned to acting, notably as the lead in the long-running TV series *The Rifleman*. He also appeared alongside the big man himself, Walter

---

* Once, Lasorda called Hooton into his office and passed over the telephone receiver. Almost beyond belief, the pitcher found himself talking to Jimmy Carter, the sitting president. "Only in LA," said the pitcher, looking back.

O'Malley, in a 1965 TV western called *Branded*, in which the owner played a bit character called "the Doctor."*

Things hadn't slowed much by 1981. Lasorda and Garvey had recently portrayed themselves on an episode of *Fantasy Island* (wherein Lasorda did most of the talking), while Steve Yeager and Don Sutton appeared in the TV series *Wonderbug*.

The walls of the manager's office were a testament to Lasorda's fixation, a shrine to the cult of celebrity to which he was so completely in thrall. Framed photos of stars, ballplayers, boxers, and even the pope adorned every inch. What each subject had in common was a place within the manager's idea of what a true celebrity looked like. The lot of them, however, couldn't hold a candle to the guy Lasorda loved most, the crooner from his childhood who became a global icon and the standard-bearer for multiple generations of Italian Americans. An entire wood-paneled quarter of the manager's office was labeled simply "Sinatra's Wall" — an entirely extraneous designation considering the 14 shots of Frank Sinatra hanging thereon.

Lasorda first met his hero as a third-base coach in 1976, when on a road trip to Chicago he was introduced by comedian Pat Henry, a friend who was opening for the singer. "To me," said Lasorda later, "this was like meeting Babe Ruth or the president of the United States." The paisans shared an instant simpatico, and before long Sinatra not only suggested that Lasorda "should be the next manager of the Dodgers," but promised to sing the national anthem at Dodger Stadium whenever that day arrived. The proclamation shot enthusi-

---

* The episode was titled "The Bar Sinister," and there was good reason to cast O'Malley. *Split Season* author Jeff Katz breaks down the episode synopsis: "The town mayor is willing to rip a beloved boy (read Dodgers) from his rightful guardian, his Native American mother (read Brooklyn). Why? To acquire land and riches, an allusion to the controversial transfer of Chavez Ravine and its environs by the City of Los Angeles that enticed O'Malley westward — parallels that made Walter O'Malley the perfect choice for the role."

asm through a guy who observers had long insisted couldn't possibly be any more enthusiastic.

It didn't take long. Alston stepped down that September 29, and Lasorda took over for the season's final four games. On September 30, he got a call from Sinatra's office: *When do you want him?* The new manager figured that opening day the following April would provide a suitable venue, and when that day came, there was Ol' Blue Eyes, Dodgers jacket on his back, crooning the anthem in Chavez Ravine.* "I really think," said Mark Heisler, who covered the team for the *Los Angeles Times*, "that Tommy's life thrilled him."

From that point forward, Sinatra became a clubhouse regular, stopping by the manager's office whenever he was in town, entourage invariably in tow. Lasorda, of course, as proud of this relationship as any he had in baseball, was perpetually eager to introduce his most famous friend to anybody he could. When Jerry Reuss found himself being ushered into the manager's office on one such occasion, he at first saw only a group of men he later described as "these big sons of bitches in three-piece suits." Then the pitcher saw him, the planet's biggest star, in the middle of the scrum. Lasorda, grinning, introduced the pitcher.

"Sorry," Reuss said. "I didn't get your name."

"Goddammit, Reuss," Lasorda moaned, "not to *him*!"

Sinatra, like most of the celebrities who found their way to the manager's office, limited his interactions mostly to glad-handing. When it came to some guys, however, full-blown performances were known to break out. One time comedian Jonathan Winters took the floor about 20 minutes before a game, diving into a routine in which

---

* It actually wasn't the first gig Sinatra did as a favor to his pal. When Lasorda was tasked with finding entertainment for baseball's winter meetings in Los Angeles shortly after taking over the Dodgers' helm, the crooner stepped up and volunteered for the gig, singing for some 1,200 people, packed to overflowing in the ballroom of the Los Angeles Hilton. Sinatra dedicated his closer, "My Way," to the beaming manager.

he pantomimed an idiosyncratic relief pitcher struggling to hold a lead. As Winters hammed it up, players throughout the clubhouse, drawn by gales of laughter from Lasorda's office, began to pack the room. So mesmerizing was the skit that before anybody knew what was happening, a clubhouse attendant raced in to inform the audience that the national anthem had concluded and first pitch was presently being delayed on account of the Dodgers having not yet taken the field. Show over, no encore, the players raced to grab gloves from lockers. "Where have you been?" plate ump Harry Wendelstedt asked a still-smiling Steve Garvey as the first baseman jogged to his position. "Jonathan Winters was doing this routine in there," Garvey responded. "I'll give you details later, at the plate." Wendelstedt was stunned. "Why didn't you tell us?" he said. "We would have come in."

Lasorda's celebrity obsession may have encouraged extra attention for a clubhouse that didn't necessarily want it, but even the reticent had to admit that it brought energy to the room. On occasion, however, the manager's enthusiasm for star power obscured his common sense. Noteworthy in this regard was a late-season game during Lasorda's initial campaign as LA's manager in 1977. The Dodgers had already clinched the National League West, and the skipper thought that it might be fun to have Don Rickles in the dugout for a game against the Braves.* Because Major League Baseball's rule 3.15 states that "no person shall be allowed on the playing field during a game except players and coaches in uniform [and] managers" (plus umpires, assorted media, and security), Lasorda dressed Rickles in a Dodgers uniform (number 40, no name) and planted him on the bench. As re-

---

* "Don Rickles would be in the clubhouse like once a week, and I avoided him for as long as I could," said reporter Peter Schmuck, knowing full well what kind of response his last name would elicit from a comedian whose career was based on insulting people. "Somebody finally introduced us, and as soon as they said my name, that was it. I never could face the man again. Every time he saw me it was 'Oh, Schmuck, Schmuck, Schmuck.' It was like that *all* of the time."

counted by Rickles, things got weird after pitcher Elias Sosa ran into trouble in the sixth inning:

> Tommy said, "Go take him out, Don."
>
> "What?" I said.
>
> "You heard me, go give him the hook. Yank him out and give the bullpen the signal for the southpaw."
>
> Why the hell not, I thought. It was a fantasy come true. I trotted out to the mound.
>
> "Sorry, fella," I told the pitcher. "You're through."
>
> "You're not the manager," he shot back. "You're not even a coach. You can't pull me out of the game."
>
> "Give me the ball," I demanded.
>
> "You're crazy," he said.
>
> Meanwhile, home-plate umpire Harry Wendelstedt, a great veteran, headed out to the mound.
>
> "What's going on here?" he asked.
>
> When he got in my face, he saw who it was and said, "I'll be damned. Don Rickles! Don, any chance of getting me two tickets to see Dean Martin in Vegas?"

Rickles told this story over and over — to *Variety* magazine, to the *Los Angeles Times*, on camera to Jimmy Kimmel and Jerry Seinfeld — but fudged a few of the details. While Lasorda did have him visit the mound, it was to speak with the pitcher, not to take him out. It was the ninth inning of a game in which the Giants led, 7–3, and the umpire in question was not Wendelstedt but John McSherry. Whether he asked for tickets is strictly conjecture.

Lasorda occasionally confirmed the account over the ensuing years, but never went into much detail. Maybe it was to protect Rickles, for whom the story gathered momentum with every retelling. Or perhaps he kept the particulars vague because that was the first time the manager's stargazing spilled onto the field — literally — and drew a stern rebuke from the front office. "Peter [O'Malley] is Mr. Conservative, and you've got P. T. Barnum in the dugout," said Dodgers historian Mark Langill. Could it have gone any other way?* *The Sporting News* went so far as to report in 1980 that "O'Malley . . . would just as soon have his manager managing and leave the public relations to someone else." It didn't stop Lasorda from dressing other celebrity guests, like Tony Danza and Mike Fratello, in Dodger uniforms over coming seasons, but they served merely as batboys, not as de facto pitching coaches.

"Tommy fetishized celebrity to a notable degree," said Heisler. "He made the manager's office like being in the door at Club 21."

A vital component of the Los Angeles scene in the early '80s was the presence of another team just across town that came to be known for its abundant excesses in ways that dwarfed the Dodgers. The Los Angeles Lakers had their own moniker — *Showtime* — that hinted not only at their fast-break pace of play but their perpetual quest for the next party. The term "Showtime," in fact, was derived from a Santa Monica nightclub called The Horn, frequented by Lakers owner Jerry Buss, which began its nightly show with a signature song: "It's Showtime." Buss himself made a reputation out of discotheque revelries — usually in the company of assorted, much-younger women — going so far as to establish his own hot spot, the highly exclusive Forum Club, within the Lakers' arena, which became a magnet for celebrities, the

---

* Rickles made a return appearance before Game 2 of the 1977 World Series (in the clubhouse this time, in street clothes), where, with the players gathered before him, he began to roast various Dodgers. To Lasorda: "Look at that stomach . . . If you guys lose, he's going to tie a rope around his neck and get work as a balloon." To the group: If you lose, "you'll all be waiting tables at the Sahara hotel in Las Vegas tomorrow night." To say that Rickles came from a different era in comedy is an understatement. He jokingly accused African Americans on the team of trying to move into his neighborhood. When he got to Dusty Baker, he said, "Don't do anything. I will give you my TV. Whatever you want." In a meeting with players some years later, he asked Pedro Guerrero, "How long are you going to make [your wife] clean hotel rooms?" and called Bill Madlock "a friendly colored guy."

young and pretty, and those who could afford not only a good time but the best of times.

The wonder of Los Angeles during that era came with attendant downside: the all-hours glitter needed fuel, and the tinder of choice was cocaine. The drug had been around in synthesized form since the 1800s — it was part of Coca-Cola's original formula — but in 1981 newfound social acceptance had only recently brought it into the open. It was a global phenomenon, but may have been felt no place more prevalently than in Southern California. "Drugs are used openly [in Los Angeles], as if old taboos had evaporated," reported the *New York Times* in 1982 in a story headlined "Pervasive Use of Cocaine Is Reported in Hollywood," which quoted a city police lieutenant describing the problem as being "at epidemic stages." It was different than the amphetamine surge of the 1960s, reported the *Washington Post*: "A lot of people began using amphetamines out of some business ethic, to work hard and keep moving, to stay awake while others were relaxing, eating or sleeping. Coke, on the other hand, is a status drug. It's not to work harder, it's almost an exotic way of showing off." The July 6, 1981, cover of *Time* magazine featured an image of a coke-filled martini glass, with the headline "High on Cocaine." The corresponding article opened with this sentence: "The 'All-American drug' has hit like a blizzard, with casualties rising."

"It seemed like everyone in Los Angeles was snorting the stuff." That one came from Dodgers closer Steve Howe.

Cocaine's price hit $2,200 per ounce that year, reported *Time*, five times the price of gold. The National Institute on Drug Abuse estimated that about 20 percent of 18- to 25-year-old Americans had used cocaine in 1979, double the number of only two years earlier, with about 10 million regular users nationwide. For the first time ever, income produced by the drug in 1980 surpassed that of marijuana, and it wasn't particularly close: $35 billion for coke as opposed to $11 billion for pot, according to the Drug Enforcement Administration. Those numbers continued to rise in '81. Wrote the *Times*: "Drug dealers, some of them riding in chauffeured limousines, make regular rounds to the homes of executives, performers and technicians in the film, television and rock music industries, some of whom are spending as much as $1 million a year on cocaine."

Ballplayers were no exception.

"There were a lot of busts back in those days, and they always say that baseball is just a smaller piece of what's going on externally," said Dave Stewart, looking back. "There's a lot to do in LA, which is no different than New York and Chicago, your major media centers and big-time party cities."

"I only know a few people that didn't try *something*," recalled Baker.

In baseball, stories circulated — and in 1985 would be told openly, in federal court — about drug dealers infiltrating major league clubhouses, at which time Mets first baseman Keith Hernandez estimated in grand jury testimony that 40 percent of major league players used the drug. No Dodgers were among the seven players directly implicated in what came to be known as "the Pittsburgh drug trials," but testimony delivered in that courtroom tied one of the primary dealers for the Pirates, a Philadelphia-based caterer named Curtis Strong, to various members of the team. It was Dusty Baker, said Pittsburgh outfielder Dave Parker, who'd introduced Strong to the Pirates.

In fact, it was Derrel Thomas who'd first made Strong's acquaintance, introduced by a friend in Philadelphia who presented the caterer as a guy with product to move. Thomas subsequently made Strong known to assorted teammates, although the significance of those relationships is up for debate. "I knew Curtis Strong, but he wasn't my kind of cat to be hanging out with," said Baker later, calling the allegation that he was responsible for turning the Pirates on to the drug dealer "straight bullshit."

"I'm a pretty good judge of character, so I didn't mess with [Strong] too much," Baker said, looking back. "We all know people, whether it's a relative or a homeboy, who's doing stuff they shouldn't be doing. Anybody who's that judgmental about you because you know somebody, well, I might could put you in that same light. They'd better look in their own houses."

Parker also testified that in 1981 another dealer, Shelby Greer, sold coke in a Pittsburgh hotel room to himself, Baker, Thomas, Steve Howe, and Pirates outfielder (and former Dodger) Lee Lacy. Upon hearing his son's name mentioned in so public a forum, Dusty's father, John Baker Sr., confronted Dusty directly, asking outright whether he'd ever tried cocaine. Yes, Dusty said, he'd tried it. Senior asked if he was still doing it. The last time Dusty had lied to his ex-military father was as a kid, when he tried to alter a report card from a D into a C. He didn't get away with it then, and he wasn't about to try it again as an adult. No, he said, issuing a promise to God and his father alike, he was not still doing it.

Ultimately, 11 major leaguers were suspended for a full season as a result of those trials, their sentences eventually commuted in exchange for community service and fines that went toward drug-use prevention. Neither Baker nor Thomas was among their ranks, although both had to undergo random drug testing for the duration of their playing careers.

Howe was a different story. Unable to escape his addiction, the reliever ended up as the poster child for drug abuse in American sports. He'd come to the Dodgers with a pedigree, as the 16th overall selection in the 1979 draft out of the University of Michigan, and made his big league debut after only 13 minor league games, all at Double-A San Antonio. Installed almost immediately as LA's closer, the left-hander saved a rookie record 17 games, allowed only one homer over 85 innings, and cruised to the National League Rookie of the Year Award.*

"The kid has ice water in his veins," marveled Lasorda at the time. "He reminds me of a young Tommy Lasorda." Howe was 22 years old.

The left-hander was also a vulnerable target at the intersection of

---

* Which may have taken a backseat to the following year's honor: being named one of *Playgirl* magazine's "sexiest men in baseball."

baseball prominence and a celebrity-oriented city. As a kid, he'd been given Ritalin to treat hyperactivity, which he later felt primed him for future abuse. In high school, Howe experimented with drugs like mescaline and LSD, but his problems took off, he said, at the press conference to announce his Rookie of the Year selection. Seeing the youngster visibly nervous at the thought of facing the assembled press — "I was used to talking with small knots of reporters in the clubhouse, but I had never faced dozens of them at once in a staged extravaganza like this," he said later — a teammate passed him a vial of cocaine. Howe snorted it, and his tension immediately dissipated, replaced by a feeling he pegged someplace between euphoria and absolute control. Soon he sought the rush constantly.

By 1981, Howe said, his cocaine use had evolved "to the point of total preoccupation." There was little apparent downside at that juncture, with infallible job security buttressing increasingly questionable lifestyle choices. The pitcher treated spring training like spring break, getting together with a handful of teammates who, he said, would split an eightball — an eighth of an ounce, or three and a half grams, of cocaine, costing up to $350 — several times per week. Chris Mortensen, then reporting on the Dodgers for the *South Bay Daily Breeze*, recalls Howe cutting a table-length line in a side room at the Dodgertown facility and snorting the entire thing by himself. The use was one thing, but the public brazenness was particularly disconcerting. The ballplayer's addiction, Mortensen said, "was borderline insanity."

The pitcher moderated his use once the regular season started, mostly limiting it to social occasions. That lasted until the strike hit. Once games were canceled, with no set schedule tethering him to reality, Howe's use skyrocketed from two grams per week to two grams per day. He later identified the period as the true marker for what became a lifelong addiction. When the schedule resumed, Howe could no longer control his habit, regularly getting high at the ballpark — not in the clubhouse, which represented too big a risk, but in the parking lot or in various hallways. "I got caught a few times," he wrote in his autobiography, *Between the Lines*, "but only by teammates. Some of them were in the tunnels on days they weren't playing, sneaking women down from the stands. When they nabbed me, I had to pay the penalty: "All right, Howzer, give me some of that stuff."

The pitcher felt that drug use among Dodgers players broke along racial lines, with most of the white guys satisfied to booze it up, while more of the black players joined Howe in coke snorting. Either way, he said, "the list of non-partiers on the 1980 Dodgers would be much shorter than the list of partiers." At the end of that season, starter Bob Welch checked into a rehab clinic for alcohol treatment. After the team's community relations representative, former pitcher Don Newcombe — a drug abuse counselor and reformed alcoholic himself — said in 1982 that "between 70 and 80 percent of professional ball-players are using some kind of mind-altering substance right now" (a stance he later clarified included alcohol), the Dodgers' team physician, Dr. Robert Woods, came out as clueless. "If there were any heavy users, they couldn't perform as well as they do," he said. "I don't think there are any kids using marijuana, or any drugs at all. I know no one is using cocaine or heroin, and none of them are on Quaaludes."

The trail of treatment told a different tale. Howe said that he spent $10,000 on coke in 1982, and the following spring took to carrying a gun around Vero Beach on account of a Florida drug dealer to whom he owed money. The pitcher went into rehab in 1982, 1983, and 1984 and was suspended three times while with the Dodgers — twice by the team and once by the league, the latter being for the duration of the 1984 season. In the interim, Los Angeles parted ways with Baker, Stewart, and Bobby Castillo, each under suspicion of being a negative influence on Howe.

Hogwash, said Baker later: "Any time you see a correlation where there's one white dude and three minorities, automatically we've got to be a bad influence. Howser didn't need any influences. If anything, we were trying to save Howser's life. We *liked* Howser. We liked Howser a lot."

Howe himself agreed. "Nobody on the Dodgers pressured me to do drugs," he recalled. "The decision and responsibility were mine. If the Dodgers thought the causes of my problem were external, they found out otherwise. Even with Stewart, Baker and Castillo gone, I was still snorting."

Things somehow grew even darker for the pitcher during a meeting with Al Campanis, which according to Howe turned into an interrogation about which minority players on the team were using cocaine. "Why do you hang around the blacks and Hispanics so much?" the GM asked him. "Why don't you hang around with Rick Monday or Ron Cey, guys like that?" The overtness of the questions was shocking, especially considering that, according to Baker, "Al Campanis was one of the more fair ones there," a guy who "took care of people of color"—an opinion shared by numerous teammates.*

The Dodgers released Howe in July 1985 after a week in which he, in order, didn't arrive to a game until the seventh inning; was a no-show at a charity dinner that he'd been slated to chair; and missed the following day's game. It was prelude to an extended run of drug-related drama that saw Howe pitch for nine teams over the next 12 years—six of them in the minors, two in independent leagues—while being suspended seven times overall and forced to sit out three full seasons.

Meanwhile, in January 1983, Ken Landreaux entered the Meadows in Wickenburg, Arizona, the same in-patient rehab facility that had hosted Howe and Welch—with the *South Bay Daily Breeze* reporting that the Dodgers were planning to approach three other players about similar possibilities. (The team denied that report, and nothing appears to have come of it.) Thomas was arrested in 1992 with

---

* Campanis's career ended after a *Nightline* interview with Ted Koppel, in which he proclaimed: "I truly believe [that African American players] may not have some of the necessities to be, let's say, a field manager, or, perhaps, a general manager . . . Why are black people not good swimmers? Because they don't have buoyancy." The Dodgers fired him two days later after a four-decade career with the organization that began during his playing days in 1940.

$151,000 in the trunk of his car that he used to try to buy 22 pounds of cocaine from an undercover narcotics agent. Later in the decade, he was fired from a managerial post with the Cincinnati Reds' Rookie League affiliate following allegations of further cocaine use. In 2000, Pedro Guerrero was brought up on charges after guaranteeing payment to a DEA informant for $200,000 worth of cocaine. (He was eventually acquitted.) "We had our own little clique of guys that we hung out with, but it wasn't anything major," Thomas recalled about drug use on those Dodgers teams. Describing consumption as "recreational," he added that "we weren't doing it on the scale the entertainers did. We heard about this guy going to a party where they had a mound of cocaine on the table, but we weren't privy to that kind of stuff. I don't know, maybe some of the guys were, but if they were, they were in the closet about it."

"It was an experimental time in our country," reasoned Baker. "There were drugs *everywhere*. You'd go to Studio 54 in New York, or to the Troubadour in LA, and there they are. We were cleaner than most because we had a responsibility to our bodies to go play. But if you're looking for saints who didn't do anything at that time, then you're looking in the wrong place."

8

Second Act

JUST BECAUSE PLAYERS had agreed to return to baseball didn't mean that they were ready to play. Spring training happens for a reason, after all, and big leaguers hadn't played meaningful games in nearly two months. The amount of time they'd be allowed to find their bearings had been included in labor negotiations, and was one area in which the owners scored a decisive victory. Allowing two and a half days of training for every week lost to the strike, as the players had initially requested, would bump the start of the season into late August, which was universally acknowledged as allowing insufficient time for the playing of stretch-run baseball.

So play was scheduled to resume eight days after the settlement, with the All-Star Game on August 9 in Cleveland. Full action would pick up a day later and follow the original script, with games that had originally been scheduled for August 10 proceeding as planned. The stoppage had lasted 50 days and wiped out 710 games, or 38 percent of the season.*

The Dodgers' group workouts had grown increasingly sporadic

---

* Among the happiest people to receive the news was Tommy Lasorda. "Me not putting on a baseball uniform is like taking a fish out of water," he'd said toward the end of the walkout. "I need something. Maybe an argument with an umpire. Are there any umpires in town?"

since the first few sessions at USC, lending their first official practice, on July 31 at Dodger Stadium, an unmistakable reunion vibe — spring training in the middle of summer. Only eight players, guys who were already in town, attended, but for Jerry Reuss, Jay Johnstone, Ron Cey, Davey Lopes, Fernando Valenzuela, Pedro Guerrero, Rick Monday, and Pepe Frías, the chance to take swings and shag flies felt exactly right. This was especially true for Johnstone, the resident prankster, who, as Reuss was being interviewed by a television news crew, exhibited midseason form by crawling on hands and knees to untie the pitcher's shoelaces, unbuckle his belt, and unzip his fly, all out of frame. The lefty never flinched as he provided unwavering discourse about strike issues, preventing those watching at home from realizing that anything was amiss. As soon as the interview ended, Johnstone could barely contain himself. "That's the mark of a true professional, to have that kind of composure after a seven-week layoff!" he yelped.

The Dodgers banged around for a week as players rolled in from across the country. Lasorda pitched a significant amount of batting practice himself — "There were lights and cameras involved," reasoned Rick Monday — offering a stream of verbal challenges with every ball thrown. "You can't hit my curveball and never could!" "If you hit this pitch, I'll give you $100!" "If you hit *this* pitch, I'll give you a Cadillac!"

"You know how many Cadillacs that man owes us?" asked Yeager, looking back. Somehow, nobody minded. "It's like, okay, we're back," reflected Monday. "Here's the little general. He's back, and so are we."

Toward the end of the first full-team workout, Steve Howe took note of the fading daylight as he stepped in to pitch the back end of batting practice — only the fifth time he'd thrown a baseball since the strike began. It was about 6:00 p.m., and the sun, sinking over the stadium's western rim, threw massive shadows between mound and plate. Howe, pitching without a protective screen, realized that he was not able to track the flight of his warm-up pitches. Steve Yeager, stepping in to face him, agreed. "I didn't even see that one," said the catcher after Howe's first offering sailed past him to the backstop.

"Neither did I," admitted Howe. "Go tell them to turn the lights on."

They didn't have time. Yeager smoked the next pitch up the middle, directly into Howe's forehead, just below the bill of his cap. Reeling, the pitcher stumbled into a nearby ball bucket and dropped to the turf. His only conscious thought, he said later, was *I told you to turn the damn lights on.* Temporarily blinded by concussion, Howe spent the night in the hospital and was held out of workouts for several days while his sight returned. When the season resumed a week later, however, he was ready to go.

The team found its game legs with an exhibition against the Triple-A Albuquerque Dukes at Dodger Stadium on August 6. For many players, the hardest part was not that Albuquerque won, 1–0, but the relentless booing from their own fans, which started with pregame introductions and barely subsided. At least the crowd size, a robust 45,000, augured well for those who feared that attendance might be permanently crippled. Then again, every ticket had been passed out free of charge, so who could tell? "The players expected it," said Bill Russell of the booing. "It's just something we will have to accept for a while. I don't think it will last all year, but we have to accept it." Of particular note in the clubhouse was second baseman Steve Sax, who was called up from Double-A San Antonio to participate — not with Albuquerque, but with the Dodgers. Those who wished to read harbingers of future roster decisions into the move weren't far off.

The exhibition capped the shortest training camp in team history. Two days later, six Dodgers made their way to Cleveland for what, everyone admitted, would be the strangest All-Star Game in which any of them had participated. LA's players composed nearly one-quarter of the 30-man National League roster — up from its usual 28 as a hedge against forcing out-of-shape players into extended action—though there were some marked differences from recent campaigns. Missing from the starting lineup for the first time since 1974 was Steve Garvey, who was batting only .279 with six homers. Dusty Baker, despite hitting .303 and running second in fan balloting among National League outfielders for much of the season, had dropped to sixth by the time final totals were released—a detail that maybe shouldn't have been surprising given that he'd never made an All-Star roster over his nine-season career, including 1980, when he finished fourth in the NL MVP vote. Both men were eventually named as reserves, joined on the bench by Pedro Guerrero, batting .325 in his second big league season and leading the Dodgers with 10 homers in 53 games.

The biggest surprise, however, was in the starting lineup, where Davey Lopes was selected by fan vote to represent the National League at second base. Lopes had widely been considered among baseball's better players at his position for much of the previous decade, but 1981 was not his year. The 36-year-old was hitting .169 when he sprained his ankle on May 16, an injury that limited him thereafter to one pinch-hitting appearance over LA's final 23 games before the schedule was suspended. Because Lopes's name was misspelled on a number of ballots, several thousand fans ended up voting for "Davey Lopez"—more, according to at least one report, than voted for Davey Lopes. "I know I don't deserve to be here," the infielder freely admitted before the game.

The most prominent All-Star of them all, of course, was Valenzuela, who, despite going 1-4 with a 6.06 ERA over his final six first-half starts—everything after that magical 8-0 opening to the season—was selected by Phillies skipper Dallas Green to start the game for the National League.* Joining Fernando was Burt Hooton, who after

---

* This despite Green's own star, Steve Carlton, being 9-1 with a 2.80 ERA. "It's been the kid's year," reasoned the manager about his decision to start Valenzuela.

his own splendid opening run (7-0, 1.96 ERA) had gone 0-3 with a 10.24 ERA over his final three starts to finish the first half at 7-3, 2.97.

The Dodgers booked an entire first-class cabin to get their traveling party — players, media members and assorted hangers-on — to Cleveland, leaving Reds starter Tom Seaver, independently commuting to the game from Southern California, relegated to steerage. Dusty Baker, on the lookout for his National League teammate, lobbied various nonplaying personnel to swap seats with Seaver, given that the right-hander was scheduled to pitch the following day. Someone eventually agreed, but it didn't seem to help; the pitcher gave up three hits and a run in one inning of work.*

Valenzuela held the American League off the board in his single inning of work, aided by Expos catcher Gary Carter, who threw out Rod Carew (on base after an infield single) trying to steal second. In the sixth inning, Hooton allowed five hits (all singles) and three runs over the span of seven batters. That he didn't surrender more was thanks to a pair of fielding plays involving two Dodgers. The first came with runners at first and second, on a one-out grounder to first base by Eddie Murray. Garvey fielded it behind the runner, which forced him to face his most notable deficiency as a ballplayer: a scattershot arm. He had a perfect angle, but his throw to second was low and tailed toward left field. He was saved by the greatest fielder ever to play the position, as Ozzie Smith, then with the Padres, managed to corral the ball while keeping his right foot on the bag for the force-out. (Smith even acrobatically relayed the ball to Hooton, covering first, but Murray beat the throw by an eyelash.)

After the next batter, Ted Simmons, singled home another run to extend the American League's lead to 4–2, NL manager Dallas Green

---

* Upon reaching the visitors' clubhouse at Municipal Stadium, the players found that the only two National League All-Stars to be separated by an empty locker were Garvey and Lopes. Perhaps their reputations preceded them.

called upon Phillies right-hander Dick Ruthven to relieve Hooton. The first batter Ruthven faced, Texas's Al Oliver, slashed a sinking flare toward center field, which Baker, in left, figured Andre Dawson would play handily. Dawson, however, lost the ball in the lights. When Smith, backpedaling, also had trouble tracking the play, Baker thought about how he really didn't want his first-ever All-Star appearance to coincide with the end of the National League's nine-year win streak. The result was a panic-fueled sprint toward the plate that ended in a full-bore dive, glove fully outstretched, to snare the ball just before it hit the turf. Baker's effort ended the inning and allowed Mike Schmidt's two-run homer in the eighth to be a game-winner, as the NL won its 18th game in 19 years, 5–4.

The next day the Dodgers hosted the Reds.

Los Angeles had barely been hanging on to first place, a half-game in front of Cincinnati, when the strike hit. On the one hand, the Reds might well have overtaken them had the strike occurred even one day later. On the other, there it was in black and white — the Dodgers' name atop the leaderboard. When play resumed, nobody yet knew exactly what that meant.

Ideas were lobbed back and forth about how to crown division champions, with no obvious solution. Playing things out as if no interruption occurred was the most straightforward approach but would lead to wildly unbalanced competition — teams with difficult first-half schedules would be at a decided disadvantage — and only five clubs supported the plan. Reds president Dick Wagner suggested pitting the overall winner against the second-half winner (a tactic that would, not coincidentally, give his team two chances at a post-season berth). Dodgers coach Danny Ozark went so far as to suggest that teams play only intradivisional games for the remainder of the truncated season, allowing those in the second division a legitimate chance to make up ground.

Most of the discussion centered on the concept of a split season, crowning prestrike and poststrike divisional champs who would meet in a five-game playoff.* It was a markedly imperfect solution. Teams would end up playing different numbers of games against far-from-uniform opponents. For Major League Baseball, of course, it would be a winner, guaranteeing postseason spots for the Dodgers and Yankees, the sport's two biggest draws, both of whom were first-half champions. That was just fine by the players in LA.

This is the plan the owners ultimately adopted, with the wrinkle that if the same team won both halves, the second-half crown would go to the team with the second-best overall record. A's manager Billy Martin immediately divined a flaw in the scenario, noting that with Oakland having already clinched the first-half title, he'd spend the second half rooting for teams he could beat in the playoffs. "I suppose it means that every time we play Seattle or Toronto I should use my second-line pitchers and save my starters for teams I have to beat," he said dismissively.

Then somebody pointed out that under such a format a team might actually benefit from losing games. Should the Dodgers hold a slim lead over Houston in the NL West toward the end of the season, for example, it might benefit Cincinnati—were the Reds playing Los Angeles in a season-closing series—to intentionally lose their final games, locking in the Dodgers as champions of both halves and throwing the next playoff spot to Cincinnati, who, in this hypothetical situation (as in reality), held a better overall record.† Less hypotheti-

---

* The benefits of the scenario were boosted immeasurably by another strike— that of the Writers Guild of America, concerning compensation for TV scripts. With the possibility of programming hours to fill, network execs jumped on the opportunity to air an extra round of playoff games. "If our own fall season wasn't in such a state of flux, we may not have said yes," admitted NBC's sports chief, Don Ohlmeyer.

† In reality, Cincinnati faced the Dodgers for the final time with two weeks remaining in the season.

cally, White Sox manager Tony La Russa stated outright that he'd do that very thing (losing games by forfeit rather than intentionally poor play). St. Louis manager Whitey Herzog concurred. "My job is to get the Cardinals into the playoffs," he said. "I would tell the public the day before the game, 'I'm sorry, but the Cardinals have to lose.'"

And so, 10 days after announcing its grand playoff plan, the league office revamped it, clarifying that should one club win both halves of the season, the other playoff position would go not to the team with the second-best overall record, but to the second-place team in the season's second half.* The move was made, said Commissioner Kuhn, "solely to eradicate any possible question of integrity."

It didn't make much difference to Los Angeles. The Dodgers' first-half crown allowed them to coast through the schedule's final months with little concern for anything but long-term health. For a team like the Reds, who'd been even with LA in the loss column when the strike hit, it was maddening. Cincinnati had won seven straight leading into the strike (including six complete games from its pitchers), and if a single game against the Giants in which the Reds led 6–0 hadn't been rained out, the division would have ended in a tie. The initial split-season format at least offered the Reds the advantage of a seven-and-a-half-game lead over Houston, but the revision stripped that away too. "Apparently, other considerations are more important than integrity," spat Cincinnati GM Wagner, intoning that a situation requiring surgery had been treated with a Band-Aid.

"There is no ideal solution," intoned Peter O'Malley, "but this is the best available solution in an undesirable situation." Dodgers players, having already been crowned first-half champs, were altogether blasé about it all, save for one detail. "Five extra days' pay," theorized Jay

---

* In such a scenario, it was decided, the dual division-winner would receive four home games in the ensuing playoff series. Otherwise, it would be split 3-2 in favor of the first-half winner.

Johnstone about the new playoff round. "That'll help." Added Ken Landreaux: "Give me my money."

Questions arose about incentive. If the Dodgers — as well as Philadelphia, Oakland, and the Yankees, the other first-half leaders — were guaranteed playoff spots with seven weeks still to play, how could they be expected to go all-out for victories? To some on the Dodgers, the insinuation was ludicrous. "Every club is going to try and maintain as much momentum as it can," said Lopes. "I mean, what athlete is going to intentionally drop a ground ball or strike out? What pitcher is going to give up three runs intentionally? A guy like that doesn't belong in pro ball."

Except that the idea had little to do with making errors or giving up hits. Critics began to examine the more subtle territory of extra effort in games that no longer mattered — things like legging out grounders and gutting out an extra inning before handing things off to the bullpen. The question wasn't even whether players would do those types of things, but whether they *should* do them, self-preservation becoming a premium-level strategy for those leading the pack. There were big games for which to prepare, but they wouldn't come until after the waning days of the regular season.

An early clinch also allowed LA pitchers to effectively treat the season's second half as extended spring training, during which they could hammer out various kinks. "I got to work on pitches like a cutter that I probably wouldn't have used otherwise," reflected Dave Goltz. "You were able to do those things without it having a drastic effect on the team, and in the long run you were better for it."

On paper, anyway, things looked good for the Dodgers. Thirty-one of LA's 53 second-half games would be at home, including 21 of the first 30, not to mention six of nine against Cincinnati. There was also the not-inconsequential detail that the Dodgers were finished with the top teams in the National League East, the Phillies and Expos, and had only 22 games remaining against other first-division opponents. (The Reds, meanwhile, had six games left against both Philadelphia and Montreal, and would play 26 of 51 on the road. Houston had it even worse, with 14 games against the Phillies and Expos, and only 23 of 53 at home.)

On August 10, *Sports Illustrated* commemorated the "new" season almost identically to the way it had back in April, running the same cover portrait of 1980 MVPs George Brett and Mike Schmidt, with slightly revised copy reading: "Here we go again!" Back in April, opening day saw Fernando Valenzuela twirl a five-hit shutout over Houston. On reopening day, Jerry Reuss — finally taking the start he should have had the first time around, on account of Fernando having just pitched in the All-Star Game — gave up three hits over six innings in a 4–0 win over the Reds at Chavez Ravine. The 35,120 fans who showed up were only 753 more than the smallest crowd of the first half . . . but at least there were fewer people there to boo. And booing seemed to come naturally to those in attendance.

With a second-half title rendered meaningless, the Dodgers turned their attention to what the roster might look like by season's end. Tommy Lasorda and Al Campanis had spent the break extensively scouting the organization's farm system, which led to conclusions about which minor leaguers were ready and how quickly they should be integrated. Within a week, the team would be bolstered by the addition of 21-year-old second baseman Steve Sax, the Texas League batting leader, at .346, who'd compiled eight homers and 34 steals in 115 Double-A games.* The closers at both San Antonio (21-year-old Tom Niedenfuer, 1.80 ERA) and Albuquerque (22-year-old Alejandro

---

* Minor controversy was stirred when Sax was promoted ahead of his Triple-A counterpart at second base, Jack Perconte, who was having an outstanding season of his own —.346 and 45 steals at Albuquerque. Perconte, who'd batted .322 and .326 at Albuquerque the previous two seasons, was irate. "I want out of the Dodgers right now, hopefully this minute," he said upon learning that he was being bypassed in favor of Sax. That winter the Dodgers traded Perconte to Cleveland; his seven-season big league career was highlighted by 60 stolen bases for the Mariners across the 1984 and '85 campaigns.

Peña, 1.63 ERA and 22 saves) were also called up, their additions—combined with Howe (age 23), Stewart (24), and Castillo (26)—giving the Dodgers one of the youngest bullpens in baseball. "Howser nicknamed us 'Canned Heat,'" recalled Stewart. "Everybody in our bullpen threw flame, and I mean threw *flame*. I threw hard, Niedy threw hard, Peña threw hard, Howser threw hard. Our bullpen was so young, and Terry Forster"—the old man at age 29—"did a great job keeping us level."

"Talk about a Kiddie Corps," said Lasorda, "we've really got 'em."

The insinuation was not subtle, nor was it intended to be. The Dodgers had a system lousy with prospects who merited use, if not immediately then before too long, and any veteran who wasn't pulling his weight was in the way. Three days into the second-half schedule, Dodgers brass made another statement by designating for assignment catcher/outfielder Joe Ferguson, who'd batted just .143 in 17 first-half games, to clear space for Peña. Ferguson had been one of Lasorda's favorite players since the Arizona Instructional League in 1968 and was an integral part of the 1974 World Series team, but at age 34 he was trending in the wrong direction.

It was easy to assume that next up on the chopping block was Davey Lopes, who had been in steep offensive decline since 1979. The second baseman's ouster seemed all but settled when, on August 17, in LA's eighth game since resuming play, Lopes—batting .178 with six extra-base hits on the season—pulled his groin and was sidelined for nearly three weeks. Sax stepped seamlessly into the lineup, making his major league debut the following day.

Like the rest of LA's infielders, Sax—a high school shortstop who had never played second base in his life prior to signing with the Dodgers—was a coconut-snatcher.* A farm boy from outside Sac-

---

* Sax didn't even play second in Little League. "When I was 10 years old, I was on the Giants," he said. "I was supposed to play second base for them, but taking infield before the opening game of the season, a ground ball came up and hit me

ramento, he didn't play college ball. He didn't play in Triple-A. He didn't even make it through a complete season at Double-A San Antonio before being summoned to Chavez Ravine. What Sax lacked in experience he made up for with uninhibited enthusiasm and an outrageous skill set. "He was like the Energizer Bunny, always bopping around, always happy," reflected Derrel Thomas. "He brought energy to the team that was starting to dwindle there in the second half. He relit that fire for us."

In his first at-bat, Sax beat out an infield single, and by the end of the eight-game road trip was hitting .364. His presence was the first legitimate threat to the longevity of LA's infield quartet, not only because of his abundant talent but because he was getting playing time never afforded to previous prospects like Iván de Jesús or Mickey Hatcher. At first, Campanis judiciously toed the company line by labeling Sax's promotion a short-term move, but within two weeks he was calling it like he saw it. "Davey took someone's job when he became the regular second baseman, and the same thing stands true," reasoned the GM in early September. "Here we've got an enthusiastic, aggressive, double-play-making, pretty good-hitting young man [Sax], and I would say that Davey has to look and say, 'Hey, that guy may be for real, he may be taking my job.'"

The other kid on the roster who everyone hoped was for real — the one who started the season 8-0 and had a mania named after him — did not take the second half by such furious storm as he had the first. Fernando Valenzuela was knocked out in the fifth inning of his first postbreak start, having given up five hits, four walks, and three runs to

---

in the eye and split my head open. I had blood all over my uniform, and I didn't get to play. I'd told my mom for weeks that something would happen, that I'd get the flu or it would rain. *Something's* going to happen, I said. It was the first time we actually got to wear the whole uniform. Now I've got a scar over my eye, and I never got to play. That was the closest I got to playing second base before I did it in the pros."

the Reds.* In his second start, against a mediocre Atlanta club, he allowed five runs over five. That put the left-hander's streak of winless starts at eight, during which time he posted a 6.46 ERA. The guy who began the season by not giving up a homer in his first seven games surrendered seven over a four-start span.

Popular theory held that what made Valenzuela's screwball so effective early on was hitters' willingness to offer at it, whether or not it was actually a strike. As reports on the rookie circulated, however, opponents began to lay off, letting the pitch tumble wide or toward the dirt, working the count in their favor while sitting on fastballs in the zone. Valenzuela, who averaged nearly nine strikeouts per start over his blazing first eight games, saw that number dive to fewer than six over his next eight. There were other troubling signs. Opponents batted .172 and slugged .212 against him over his first eight games, stats that climbed to .254 and .420 thereafter. Fernando's line-drive percentage — the number of balls hit hard against him — more than doubled, from 5 percent to 12.

"He's hanging his pitches a lot more," posited Atlanta third baseman Bob Horner, who hit one of Atlanta's three homers against the phenom on August 16. "He's throwing offspeed stuff over the middle of the plate. When he went around the league the first time, nobody knew him, nobody knew what to look for, what he threw, how he threw it. Since then the hitters have smartened up. The first time around, when he hung a screwball people didn't know what to expect. Now if he hangs one he's going to get beat."

Valenzuela finally righted the ship in his third poststrike start, fanning 12 in St. Louis on August 22 while falling one out short of a complete game in a 3–2 victory. That made him the National League's first 10-game winner, but by then the Dodgers were a dozen games into

---

* The game was carried by 38 stations on the Dodgers Spanish-language network, many of them in Mexico, for an audience estimated by broadcaster Jaime Jarrín to be as high as 20 million, because "Mexico is baseball crazy now."

the second season, and — in case anyone needed an indicator of how already clinching a playoff berth might have affected their urgency — it was the first time since June 1 that they'd won back-to-back games.

The Dodgers needed a jolt, something beyond the youthful energy of Steve Sax. Luckily, they had an ideal jolter in their clubhouse. Reggie Smith wasn't the same player he'd been even recently, his damaged shoulder leaving him unable to throw and limiting him to pinch-hitting duty in every one of his 20 appearances through mid-August.* Dodgers trainer Bill Buhler began discussing Smith's injury in retrograde terms, saying that it was back to where it had been during spring training, five months of rehab be damned. Smith, one of the team's undisputed leaders, was visibly frustrated, unable to do much of anything to aid a winning cause. He had lost all three of the World Series in which he'd participated — with Boston in 1967 and with the Dodgers in 1977 and '78 — and now that he had a chance to rectify it, he couldn't help but wonder whether he was a burden to the roster. This made him angry.

On August 25 at Pittsburgh's Three Rivers Stadium, the 16-year veteran reached the limit of his ability to keep his frustration contained. He wasn't in the lineup, of course, because he was never in the lineup. Hell, Smith had batted only three times in the two weeks since play resumed, striking out twice and grounding into a double-play. Just over a month remained in the schedule, and despite having been on the active roster since opening day, he'd collected four hits *all season*. Of course he was angry. This may have explained why the guy who was already the least likely Dodger to abide an opponent's shenanigans had so little tolerance when Pirates pitcher Pascual Pérez — a 24-year-old only recently recalled from Triple-A — nearly hit Dusty

---

* Smith wouldn't play the field until he took over at first base midway through a game against Atlanta on September 16, using Mike Marshall's glove. It was one of two non-pinch-hitting appearances he'd make on the year.

Baker in the first inning, then did hit Bill Russell in the sixth, then four batters later nearly hit Baker again, then actually *did* hit Baker one pitch after that.* Dusty took it in stride and calmly headed toward first base, but on the bench Smith spun into a tizzy. "I'll see you after the game," he shouted toward the mound after Pérez struck out Steve Garvey to end the inning. The slender Pérez, 20 pounds lighter than Smith despite being two inches taller, was uncowed. "How about right now?" he responded.

"Reggie had that voice that carried a little better and a little louder," recalled Jerry Reuss. "And Pérez was one of those guys who'd hear everything you'd say and respond to it."

Smith was one of five Dodgers who grew up in or around Los Angeles,† a product of Centennial High School in Compton. He was a switch-hitter with power, possessing (before his shoulder injury) one of the strongest outfield arms in the sport, not to mention one of the keenest minds. Smith was a big leaguer with Boston at age 22 and from the very beginning brought more intensity to a ballfield than some of his teammates knew how to handle. The catch was that he rarely cared whether he might be rubbing people the wrong way. Smith got into tiffs with the media and Red Sox management, and fought with teammate Bill Lee. When he intoned that racism was an issue in New England — primarily because racism was an issue in New England — a fan base that had already started to sour on his off-field drama doubled down. "Bottles were thrown at my house," Smith said. "My son heard nasty things said about me in school. Someone scratched my car with a key. I was called all kinds of names. Well, Boston is a racist city."

---

* Pérez's fastball naturally tailed in to right-handed hitters, and the pitcher didn't exactly mind working the inside corner. He'd drawn similar complaints in every one of the five games he'd pitched since coming up from the minors.

† Bobby Castillo, Ken Landreaux, Rick Monday, and Derrel Thomas were the others.

"Reggie was a proud man, and he was scarred by the Boston experience, there's no question about it," reflected reporter Chris Mortensen. "I remember thinking that somebody pissed off the wrong guy."

Never mind that in six full seasons with the Red Sox Smith was runner-up for Rookie of the Year, made two All-Star appearances, earned a Gold Glove, and picked up MVP votes four times; Boston couldn't unload him quickly enough. Five days after the 1973 World Series, the Red Sox flipped him to St. Louis for Bernie Carbo and Rick Wise.

Immediately feeling more comfortable in the harder-edged National League, the outfielder said that American Leaguers "took my aggressiveness as being mean" — a sentiment valid only when his aggressiveness wasn't actually intended to be mean. With one of the most intimidating men in baseball, it was sometimes difficult to tell. Speaking about Smith's short fuse, Dave Goltz said that his teammate "can go off the deep end real quick for a very little thing." Jerry Reuss compared Smith to Reggie Jackson. "If you have a Reggie bar in New York, you open it up and it tells you how good it is," he said. "If you have a Reggie bar here, you open it up and it punches you."

Smith earned an All-Star berth in each of his two full seasons with St. Louis but injured his left shoulder on the second day of the 1976 campaign and batted just .218 thereafter. He had been in a dispute with Cardinals brass over deferred salary payments, and the team seized his decline as an excuse to rid themselves of a headache, sending him on June 15, 1976, to Los Angeles in a deadline deal involving Joe Ferguson.[*] Despite rumors out of St. Louis that Smith hadn't been injured as severely as he claimed (started, said Smith, by the Cardinals themselves), Dodgers doctor Frank Jobe surgically repaired loose cartilage in the outfielder's left shoulder after the season.

Smith might not have seemed like the ideal target for Tommy

---

[*] Ferguson would be reacquired in 1978 from Houston, for then–minor leaguers Jeffrey Leonard and Rafael Landestoy.

Lasorda's brand of feel-good motivation, but when he arrived in Los Angeles, it worked. "Lasorda came to me and said, 'I need you,'" the outfielder recalled. "No one in baseball ever said that to me." Smith became one of LA's quartet of 30-homer hitters in 1977 and led the team in home runs in 1978, finishing fourth in the NL MVP vote both times as the Dodgers won back-to-back National League pennants. Bill Russell called Smith "the difference between first and second place for us." Dusty Baker positioned the outfielder as "the second-best player I ever played with," behind only Hank Aaron.

Then Smith's familiar bugbears arose. As the Dodgers struggled in 1979, losing 31 of 41 to enter the All-Star break dead last in the NL West, Smith scuffled similarly. Hitting .163 well into May was one thing, but getting into a public contract battle with Al Campanis opened an avenue of dialogue that people throughout the organization would have preferred remain shut. Smith proclaimed that he had signed his contract with assurances that among the Dodgers, only Steve Garvey would ever receive a higher salary. At the time of his objection, Smith's paycheck ranked fourth on the team. He complained about being lied to, then surprised everybody by adding that "I can't seem to find the concentration this year," while admitting that "my mind is elsewhere." As if to up the shock value even further, he then claimed that, surrounded by what he perceived as acceptance of losing, "it is very difficult for me to care whether we win or not."

Talking openly of retirement, Smith missed meetings and BP sessions. This did not sit well in the clubhouse. Teammates openly labeled him a quitter, anonymously suggesting in reports in the *Los Angeles Herald Examiner* and the *Long Beach Independent Press-Telegram* that the Dodgers would be well served by ridding themselves of his baggage. That July, Smith called a clubhouse meeting at Dodger Stadium, during which he spent the better part of an hour shouting about the injustice in his midst. The very next day he reinjured his ankle and collected only a single at-bat through the rest of the season.

"Reggie was a force in every way, on the field and off the field," said reporter Lyle Spencer. "He had high standards and great integrity. He was a guy who didn't have the capacity to be political and was totally honest all the time. That was seen as being difficult, but in reality it was just his nature, being honest. He would never back down from his point of view, and that would occasionally get him in trouble."

Players who make a lot of noise while failing to perform rarely find steady employment. As Smith proved in 1980, however, solid character and a robust stat line will mitigate all manner of outburst. His early season was a return to form: a .328 batting average, 15 homers, and 51 RBIs were good enough to make his seventh All-Star team as the Dodgers entered the break with the most wins in the National League. Two weeks later, however, Smith's shoulder acted up again, the latest flaring of a chronic injury that made the joint pop out of place, and would ultimately require the reconstructive surgery that not only wiped out the remainder of Smith's 1980 season but limited him to pinch-hitting duty in 1981.*

Smith didn't have to throw a baseball, however, to put a scare into a hothead like Pascual Pérez. As he lobbed threats toward the Pirates pitcher throughout the inning, it didn't bother Smith a bit that Pittsburgh — featuring enormous players like Dave Parker, Jim Bibby, and John Candelaria — was the league's most physically intimidating team. When Pérez pointed toward the grandstand — an obvious invitation to meet out of sight, in the stadium bowels — Smith didn't

---

* After the procedure, Smith was visited in the hospital by Jerry Reuss and Don Stanhouse, who borrowed white jackets from the staff and taped paper towels across their faces in lieu of surgical masks. The ersatz doctors laid out a cornucopia of fried chicken, barbecued ribs, and a bottle of scotch atop a gurney, covered it with a blanket, and entered the outfielder's room as if important medical business was at hand. Smith immediately burst into laughter, even as his family members wondered what the hell was going on. There's something to be said for bedside manner, but the pitchers ended up feeding Smith so much scotch that his blood-sugar levels destabilized and he had to remain hospitalized for an extra day. "It wasn't our nature to be low-key," smiled Reuss, looking back.

hesitate. Each man raced for his dugout stairs, which led to the interior hallway that connected the clubhouses. Players from both teams scrambled to follow, the benches emptying not toward the field but away from it, a reverse brawl, spikes echoing off the concrete floor. Baker, far from the action at first base, sprinted to catch up to the rest of the Dodgers, shoving past Lasorda "like a wild buffalo," the manager said later.

In the press box, reporters were baffled. Knowing something was afoot but having little idea what it might be, a passel of media members hopped an elevator for some on-the-scene reporting. Unfortunately for them, the elevator shaft, located directly between the clubhouses, opened onto the spot toward which, at that very moment, each team was charging.

"On one side is Pascual Pérez and the Pirates, who were the hugest team in history," recalled Peter Schmuck of the *Orange County Register*. "Pérez has a bat in his hand. We look the other way, and here's Reggie Smith and the Dodgers coming out of this other hallway. We're standing right in between them." Pirates manager Chuck Tanner screamed for security to clear out the reporters, more of whom were emerging from a nearby stairwell. He didn't have to ask twice. "It was like, push the elevator button!" said Schmuck. "Get that elevator back!"

In the hallway, which was no more than 10 feet wide, Willie Stargell and Bill Madlock blocked Smith's path to Pérez. That might not have been a bad thing. Pérez raised his bat as if to swing, but was stymied when teammate Bill Robinson grabbed his arm. Smith went straight to negotiation. "Pops," he said, referring to Stargell by his nickname, "this has nothing to do with me and you, so get out of the way." Stargell, though, was captain of the Pirates for good reason. "Come on," he said sternly to Smith, "there ain't gonna be none of that."

Smith was uncowed. "If I have to go through you, Pops," he snarled, "I'm *going* to go through you." Whatever Smith's purpose, however, no matter how intent he was on getting a piece of Pirate, the hallway was simply too tight for a group brawl. Amid the crush of bodies, the outfielder couldn't so much as effectively draw his fist back, let alone throw a punch. Never mind that the Dodgers were wildly outmanned when it came to BMI — "a bunch of little guys trying to look over a fence," is how Dave Stewart put it.* All Dusty Baker could think about was the five-foot-ten Garvey, the five-foot-ten Cey, and the five-foot-nine Lopes going up against an NFL-sized front. Even the best fighter of the bunch, Smith himself, was markedly smaller than fully half of Pittsburgh's roster.

"It was like a scene from *Braveheart*, little guys against big guys," said Garvey, looking back. "It had no future. You're thinking to yourself, 'I wasn't involved in this. I'm going to help my team, but this is crazy.'"

"All the years we'd been in that stadium, we thought those hallways were somewhat wide," recalled Rick Monday. "It's amazing how small they got in a hurry." Those at the front lines ended up nose to nose with the opposition, but things pretty much ended there. Pérez stayed safely behind his wall of teammates, and before long players coaxed each other back toward the field. "Let's put it this way," said Monday. "Air traffic controllers don't let jets get that close."

The Dodgers, ahead 6–1 at the time of the incident, held on for a 9–7 victory — nobody was even ejected — in the second game of what would become a five-game winning streak, LA's longest such stretch since mid-May. Maybe Smith was on to something. The Dodgers had stretched the streak to 11 wins in 16 games when they hosted the Giants a couple of weeks later, on September 9. LA had already taken the first two games of the series and led the National League West by four games with less than a month remaining. A clean sweep of both

---

* One report had Dodgers utilityman Pepe Frías wielding a knife in the rear of the scrum. Perhaps it would have evened the odds in the eventuality that things grew truly homicidal. Thankfully, if it happened, most of the people there didn't even see it.

halves of the season was looking increasingly likely, leaving Cincinnati and Houston to battle for second.

Then Tom Griffin broke Ron Cey's arm.

Dating back to 1890, when both teams were based in New York,
Dodgers versus Giants had been one of the most fraught rivalries in
baseball. Lasorda himself bought into it early, posting a sign in the
Ogden clubhouse during his Pioneer League tenure in the 1960s that
read, LOVE BASEBALL, HATE THE GIANTS. In recent years, however,
it had been a decidedly one-sided affair, the Dodgers finishing higher
in the standings for nine straight seasons and making it to three
World Series while San Francisco finished a cumulative 63 games under .500 and an average of 21 games out of first place. It was more of
the same in '81, although the Giants' attitude appeared to be changing
under first-year manager Frank Robinson, who had his club playing
increasingly hard-nosed baseball.

Cey was of particular interest to San Francisco's skipper given the
thoroughness with which he battered the Giants, hitting .364 against
them over the preceding four seasons, with 21 homers and 57 RBIs.
When Griffin—who would lead not only the Giants in hit batters in
1981, but the entire National League—faced Cey at Dodger Stadium
on September 9, the Penguin had already gone 3-for-6 with two homers over the first two games of the series. The third game is where
things changed.

In the fourth inning, Griffin ran a pitch directly toward Cey's face,
which crashed into his left wrist when the hitter reflexively threw up
his arm in defense. The pitch connected with such force that it didn't
break the bone where it connected, but the one opposite, on the far
side of the arm—"a medical first," said Cey later. Awash in pain, the
third baseman spiked his helmet in frustration. He was taken to Centinela Hospital, where he was told that recovery would be a six-week
process. If everything went well, said the doctor, Cey might be able
to ditch the cast in three weeks. The key would be calcium deposits
along the fracture—if they developed as hoped, it would signal that

healing had begun and could point to an early return. Until then, Cey could do little but hope for the best.

The injury knocked out LA's club leader in home runs, slugging percentage, OBP and OPS for the remainder of the regular season. That was the best-case scenario. With the Dodgers already locked into the playoffs, they had little idea whether their best power threat would be able to join them there.

Oh, how the Dodgers missed Cey. They lost that game to the Giants, and their next two, and nine of 13, during which they watched as their lead shriveled, then disappeared entirely.* By the time they traveled to San Francisco for a rematch two weeks later, they were riding a three-game losing streak and in second place, a game behind Cincinnati.

That Tuesday, Valenzuela lost the opener to the Giants. Four straight losses, one and a half games back.

That Wednesday, Goltz lost the second game to San Francisco. Five straight losses, two and a half back.

The Giants were out of the postseason hunt by then, but the latter win brought their record to an even .500. Perhaps they were feeling cocky. In the third inning, Dusty Baker was motoring into third on a hit-and-run single by Garvey when San Francisco third baseman Darrell Evans, pretending to have the ball, threw down a phantom tag — a decoy, or "deke" in baseball parlance. There was little reason for it; the ball had actually been thrown to second base, and Baker, safe at third regardless, was no threat to score on the play. By making him think an unexpected play was taking shape, however, Evans forced Baker into a hurried, defensive slide. Already hobbling on a balky knee, Dusty stumbled into the base and nearly exacerbated the injury.

---

* Pedro Guerrero, who'd been a minor league infielder until he was coconut-snatched to the outfield in 1977, made a relatively seamless shift to third base to cover for the Penguin. Nobody was about to mistake him for Brooks Robinson, but as a stopgap measure he worked just fine. Rick Monday came off the bench to cover Guerrero's spot in right field.

It was an inexplicably dirty play as far as Baker was concerned, especially considering that he and Evans had been teammates for seven seasons with the Braves, and Baker considered him a friend. "D, what are you trying to do to me?" he said incredulously as he rose from the dirt. Evans had no good answer.

By the time Evans was scheduled to bat five innings later, the Giants led 8–4, and Baker pulled reliever Tom Niedenfuer aside. "Drill him in the elbow," he instructed. The pitcher complied. Evans went down, left the game two innings later, then missed San Francisco's next four contests.*

That was only the beginning of the chippiness. It continued in Thursday's series finale, when Baker singled against Griffin in the first inning and, before anybody knew what was happening, found himself in a shouting match with Frank Robinson as the manager subsequently made his way to the mound. As best as anyone could tell, Robinson was angry with first-base coach Manny Mota, whom he accused of stealing signs. "Shit," yelled Baker toward the Giants skipper, "we don't need no fucking signs to hit your sorry pitchers."† Robinson didn't like that. The following inning, Griffin plunked Rick Monday, and though it was almost certainly accidental — a slow curveball that bounced off of the hitter's foot — history counts for something in these situations. Given that Griffin had ended Cey's season only days earlier, Bob Welch responded by knocking the pitcher to the dirt during his next at-bat. Cumulatively, it served as a tension-filled backdrop to what went down in the sixth inning.

It started when Reggie Smith was stretching alongside the dugout

---

* The following day, Evans tracked down Baker on the field and asked whether he'd been drilled on purpose. "Of course not," Baker lied.

† If Mota was relaying anything it was likely location, which has to do with where a catcher sets up, not with the pitches he calls. The typical baseball response involves simply having the catcher set up later in the sequence, once it's too late to inform the hitter about it. In this and many other ways, Frank Robinson was atypical.

and an inebriated fan in the second row began hectoring him with such ferocity that Lasorda felt the need to summon a security guard. The fan was ordered to pipe down. The fan did not pipe down.

"You stink," he yelled at Smith. "You have no class." It was typical fodder from a partisan Candlestick Park regular, the likes of whom loved nothing more than to rile their more successful neighbors to the south. Smith, however, was not long on tolerance. "No class?" he responded. "What does that make you, if you're talking to me?" Before anybody in the dugout knew what was happening, Smith and the fan, a 37-year-old from nearby Menlo Park named Michael Dooley, were in a high-volume shouting match. "Come on up here," Dooley challenged. That he was six-foot-four and nearly 220 pounds did not intimidate Smith a bit, but the player knew better than to leave the field of play. "I can't come up," he responded. "Why don't you come down here and we'll settle it?"

"What will it take to get you up here?" Dooley taunted. "What if I take off this helmet and throw it at you?" It was souvenir helmet giveaway day at the yard, and the fan waved his at Smith.

"You can't possibly be that stupid," Smith intoned. Yes, as it turned out, he could. With a smirk, Dooley hurled the helmet toward Smith, eliciting precisely the response for which he'd been begging. With no further consideration of consequences, the player leaped into the stands — "like he was Bruce Lee," marveled Baker later — determined to drag Dooley onto the field, where he could finish him off. It was a shortsighted move, of course; Smith was wildly outnumbered and, in his Dodgers uniform, not just a little conspicuous.

Perhaps Dooley would not have so thoroughly provoked Smith had he known the player's history in similar situations. There was the heckler Smith had decked in Vero Beach earlier that spring. In June, at the Airport Marriott where players were discussing strike issues, he had a run-in with Los Angeles sportscaster Ted Dawson over Dawson's on-air comment that maybe Smith should have played through his shoulder injury. (Smith invited Dawson to step outside;

Dawson wisely declined.) Three years earlier, Smith had started toward the stands in Wrigley Field for a confrontation similar to the one at Candlestick, only to be corralled by Baker before reaching his mark.

"Oh shit," said Johnstone when Smith vaulted into the Candlestick grandstand. "Oh shit," said Rick Monday, standing alongside Johnstone. Monday flew toward the railing, along with most of the bench. Johnstone, however, went the other way, climbing atop the far side of the dugout to more easily reach his marauding teammate, his cleats slipping atop the painted concrete dugout roof as he tried to run. Not that Reggie needed much help. Upon reaching his mark, he connected with a solid right, knocking Dooley forward toward the rail. On the field below, Landreaux called for Smith to toss the guy down. Dooley resisted as best he could, putting a choke hold on the railing even while continuing to threaten bodily harm to anybody who touched him.*

With large numbers of Giants faithful closing in, Johnstone arrived at Smith's side just in time to see, in his own words, "a big black guy with glasses" racing toward them. Without hesitating, he grabbed the man by the arm and slung him backward up the steps. By that point, police were descending on the pile. Even as Smith was jostled back onto the field, Dooley refused to release his grip on the rail despite direct orders to do so from authorities. The fan was in a tough spot: if he complied, the Dodgers were as likely to drag him onto the field as the cops were to drag him away from it. Eventually, officers beat his knuckles with their batons until he let go, then arrested him on charges of battery, disturbing the peace, disobeying an order from a

---

* "You do that in Philadelphia or New York or San Francisco, you're going to get beat up," reflected Steve Garvey. "In San Diego you'd probably eat somebody's fish tacos, and you'd be all set."

police officer, and resisting arrest.* Seven other fans were charged with similar indiscretions.

Smith was ejected, which didn't matter since he wasn't playing anyway (he was later fined $5,000 and suspended for five days), and the Dodgers held on to win for the first time in six games, 7–3. In the clubhouse afterward, Johnstone and Smith were recounting the drama when the black guy with glasses Johnstone had dispatched in the grandstand approached with a scowl. Looking at Smith and pointing at Johnstone, he screamed, "That's the guy!" It turned out to be Smith's cousin, who had been racing forward to help.†

It was heady stuff, just the latest example of what made the Candlestick Park experience so vibrant — and so terrifying — for the Dodgers. Hell, Smith wasn't even the first member of the Dodgers to turn that particular trick in San Francisco. In 1976, Derrel Thomas went into the Candlestick grandstand after a heckling fan made unkind comments about his mother; the catch was that he was playing for the Giants at the time. Unlike Smith, Thomas was restrained by teammates before he could get both feet over the railing, and no punches were thrown. Throughout the 1970s and well into the '80s, Giants fans, having long since given up hope for championship contention, ranked success mostly by how frequently their team could beat Los Angeles.‡ So combative was the rivalry that when Campanis once donned a Gi-

---

* Dooley ended up suing Smith, Johnstone, Lasorda, Lopes, and Peter O'Malley for $5 million. They settled out of court in 1986.

† Afterward, Frank Robinson tried to pin the trouble on LA's manager. "If Lasorda would keep his club in the dugout, it wouldn't have happened," he said. "But he's got his head in the TV camera. If the players had stayed in the dugout, it wouldn't have happened."

‡ When this author was a teenager in the Bay Area, he took particular pride in wearing his DUCK THE FODGERS T-shirt to Candlestick Park . . . where it usually ended up buried under several layers of sweatshirts because it was summer in San Francisco. Still, booing Lasorda was booing Lasorda.

ants-branded overcoat in the press box to ward off the typical Candle-stick chill, he felt the need to proclaim surprise that a Giants jacket could even give off warmth — and then took it off when an outsider noticed him wearing it.

Lasorda fully embraced the dynamic, spending his career inton-ing to Dodgers players the evil ways of the Giants and promoting the necessity of burying their rivals as frequently as possible. The pecu-liar layout of Candlestick Park — because the visitors' dugout was not connected via tunnel to the clubhouse, opponents had to walk across the field to reach their bench — allowed Lasorda to lap up scorn that Giants fans were only too happy to heap upon him. He reveled in those outfield walks, blowing kisses to the lustily booing crowd every step of the way.*

The core of the Dodgers was unassailable, a veteran bunch that had led the team to three World Series in seven seasons. The influx of kids, however, was something new, a visceral threat to the established order, the likes of which hadn't been seen since the team's veterans were kids themselves. The longer-toothed among them had different ways of dealing with it.

On September 7, Jerry Reuss held a postgame lottery in which

---

* Jerry Reuss threw a no-hitter at Candlestick in 1980 and ended up surprised when a group of fans applauded him the following day. He offered a friendly wave as he headed to the dugout and was surprised again upon reaching the bench when Lasorda informed him that he was being fined $50 for acknowledg-ing Giants fans. Understanding the futility in pointing out the overt hypocrisy of the manager's decision, Reuss took a different tack. "I did not acknowledge Giants fans," he said, at which point Lasorda called him a liar and doubled the fine to $100. "I watched you all the way from the clubhouse, waving at them," the manager said. "Tell me how you weren't acknowledging them." Reuss asked the skipper to look into the grandstand. "You see those four people wearing Dodgers jackets?" he said. "I was waving to them and nobody else." By this point, half the dugout was laughing at the absurdity. "You know," said Lasorda, "I'm the idiot for arguing with you."

players selected slips out of a cap to determine who should get more playing time, Lopes or Sax. Every entry, of course, bore Lopes's name. "That's it," said the pitcher, clapping his hands upon tallying the total. "He's our second baseman for the rest of the summer."

In reality, Lasorda had already taken care of the matter, pulling Sax aside on September 5 and laying out the pecking order in no uncertain terms. With Lopes sidelined, Sax was batting .286, had just hit safely in his seventh straight game, and stole five bases, mostly from the leadoff spot, in 17 starts. Most importantly, the Dodgers went 11-7 during that span.

The rookie had no chance. It did not matter that Lopes was hitting well under .200. He was ready to return from his ankle injury, and he was Lasorda's guy. On September 6, the veteran started his first game in nearly two weeks and connected for three hits, driving in a pair and stealing his 17th base of the season.* After the game (the Dodgers beat St. Louis, 5–0), reporters peppered Lasorda with questions about his plans for the position moving forward.

"Who was the second baseman before Sax?" the manager asked the gathered crowd. "And who was the second baseman before Davey got hurt?"

He waited until somebody responded: *Davey Lopes.*

"Okay," he said firmly, "you've got your answer."

When reporters questioned Lopes about it, he conceded that the job would one day belong to Sax, even while insisting that such a time was not yet upon them. "I'm not going to let people bury me," he grumbled.

---

* Also noteworthy during the game was the continuing resurgence of Fernando Valenzuela. After the left-hander's miserable eight-game stretch following his magical beginning (eight starts, 6.46 ERA, 1-4 record), his four-hitter on September 5 capped four starts in which he averaged *more* than nine innings per game (two complete games, one in which he went eight and two-thirds and one where he went ten), gave up a total of three runs, and struck out 37 while walking eight. LA won all four. Fernando, it appeared, was back.

Lopes was 27 years old when he reached the majors, and 28 when he first made the team out of spring training. Lasorda named him captain in 1978, only the fifth time such an honor had been bestowed in the team's Los Angeles history, the second baseman joining storied names like Pee Wee Reese, Duke Snider, Maury Wills, and Willie Davis. The arrangement didn't last two seasons.

At the 1979 All-Star break, LA was 21 games under .500 and in last place, 17½ games behind the Astros. After the blowup in which Reggie Smith shouted at the team about being labeled a quitter, Lopes one-upped him and actually did quit, renouncing his captaincy effective immediately. "Some things were said at the meeting, and I felt this was the best time to do it," he explained afterward. "This way we're all equal. I have no title. Nothing more is expected of me than from anyone else."

Still, he was Davey Lopes. Removing the "C" from his jersey did little to remove the chip from his shoulder. Once outspoken, always outspoken, the second baseman continued to exert influence over a clubhouse that frequently needed it.

With Lopes, it was rarely easy. In 1980, the Dodgers gave his leadoff spot to rookie outfielder Rudy Law, at least until Law struggled enough to give it back. Even then, Lasorda put Law, a .260 hitter who rarely walked, into the number-two hole behind the former captain. Because Law was not the type of situational hitter Lopes could use to his advantage while on the basepaths, he rarely ran — and those occasions when he did run were frequently under less-than-ideal circumstances. By season's end, Lopes had stolen only 23 bases, about half as many as his worst season and fewer than a third of his best season, while getting caught at the highest rate of his career. Even the team's ensuing media guide described his campaign as "disappointing." That winter, the Dodgers reportedly offered top minor leaguer Mickey Hatcher to Toronto in exchange for second baseman Dámaso García.

Things weren't too much better by September 1981, but at least

Lasorda knew how to maintain and contain the mercurial player. By publicly insisting that the starting job belonged to Lopes, the manager ensured peace from that corner of the clubhouse, but Lasorda was no dummy. As part of the conversation in which he informed Sax about his plans to reinstate Lopes once the veteran was healthy, he told the rookie one thing more. "If you don't mention anything about it," Lasorda said quietly, "and if I'm the manager next year, you're my second baseman." The proclamation took Sax by surprise. "Yes, sir," was all he said.

The 12 games thereafter represented Lopes's best stretch of the season. He hit safely in the first six of them, spurring his batting average over .200 for the first time all year. He went 3-for-5 against the Reds and 4-for-6 against the Padres, his 17 hits during that span coming close to matching the 27 he'd compiled all season prior to that point. The boos he'd been hearing at Dodger Stadium disappeared entirely. Lasorda was right. Again.

Lopes's hot streak limited Sax to a pair of pinch-hitting appearances over a 17-day stretch. It wasn't until the veteran's back acted up, sidelining him for five games late in the month, that his young counterpart again saw the field.

Nonetheless, Al Campanis increasingly began to talk about the next wave of players — the "Mod Squad," as Lopes jokingly dubbed them — in present tense rather than future. The key name when rosters expanded in September was Mike Marshall, who'd just won the Triple-A triple crown with a .373 average, 34 homers, and 137 RBIs. Joining him on the roster were Albuquerque teammates Candy Maldonado (.335, 21 homers, 104 RBIs), Jack Perconte (.346, 45 steals), and Ron Roenicke (.316, 15 homers, 25 steals), plus Mark Bradley (.316, 20 homers, 28 steals) from Double-A San Antonio. They, along with Sax and the baby relievers, Peña and Niedenfuer, formed a litany of players younger than 25 that also included Valenzuela, Stewart, Howe, Welch, Scioscia, and Guerrero, and cast little doubt about which direction the team was headed when it came to roster construction. "If you've got the talent," said Campanis with no small amount of foreboding for the team's veterans, "the timing will take care of itself."

Garvey's contract would be up in '82, and Marshall was waiting. Cey was seen as increasingly expendable with every inning Guerrero spent subbing for him at third. The contracts of Reggie Smith, Rick Monday, and Jay Johnstone were about to expire. One free-agent bust, Don Stanhouse, had been cut loose before the season started, and another, Dave Goltz, was expected to depart shortly after it ended. Even the 1979 NL Rookie of the Year, Rick Sutcliffe, had been relegated to a spot-starter role in order to accommodate the team's abundance of young pitching.

This didn't mean that the vets took things sitting down. On September 12, the team's age-based factions — which came to be known as the Old Goats and the Young Studs — began squaring off in early batting practice, with judges like coach Danny Ozark and bullpen catcher Mark Cresse deciding what counted as hits and how many points they were worth. To make things interesting, the players wagered $20 per head — not a good idea for the Young Studs, as it turned out. "It was like taking candy from a baby," gloated Monday after the Old Goats swept the contest's early rounds. Buoyed by their success, the veterans called for a fee increase, to $50, which the Studs prudently declined.* "The Old Goats beat their ass every day out there,"

---

* There was also, of course, copious hazing. Sax, for example, fell for the ages-old "three-man lift," in which a veteran — in this case, Jerry Reuss — claims to be strong enough to lift three teammates at once. So bidden, a rookie is positioned on the floor, lying between two veterans — in this case, Rick Monday and Mark Cresse — the three of them interlocking arms for support. Instead of lifting the trio, of course, the veteran douses the rookie with whatever sticky substances he can find — everything from peanut butter to shaving cream to orange juice was thrown at Sax. The rookie, held firmly on either side, was helpless. "What was really funny," grinned Sax, looking back, "was that Alejandro Peña fell for it *twice.*"

recalled Yeager with no small pride. "That's a fact. We just beat the dogshit out of them."

"Oh my God, you had Reggie Smith, you had Yeager, you had Monday," recalled Scioscia, a member of the Studs. "We were ready to fight at times because of rulings that Danny [Ozark] would make on a fly ball, about whether it was an out or a double. If you won that game with a home run, you felt like you just won a regular-season game. It was unbelievable."

Ultimately, according to some of the Old Goats anyway, the contest grew so lopsided that players began to lose interest. Still, the game was more than a simple way for players to pass time. "That group of guys — Davey and Yeager and Rick Monday — had been through the World Series before and wanted to win no matter what," said Scioscia. "They were very competitive, and that's why they had a lot of success. If they were playing Tiddlywinks, they wanted to win, and that made an impression on us. I'll tell you, it was a big reason we went so far that October."

Yeager, thinking about the BP confrontation years later, distilled it into a single sentiment. "There's something to be said," he proclaimed, "for old goats."

Despite the abundance of September drama — or perhaps because of it — the Dodgers failed to find their footing down the stretch. They went 4-6 in the 10 games remaining on the schedule following Smith's foray into the Candlestick Park grandstand, watching their deficit balloon to as many as five games. Things hit a nadir on September 26 in Houston, when LA fell victim to Nolan Ryan's record fifth no-hitter, in which he struck out 11 and retired the final 19 hitters he faced.

The very next day old pal Don Sutton tossed a two-hitter in a 4–1 Astros victory. At one point in that game, Bill Russell, recently returned from a six-game absence to rest a stress fracture in his right instep, accidentally let go of his bat, which landed near the mound.

Sutton joked, "This is too heavy for you," as he returned it to his former teammate. Russell playfully chucked Sutton in the stomach with the butt end, then proceeded to strike out. Sighed the shortstop afterward, "Maybe it *was* too heavy."

A 2–1 loss to the Braves the following day was LA's eighth in 10 games. Using a lineup increasingly reliant on call-ups — the Dodgers featured four rookies plus utilityman Derrel Thomas against Atlanta, and Jay Johnstone at first base instead of Garvey from the second inning on — they extended a run in which they totaled eight hits over the course of three games.*

In their next series, the Dodgers were shut out twice by the last-place Padres, stymied by somebody named Steve Fireovid in his fourth career start, and by Fred Kuhaulua, in his fifth.† Across the lineup, stat lines crumbled. A 13-for-72 stretch (.181) dropped Scioscia's batting average from a season-high .308 on September 3 to .276 by season's end. Ken Landreaux tumbled from .284 on August 8 to .256. Pedro Guerrero slipped 22 points in September to finish at an even .300, and hit only two homers over his final 51 games. Cey didn't play at all, with the Dodgers going 9-14 while he was sidelined with his broken arm. During one six-game stretch toward the end of the month, LA scored only seven runs.

Were there a saving grace, it was the starting rotation. A resurgent Valenzuela posted a 2.11 ERA in September, Hooton 2.20, Reuss 2.43, and Welch 2.72. Ultimately, it barely mattered. The Dodgers lost 15 of their final 24 to limp home with a 27-26 record in the second season, four games behind Houston. Cincinnati, meanwhile, ended up with the National League's best overall mark at 66-42 but missed the

---

* The lineup on September 20 included Garvey and Scioscia as the only regulars, plus pitcher Ted Power making his first major league start. LA fell to the Reds, 5-1.

† And last.

postseason entirely given their failure to capture either first- or second-half crowns.*

The Astros clinched a playoff spot during the last series of the schedule, at Dodger Stadium, despite LA winning the first two games, 6–1 and 7–2. The results shouldn't have been too surprising, as Houston had won only once in its last dozen games at Chavez Ravine — the playoff that ended the Dodgers' 1980 season.† Even the Astros' 5–3 victory in the season finale came only after they scored three runs in two innings against Dave Goltz, long since relegated to mop-up duty, to put a cap on a month in which he posted a 9.60 ERA. That last game was so dull, wrote columnist Scott Ostler in the *Los Angeles Times*, that the normal paradigm of Dodger Stadium ushers confiscating beachballs from the grandstand was turned on its head. "Sunday," he wrote, "the ushers confiscated the baseball because the game was becoming a distraction to people trying to watch the beachballs." At one point, the LA dugout was completely empty save for coaches Manny Mota and Danny Ozark.

Houston's losing streak in Los Angeles made things interesting. The Astros would be the Dodgers' opponent in the first-ever divisional playoff two days later, where the irresistible force of their SoCal failures would be pitted against the immovable object of LA's woeful offense and 10-losses-in-13-games slide. It was a perverse bat-

---

* Something similar happened in the National League East, where St. Louis posted the division's highest overall winning percentage at .578. Their 59 wins trailed Montreal's 60, however, owing to the fact that the Expos played six more games than the Cardinals. That made a difference when St. Louis finished the second half tied with Montreal in the loss column, but won one game fewer — having played one game fewer in the second half — and missed the playoffs entirely.

† The Astros didn't even clinch with a win, but when the Reds eliminated themselves with a loss to Atlanta. "We've won one game [at Dodger Stadium] in our last 12 here, and we've celebrated twice," said befuddled Astros pitcher Joe Niekro afterward.

tle of anti-indomitability: a team that couldn't win against a team that couldn't beat them.

More important to Houston's long-term prospects was the fact that, in the third-to-last game of the season, Reuss hit Don Sutton in the knee with a fastball, fracturing a bone and sidelining the pitcher until 1982. Sutton had been squaring to bunt, which itself was noteworthy given his off-season change of scenery from Los Angeles to Houston. The Astros were old-school, instructing their hitters to fully face the mound while bunting, a stance the Dodgers had long since abandoned because it put hitters into a dangerous position. Sutton inadvertently planted his right spike on the inside corner of the plate while squaring, which is exactly where Reuss's pitch ended up. Still unused to his new stance after 15 years of doing it differently in LA, the right-hander was not able to react quickly enough to bail out.

"Hell, I knew he was apprehensive about bunting, and I wanted him to be even more afraid so that he would bunt it straight up and we'd get a quick out," said Reuss, looking back. "If it was a little too inside, I figured he could get out of the way, but when he put his weight on that right leg leaning out over the plate, he had nowhere to go. God, I felt terrible." The irony was difficult to miss. Before bolting Los Angeles for the Astros, Sutton had missed only four starts in 15 years. Now, on the cusp of the playoffs, Houston would be without one of the two future Hall of Famers in its starting rotation.

The day before the season's final game, the Dodgers announced their playoff roster. It included few surprises save for the absence of 1979 National League Rookie of the Year Rick Sutcliffe. The onetime star-in-the-making had gone through a rough two-season stretch, a horrid 1980 (3-9 record, 5.56 ERA) having been followed by a mediocre 1981. For the second straight year, Sutcliffe was dropped from the rotation after only six starts. In 1980, the pitcher's 8.33 ERA made it justifiable. In '81, though, he'd been at only 3.45, and even that was mostly the function of one terrible outing. Sutcliffe was used exclusively in relief for the rest of the season, and only sporadically at that, getting into a single game in August, and then two in September while he dealt with a foot injury. When Lasorda gave late-season starts to a rookie (Ted Power), a reliever (Bobby Castillo), and a retread (Dave Goltz) instead of to Sutcliffe, the pitcher stewed. When the manager informed him on the season's second-to-last day that he was being omitted from the playoff roster, Sutcliffe snapped. The two were in Lasorda's office, and the six-foot-seven pitcher's first move was to shove everything on the manager's desktop onto the floor. Screaming profanities, he moved toward the liquor cabinet and, one after another, began hurling bottles at the opposite wall. Lasorda, terrified, crouched behind his desk while imploring the right-hander to calm down.

After the manager's liquor supply had been distributed via airmail, Sutcliffe lifted a chair over his head and turned to exact his vengeance on new territory — the adjacent wall, dedicated to photos of Frank Sinatra. This is when Dusty Baker raced in and saw what was about to happen. "Hey, man, you're already in trouble," he shouted, "but not the kind of trouble you'll be in if you tear up that Sinatra wall." Sutcliffe was furious, but he was not stupid. Pausing to consider the truth of his teammate's warning, he instead sent the chair skittering in the opposite direction before being hustled from the room by assorted teammates. Back at his locker, Sutcliffe made his stand, proclaiming for the media that "I will never play again for Tommy Lasorda" and demanding to be traded.* The pitcher cleared out his locker and did not return to Dodger Stadium for the season finale.

It was an awkward end to a shaky season, but overall assessments were positive. The Dodgers stank up the joint down the stretch, but part of that was by design, as veterans rested and rookies were showcased. Clinching a playoff berth in June will do that to a team.

Despite their offensive woes in September, the Dodgers still led the

---

* After the season, he was sent — along with another malcontent, Jack Perconte — to Cleveland in exchange for three players who would barely contribute.

National League in home runs and finished second in hits and fourth in batting average and runs scored. Cey missed the last three weeks but nonetheless finished tied for 10th in the league with 13 homers. Pedro Guerrero finished one back, with 12. Rick Monday, pressed into emergency service after Cey's injury, blasted 11 homers in only 130 at-bats. For the first time since 1973, somebody other than Garvey led the team in hits, as Dusty Baker's 128 topped the first baseman's 122. On the mound it was even better, as Valenzuela, Hooton, and Reuss helped LA's staff to second-in-the-league finishes in ERA, wins, and strikeouts.

Also noteworthy was the attendance at Dodger Stadium, which, despite a marked poststrike drop-off, averaged 42,523, the highest mark in major league history. The Dodgers lost 26 home dates to the strike yet still, at 2,381,292, boasted the 25th-best such season ever.

All can be forgiven, it seems, for a winner.

Portrait of an eager young pitcher: 26-year-old Tommy Lasorda in Vero Beach, Florida, March 1954. He'd make his first appearance for the Brooklyn Dodgers five months later.

© Jim Kerlin / AP / Rex by Shutterstock

Where the magic happened: Tommy Lasorda kicks back in his Dodger Stadium office shortly after the 1981 World Series. *Rasmussen / AP / Rex by Shutterstock*

The old left-hander could still bring it on occasion. He let hitters know it too.

F. Carter Smith / AP / Rex by Shutterstock

Reggie Smith gets stretched by trainer Bill Buhler (left) and Davey Lopes as spring training gets under way in Vero Beach. *Mark Foley / AP / Rex by Shutterstock*

"It is incredible, it is fantastic, it is Fernando Valenzuela," said Vin Scully on a Dodgers broadcast in 1981, reserving more ordinary adjectives for more ordinary pitchers.

Los Angeles Times, *Oct. 20, 2010*
Anonymous / AP / Rex by Shutterstock

Fernando and his screwball whisperer, Bobby Castillo, in Philadelphia, May 1981. Valenzuela had made eight career starts at that point, going 8-0 with seven complete games and five shutouts. His ERA on the season was 0.50.

Rusty Kennedy / AP / Rex by Shutterstock

Even nuns loved Fernando. Especially nuns loved Fernando. *Rasmussen / AP / Rex by Shutterstock*

The pitcher as a young man: Valenzuela contemplates his career before his first-ever start at Shea Stadium, May 8, 1981. *Richard Drew / AP / Rex by Shutterstock*

Steve Garvey, Dodgers first baseman/third baseman, 1969–1982. Two-time National League hits leader, eight-time All-Star (plus two more with San Diego), 1974 National League MVP, National League record-holder for consecutive games played. *Rusty Kennedy / AP / Rex by Shutterstock*

Ron Cey, Dodgers third baseman, 1971–1982. Six-time All-Star. 1981 World Series co-MVP. *Rasmussen / AP / Rex by Shutterstock*

Davey Lopes, Dodgers second baseman, 1972–1981. Two-time National League steals leader, four-time All-Star. *Anonymous / AP / Rex by Shutterstock*

Steve Garvey holds up his handiwork after Fernando Valenzuela picked Houston's Art Howe off of first base in Game 1 of the 1981 National League Division Series. Making the call is umpire Jim Quick.

Anonymous / AP / Rex by Shutterstock

Bill Russell, Dodgers shortstop, 1969–1986. Three-time All-Star. *Richard Drew / AP / Rex by Shutterstock*

Mike Scioscia doing what Mike Scioscia does: absorbing undue punishment in an ongoing effort to keep opponents away from the plate. Battering him is Houston's César Cedeño, who was tagged out to end the fifth inning of Game 2 of the National League Division Series. *Everett / AP / Rex by Shutterstock*

Dusty Baker rolls into second base with a first-inning RBI double to open LA's scoring in Game 3 of the National League Division Series. It was the Dodgers' first lead of the series. *Anonymous / AP / Rex by Shutterstock*

Steve Garvey and Expos catcher Gary Carter both watch Garvey's eighth-inning home run in Game 4 of the National League Championship Series in Montreal. The two-run homer provided the winning margin as the Dodgers tied the series at two games apiece. *Rusty Kennedy / AP / Rex by Shutterstock*

Jay Johnstone as we remember him best: clowning around in Tommy Lasorda's jersey during a rain delay in Montreal during the National League Championship Series.

Barrett / AP / Rex by Shutterstock

Rick Monday watches his ninth-inning homer in the decisive Game 5 of the NLCS, which sent the Dodgers to the World Series and relegated a generation of Expos fans to rue what came to be known as "Blue Monday." *Rusty Kennedy / AP / Rex by Shutterstock*

Game 5 heroes of the NLCS: Valenzuela and Monday. *Mac Alpine / AP / Rex by Shutterstock*

Steve Garvey, sporting a shirt given to him by a longtime Dodgers fan, celebrates LA's NLCS victory over the Expos. *Rusty Kennedy / AP / Rex by Shutterstock*

Tom Lasorda, as it turns out, can be quiet for moments on end. Here he waits patiently for his turn to speak as Yankees manager Bob Lemon answers questions at a news conference in New York after Game 6 of the World Series was rained out. *BH / AP / Rex by Shutterstock*

Ron Cey tests his head in a pregame workout prior to Game 6 of the World Series, after being beaned in the helmet by a Goose Gossage fastball in Game 5.
Anonymous / AP / Rex by Shutterstock

Steves unite! Steve Howe, Steve Yeager, and Steve Garvey revel after the Dodgers clinch the World Series in six games. *Anonymous / AP / Rex by Shutterstock*

Nobody was spared in the celebratory postgame food fight after the Dodgers' victory at Yankee Stadium.
Anonymous / AP / Rex by Shutterstock

MVTrio: Pedro Guerrero, Steve Yeager, and Ron Cey pose as part of the first three-way MVP vote in World Series history.
Anonymous / AP / Rex by Shutterstock

9

Houston-Ho!

As LA PREPARED for the Astros in baseball's first-ever divisional playoff round, participants could not help but recall the teams' showdown the previous September, when the Dodgers clawed back from three games down with three to play, a trio of one-run victories—two of them come-from-behind—spurring increasingly vibrant drama that was shattered in short order by the should-have-started-Fernando playoff meltdown.

Now here they were again, jetting to Houston for the postseason opener. The previous year's do-or-die face-off had been a rush job, foisted upon the Dodgers the day after the regular season ended. There was no time to think about it, let alone adequately prepare. In 1981, however, LA was working with an abundant calendar, 117 days over the three-plus months since the strike was called to mull over playoff positioning.

Houston presented unique problems. It was a pitching-driven club that was downright deadly at home, with a collective 1.70 ERA in the Astrodome, spurred by Nolan Ryan (1.11), Bob Knepper (1.22), and Joe Niekro (1.94).* Even without Don Sutton and longtime stalwart J. R. Richard, who the previous season had suffered a stroke that would

---

* Steve Garvey long suspected the Astros of fostering an additional home-field advantage by dimming the lights in the dome whenever their power pitchers started.

claim his career, the rotation boasted three current or former All-Stars, plus another in closer Joe Sambito.

The Astros had benefited from the split-season format more than anybody, the strike rendering inconsequential the fact that they staggered to a 3-15 record out of the gate. Houston shored up its offense midway through the season by acquiring Phil Garner from Pittsburgh and Tony Scott from St. Louis, but even then the Astros earned their paychecks more through scrappy play than anything else. Despite hitting fewer homers than every club save last-place San Diego, Houston's second-half record was a National League–best 33-20. Theirs was a perfect offense for their massive home ballpark, which served to negate much of LA's power while playing to Houston's strengths.

The Dodgers opened with Fernando Valenzuela. That was a good thing. The Astros countered with Nolan Ryan. That was better.

Apart from each putting up spectacular numbers in 1981, the pitchers had little in common. Ryan was 34 years old, a lean, right-handed, flamethrowing veteran of 14 big league campaigns. He'd pitched in four postseason series with three different teams, winning the World Series with the Mets in 1969. Before he was through, he'd toss a record seven no-hitters and strike out more men than any pitcher ever by a ridiculous margin. If any player in the league had seen it all, Ryan was the guy.

Valenzuela, on the other hand, was not yet old enough to drink legally in the United States and still barely spoke English.* In contrast to Ryan's heat, Fernando baffled hitters with command and movement. The day before his first-ever playoff start, the lefty spent time on the Astrodome turf juggling baseballs with his legs as he once did soccer balls on the Mexican plain. *Todo esta tranquillo.*

One other notable difference between the pitchers: in Fernando's previous appearance against Houston, on September 27 — his second-

---

* Mike Scioscia, asked whether Valenzuela's English was improving, said, "What you should be asking is, are we picking up any Spanish?"

to-last start of the season — he gave up four runs over seven innings and lost the game. In Ryan's last outing against the Dodgers, on September 26, he threw a no-hitter.

Valenzuela and Ryan would finish first and fourth in the National League Cy Young voting, respectively, and went out and pitched like it. Through eight innings each team was able to score only once, the Astros on two hits and a walk in the sixth, the Dodgers on Steve Garvey's homer a half-inning later.* With Valenzuela set to lead off the ninth and the game tied 1–1, Lasorda took a gamble and sent up Jay Johnstone as a pinch-hitter. It made little difference to Ryan, still throwing 97 miles per hour, who blew through the Dodgers in order for the seventh time in the game.

To pitch the 10th, Lasorda tabbed rookie Dave Stewart, hoping that his gas would provide an effective contrast to Valenzuela's more deliberate approach. Stewart hadn't given up an earned run until June, all his appearances coming in relief, and going into September his ERA sat at 0.93. The season's final month, however, raised some concerns. The right-hander surrendered late-game homers to St. Louis's Sixto Lezcano, Cincinnati's Johnny Bench, and Pittsburgh's Dave Parker, putting up a 5.65 ERA over his final 14 appearances, during which the Dodgers went 6-8. It's difficult to say that a pitcher who'd thrown only 43 innings on the season and received a two-and-a-half-

---

* Houston's run was preventable. After Terry Puhl singled with two outs and nobody on, Lasorda ordered two straight pitchouts with Phil Garner at the plate, in addition to multiple pickoff attempts. Valenzuela had not walked anybody all night, but put into a hole, he ended up walking Garner. The next hitter, Tony Scott, flared a soft pop-up to short right-center field. Davey Lopes was well within range but took a bad angle and got turned around trying to adjust. The ball fell, and Puhl scored. "What the hell you gonna do?" said Lopes afterward. For Fernando, it was not exactly unusual. Two of his seven losses included different Dodgers right fielders misplaying fly balls into inside-the-park homers, and his final defeat on the season was by a 1–0 score.

month break smack in the middle of things was getting tired, but that appeared to be the case.

Stewart was drafted by the Dodgers in 1975 but was born to play for the A's.* The right-hander grew up a 10-minute walk from the Oakland Coliseum. He was a run-down kid in a run-down neighborhood — a self-described menace. "They couldn't contain me," he said later. "My mom kept switching me to different, stricter schools, but I didn't get any better." It was a people problem, he said. He didn't like them. Stewart's father, David Sr., a longshoreman, died in 1972, when his son was 15, but not before discouraging sports as a potential career. It was Dave's older brother, Gregory, who taught him how to play baseball. That was a good decision.

Sports kept Stewart tethered. He was a teenage member of Reggie's Regiment, the bleacher-based fan club of A's outfielder Reggie Jackson, and spent nearly every day at the Oakland Boys' Club. Stewart was on a field or a court year-round at St. Elizabeth High School, picking up 26 football scholarship offers upon graduation in 1975. Instead, he signed with the Dodgers after being drafted in the 16th round.

In the grand tradition of coconut snatching, the Dodgers shifted Stewart from catcher, where he'd played through high school, to the opposite end of the battery. A 95-mile-per-hour fastball will do that for a guy. Unfortunately, the pitcher they called "Smoke" (profound heat inspires nicknames) didn't possess much in the way of secondary pitches. That's why Stewart began his big league career in the bullpen, and why, of his 32 appearances in 1981, only two lasted more than two innings. "The only way you can get by with nothing but a fastball is in short relief," he admitted. The pitcher did not yet possess the weapons to effectively alter course.

One thing Stewart did possess was an intimidating gaze, cap pulled

---

* Stewart eventually spent the bulk of his career in Oakland, where he won 20 games in four straight seasons, garnering top-five Cy Young finishes each time.

low over his eyes, which would come to define him in future seasons. Any questions he might have had about its efficacy were answered one night while out on the town with Dusty Baker and Philadelphia's Gary Matthews. "You need to raise that goddamn cap up," Matthews scolded the rookie. "I can't even see your fucking eyes, so how in the fuck do you know where the ball is going?" This pleased Stewart, who'd long subscribed to a simple lesson taught to him years earlier in the Instructional League by none other than Sandy Koufax. "The key to getting a hitter out," the legend informed him, "is one inch of fear." That was it. Starting with his cap, Stewart spent the rest of his career trying to put one inch of fear into hitters.*

Upon being inserted against Houston, the rookie looked at first like an inspiration. Stewart easily handled the inning's first two hitters, striking out César Cedeño and retiring Art Howe on a flyball to center. The next man up, pinch-hitter Craig Reynolds, bounced an ill-considered curveball up the middle for a single, but it was hardly cause for alarm. The right-hander had only to retire eighth-place hitter Alan Ashby to escape the frame. Hell, even if Ashby managed to reach base, Astros manager Bill Virdon would then have to pinch-hit for Ryan, and the Dodgers offense would get new life in the 11th. Stewart, however, ended up with option number three.

Ashby had hit four home runs all season, and only 30 over an eight-year career, but when a pitcher throws primarily fastballs it's not hard for a hitter to guess what's coming. Ashby — who'd grown up a die-hard Dodgers fan in San Pedro, California — did exactly that, sending an inside fastball on an arc down the right-field line, well into the Astrodome bleachers. As soon as ball left bat, Scioscia turned and headed for the dugout. He knew. Final score: Astros 3, Dodgers 1.

Afterward, Stewart was disconsolate. "[The Astros are] not a

---

* Later, Koufax introduced Stewart to the notion of separating his fingers on his fastball grip, which lent downward movement to the ball. That grip eventually evolved into the forkball that Stewart used to outstanding success in Oakland.

home-run hitting team," he said in the postgame clubhouse. "If they are going to beat you, you have to make them beat you doing what you do best." That was exactly what the pitcher had tried to do, and they beat him anyway.

The Dodgers' best wasn't good enough in Game 1. The question at that point was whether it might be going forward.

Things got no easier in Game 2. Starting for Houston was knuckleballer Joe Niekro, whose junk-heavy repertoire was as distinct from Nolan Ryan's heat as could be found in baseball, yet whose success — fourth- and second-place Cy Young finishes the previous two seasons — was entirely comparable. Niekro was more hittable than Ryan (who wasn't?), but that was part of his appeal. The Dodgers managed to put 10 runners on base against the right-hander over eight innings, but could do nothing with them, Niekro wriggling out of trouble in scoreless frame after scoreless frame.

The good news for the Dodgers was that Jerry Reuss was equally effective, surrendering only five hits through nine innings while matching Niekro, zero for zero.

Houston nearly scored in the fifth when, with one out, César Cedeño reached second on a walk and a stolen base, achieved after Bill Russell dropped a throw from Scioscia that had arrived in plenty of time. The shortstop atoned for his error one out later with his play on a Dickie Thon smash deep into the hole at shortstop. It would have been a clean single in a regular-season game, but this was the playoffs, and Russell, avowed anti-diver, laid out for it, spearing the ball as it was about to skitter past. Cedeño, going all out, ignored the stop sign put up by third-base coach Don Leppert, and stood no chance. The shortstop's throw beat him to the plate by 30 feet.

LA's best opportunity came in the seventh, when Davey Lopes hit a leadoff double and was sacrificed to third. With their two best hitters coming up and needing only a sacrifice fly to bring home their most capable base runner, the Dodgers whiffed, Baker grounding out to third, and Garvey grounding out to shortstop. Scioscia called the lack of execution "criminal."

In the bottom of the ninth, the Astros managed to get the winning run to second with one out. Reuss, exhausted but determined, pumped all he had into his final pitches, retiring Cedeño and Art Howe without allowing a ball out of the infield. Mission accomplished, he shuffled into the dugout and informed Lasorda that he had nothing left and the team would be better served with somebody fresh.

That somebody was closer Steve Howe, who worked a scoreless 10th. In the 11th, Lasorda turned to Dave Stewart in crunch time for the second straight game.* For the second straight game, Stewart let him down. A day earlier it had been a home run. This time it was a dink-and-dunk death, with leadoff singles by Phil Garner and Tony Scott putting runners at the corners, making it four straight hits given up by the right-hander over his two appearances. Lasorda wasn't going to give him the chance for five. The manager brought in southpaw Terry Forster to face lefty-swinging José Cruz, and drew in every defender on the diamond. Forster did his job, inducing a pop-up to left fielder Dusty Baker, who was effectively playing a deep shortstop. One down.

With four straight right-handed hitters due up, Lasorda turned to another rookie, Tom Niedenfuer, who intentionally walked Cedeño to load the bases and set up a force at the plate. Then he fanned Art Howe. Two down.

Houston's victory in Game 1 had been expertly navigated by manager Bill Virdon with a canny selection of pinch-hitters. In Game 2, he went right back to it, sending up lefty Denny Walling to hit for Dickie Thon, then smiling as Walling smacked a 1-1 fastball into right-center

---

* The Dodgers wasted another rally in the top of the frame, putting runners at first and second with one out against reliever Joe Sambito, who then struck out pinch-hitters Reggie Smith and Mike Marshall.

field, over the head of Derrel Thomas.* The ball hit the wall on two bounces as Garner trotted in from third with the winning run.

In the Dodgers clubhouse, Stewart sat stone-faced and tried to make sense of the previous two days. "I haven't done anything good in this series," he said quietly to reporters. "I'm zero and two, and we are zero and two. I wanted to be in there, trying to redeem myself for yesterday. Then the situation got out of hand before I knew it." Lasorda hunkered down in his office, stunned by his pitcher's collapse. Stewart would not see the mound again with a game on the line until 1982.

The Dodgers had followed their anemic September by scoring once over 20 postseason innings against Houston, a dearth made all the more glaring by Cey's absence. LA had received two outstanding pitching performances and owned a two-game deficit to show for it.

The Astros packed with confidence for their trip to Southern California, needing to win only one of the three games remaining to advance to the National League Championship Series. They had matched up almost precisely with the Dodgers through the first two, yet Houston—with a slight edge in pinch-hitting and relief pitching—was comfortably in charge. "We did what we do best . . ." said Walling. "We got enough runs."

At least the Dodgers were headed home, where they played far better baseball than on the road. Hell, Pedro Guerrero had hit three flyball outs at the Astrodome that would likely have been home runs at Dodger Stadium. Chavez Ravine was the site of the Dodgers' epic,

---

* Walling had noted on the bench that Thomas was playing extremely shallow, which was little surprise since that was the outfielder's preferred positioning. In 1979, his first year with the Dodgers, Thomas's refusal to adjust his station in center field in accordance with instructions from the dugout—Lasorda frantically tried to wave him over, and Thomas simply waved back—led to a clubhouse argument with Reggie Smith, during which Smith punched a glass cooler door and ended up with 60 stitches in his arm. Still, Thomas insisted—as did coach Danny Ozark, in charge of positioning the outfielders—that he'd been at normal depth for this one.

end-of-season comeback against Houston a year earlier, part of a streak in which the Astros had lost 11 of 13 in LA. That, too, seemed like a hopeful detail. Reported the *Los Angeles Times*: "No team has ever come from 0-2 down in the history of the division playoffs, which is not surprising since the history of the division playoffs is only two days old." The Dodgers would make history one way or another.

In the aisle of the Kay-O II, just before the plane landed at LAX, Lasorda sidled up to Garvey. "Want to go grab some dinner?" he asked. Dining out with the manager was always an experience, and this evening would be no different. The pair of Dodgers headed directly from the airport to Musso & Frank Grill on Hollywood Boulevard, where they were led to a private room. Already seated were Frank and Barbara Sinatra, and over the course of two and a half hours the group talked about anything but baseball. Finally, Sinatra broke the ice. "You guys aren't going to lose this next one, are you?" he asked. Lasorda didn't hesitate. "Nah," he responded, "we went up against some good pitching. We have them at home now."

"Mr. Sinatra, we've got them right where we want them," said Garvey. "I guarantee it."

Back in 1980, when the Dodgers and Astros met in Los Angeles for the final three games of the regular season, LA needed to win all three to force a divisional tie. Whatever relaxation Houston may have felt at the time was exemplified by third baseman Enos Cabell, who grew up in nearby Gardena and made his off-season home a block and a half from Jerry Reuss.* Because Cabell's was a one-car family, he asked Reuss whether he might be able to hitch a ride to the ballpark. Reuss viewed the request with some trepidation—traveling to a make-or-break game with a member of the opposition could easily garner side-

---

* Cabell was also a cousin of Ken Landreaux, though Landreaux had not yet joined the Dodgers at that point.

ways glances from teammates — but after talking it over with carpool partner Rick Monday, he agreed.

Monday drove a sports car with a tiny backseat, which is where Cabell folded himself for the commute. He was breezy and confident, and had every reason to be, even after the Dodgers won the series opener. The following day, Cabell again asked to tag along, though this time his tone was less assured. The Dodgers won again.

Cabell found his own way to the ballpark for the series' third game.

A year later, the teams were back at it, again in Southern California for a trio of elimination games for the Dodgers.* Cabell wasn't even on hand, having been traded to the Giants for pitcher Bob Knepper — who, coincidentally, would start Game 3 against Los Angeles. Knepper had flourished in Houston, where a 9-5 record and 2.18 ERA led to the first All-Star selection of his six-year career. Those numbers, however, were heavily skewed by the Astrodome, where the left-hander went 8-2 with a 1.22 ERA. In eight road starts, Knepper was a paltry 1-3 and 4.47; he'd just given up three runs over four innings in his last appearance of the season, October 4, at Dodger Stadium.

For Los Angeles, Tommy Lasorda was rethinking his decision to go with Bob Welch, long since announced as the Dodgers' starter. Welch's numbers were solid — 9-5, 3.44 — and he'd won his last five decisions, but with the season on the line, turning to Burt Hooton on short rest made sense. Welch's strong arm would bolster a bullpen full of question marks, while Hooton provided considerable and proven firepower, his 11-6 record and 2.28 ERA augmented by a 3-0 mark against Houston, including a four-hit shutout at the Astrodome two weeks earlier. The deciding factor for Lasorda was that the move set up Valenzuela to take Game 4, and Reuss Game 5, if the Dodgers made it that far.

---

* Garvey made sure to point out that the '81 series against Houston presented an easier task than the previous year's version. "All we have to win is three games in a row this year," he said. "Last year we had to win four."

Aiming for inspiration, the manager tabbed Ron Cey, still disabled, to throw out the ceremonial first pitch. Lasorda also delivered a pre-game pep talk to the clubhouse, the theme of which he later described as *I believe more than anything in my life that we are going to win*, and which Garvey later described as "nothing we hadn't heard before." ("Believe me," the first baseman said, "we've heard a lot before.") After Lasorda finished, as players were grabbing their gear, Garvey channeled actor Bill Murray from the 1979 film *Meatballs* and began to chant, "It just doesn't matter, it just doesn't matter, it just doesn't matter." It was his way of breaking some tension, and a number of players picked it up as they headed out to the field. "I thought it went over pretty well," the first baseman said, looking back.

It didn't take long for the Dodgers' comfort at home to manifest. In the very first inning, a walk, a double, and a Garvey homer on a hanging Knepper curveball produced three runs—two more than LA had scored across two games in Houston. Knepper settled down thereafter, limiting the Dodgers to two hits over the next four innings, which was followed by two perfect frames from reliever Frank LaCorte. The way Hooton was pitching, it would not matter. It was the kind of performance that had been anticipated from the beginning for the right-hander, though it turned out to be years in the making.

Hooton had been a Texas prep phenom, pitching Corpus Christi High to a state championship in 1967 with a 15-1 record, followed by a 35-3 mark over three years at the University of Texas, where his prospect status shone brightly enough to merit a feature story in *Sports Illustrated*. After the Cubs took him second overall in the secondary phase of the 1971 draft, Hooton became the third player ever to jump directly from the amateur ranks to the big leagues. He was sent to Triple-A Tacoma after one abbreviated outing in Chicago, but the next three starts of his big league career—two after being recalled that September, one the following season—were so sublime as to set absurd expectations. The first, against an above-average Mets team, saw Hooton strike out 15 in a complete-game victory. In the second, his final start of the 1971 season, he tossed a complete-game, two-hit shutout, also against the Mets. Then, on the second day of the 1972 season, he no-hit Philadelphia. Hooton's secret was the unique and devastating knuckle-curve he'd been throwing since high school, which he held like a traditional knuckler, with the fingernails of his index and middle fingers flat against the horsehide. Instead of trying to eliminate spin by pushing out with his fingers upon release, however, the right-hander utilized a downspin-heavy fastball delivery that lent the pitch such abundant dropping power it was occasionally mistaken for a spitter.* "I imagine somebody must have had a pitch like this sometime, somewhere," said Cubs coach Pete Reiser, "but I can't think of anybody."

Hooton was pitching for the Cubs, of course, so the success was not to last. While his three full seasons in Chicago weren't quite a disaster, neither were they the stuff upon which the pitcher's Texas legend had been built. Three managers and five pitching coaches unsuccessfully tried to integrate a sinker and a slider into the repertoire of a guy who'd built his success throwing everything with four seams, the experiment leading to a 32-42 record and an increasingly frustrated pitcher. "Three and a half years after I got there," said Hooton, looking back, "I wasn't any good." The right-hander lost motivation and put on weight. He couldn't sleep. His ERA ballooned from 2.84 in 1972 to 3.68 in 1973 to 4.80 in 1974. He was periodically demoted to the bullpen. Things grew so bad that Cubs owner Philip Wrigley publicly labeled the pitcher lazy and charged him with negatively af-

---

* Back in Corpus Christi, the pitch was known simply as "The Thang." When the Dodgers acquired Dave Goltz, they became the rare team with *two* knuckle-curve pitchers. Goltz's was far different from Hooton's, however. Whereas Hooton's secret lay in his overhand delivery, Goltz relied on wrist snap, meaning that while Hooton's ball broke mainly down, Goltz could get his to move from side to side. It also meant that his version was considerably slower than Hooton's.

fecting the rest of the team. Chicago went from 85 wins in Hooton's first season to 96 losses just two years later.

As an outsider, Tommy Lasorda could not imagine what had happened to a guy for whom he'd envisioned immediate and enduring stardom. During Hooton's brief stint in the minors he'd struck out 16 against the Lasorda-led Spokane Indians, inspiring the manager to call him "the best young pitcher I've ever seen." It got Lasorda thinking. One day in the midst of the right-hander's struggles in 1974, the Cubs were in Los Angeles and Lasorda — the Dodgers' third-base coach at the time — cornered him near the batting cage. "What happened?" he asked. "You were the best-looking guy I've ever seen coming out of college, and now you're an also-ran." The comment was genuinely inquisitive, intended in no way as an insult. When Hooton failed to come up with a satisfactory answer, Lasorda asked whether the pitcher might like to join his Licey team in the Dominican Republic that winter.

"I'm thinking, there ain't no way I'm playing for this guy," recalled Hooton, who as an opponent was no fan of Lasorda's outsized personality. "Then my teammate, Billy Grabarkewitz, talked me into it. He played for Tommy in the minors and said that I needed to do it." So the pitcher did.

When Hooton arrived in the Caribbean, Lasorda was amazed by his lack of conditioning — the pitcher himself admitted to being "a big blob" — and quickly put him on a program that had the pitcher running laps around what to him seemed like the entire island. Lasorda also prescribed a strict diet, all but convulsing when he caught Hooton eating baked Alaska — a concoction of ice cream, cake, and meringue — while out to dinner one night. Right there at the table the manager banned desserts from that point forward, then made Hooton walk the two miles home. By winter's end, the pitcher had dropped 25 pounds.*

_____

* Under the headline "Whale to Barracuda," the Dodgers' own 1981 yearbook re-

Hooton returned to the Cubs for the 1975 season but struggled with a diminished fastball, thanks to his newly missing body mass. When he put up an 8.18 ERA over his first three starts, the Cubs couldn't unload him quickly enough. They found a willing trade partner in Los Angeles, with the Dodgers giving up young pitchers Geoff Zahn and Eddie Solomon for somebody Lasorda viewed as a potential staff ace.

LA was coming off a World Series appearance and brimming with confidence the likes of which Hooton rarely saw on the north side of Chicago. Pitching coach Red Adams quickly scrapped the subpar sinker and slider that the right-hander had been ordered to throw, and convinced Hooton to develop a changeup. The pitcher was anxious upon first taking the mound for the Dodgers, allowing a nerve-wracked five runs in two-plus relief innings in his debut with the team — "If you ain't shot for a while," he posited in his Texas twang, "you cain't shoot straight" — and was up and down for 15 starts thereafter. From that point forward, however, the pitcher was settled and sublime, going 12-0 over his final 14 outings, with a 1.83 ERA, two shutouts, nine complete games, and one more in which he went 11.*

Through it all, Hooton maintained the same taciturn facade that led to the nickname that would stick with him through the remainder of his career. It came about back in the Dominican, during a New Year's Eve party in Lasorda's suite at the Jaragua Hotel. The pitcher, having little interest in revelry, found a quiet corner and a deck of cards, and set to an extended session of solitaire. "Look at him," said Lasorda to a group of players, nodding toward the guy who hadn't said a word to anybody for hours. "Isn't he happy?" From that point forward, "Happy" it was.

---

ported that "[Lasorda's] vision pierced Hooton's blubber and detected the makings of a trim major league pitcher."

* Hooton fully embraced the California lifestyle by visiting celebrity hypnotist Arthur Ellen, who'd previously worked with Maury Wills, Nolan Ryan, and Roberto Clemente. The pitcher said that it helped his confidence.

It was funny, of course, because it fit. "Happy's idea of a high-five is standing up and nodding," said Rick Monday. Columnist Jim Murray wrote that Hooton got his nickname because he smiled . . . once. Vin Scully summed up the pitcher by saying that he celebrated by going out and "painting the town beige."

Now, against Houston, the destiny Lasorda envisioned for the pitcher was playing out fully. Hooton held the Astros to three hits into the eighth, his knuckle-curve dancing away from bat after bat. Art Howe's homer leading off the third was the only real damage Houston managed, and by the time Hooton walked Howe to open the eighth, LA led, 3–1. Lasorda brought in Steve Howe (no relation) to close out the inning, and Bob Welch, in his first relief appearance in two years, threw a perfect ninth. The three runs the Dodgers scored in their final at-bat were entirely extraneous in a 6–1 victory. It was LA's 12th home win against the Astros in their last 14 games.*

Houston still led the series and still needed to win only one of the next two to eliminate the Dodgers, but to judge by the questions asked in their postgame clubhouse, it was the Astros who were on the defensive. What was it about Dodger Stadium that affected them so? What happened to their bats, not to mention their nerves, whenever they traveled to Los Angeles? "There are probably some jitters here," admitted Houston catcher Alan Ashby. "Maybe there is a psychological factor." It was easy to think back to the Astros' three-game implosion in Los Angeles a season earlier, the turning point of which, wrote Kenny Hand of the *Houston Post*, "was when the Astros plane landed."

On the Dodgers' side, Steve Garvey confused some 60 reporters in the interview room by answering a question about his home run with

---

* Visitors in the postgame clubhouse included Lasorda's old friend, legendary USC baseball coach Rod Dedeaux. "You played like a Trojan!" Dedeaux enthusiastically told Ken Landreaux, who'd played collegiate ball at rival Arizona State. The outfielder offered a faux scowl in response. "Horseshit," he spat.

the phrase, "Thanks, Jerry." Nobody knew it, but he was talking to Jerry Reuss, standing on the opposite side of the room's partition, in the closed-off portion where the Dodgers kept their workout equipment. Upon realizing that only Garvey could see him through the opening, the pitcher immediately dropped his pants.

When it came to actual answers, the most pertinent one had to do with Houston's next starting pitcher. Game 4 was custom-built for Nolan Ryan, with a twilight start that made the baseball all but impossible to pick up over the game's early innings. "My son is tough to hit in twilight," theorized Rick Monday about his nine-year-old, wondering how he'd ever catch up to one of baseball's hardest throwers.

There was, of course, a catch. Were Ryan to take advantage of the setting, it would have to be on short rest—something he hadn't done all season. Astros manager Bill Virdon also could not help but consider that if Houston managed to win without Ryan, his ace would get three extra days' rest prior to the National League Championship Series. Holding a two-game lead meant that even if the Astros lost without him, Ryan would be at full strength for the decisive Game 5. So Virdon went with 30-year-old right-hander Vern Ruhle (Houston's fifth starter until Sutton went down), who'd posted a 2.91 ERA across 15 starts. Unlike Knepper, Ruhle was equally effective on the road as he was at home.

By this point, Fernando Valenzuela was accustomed to working with only three days off and was more than pleased to pick up the slack for Los Angeles. From his very first pitch, the lefty was dominant, striking out two of the first three men he faced, his screwball spinning away from Astros hitters who could not resist it. Fernando set down the side in order in the first four innings, and all Houston could scrape together through eight was two scattered hits and a walk.

Ruhle was nearly as good, allowing only four hits over eight innings, but he slipped just enough to matter, allowing a solo homer to

Pedro Guerrero in the fifth (no Astrodome to swallow that one) and a two-out RBI single to Bill Russell in the seventh. The Dodgers led, 2–0, heading into the ninth. They'd need both runs.

Valenzuela, on the cusp of shutting out Houston for the third time on the season, was tiring noticeably even before he opened a cut on the middle finger of his left hand — the result of eight innings' worth of friction from baseball seams on his screwball release.* So hampered, the lefty allowed a one-out double to Terry Puhl, who was brought home by a two-out single from Tony Scott. Now LA led 2–1, with the winning run at the plate and the season on the line. Lasorda had a quick decision to make: stick with his fading superstar or go to a bullpen that had yet to conclusively answer any postseason questions about its trustworthiness. Eyeing Houston's cleanup hitter, José Cruz, the manager, ever dogged, stuck with what worked. He left Valenzuela in.

Fernando made him look good by inducing Cruz to pop up to Scioscia behind the plate. Game over, series tied. "I wish I'd had that kind of poise when I was 20," marveled Ryan in Houston's postgame clubhouse. With a decisive Game 5 now set for the following day, pundits began to wonder whether the Astros' struggles in Los Angeles were not merely mental. Dodgers players weighed in. "They can afford to challenge you in the dome," posited Garvey, explaining that Houston's spacious stadium allowed pitchers to keep their offerings over the plate in ways that were less effective in smaller ballparks. Guerrero's would-be homers in Houston served as three examples, and Garvey's Game 3 homer at Dodger Stadium — "that ball would not have gone out of the Astrodome," said Baker after the game — was another.

"I'm sure if you ask them," said Garvey about the Astros, "they are

---

* When asked to display the wound for the media after the game, Valenzuela considered the possibility of what he was about to do and then, with a wide smile, flipped reporters the bird, exactly as requested.

concerned." He was right. They *were* concerned. Which is exactly how the Dodgers wanted it.

It's not like Houston was conceding. Solid as Ruhle had been for the Astros in Game 4, his real contribution was in allowing Virdon to save Nolan Ryan for the series finale. It didn't seem fair. Ryan no-hit the Dodgers in his only regular-season start against them, then two-hit them 10 days later in the playoff opener. He was rested and ready.

Los Angeles countered with Jerry Reuss, whose success against the Astros — 26 regular-season innings included a shutout on short rest and a total of two runs surrendered — was comparable to Ryan's against the Dodgers. Like Valenzuela before him, Reuss was pitching a day earlier than his regular schedule mandated.

It did not begin well for the left-hander. With Reuss looking like he was "trying to throw the ball through the backstop," according to Davey Lopes, the pitcher allowed eight base runners — four hits, three walks, and an error — over the first six innings while striking out only one and consistently running deep into counts.

Still, Reuss kept Houston off the board. Two runners stranded in the second. One each in the third, fourth, and fifth. Two more in the sixth, plus another caught stealing. With the game still scoreless, it would have been easy to suppose that the pitchers were on equal footing, but that simply wasn't true. Ryan was typically dominant, allowing only one hit and one walk to that point while striking out six. Still, his curveball wasn't as sharp as it had been in his earlier starts against the Dodgers — the right-hander threw four breaking pitches in the first inning, none for strikes, and that was essentially that — but with his fastball crackling as usual it didn't much matter. "He throws it and you can't see it," said Lopes. "He just paralyzes you."

Ryan's undoing came in the sixth, and it started with poor fielding. With one out, Baker sent a foul pop-up soaring down the first-base line, a difficult play in a sun field that had earlier cost Steve Garvey a shot at a similar ball. Houston first baseman Denny Walling, blinded and flailing, could do no better, the ball falling harmlessly to the turf nearby. Baker ended up walking, then took third on a hit-and-run single by Garvey. With pressure mounting in a scoreless game, Ryan did what Ryan did best, overpowering Monday with a pair of fastballs, each of which the hitter fouled off weakly. "I felt like calling the National Guard for help," he admitted afterward.

He didn't need it. Ryan's third pitch, also a fastball, caught just enough of the plate for Monday to send it on a line into right field for a run-scoring single. One-nothing, Dodgers.

One out later, Ryan made an ill-considered decision to revisit his curveball, which Scioscia pounded into center field for another single, bringing home Garvey to extend the lead. The next hitter, Russell, extended it further when, racing down the line after hitting an infield grounder, he knocked the ball out of Walling's glove as the first baseman reached for a wide throw. It was Houston's third error of the game, and the Dodgers' third run.

"Something changed with Nolan," said Reuss, who noticed it later while watching game tape. "Suddenly the guys were swinging differently. Their approach was different. It was like they knew what was coming, and they knew the location. They were reading *everything*." That probably had less to do with Ryan tipping pitches than the fact that it was LA's third time through the order, and the twilight shadows had disappeared. Looking back, Dodgers hitters claimed to a man that they were simply more comfortable against Ryan than they'd been earlier in the game. It was enough.

That was all the rope Ryan was given. Virdon pinch-hit for him in the seventh, and LA touched the Astros bullpen for another run when Garvey tripled in Ken Landreaux in the bottom half of the frame.

Granted a late 4–0 lead, Reuss recalled a pep talk he once received about the hazards of going all-out — something about being able to run faster at 95 percent effort, because at 100 percent everything tightens up. He couldn't remember who told him that. It sounded like Koufax. So the left-hander intentionally eased up in the game's latter portion, and damned if it didn't work. Reuss notched three of his four strikeouts across the eighth and ninth innings while yielding only one hit. The four runs Los Angeles had given him turned out to be three more than they needed.

The game's final play, a swing and miss by pinch-hitter Dave Roberts, was nearly overshadowed by the fact that the ball escaped Scioscia and rolled all the way to the backstop. Roberts, who at first didn't notice, took off only belatedly as Reuss hopped madly on the mound, frantically stabbing a finger toward first. Fans had already begun to storm the field by the time Scioscia corralled the ball and fired it to Garvey, just ahead of the diving Roberts. "I was thinking shades of Mickey Owen there for a while," said the relieved catcher afterward.* The ninth inning was Reuss's 18th straight scoreless frame of the series. He'd thrown almost nothing but fastballs along the way in securing the clinching victory with a five-hit shutout. The Dodgers would now face the Montreal Expos, who'd clinched their own series with a victory in Philadelphia earlier in the day.

In the celebratory postgame clubhouse, Tommy Lasorda was tackled to the ground and had beer poured down his pants. Reported the *Los Angeles Times*: "Fernando Valenzuela, who led the team in the champagne-poured-on-your-head category, staged a champagne fight with Reggie Smith. It was a draw."

It was the only draw to be found in Dodger Stadium that day. LA had staged its second annual late-season, three-game sweep of the

---

* Old-time Dodgers catcher Mickey Owen is best known for the infamous moment during the 1941 World Series when he allowed a passed ball after New York's Tommy Henrich struck out for what should have been the final out of Game 4. Instead of tying the Series at two games apiece, Henrich was safe at first and the Yankees rallied for four runs, winning both the game and, eventually, the championship.

Astros, but unlike 1980, this improbable comeback ended with a win. "I believe in something called the last breath," enthused Dusty Baker. "You haven't beaten people until you've taken away their last breath. We were still breathing, even after we lost those first two games."

Now the Dodgers were on to Quebec, with breath aplenty, to play for the right to go to the 1981 World Series.

10

Tundra

IN 1981, TO judge the Montreal Expos by their brief history would have been an injustice. The franchise was only a dozen years old at that point, the first decade of which saw the team finish a collective 202 games under .500 and an average of 23 games out of first place.

Recently, though, things had changed. The Expos had never made the playoffs but nonetheless held the National League's best record over the previous two seasons, 1979 and '80. Their back-to-back second-place finishes were by a total of three games, which mostly served to make abundantly clear that this team was due. That was the theory anyway. Led in 1981 by young stars like Gary Carter and Andre Dawson and buoyed by the ascension of rookie outfielder Tim Raines (all three would make the Hall of Fame), the Expos were a team on the come . . . until their roster was struck by a spate of injuries and an unmistakable sense of malaise. An 11-2 start was completely undone by multiple losing streaks, with Montreal sinking as low as fourth place, just two games over .500, days before the strike hit.

When the schedule resumed and things didn't improve—the Expos went 13-12 across August and early September, despite new hope delivered by the split-season format—fifth-year manager Dick Williams was canned. Replacing him was the team's VP for player development, Jim Fanning, who not only had never managed in the majors, but whose last full-time gig as a skipper was in the Class-C Northern League, a division that hadn't existed since 1962.

The Expos responded. Behind Dawson (.302, 24 homers, 26 steals, second-place finish in NL MVP voting) and Carter (Gold Glove and Silver Slugger awards, sixth-place MVP finish), Montreal won 11 of its final 15 to clinch the NL East's second-half title. Raines lent explosiveness to the top of the order with 71 stolen bases in 88 games, prevented from approaching Lou Brock's record of 118 steals only by the strike and a late-season hand injury that cost him 30 games. "He is so fast," wrote Jim Murray in the *Los Angeles Times*, "it is widely reported only three people in his hometown are sure what he looks like. What he usually looks like is a guy who just heard the dam break."* Raines set a record by successfully swiping the first 27 bases of his career without being caught — seven during brief call-ups in 1979 and '80, and 20 in 1981 — only eight off the all-time mark of 35, set by Davey Lopes in 1975. Only six catchers threw him out all season. Mike Scioscia was the first.

Behind superlative pitching in the National League Division Series from Steve Rogers — two starts, 17⅔ innings, one earned run, 0.51 ERA — the Expos upset highly favored Philadelphia in five games. It was Montreal's first-ever playoff series, and the taste of success left them wanting more.

For LA, three straight elimination games in the NLDS lent the blank slate of the championship series a distinct aura of relief. Then again, while the Dodgers had proven that they could respond with their backs against a wall, critics wondered whether they could keep it up now that the footing was even. Burt Hooton offered a decisive answer. On a sunny afternoon at Dodger Stadium, the right-hander shut down the Expos into the eighth, in a game that was effectively over by the second inning, when LA scored two runs off of Expos right-hander Bill Gullickson. They were the only two runs he'd allow,

---

* The columnist didn't stop there with the puns. "Raines signed with Montreal four years ago clear down in the fourth round," Murray wrote. "Some say it took them three rounds to catch him."

but with the way Hooton teased Montreal the game never seemed close. After Pedro Guerrero and Mike Scioscia hit back-to-back home runs against reliever Jeff Reardon in the eighth, it actually wasn't close, the Dodgers rolling to a 5–1 victory.

Credit could be distributed across the Los Angeles clubhouse. Hooton worked effectively without his best stuff, throwing fastballs so slow that Scioscia mistook them for changeups. "Anyone can go out with good stuff and win," the catcher theorized after the game. "A guy who wins with mediocre stuff, *that's* a good pitcher." As a staff, the Dodgers had allowed three runs over their last four games, all victories, pitching 43 shutout innings out of a possible 47. (When somebody asked Lasorda, "Are your pitchers at their peak?" he answered, "I hope not.") On the offensive end, Bill Russell squeezed in a run. Davey Lopes, despite a bad back and a bone bruise on his right hand, stole two bases. Best of all—and on this, everyone agreed—was the return of the Penguin.

Ron Cey hadn't appeared in a game since breaking his arm against the Giants in September, at which point any possible comeback was immediately pegged to how deep into the playoffs the Dodgers might play. By beating the Astros, the team held up its end of the bargain. Cey was determined to respond in kind.

The third baseman had been with the club throughout the first round, working out in the cage and on the field, then sitting on the bench, in uniform, during games. To protect himself during drills he wore a plastic shield over the outside of his forearm while batting, which he flipped around to the inside, to cover the break, while playing defense. "I've done my work, and now I'm in a position to take advantage of it," he told reporters before the Expos series. "I'm ready to dive for balls. I won't know 'till it happens, but I'm ready."

What Cey was attempting—returning from the most serious injury of his career, on the biggest stage he'd seen since the 1978 World Series, having missed nearly five weeks without so much as a minor league rehab assignment in between—was formidable. Hell, his cast had been off for only a week. It was possible that Cey's readjustment to game action could last the duration of the playoffs, costing the Dodgers a more capable player in his place. His teammates didn't care a bit. "When you get a player back that's done what Ronnie Cey's done," said Yeager, "you have to feel a little bit better."

To accommodate the third baseman, Lasorda returned Pedro Guerrero to right field, which meant sending Rick Monday back to the bench. This was no easy decision. From the day Cey went down until the end of the season, Monday had hit .415, with six homers in 18 games. It was the most productive stretch of his career, but he took the decision without complaint. "There's no question we're a better club when the Penguin is at third base," he said.

Cey wasted little time proving Monday correct, driving in Game 1's first run with a second-inning double, then starting a two-out, three-run rally in the eighth with a base hit. "I was ready to play," he said, looking back. "It was a matter of how many games or how many pitches or how many at-bats it would take me to get into a comfort zone." The answer to all those questions fell someplace between "not many" and "zero."

"He's amazing," Lasorda said afterward of his third baseman. "They said he was talking to his arm. That was OK with me, but I would have started worrying if he told me it talked back."

The loss continued a baffling streak in which the Expos had gone 1-19 over their last 20 games in Los Angeles, a record of futility that could not be fully explained by anyone on either club. At least part of it lay in the fact that Montreal, while a world-beating 38-18 at home in 1981, was merely 22-30 on the road — a worse mark than all but the three worst teams in the National League — and went 23-33 against clubs with .500-or-better records.*

---

* In the context of Montreal's putrid record at Chavez Ravine, the *Los Angeles Times* pointed out that USC, in its annual February exhibition game against the Dodgers, had managed to go 7-2-1 over the prior decade at Dodger Stadium.

After their victory, the Dodgers welcomed to the locker room singer Carl Carlton, whose single "She's a Bad Mama Jama" was peaking at number 22 on the US singles chart. Usually, clubhouse celebrity sightings were limited to the manager's office, but when Carlton — about to be nominated for a Grammy Award for best R&B vocal performance — heard Dusty Baker proclaim that his was the team's theme song, he had to swing by to check things out for himself.*

This was how it was supposed to be. The sun was shining in Los Angeles, the Dodgers were winning, and pop stars had joined the party. The good vibes seemed like they might never end. Then they did, the very next night.

The Dodgers understood the odds. They knew how poorly the Expos fared in Chavez Ravine. They were also aware of how well the Expos played in Montreal — the-best-home-record-in-baseball well — never mind the frigid inhospitality of Quebec in October. Making things even more difficult was that Expos ace Steve Rogers — who'd been biding his time since pitching his team's NLDS finale against Philadelphia — awaited once the series returned to Canada. For Los Angeles, the need to win Game 2 at home in this best-of-five series was profound.

Standing in the way was 31-year-old right-hander Ray Burris, a journeyman starter who in nine seasons with three teams had a losing record and a 4.26 ERA. Over a single two-month span earlier in his career, he'd been cut by the Mets and waived by the Yankees.†

---

* The Expos countered with their own celebrity fan, actor Donald Sutherland. A New Brunswick native, Sutherland made a point of attending every one of Montreal's games down the stretch, home and away, and ended up in the celebratory clubhouse when his team clinched a spot in the playoffs.

† Burris had come on strong in the season's second half, when a 3.10 ERA and 6-2 record over his final 11 starts solidified Montreal's rotation down the stretch. Still, the most interesting thing about his campaign was his documented love of eating, enabled by teammate Woodie Fryman. The duo came to be known as the

Burris's only playoff experience was a division series start against Philadelphia five days earlier, in which he'd given up seven hits, four walks, and four runs while failing to escape the sixth. The pitcher was winless against the Dodgers on the season, going 0-1 with a 5.79 ERA in two starts—numbers that stood in stark contrast to his Game 2 opponent, Fernando Valenzuela, who beat Montreal in both of his starts, yielding only three runs across 18 innings. (After being dominated the first time around, Gary Carter said that the rematch would prove some things. In the rematch, Valenzuela tossed a three-hitter.) The mismatch was obvious.

This, then, is why they play the games.

Burris did his best impersonation of Cy Young there in Chavez Ravine, stifling Los Angeles on five hits in a complete-game shutout—his first since 1978—for a 3–0 victory. Only twice did the Dodgers get a runner as far as second base. "Ray Burris," marveled Ken Landreaux, years after the fact. "Can you believe that?"

Montreal's strategy against Valenzuela mirrored what other teams had done late in the season: lay off the screwball and force fastballs into the zone. Over recent weeks, however, Fernando had foiled the tactic by throwing his screwball for strikes. This, however, was his third start in nine days—the first time he'd ever thrown that much, that frequently—and he was beginning to feel the strain.

Valenzuela wasn't terrible, but neither was he dominant, the very first batter he faced serving as a representative example for the 24 to follow. Tim Raines—who, prior to Game 1, had last batted on Septem-

---

"Beast Brothers," owing to the fact that they seemed to be appetized by pretty much anything they could fit into their mouths. "You can't pitch undernourished," reasoned Fryman. "We eat barbecue ribs, chicken, pancakes, just about anything . . . You have to work so you can enjoy what you like to do. What we like to do is eat." After Burris's Game 2 start against the Dodgers, he admitted that he spent the middle innings thinking about cheeseburgers. "I wish I'd had one," he said. "It might have put an extra five miles an hour on my fastball." For all the attention given to Lasorda's appetite, the manager had nothing on this pair.

ber 13, when he injured his hand—stroked a single to left on Fernando's second pitch of the game, immediately putting the left-hander into the stretch. Valenzuela, of course, was cooler than any player this side of the NHL and was ready for the major league's stolen base leader. Raines took off as Valenzuela prepared to deliver his second pitch to Rodney Scott, and Fernando fired a pickoff throw to first. With the base runner streaking toward second, players watching from the Dodgers bench grew nervous. Garvey's throws were frequently a gamble, but this one was perfect, his peg to Russell on the money and in plenty of time to retire Raines. The up-and-down nature of the inning, with Valenzuela doing just enough to muddle through (and sometimes not that much), would take a familiar pattern.

In the second inning, Fernando yielded, in order, two singles, a double, a walk, and another single—which somehow accounted for only two runs after Guerrero gunned down Warren Cromartie at the plate for the inning's third out. The Expos put up another run in the sixth, Valenzuela's final frame, on two singles—the sixth and seventh hits surrendered by the lefty—and a wild pitch.

Burris, meanwhile, was imperturbable. Even when a Montreal error put two Dodgers on base with one out in the ninth, bringing Pedro Guerrero to the plate as the tying run, Burris was able to induce a line drive to shortstop Chris Speier, who promptly doubled Garvey off second to end it, 3–0 Expos. The series was even at one game apiece.

With the teams now headed to Canada, the weather—forecasts warned that temperatures might dip into the 30s—became a prominent discussion topic. "Gentlemen, bring your long underwear," proclaimed Gary Carter, "because it's going to be cold."* Even the *Los*

---

* People immediately turned to former big leaguer and current Angels broadcaster Ron Fairly for comment, given that he spent the first 11 seasons of his career with the Dodgers before being traded to Montreal, where he spent the next six. Fairly did not disappoint. "The best way for me to describe the weather in Montreal is to tell you how the weather report went," he said. "It's like the old story, is the glass half-empty or half-full? They would come on, half in French,

Angeles Examiner got into the act, its headline in the following day's paper reading, "From Burris to B-r-r-r." The *Boston Globe* mentioned that in Montreal's previous series, Pete Rose had requested that a ball be pulled from the game for his collection, what with it being the first hit he'd ever gotten in the snow. And how the tobacco in the back pocket of Expos third baseman Larry Parrish froze solid. And how the grounds crew had to use a blowtorch to uncover home plate.

The Dodgers did their best not to be psyched out, saying things like, "The less you talk about it, the better" (Garvey) and "We just have to put it out of our minds" (Baker). Lasorda theorized that "at least we have a Penguin on our team." Dodgers equipment men packed sweatshirts, parkas, and mittens in dreary anticipation.

At least Los Angeles would have Jerry Reuss, a Missouri native used to harsh winter weather, on the mound. Even then the Expos had a perfect counter: Steve Rogers, making his first start of the series, also grew up in Missouri. In fact, Reuss and Rogers had squared off as teenagers — Rogers's team from Springfield beating Reuss's team from St. Louis in the 1966 American Legion state finals, and Reuss returning the favor the following season, shutting out Rogers's high school team in the state semifinal.

That, though, had been more than 1,000 miles away and a lifetime earlier. Now each man was a major league All-Star, pitching in the biggest game of the season. Leave the schoolkid stuff to schoolkids.

---

half in English, and they would say, 'The weather is not too bad for this place, eh?' We had such bad weather in one stretch, they said, 'We are going to have scattered daylight with intermittent sunshine.' I played one game at 34 degrees, but with the wind chill factor it was about 15. One guy was treated for frostbite, a fan. You know those heaters that blow out, almost like a flame? We had two of those in the dugout in Jarry Park. There were a few weeks when we ran off the field and right into the sauna, and turned it up to about 270 degrees. We went in there, uniforms and all. I remember one day when it was windy and cold, and the next day I woke up and it was crystal clear. I thought, 'Oh my gosh, a heatwave.' I walked outside and it was 10 degrees. We didn't play that day."

This was Montreal on the cusp of winter, and the Dodgers had yet another test to face.

Olympic Stadium had been problematic from the beginning. From the very first inkling that major league baseball should be played in Montreal, it was clear that unless the municipality was willing to build a domed stadium, a retractable roof would be necessary to mitigate the harsh northern weather of early spring and late fall. What the city ended up with fell glaringly short. The stadium, designed for the 1976 Olympics (thus the name), was known not only as the Big O but the Big Owe, given its cost overruns. It opened in time for the Games, yet even then wasn't fully finished; the Expos didn't move in until 1977. Designs called for a tower from which a hinged, lidlike roof could be harnessed via cables, but the installation wouldn't be completed for another decade. Thus were the 1981 playoffs exposed to the elements.

That was hardly the limit of the stadium's offenses. Its artificial turf was thin as a bedsheet and sat atop a concrete substrate so unforgiving that players would do pregame running at a nearby park for fear of damaging their knees. The padding on the outfield walls was similarly nonexistent, leading to the possibility of injury for hard-charging outfielders. Patches of ice were known to develop on the field both early and late in the season, leading to a variety of traction problems, let alone the fact that the only substance harder than Olympic Stadium turf was Olympic Stadium turf when it was frozen solid. As if to make things worse for the Dodgers, the Expos were expert at taking advantage of these quirks. They weren't just the best home team in baseball in 1981, but over the previous three seasons combined, at 145-72.

When the teams arrived for Game 3, the weather wasn't quite as consuming as had been forewarned, but the mid-40s chill settling across Montreal was still more frigid than most of the Dodgers had experienced for a ballgame. It was cold enough for Expos players to emerge for batting practice wearing team-branded ski caps and for the Dodgers, inside the concrete-bunker visiting clubhouse, to wrap themselves in parkas intended for outdoor use.

Then Lasorda got an idea. Just before the Dodgers were to take the field for pregame introductions, he stormed into the locker room and made an announcement: *Put away the jackets, boys, we're going out in our shirtsleeves.* When the manager punctuated his edict by shrieking, "This is our weather!" nobody could believe it ("This is not a good decision," muttered Cey), but everyone obeyed. Upon reaching the field, they could see appropriately bundled Expos players in the opposing dugout. "We're out there freezing our asses off just to show them that the weather wasn't going to bother us," recalled Yeager. "We had to stand on that line, freezing, for the introductions of both teams and two anthems. Shit." As they waited, Lasorda turned to Lopes and reminded him, "Whatever you do, don't shiver."*

At least the manager knew what he was getting his team into. He spent nine years as a pitcher in Montreal, back when its team was the Triple-A Royals and its ballpark was Delorimier Stadium. Lasorda won 107 games for that team while saying things like, "Center field in Montreal is the closest position in baseball to the North Pole," and claiming that he was denied five victories over the years in games "where I was ahead when it started snowing."†

So . . . did his jacket-free plan work? "It worked for me freezing my ass off," said Ken Landreaux, speaking for the majority.

Playing mind-games with the Expos certainly didn't help LA play baseball. Steve Rogers was by that point the best pitcher in Montreal

---

* At least one of the Dodgers remained entirely unfazed. "Coming from Minnesota, it was not a big thing for me," said Dave Goltz. Temperatures in the 40s, he said, "were spring baseball back home." Goltz was the only Dodger interviewed for this book to not even recall having to stand for introductions sans jacket.

† Because he was Tommy Lasorda, he couldn't let it go at that. "I just missed a few no-hitters," the manager said about his time in Quebec, pausing before delivering the punch line: "Usually in the first inning."

history, following All-Star appearances in 1978 and '79 with a fifth-place showing in the Cy Young vote in 1980. He'd finished the 1981 campaign on a roll, racking up a 1.72 ERA over his final 10 appearances, during which he yielded three earned runs, total, over his last three starts. The right-hander continued the streak with two dominant starts against Philadelphia in the division series and showed no signs of slowing against the Dodgers. Over his first five innings of work in Game 3, Rogers gave up five hits, all singles, cracking only a bit in the fourth, when LA turned two of those singles into a run.

It wasn't much, but it appeared like it might be enough. That's because Jerry Reuss was even better, allowing only three scattered singles, his slider moving with such ferocity that by one estimate the left-hander broke nine bats.* It was remarkable, really, how much LA's postseason run had hinged on the pitcher's performance. Forget even his 18 shutout innings against the Astros in the playoffs' first round — if Reuss hadn't beaten St. Louis with a complete game in his final start of the season's first half, LA would have gone into the strike trailing Cincinnati by a half-game and probably wouldn't have made the playoffs at all.

Acquired from Pittsburgh three days into the 1979 season, Reuss finished second in the NL Cy Young Award voting in 1980. That kind of success had been anticipated for him from the outset, yet it somehow took him 10 years and four teams to achieve it. Reuss had been the schoolboy pride of St. Louis, his Ritenour High School team winning back-to-back state championships before the hometown St. Louis Cardinals selected him in the second round of the June 1967 draft. The six-foot-five, 200-pounder was mostly middling, however,

---

* A bit of a kerfuffle erupted mid-innings when it became clear that the Expos — like the Giants before them — suspected first-base coach Manny Mota of tipping LA hitters to the location where catcher Gary Carter was setting up. Rather than confront the coach, however, Carter simply mixed things up, occasionally setting up outside for pitches he wanted in, and vice versa.

and at age 23 was traded to the Astros, less because of his 22-22 lifetime record and 4.43 ERA than for his outspoken nature and blond mustache, which irked Cardinals owner August Busch to no end.* In Houston, Reuss butted heads with old-school manager Leo Durocher, who, calling the pitcher "the asshole of all time," shipped him to Pittsburgh after two seasons. Reuss managed to make an All-Star team in 1975, but his standing with the Pirates fell so precipitously over the ensuing seasons that he ended up spending much of the 1978 campaign in the bullpen, sitting idle for as long as 19 games at a stretch. The Dodgers, experiencing a shortage of left-handed pitching, acquired him during the first week of the 1979 season in exchange for former All-Star Rick Rhoden.† "It wasn't like, 'Oh, we got Jerry Reuss!'" said Dodgers historian Mark Langill. "It was, 'This guy's left-handed and he used to be good.'"‡

Reuss was 29 years old and at a career crossroads. Lasorda started him off in the bullpen but, unlike Pirates manager Chuck Tanner, actually used him there. Leaning on his fastball during short stints helped Reuss discover that releasing his four-seamer on the inside of his middle finger allowed him to cut the ball in on the hands of right-handed hitters. He was, he said later, "like a kid with a new toy." By

---

* It was the season before the Oakland A's mustache gang exploded baseball's anti-facial-hair hierarchy.

† Of the three lefties on the Dodgers staff, Terry Forster was hurt, and Doug Rau and Lance Rautzhan would soon be off the team. LA immediately offered Reuss a guaranteed five-year contract that included a 50-percent pay raise. The pitcher couldn't agree quickly enough.

‡ On Reuss's first day as a Dodger, while wearing only a towel in the clubhouse, he grabbed a handful of popcorn from a tray in the middle of the room. "That's a fine!" shouted Davey Lopes, invoking a team rule about taking communal food while naked. Tommy Lasorda immediately docked the pitcher $10. When Reuss protested that he'd been draped in a towel, Lasorda doubled the fine to $20. "Okay," said the pitcher, letting the towel fall and sitting bare-assed on the popcorn tray. "How much is this?" First impressions, it turns out, can go a long way.

early June he had joined the rotation, and over his last 13 starts put up a 2.11 ERA.

Still, the Dodgers had holdovers Don Sutton, Burt Hooton, and Bob Welch in camp the following spring, plus defending Rookie of the Year Rick Sutcliffe and their first foray into the free agent market, Dave Goltz. That made five starters, which relegated Reuss to serve as the bullpen's primary lefty through the season's first five weeks, until Goltz came down with the flu and Sutcliffe pitched his way out of the rotation. Given an opportunity, Reuss won his first three starts and tossed shutouts in four of his first nine. On June 27, he no-hit the Giants* — he was one Bill Russell throwing error away from a perfect game — which extended his string of shutout innings to 24⅔. Reuss was striking out hitters at his usual rate while issuing the fewest walks per start of his career. Between a new fitness program,† a devastating cutter, and a revamped approach on the mound, the southpaw had remade himself almost entirely.

"I'm stronger," said Reuss. "I'm keeping the ball down in the strike zone. I have much better extension now than I had earlier in my career. It's a completely new pitching style. Before, I was a high-ball pitcher. Now I'm keeping everything down."

He did it almost exclusively with fastballs. One 82-pitch outing against St. Louis featured 80 of them. His no-hitter in San Francisco included only five breaking pitches. (When a reporter commended Yeager afterward for calling a splendid game, Reuss replied that "It doesn't take a Rhodes scholar to hold one finger down all night.") The pitcher ended the season 18-6 with a 2.51 ERA and a league-leading six shutouts.

---

* Peter O'Malley rewarded him with a TV so big that Reuss couldn't fit it into his house. So Lasorda kept it.

† Shortly after Reuss first arrived at Dodger Stadium, Don Sutton pulled him aside and explained that Dodgers pitchers maintained fitness by alternating distance running with sprinting, a regimen that had started in the days of Koufax and Drysdale. Reuss bought in immediately.

In 1981, Reuss was even better, going 10-4 with 2.30 ERA, but there on the mound in Montreal, trying to protect a 1–0 lead, the approach that had recently worked so well for him came to a grinding halt. With two outs in the sixth inning, he gave up a single to Andre Dawson. Then he walked Gary Carter. Another single, by third baseman Larry Parrish, brought home Dawson. Tie game. Maybe the weather was having an effect after all. The next hitter, Jerry White, wasn't exactly known for his power, having hit three homers all season and only 18 across his seven-year career. He'd batted just .218 in 1981, while driving in only 11 runs. "If you'd have given me a look at the lineup and I would have told you the guys I thought could hit a home run, [White] wouldn't have been first, second or third," said Reuss. "He wouldn't even have been fifth or sixth."

Guess what happened?

In the battle of Jerrys, White seized a decisive victory, his three-run homer giving the Expos all the offense they needed in a 4–1 victory that put the Dodgers in a two-games-to-one hole.* Starting with White's homer, Montreal fans began to sing the team's theme song, "The Happy Wanderer," in earnest, its "Val-de-RI, val-de-RAHs" echoing off the concrete bowl of Olympic Stadium. The chant grew especially raucous when Rogers wrapped things up by striking out Scioscia to cap a complete-game seven-hitter. Even ensconced behind their closed clubhouse doors, the Dodgers could clearly hear the song reverberating through the building. For the second straight series, LA would face a do-or-die game. If things went well, they'd face two. In his office, Lasorda seized motivation wherever he could. "I never heard of a team holding a damn celebration after winning two games in a row," he simmered as the arena rocked around him.

---

* So empty was White's stat sheet that when Andre Dawson was asked after the game to comment on his unexpectedly heroic teammate, the most enduring compliment he could come up with was: "Best dresser in the league."

"They still have another damn game to win tomorrow — and they're *not* going to win."

It was brash, but fully in character, Lasorda channeling frustration the best way he knew how. His anger was communal, felt by everyone on the team. Some of his players found a different way to express it.

Back at the hotel after the game, a number of Dodgers veterans congregated with their wives in an upper-floor lounge. It was not a cheery place. The Yankees had already swept Oakland to clinch the American League pennant, setting up an opportunity for Los Angeles to avenge its World Series losses in 1977 and 1978 . . . if only the Dodgers could make it that far, which seemed increasingly less likely with every game they played. To dull the compounding pressure, players began to knock back cocktails at an alarming pace. Only three teams had ever come back from a two-game playoff deficit, a detail about which everyone was all too aware, and an already somber mood became incrementally surlier with each drink put down. After so many years together, these teammates could be counted upon to speak their minds, which they began to do with increasingly little care for whose feelings might be hurt in the process. Voices grew loud and tempers rose, players overtly sniping at one another. Growing weary of the tension, Reuss, the losing pitcher, decamped to the restroom to clear his head.

Once there, he couldn't help but notice his reflection in the full-length mirror. Trying to think about anything but baseball, the left-hander took to examining the overcoat he'd been wearing all evening. Somehow he'd never realized quite how short it was. Far shorter than it should be, he thought. Reuss's reverie was broken by the voices of his teammates, filtering up the long spiral staircase leading to the washroom. They appeared to be shouting at each other.

Continuing to eye his jacket in the mirror, and without stopping to consider what he was doing, Reuss removed his pants and folded them across his arm, like a waiter bearing a towel in a fine restaurant. He buttoned his coat over his bare legs and steeled himself. His was a team that needed shaking up, and shaking things up was Jerry Reuss's specialty. This was his moment.

The stairs down to the bar were illuminated by a series of spotlights of which Reuss took full advantage, posing every few steps while gazing off into the distance, doing his best impression of a fashion model. That is how he descended, in silence, a few steps at a time, pants still folded across his arm. They'd notice soon enough.

Reuss was the tallest man on the team, and his pale legs seemed even longer than usual. With each pause, he alternated his direction, facing left, then right, then left again, trying to cultivate what he later described as "a Loretta Young–type moment." The voices below raged on . . . and then all stopped at once. Refusing to avert his gaze from the horizon, Reuss couldn't see his teammates, but he knew that they'd finally caught on. A couple of wives giggled.

Nobody had said a word by the time the pitcher made his way back to the bar, so he seized the opportunity. "Since all of you have opinions to express, I beg for one more," he proclaimed, spinning in a full circle. "Is this topcoat too short for a man of my height?"

That was all the group needed. The players broke out in laughter. It was something anyway. Nobody wanted to undo Reuss's legwork, both literal and figurative, by reigniting the conversation in which they'd been so angrily engaged. Before long the players smilingly returned to their rooms. There was a game to play the next day.

Before the Dodgers left their hotel for Olympic Stadium, traveling secretary Billy DeLury issued standard orders for the final game of a road trip, which were tough to swallow with two potential games remaining in Montreal: "All bags in the lobby by 10 a.m. Check out and pay all extras." If the Dodgers lost, they'd be going home directly from the ballpark. As such, suits — the team's mandatory travel wardrobe — were required. Dusty Baker was having none of it. He showed up at the ballpark wearing standard street clothes, and when his teammates inquired about it, he laid it on the line. "I'm going to New York either way," he said, noting that his suitcase had not been among those gathered by the team at the hotel. "I'm going to the World Series if I have to sit in the stands. I'm *not* going home."

The outfielder did not leave it at that. The Dodgers needed some sort of boost, a karmic jolt to inspire them toward salvation, or at least toward the Bronx. They were staring at a pair of elimination games if the series even lasted that long. Sure, they'd come back from the precipice against Houston, but that was lightning in a bottle. And what was it people said about lightning striking twice?

Baker wanted to offer words of inspiration to his teammates, but preferred to do so anonymously, feeling that attaching his name would detract from their power. So he handed Tommy Lasorda a slip of paper to read, with a specific request that the manager refrain from mentioning his source. As soon as Lasorda entered the clubhouse, of course he announced, "Hey, Dusty gave me this parable." The outfielder could only shake his head.

The parable in question was actually a Bible passage, Romans 5:3–5: "Suffering produces endurance, and endurance produces character, and character produces hope, and hope does not disappoint us."*

Hope does not disappoint us.

Although the passage was biblical, the moment was not spiritual per se. No prayers were offered. Lasorda, of course, contributed his own holy addendum, saying, "That means that we all got to go out there and hope that we win." When the players burst out laughing, the manager seized the moment and placed a baseball in the hand of starting pitcher Burt Hooton. "Go get 'em," he urged.

Tom Lasorda was a religious man, but he was not about to relegate his team's destiny strictly to the power of scripture. Ken Landreaux had slumped badly since play resumed in August — batting .176 with-

---

* "I know my Bible pretty good," reflected Baker, who was a junior deacon as a kid, spending virtually all day at church on Sundays — classes in the morning, sermon at 1:00 p.m., and back for the 6:00 p.m. late service.

out a homer in September, then going 4-for-20 against Houston and 1-for-10 over the first three games against Montreal—and so was shown the bench. Lasorda shifted Pedro Guerrero into center field and inserted Rick Monday into right.

That last point delighted the manager. When the season began, Monday was almost exclusively a late-inning mop-up guy, compiling only 61 at-bats over 31 appearances in the 57 games before the strike. At age 35, he'd accepted his diminished role and performed capably, but that was mostly prelude for what came next—a .348 batting average in the season's second half, including a .372 mark in September and .415 after Cey was sidelined with his broken arm. Those numbers made it difficult for Lasorda to pull Monday from the lineup when Cey returned . . . and easy to put him back when Landreaux slumped. The veteran would bat sixth in the Game 4 lineup, between the Penguin and Guerrero.

The game's early story, however, was starting pitching. Hooton and Bill Gullickson were mainstays on their respective staffs, and in a rematch of Game 1 they showed why. Eight innings' worth of zeros were interrupted only when Dusty Baker doubled home Russell in the third and when Warren Cromartie singled home Gary Carter in the fourth. (Both runs were scored by men who reached on errors by third basemen, Larry Parrish and Ron Cey, respectively.)

That the Dodgers didn't score more was driving Hooton crazy. In the first inning, Lopes reached third with one out on a single, a steal, and a sacrifice, but was stranded.

In the second, the Dodgers put men on first and second with nobody out, and at first and third with one out, and did not score.

In the fifth, Scioscia reached second with one out and advanced no further.

In the sixth, LA put runners at the corners with nobody out. Dusty Baker, breaking for the plate on contact, was thrown out on a grounder to third, reduced to running as upright as possible, shoulders back, in hopes that Parrish's throw would hit him in the back. (No such luck.)

Gullickson then struck out Monday (looking) and Guerrero (swing-ing) to end the rally.

Hooton, desperate for support, grew increasingly agitated, even-tually talking out loud to himself in the dugout, saying things like, "I wish somebody would get me some runs," and, "It sure would be nice to go out there and pitch with a lead." On the mound, though, the guy was all business.

With the game knotted 1–1 in the eighth, Baker reached base for the third time with a one-out single. It was nice, but based on recent results there seemed to be little chance that he'd score. Then Gullick-son made one of his only mistakes on the day, feeding Steve Garvey —who on the bench only moments earlier had told Jay Johnstone, "If he throws me a slider on the first pitch, I'm going to drive it"—a slider. Garvey responded as promised, popping the ball into the left-field bleachers for a two-run home run and a sudden 3–1 lead. In the dugout, Monday led the Dodgers in a mocking rendition of "The Happy Wanderer."

The lead gave Lasorda leeway to pull Hooton in the eighth, at the first sign of trouble, with Bob Welch and Steve Howe coming on to retire all five of the batters they faced to close things out. Three Expos relievers, meanwhile, yielded a bunch of superfluous offense in the ninth—five singles, two walks, and four runs, making the final score 7–1. With every run, the "Val-de-RI, val-de-RAHs" in the Dodgers' dugout could be heard just a little more clearly from the grandstand.

The victory ran Hooton's playoff record to 3-0, each win coming on three days' rest—an especially impressive statistic considering that two of them were elimination games. The right-hander had given up one earned run over his last 18⅔ innings. Afterward, Lasorda did his best to explain how difficult it can be for a pitcher when his team continually whiffs with runners in scoring position, saying that had he been on the mound, he wouldn't have handled things as elegantly as Hooton. "Oh man, I'd have been screaming," Lasorda admitted. "I'd have been hollering. I'd have been telling those guys to score some runs. I'd walk up to guys and punch them right in the nose because they didn't drive in any runs."

Come on, said the assembled media. *You don't really mean that.*

"You're damn right I do!" the manager replied. "I remember grabbing Sandy Amoros by the throat one time and squeezing him until his eyeballs were popping out!"

When reporters approached Hooton for comment, the guy they called Happy kept things typically bland. "I like going out and beating the Montreal Expos in the fourth game of the championship series," he said, and left it more or less at that. Landreaux, at least, got philosophical. "The true essence of a competitor," he said, "is found in competition."

The next day the Dodgers would compete once more, in Game 5, and then get on an airplane. As improbable as it might have seemed several days earlier, whether they headed east or west was entirely up to them.

Game 5, make or break, broke. At least the weather did. Preparations were in full swing only minutes before game time, with the stadium filling up and NHL legend Maurice "Rocket" Richard throwing out the ceremonial first pitch. And then . . . nothing but drizzle. Scheduled starter Fernando Valenzuela tossed a baseball to himself on the bench while the teams waited it out. Everybody, fans and players both, sat around, hoping for something to change.

A rainout appeared to benefit Montreal more than the Dodgers, allowing Game 2 hero Ray Burris to pitch on full rest and Game 3 hero Steve Rogers to come out of the bullpen. The Expos front office was aware of this detail. A couple of hours after the delay began, Montreal's traveling secretary, Rodger Brulotte, picked up a weather report from the bureau at Dorval Airport calling for a cessation of rain within the hour — yet, on instruction from Expos manager Jim

Fanning, strode into the umpires' dressing room and proclaimed that the storm would continue throughout the day. Three hours after its scheduled start, the game was canceled.*

For the Dodgers, it was maddening on a number of levels. For one thing, the rain stopped an hour later, as predicted. For another, had the game begun in the early afternoon as originally planned, the weather would not have been a factor. Instead, NBC asked that first pitch be pushed back to accommodate an NFL broadcast. As if that wasn't enough, Olympic Stadium was supposed to have featured a retractable roof, but when the building began to settle into its foundation, questions arose about the structural integrity of the tower designed to lift the lid. The building material — already selected and paid for — sat in storage in Le Havre, France. "The roof was supposed to be on five, six years ago," said National League president Chub Feeney, fruitlessly attempting to explain the rain delay to reporters. "They're still working on it. Sometimes these things take some time. I assume there will be a roof in the next couple of years." The lid would not be installed until 1987, and it wouldn't be able to retract until 1988, by which point the 1981 NLCS was little more than a distant memory. There would be no baseball until the following day.

It was drizzling again on Monday when the teams arrived at the ballpark, though only enough to delay the game by 26 minutes. Still, the weather had a profound effect. When Ray Burris released his first pitch — 21 hours after he was originally slated to do so — the temperature at Olympic Stadium was 41 degrees. During pregame warm-ups,

---

* At least one person in LA's camp was pleased by the decision. Broadcaster Vin Scully was in Minneapolis when the rain started, fulfilling a contract with CBS-TV that had him working the NFL's Vikings-Eagles game. So vested was Peter O'Malley in having Scully on hand for Game 5 that he chartered a jet to ferry the voice of the Dodgers to Montreal immediately afterward. Without the delay, there would have been no way for Scully to have made it in time.

outfielders warily tested the nearly frozen turf. Defense would be an adventure.

On full rest, Burris did not disappoint, allowing six hits and a walk over eight innings. The only run the Dodgers scored was courtesy of Fernando Valenzuela, whose one-out grounder to second brought home Rick Monday in the fifth inning. It was the only frame in which Burris allowed more than one Dodger to reach base.

Valenzuela was not to be outdone. The meteoric beginning to his season had given way to a terrible middle, which had itself given way to a splendid conclusion — a 1.85 ERA over his final nine regular-season starts. The lefty had pitched two marvelous games against Houston in the NLDS and turned in a workmanlike performance despite mediocre stuff in his Game 2 loss to the Expos. Game 5 would be a full return to form for Fernando, a revisitation of the early part of the season, when his name was uttered in awe at breakfast tables across the country after every gem he twirled. Valenzuela's approach in the deciding game against Montreal was obvious from the start: he leaned on his screwball from the beginning as hitters — instructed to lay off it in hopes that it would fail to catch the strike zone — watched helplessly as the pitch touched edges and corners. The lefty yielded only three hits through eight innings, with Montreal scoring its only run on a double-play grounder by Andre Dawson in the first.

With each pitcher refusing to yield, the game went into the ninth tied, 1–1. Burris wasn't exactly tiring — he'd allowed only an infield single to Lopes since the fifth inning — but with Rogers rested and ready in the Expos bullpen, Fanning opted for action in the bottom of the eighth, sending up Tim Wallach to pinch-hit for the pitcher. The rookie hit a tapper back to the mound for the second out in a three-up, three-down frame and helped set the table for history.

At first, Fanning's decision seemed solid. In the ninth, amid increasingly fervent chants of "Steve, Steve" (pointedly *not* directed toward the inning's leadoff hitter), Rogers got Steve Garvey to pop up to second, then induced an easy fly ball to left field from Cey. The right-hander had compiled three postseason victories over the previous 13 days and was going all-out for a fourth. Up stepped Rick Monday. He was, in many ways, perfect for the moment.

Like several of his Dodgers teammates, Monday was a Southern California kid, a prep standout at Santa Monica High School. He had been the first of the 1981 Dodgers to play for Tommy Lasorda,* having joined a youth team called the Dodgers Rookies, helmed by his future big league manager back when Lasorda was just a scout.† By Monday's senior year of high school in 1963, six colleges and eight pro teams were vying to sign him. The Dodgers — and their vociferous scout — were prominent among the ranks.

Lasorda knew Monday well enough to understand that talking the player into signing would mean nothing if Monday's mother, Nelda, was not similarly convinced. So the scout got himself invited to dinner, did some sweet talking, and set a contract on the table. It was the first offer the family had seen in writing.

Nelda was unswayed. She wanted her son to attend college, insistent that Rick have a fallback option in case baseball didn't work out. When she turned the offer down, Lasorda reached over, crossed out the dollar amount, and replaced it with a more robust figure. Again Nelda refused.

Tommy Lasorda did not handle rejection well. Again he grabbed the contract, and again he increased the offer, this time to more than double the original amount. It was, recalled Rick, "a number that my mom would have had to work for years to make." It mattered little. Nelda was dictating terms, not negotiating them. The contract would remain unsigned. To show her appreciation, however, she made

---

* A significant distinction, given that Russell was on the second pro team Lasorda ever helmed, in Ogden in 1966.

† Other alumni of the club included, at various times, Wes Parker, Jim Lefebvre, and Rollie Fingers. (All were area locals. Parker and Lefebvre ended up signing with the big league Dodgers as well.) In addition to Lasorda, managers over the years included scouts Lefty Phillips and Kenny Myers.

a goodwill offer: When Rick was ready to go pro, it would be with the Dodgers and the Dodgers only. Lasorda didn't like to lose, but he knew when he was beaten. Reluctantly, he agreed.

So Monday decamped for Arizona State, where he was named *The Sporting News* Player of the Year and helped the Sun Devils win the 1965 national championship in his only season with the varsity program. It was enough to convince him (and his mother) that he was good enough to make it as a professional. Unfortunately for Lasorda, that was also the inaugural year of baseball's amateur draft, in which the outfielder was selected first overall by baseball's worst team, Charlie Finley's Kansas City Athletics. Lasorda would have to wait.

Being baseball's first-ever draft pick was one of two things for which Monday came to be known. The other happened at Dodger Stadium in 1976, when the slugger was playing for the Chicago Cubs. In the fourth inning of a Sunday afternoon game, two fans ran into the outfield and doused an American flag in lighter fluid. As they struggled to ignite a match, Monday, who spent six years in the Marine Corps Reserve, did not hesitate, sprinting from his post in center field to grab the flag away from the miscreants. After he jogged it to safety in the Dodgers' dugout, the crowd offered a standing ovation and the scoreboard flashed: "RICK MONDAY — YOU MADE A GREAT PLAY." Soon, President Gerald Ford was commending the outfielder, and newspapers around the country were running headlines like "The Newest American Hero."

In between those moments — rejecting Lasorda's offers at the dining room table and taking a hero turn at Dodger Stadium — Monday lost much of his luster as a player. The attendant expectations of being the top overall pick melted into a .267 batting average in five full seasons with the A's, during which he averaged 12 homers and 51 RBIs. Monday was traded to Chicago for pitcher Ken Holtzman prior to the 1972 campaign, and though his numbers improved, they were never enough for him to make an All-Star team with the Cubs.

After that 1976 season, Chicago, in the face of Monday's demand for a multiyear contract, sent him to Los Angeles in exchange for Bill Buckner and Iván de Jesús. That the outfielder was 31 years old made little difference to the Dodgers, who immediately locked him up for five years and $1 million.*

Things weren't easy for Monday at Chavez Ravine. He fell while diving for a ball against the Astros early in the 1977 season, leading to back issues that plagued him throughout the year and resulted in a .230 batting average with diminished power. He tore his Achilles tendon in April 1979, mandating surgery and limiting him to 12 games all season. By 1980, Monday was 34 years old and a clear-cut part-timer, but the role seemed to suit him. Playing in only 96 games, his batting average, slugging percentage, and OPS were all higher than his career marks. "Rick Monday was an underrated tough guy on a team of tough guys, and people knew it," reflected reporter Lyle Spencer. By 1981, Monday was one of the team's most valuable bench play-

---

* When Monday joined the Dodgers for his first spring in Vero Beach, he asked Lasorda a question that had been on his mind for more than a dozen years. "When I was 17, the Dodgers Rookies went down to San Diego and played against the Marine All-Star team," he said to his manager. "You had me batting second. You're not going to remember this, but the first guy walked on four pitches, and none of the pitches were even close. You were coaching third, and when I got to the plate you gave the hit-and-run sign. I *had* to swing. The runner takes off, here comes the pitch, up high by my forehead. I had to swing at it, so I did — and I hit it out, a home run. Well, something's really been on mind. Every time somebody hits a home run or does something good, you're the first one out there grabbing their hand and slapping them on the rear end. Well, you didn't on that day. You backed up from the third-base coaching box and walked away when I came around. It struck me as strange." Lasorda exploded. "Remember it?" he shouted. "I remember it! And I'll tell you why I walked away! There were 12 major league scouts in the stands. After that first guy walked, I put the hit-and-run on, wanting you to look bad because I was trying to sign you to the Dodgers. I wanted those guys to think, 'He's got no discipline at all.' Then the pitch comes in up here and you go and hit a home run. Boy was I pissed! *That's* why I didn't shake your hand! Remember it? Goddamn right I remember it!"

ers . . . right up until Cey went down, at which point he became one of the team's most valuable starters. Now, with Landreaux slumping, here he was again.

Perhaps it mattered that Rogers was making his first relief appearance in three seasons. Maybe he hadn't yet adjusted to bullpen duty, or wasn't properly warmed up on a frigid day. Whatever it was, when the right-hander ran the count on Monday to 3-1, he turned to his out-pitch, the sinker. Not wanting to issue a walk, he threw it over the plate. Trouble was, it didn't sink. Monday's eyes widened as he saw the pitch sail in chest-high, slower than a typical fastball but traveling on a similar trajectory. His lefty swing caught the ball flush, sending it on a high arc deep toward center field. At first, Monday wasn't even sure where it went. He figured he'd pulled it somewhere toward right. It wasn't until he saw Andre Dawson giving chase near the fence that he was able to home in on the action. "I saw Dawson looking up," Monday said later. "If you're a center fielder, you know that look well. It's the look you get when you reach in your pocket and your wallet's gone." In this case, the wallet was a baseball, and it was gone over the center-field fence, just barely, landing beneath the raised bleachers beyond. For the first time all game, the Dodgers led. A few steps past first base, Monday leaped midstride, punching the air with a celebratory fist. Upon reaching the plate, he was met by a scrum of deliriously happy — and not just a little violent — teammates. "A lot of things go through your mind when you get to home plate and your teammates start beating the hell out of you," he smiled afterward. Meeting the Yankees in the World Series was foremost among them.

"I didn't think that it was possible for anybody to send one out of the park on the deep end of things toward center field, but Monday was able to do that," marveled Cey. "Down the line, I suppose, but the weather was so cold, that ball was not going to carry very well."

The game wasn't over, of course; after Rogers struck out Guerrero to end the inning, the Expos still had an at-bat remaining. In the bottom of the ninth, Valenzuela appeared to have things in hand, retiring Rodney Scott and Andre Dawson in short order to bring the Dodgers one out away from a 2–1 victory. Then the lefty ran into trouble.

First, he walked Gary Carter on a full count. Then, after putting Larry Parrish into an 0-2 hole, he threw four straight balls, later admitting that the adrenaline of the moment had him "putting a little bit extra on my pitches." Now the tying run was in scoring position, with Jerry White, whose three-run homer won Game 3 for the Expos, coming to the plate. Lasorda found himself making a mound visit that moments earlier seemed entirely unnecessary. The Expos had put runners on the corners with nobody out back in the first, but that was as much pressure as they could muster against Valenzuela all game — until the ninth anyway. Fernando had allowed only three hits and a run, but he'd faced 32 batters and appeared to be tiring. It was not a stretch to imagine that another base hit could cost the Dodgers the pennant. Lasorda climbed the dugout steps, and, as he walked to the mound, turned toward the bullpen and touched his right arm. He wanted Bob Welch.*

Fanning had turned to his own starter for relief work only a half-inning earlier, and the strategy backfired badly. Lasorda was unfazed. Every one of Welch's 23 appearances during the regular season had been a starting assignment, but things were different in the playoffs. Never mind the pitcher's long-standing claim that the pressure of relief work helped fuel his unchecked alcoholism in the late 1970s — the Dodgers were utilizing a three-man postseason rotation, and the bullpen was where they needed him. Welch had been sober since February 1980 and had his manager's faith. By going with a right-hander, Lasorda forced the switch-hitting White to shift to his weaker side.†

It took Welch only one pitch. White bounced the first offering he

---

* When Lasorda reached the mound he said, in mangled Spanish, "It's time for a fresh horse." Valenzuela burst out laughing.

† Valenzuela greeted Welch's arrival on the mound with one of the snippets of

saw to second base, where Lopes, ranging far to his left, fielded it only about 30 feet from Garvey. The throw to first came in low, and Garvey sank with it, ending up in splits atop the dirt of the cutout, right foot tethered to the bag. Game over, pennant secure. By the time Garvey scrambled to his feet, Welch and Scioscia had raced to his side. The first baseman leaped into Welch's arms, and the pitcher carried his shorter teammate several steps before the rest of the club reached them. It was the fifth time in 10 games that the Dodgers had to win or go home. It was the fifth time they'd won.

In the giddy postgame clubhouse, as players began another round of "Val-de-RI, val-de-RAH," Scioscia described Welch's decisive pitch — his *only* pitch — as a "180-mile-per-hour fastball." When the right-hander heard about it, he smiled. "He's only about 100 miles per hour off," he clarified.

Burt Hooton was named series MVP for his winning turns in Games 1 and 4. Valenzuela was as cool after the game as he was during it, spilling the same sorts of platitudes that had long since become rote for him. "I feel very glad that in my first major league season I have done so well," he told reporters through interpreter Jaime Jarrín. "I feel nice to have started the opening game of the season for the Dodgers, and to have started the All-Star Game, and now to be going to the World Series." The media would have to make do with outstanding pitching from the guy, because they weren't getting much in the way of insights.

Monday discussed with reporters the idea that, had the Dodgers lost, it might have been his final game as a big leaguer. His contract with Los Angeles was up, and he'd already decided that if the Dodgers did not want him back he'd retire to pursue a career in broadcasting. Dusty Baker didn't give up on Monday so easily, saying about his teammate's homer what Monday would not say himself: "That was a

---

English that had been so exactingly imparted to him by Reggie Smith: "Go get 'em, you fuck."

contract swing — a two-year contract swing."* Monday had driven in the winning run in the decisive games of both playoff series, the second one after being pulled from the starting lineup to accommodate Cey's return.

The Expos, meanwhile, would never make it closer to the World Series than in 1981, a detail that inspired a generation of Montreal fans to label Game 5 "Blue Monday."†

After champagne was consumed and showers taken, Dusty Baker, Ken Landreaux, Derrel Thomas, and their wives made their way from the clubhouse to the stadium parking lot, still engulfed in the giddiness of the moment. They were to meet a friend of Baker's who was to take them to the airport to meet the team plane. Thomas and his wife Liz were several steps ahead of the pack, lost in conversation, when they rounded a corner and were surprised by a trio of Expos fans, who unexpectedly rushed them. Liz was pushed backward, over her suitcase, which was what Baker saw when he rounded the corner: Liz Thomas's legs in the air, and her husband preparing to fight a cadre of Canadians, one of them wielding a bottle. Dusty raced toward the scrum while Landreaux circled around to cut off the assailants' flank.‡

Baker dropped one of the attackers quickly with a flurry of punches,

---

* Sure enough, after the season, Monday signed a new contract and played with the Dodgers until retiring in 1984, at age 38.

† The fact that it actually fell on a day-of-the-week Monday didn't hurt. For years, Monday (the player) felt resentment toward him whenever he was in Montreal. At a restaurant with Steve Yeager the following season, a waiter told the pair, who had not yet ordered, that they'd have to leave. When asked why, he said simply, "I don't want any fights here." Monday explained that he and Yeager were as peaceful as could be. "I'm not worried about *you*," replied the waiter, "but there are six other guys here who want to jump all over you."

‡ Incredibly, it wasn't the first time a Dodger had recently been assaulted with a bottle. In 1978, two fans attacked Reggie Smith in the Dodger Stadium parking lot, one of them hitting him over the head with an empty beer. Smith beat them up regardless, and they were arrested and charged.

which scared the others off. Landreaux, surveying the landscape, was incredulous about what had just gone down. "I had enough of that kind of thing growing up in the 'hood," recalled the Compton native. "I couldn't believe I had to go through it in freaking Montreal."

Later, Baker limited his account of the fight to sentence fragments. *How long did it last?* he was asked. "It didn't last very long." *Who won?* "We did."

The outfielder was terse because he was unhappy. He was unhappy because fallout lingered. Though the fight itself was of little consequence, Baker had jammed his right wrist while landing a punch. By the time the team boarded its flight to New York, it throbbed so badly that he thought it might be broken. "Uppercuts—I threw a lot of uppercuts," he recalled. "You risk hurting your wrists when you throw uppercuts." The Dodgers were already without one of their best hitters in Reggie Smith. To lose Baker too would be devastating. Dusty told Lasorda about it on the plane and was surprised to find the manager entirely unwilling to deal with reality on its own terms. Baker would play with anything short of a break, Lasorda informed him, because the threat he presented in the heart of the lineup was better than not having him in the lineup at all—even if it was entirely subterfuge. "We ain't the same if you ain't out there," he said to the morose slugger. Moreover, the manager told him, the less Baker said about it, the better. If the Yankees never caught on to how hurt he was, there was less chance they'd pitch around somebody to face him.

Dusty wasn't Baker's real name, of course. He was born Johnnie B. Baker Jr. (the "B" standing for nothing but the letter B, the "Jr." standing for a wondrous, if complex, relationship with his father, John Baker Sr.). The name Dusty was acquired in the family backyard in Riverside, California, where the lad consistently eschewed the lawn in favor of a patch of dirt. "There were a lot of baths," recalled John Sr.

The elder Baker was an Air Force sheet-metal technician who, the year Dusty was born, shattered his knee in a fall from a Douglas C-47 Skytrain that he was wrenching on. The accident left him with a limp but did nothing to reduce the military precision with which he ran his household. Cursing was banned all the way down to "darn it," as were drinking and smoking. When Dusty was old enough, he helped his father earn extra income by mowing lawns, a part-time job for which he was compensated in regular meals and clothes that fit. John Sr.'s approach to neighborhood kids was much the same. Dusty's house was home base for driveway basketball . . . right up until John Sr. came home from work, at which point kids would fly in every direction. "My dad saw my friends as free labor," Dusty recalled. Nobody wanted to be recruited.

The Bakers lived in a middle-class neighborhood, predominantly black and Hispanic, until Dusty was 14 and John Sr. got a job at McLellan Air Force Base, just outside Sacramento. Junior's new school, Del Campo High, required some adjustment for a kid who'd grown up in a thoroughly multicultural environment. "I asked my brother Victor on the first day of school, 'Hey, you see any other black kids here?'" Baker said. "'Nope. Just us.' It was enlightening. I learned to get along with everyone, to be strong."*

The Baker family's move coincided with the Summer of Love, the center of which—San Francisco's Haight-Ashbury district—was only a couple of hours south on I-80. Dusty and his friends immersed themselves in the hippie movement, even as his mother opened up his consciousness to a world of black writers like W. E. B. Du Bois, James Baldwin, and Marcus Garvey. Christine Baker's graduation gift to her son was time and distance—use of the family station wagon to head down the coast to the Monterey Jazz Festival for which he was provided tickets to see Jimi Hendrix.

The gift came from his mother alone, since his parents had sepa-

---

* Decades later, Baker kept two framed photos on his wall—one of his fourth-grade class in Riverside, which contained a tableau of faces of every hue, and one of his Del Campo High football team, in which Dusty is exceedingly easy to spot given his position as the lone African American.

rated during Dusty's senior year of high school. The separation led to spectacle when the teenager, an all-county basketball player, was offered a scholarship to nearby Santa Clara University, which his father accepted on his behalf. Basketball may have been Junior's primary sport, but when the Atlanta Braves made an offer of their own — complete with a $15,000 signing bonus — Dusty decided he'd had enough of being told what to do. He'd abided John Sr.'s bans on booze, drugs, and cursing. Hell, he'd even avoided venturing into Berkeley because his father didn't want him corrupted by the Activist Left. But this? This was too much.

Bucking his father, Dusty signed Atlanta's contract, his mother putting her name alongside his. John Sr. was so outraged that he went to court in an effort to invalidate it. Dusty eventually agreed to defer half the bonus money until he was 21 and put the other half in a trust, while adding a clause to the contract stipulating that the Braves would pay his tuition should he ever decide to go to college. Meanwhile, the 18-year-old reported to Double-A Austin of the Texas League. It would be three years before he and his father talked again in a meaningful way.*

In the meantime, the kid received a crash course in race relations. Minor league stops in Texas, Florida, South Carolina, Louisiana, and Virginia placed him front and center with, alternately, a black population at the tail end of the civil rights movement and a white population that tended to hold his skin color against him. Dusty bought in and began to talk openly of becoming Muslim, while scorning his white friends from back home.

Shock value may have been a factor when Dusty called John Sr. to tell him about the influence of Malcolm X on his life. What he heard from his father was of far more lasting import. "Son," John Sr. said with conviction, "a black man who hates white people and a white

---

* This period, not coincidentally, lined up with Baker becoming old enough to claim the remainder of his signing bonus.

man who hates black people are identical twins." Dusty wasn't raised to think that way, his father told him. The conversation lasted three hours and drew the two men closer than they had been in years.

Baker reached the big leagues for good in 1971, and though he came of age as a ballplayer in Atlanta, he never stopped agitating for a return to California. Nothing about his style, from music to wardrobe to the way he talked, meshed with conservative Southern culture. Calling himself "arrogant," Baker admitted later that "I liked to talk a lot, and much of it was the wrong talk, both to the press and my teammates."

He slipped from a .321 batting average in 1972 to .288 in '73, to .256 in '74. When he hit only .261 the following season with diminished power, the Braves took Dusty up on his long-standing suggestion and traded him to LA before the 1976 season for a handful of capable play-ers.* He was 26 years old. "I always wanted to be a Dodger," said the kid who grew up in Riverside, 60 miles from Dodger Stadium, and spent his formative years listening to Vin Scully on the radio. "I heard the Dodgers had the best athletes, pretty uniforms and good bodies. I was like, shoot, you're talking about *me*."

Less than two weeks after being acquired by LA, however, Baker hurt his knee playing pickup basketball with, among other people, Detroit Tigers infielder and Sacramento-area native Jerry Manuel†. Not wanting to destroy his reputation before he even had a chance to suit up for his new team, Baker fed the press a story about sustain-ing the injury while running his dog on the beach. (Upon examining Baker's knee, Dodgers trainer Bill Buhler wasn't fooled for a second. "Did your dog get an assist on the play?" he asked the sheepish pa-

---

* "Tommy [Lasorda] didn't really tamper, but he told me that I was Dodger ma-terial back when I was with the Braves," recalled Baker. "I was cocky and he was cocky, and back then, almost everybody on the Dodgers had that appearance of being cocky. It was a situation where nobody liked them, but a lot of people would have loved to play for them."

† Who as a backup on the Expos in 1981 collected one at-bat against the Dodgers in the NLCS.

tient.) The resulting season was the most difficult of Baker's career. He homered in his very first at-bat for the Dodgers, against the Giants on opening day, and then went until July 15 — 77 games and 295 at-bats — before hitting another. He ended the season batting .242 with only four home runs, easily his worst marks since becoming a regular, and Walter Alston benched him for much of August and September. The booing at Dodger Stadium got so bad that Dusty would wait in the dugout as long as possible before going up to pinch-hit late in the season. "From the dugout to home plate at Dodger Stadium was a long way," he recalled. "I was like, dang, I've got to run out there with all these boos?" Angry fans broke the lights in the sconces outside his house and scratched his Porsche.

The ascendance of Tommy Lasorda to the manager's office, however, combined with surgery on his knee, worked wonders for the embattled outfielder. Lasorda called Baker during the off-season and told him that he would be the starting left fielder no matter what. Dusty responded with the best four-year stretch of his career . . . not that anybody noticed. Early in his career Baker had played under Hank Aaron's shadow — a notable detail on a mediocre team that invariably sent only one player, Aaron, to the All-Star Game. In Los Angeles, Dusty found himself similarly concealed, this time by too much talent. During his 1977 breakout he became one of the first-ever quartet of 30-home-run hitters on the same team, but even then was the last of the foursome — Steve Garvey, Reggie Smith, and Ron Cey were the others — to turn the trick, finally reaching 30 in his final at-bat of the season.* Despite a string of outstanding campaigns — including in 1980, when he batted .294 with 29 homers and 94 RBIs and finished

* "Lasorda kept telling me, 'Dusty, God isn't going to let you hit 29 homers and not 30,' . . ." Baker recalled. "Tommy kept saying, 'You're gonna hit it, you're gonna hit it.' I was tired, and there was a lot of pressure. Most of the other guys were resting up for the playoffs, but I was still in there." Baker's homer was historic, but true history was made immediately afterward, when his teammates raced out to congratulate him. Outfielder Glenn Burke was so excited that he

fourth in the National League MVP voting — he failed to make an All-Star team prior to 1981.

Still, Baker was popular with fans, who took to calling the left-field bleachers "Baker's Acres." In informal polling about leadership in a clubhouse with no clear leader — or more accurately, with many leaders, leading in many ways — Dusty's name was the most frequently mentioned, by far. He was a bridge between races and positions, between English and Spanish, between partiers and loners. "Everybody probably had a complaint about somebody in that clubhouse, but I don't think anybody complained about Bake," reflected reporter Chris Mortensen.

"Dusty was the unifier," said Lyle Spencer, who covered the team for the *Los Angeles Examiner*. "He was the guy who kept everything together in a clubhouse that really could have fractured over personality conflicts. He was the guy to get people beyond the pettiness, to say that we're in this together. Because he spoke Spanish, he was like a big brother to the Latino players, the guy they all leaned on for advice."

Before the 1981 season, Los Angeles signed Baker to a five-year, $4 million contract, the richest in club history. And now here he was, landing in New York about an hour before midnight, due to arrive at Yankee Stadium for Game 1 of the World Series the following afternoon, his wrist throbbing beyond belief. Baker spent the night in his hotel room plunging his hand alternately into a bucket of ice water and a steaming-hot bathtub. Cold, hot, cold, hot, into the wee hours. It's not like he had other things to do; his wrist was too painful for sleep.

For Baker, the hardest part of his night wasn't restlessness but coming clean to his father about what had happened, which he did with a phone call shortly after checking into the hotel. If John Sr. happened

---

raised his hand high into the air; without any idea about what to do in response, Baker instinctively slapped it. Thus was born baseball's first-ever high-five.

to hear about it from somebody else first, there'd be hell to pay. "Boy," said his father upon hearing the news, "I told you about fighting." He had. Ever since Dusty was a boy, John Sr. had warned him against physical confrontation, even fights he might win, and how there was always a better way to handle his business. Senior called him hard-headed. "This is going to cost you something," he told his son. Of that, Dusty was already aware. The only question was, how much?*

In the morning, Baker went to see a hand specialist in Manhattan, who delivered what he figured would be taken as good news: there was no break. The doctor told Dusty that he'd be good to go in about six weeks. "Six weeks?" yelped the outfielder. "Man, I don't have six *hours!*"

When Baker got to the ballpark, coach Manny Mota gave him a wrist brace made for bowlers to help stabilize the joint, and some di-methyl sulfoxide — DMSO, foul-smelling horse liniment. When Dusty tried to swing a bat the pain was intense, and he could draw no power from his top hand. So he skipped batting practice, and hoped.

For LA's number-three hitter, it would have to suffice. The Dodgers were in New York, and big things were expected.

---

* Did Dusty learn any lessons from the incident? "I learned to lock my wrist in-stead of cock my hand when I'm uppercutting," he said later.

11

Doodle Dandy

GETTING TO THE World Series was special. Getting to play the Yankees was something else entirely.

The Dodgers and Yankees had shared copious World Series history, though it rarely ended well for the boys in blue. The most recent developments, in 1977 and 1978, saw New York winning in increasingly painful fashion. In '77, Lasorda's first year as manager, Reggie Jackson cemented his status as a postseason legend with three home runs in three swings in the deciding Game 6. In '78, the Dodgers won the first two games at home and then, despite a palpable wave of possibility, dropped four straight, the key moment being Jackson's hip-check of Bill Russell's relay throw.

Three years later the wound still stung, especially for those LA players remaining from the '78 squad who were trying to find perspective on the upcoming series. "That flight coming home from New York in 1978 was the longest that I can ever remember in my whole life," said Dusty Baker, looking back. "We didn't want to get off the plane. For two weeks I didn't go out. I didn't go to the grocery store, or to a bar, or anywhere, because I was down and out and ashamed. I didn't want that feeling again in 1981."

Tommy Lasorda put it in religious terms. "Because God delays does not mean that God denies," he said. "Well, he delayed, but he didn't deny. We got the Yankees again."

It would be the 11th time the Dodgers and Yankees had met, in a lopsided postseason rivalry that ranked eight to two in New York's favor. More pertinent to the modern era was that this almost certainly was LA's final chance at redemption, at least in its current configuration. Of the 24 players on the Dodgers roster in 1981, half had faced the Yankees in '78. Of those, only five—the four infielders plus Yeager—were with the World Series club of 1974. They were also the five most likely players to find themselves wearing new uniforms in the near future. All were on the wrong side of 30, and each felt pressure from an abundance of minor league talent salivating to take over. "We knew that most of us were going to be gone," recalled Yeager. "If we were ever going to win a Series together, we had to do it then. That was on most of our minds."

Like the Dodgers, New York put up a dominating first-half record before sagging in August and September, eventually finishing the second season at 25-26 and in fifth place in the American League East. (Had divisions been decided by overall records, the Yankees, like Los Angeles, would have missed the playoffs entirely.) New York, featuring standbys like Jackson, Graig Nettles, and Ron Guidry, had recently added free agent Dave Winfield, who in his first season in the Bronx made his fifth straight All-Star team and finished seventh in the American League's MVP voting. After taking down the Brewers in the division series, New York steamrolled Oakland in the ALCS, winning three straight by a cumulative score of 20–4. The Yankees had been resting since the Dodgers arrived in Montreal.

New York seemed to have the advantage in ways big and little. The Yankees boasted eight players with World Series rings, while the Dodgers had only one—and even then Jay Johnstone had earned his while with the Yankees in 1978. The Dodgers were coming almost directly off a flight from Montreal, with no time to decompress between games. They had Jerry Reuss slated for Game 1 on only three days' rest, and after him the rest of the rotation was up for grabs. Hooton was a possibility for Game 2, though it would mean a third straight start on short rest. Valenzuela, the primary reason the Dodgers made it so far in the first place, was unavailable until Game 3 at the earliest. Welch, who had yet to start a game in the postseason, was also a possibility.

The guys giving the pitchers targets would probably be different than against the Expos and Astros. The catcher platoon Lasorda employed throughout the season — Steve Yeager against left-handers, Mike Scioscia against righties — had limited Yeager to only five at-bats against Houston and two against the Expos. With the Yankees boasting a southpaw-heavy rotation, however, things were about to change.*

Yeager's defense — both his handling of pitchers and his arm behind the plate — was beyond reproach. The catcher had suffered a panoply of injuries over recent seasons, however, and his offensive output nosedived correspondingly: a .209 batting average in 1981 followed seasons of .211, .216, and .193. He was about to turn 33 and, with the end of his career visible on the horizon, had been thinking about the Yankees' left-handers for more than a month, telling his teammates in September, "Just get me to the Series, just give me a chance to play."

For Yeager, the feeling of being overlooked was familiar. Drafted a year before the storied class of 1968, he played minor league ball with some combination of Garvey, Lopes, Russell, and Cey at each minor league level save for the Rookie League, and had been with them every step of the way for their record-breaking run of longevity in Los Angeles. Still, for reasons beyond his control Yeager was rarely mentioned when people spoke of the historically durable infield. Even within his own family he took a backseat to cousin Chuck Yeager, the

---

* Yeager ended up facing about an equal number of left-handers and righties on the season, but of Scioscia's 335 plate appearances, only 16 came against southpaws. So dissatisfied was Yeager with the situation that in an interview with Howard Cosell that aired during the World Series he specifically asked for a trade. "I had a good spring training, and that's what they wanted me to do," the catcher said. "To sit on the bench and have 86 at-bats all year long, I would like to go someplace and play every day."

U.S. Air Force pilot who became the first man to break the sound barrier, portrayed by actor Sam Shepard in an Oscar-nominated role in the 1983 film *The Right Stuff*.*

Despite having once been called by *The Sporting News* "the brightest catching prospect to come through the Dodgers' ranks since Roy Campanella," the Ohio native was continually forced to fend off challenges for his starting role, first from Joe Ferguson (whose 25 homers in 1973 set a Los Angeles Dodgers record for a catcher), then, beginning in 1980, from Scioscia. There was no questioning Yeager's ability, but his commitment to late-night revelry struck many as having taken a toll on his long-term performance. "No ballplayer ever led a more active social life and survived," said an awed Jay Johnstone.†

Now, with Rick Reuschel being the only right-hander in New York's rotation, Yeager was due to see extensive playing time. The development may have been good for the catcher, but it was troubling for his team — not that Yeager was playing, but the reason therein: New York's lefty-heavy staff was simply elite, its 2.90 team ERA the only such mark in the American League below 3.30. The Yankees struck out more hitters and walked fewer than all but one team. Guidry con-

---

* One area in which Yeager stood alone was as an innovator in the pantheon of catcher's gear. In 1976, while standing in the on-deck circle at San Diego's Jack Murphy Stadium, he was struck in the throat by a jagged shard of Bill Russell's bat, which had shattered on impact during a swing. The catcher underwent 98 minutes of surgery to remove nine pieces of wood, some of which missed his jugular by inches. With that area now compromised, Yeager, along with Dodgers equipment man Bill Buhler, invented a throat protector that dangled from the lower bar of the catcher's mask to prevent further such mishaps while he was behind the plate.

† Yeager once explained away a pregame meal of doughnuts, coffee, and a cigarette with the rationale that "I'm eating from the four food groups — sugar, fat, caffeine, and nicotine." Said Dusty Baker: "I've never seen a guy who could smoke and drink coffee naked in the shower and never get his cigarette wet." The catcher's nickname around the clubhouse was "Unlikable Hero," derived when a newspaper once referred to him as an "unlikely hero," a moniker Yeager misunderstood. "Unlikable?" he said in shocked response. "I'm not unlikable."

tinued to be among baseball's best pitchers, following his 1978 Cy Young Award with top-10 finishes the next two seasons. At 31 years old, he'd lost some speed off a fastball that once topped out at 98 miles per hour, but nonetheless struck out four times as many men as he walked in a season in which he finished fifth in the league in strikeouts. Guidry allowed fewer base runners per nine innings than any other American League pitcher.

New York's number two starter was no less formidable, though he was much more familiar. Tommy John had only recently concluded seven seasons with the Dodgers (including 1975, which he spent recovering from the revolutionary elbow ligament surgery that would come to bear his name) before jumping to the Yankees as a free agent in '79. A guy who'd pitched for 12 seasons before surgery without garnering a single Cy Young vote had since earned top-10 finishes over his last two seasons in LA and top-five finishes in his first two in New York, during which time he was the American League's winningest pitcher.

Rounding things out were Dave Righetti, whose 8-4 record and 2.05 ERA would earn him the American League Rookie of the Year Award (whose appearance would mark the first time a team started three straight left-handers in the World Series since 1918*), and Reuschel, who posted a 2.67 ERA, a full run below league average, in 11 starts after being acquired from the Cubs midseason.

For all the star power of New York's starting rotation, though, it was the bullpen that truly amazed, highlighted by closer Goose Gossage's 99-mile-per-hour fastball and 0.77 ERA. Ron Davis made the All-Star team as a setup man. George Frazier's ERA sat at 1.63.

The New York press, decidedly biased, called for a rout, with the *Post* favoring the Yankees in eight of 10 categories (with one draw)

---

* The Cubs started southpaws in all six games against Boston, although it was actually only two pitchers — Hippo Vaughn and Lefty Tyler — who made three starts apiece.

and the *Daily News* doing similarly in seven out of 11. In ABC-TV's pregame coverage, Howard Cosell gave the edge to the Yankees at every position save first base, including starting pitching, relief pitching, and bench play. That even a backup, Larry Milbourne — filling in for the injured Bucky Dent — was unanimously ranked higher than Bill Russell was telling.

For all that, Dodgers up and down the lineup agreed that the key to New York's victory in 1978 had been the wondrous fielding of Yankees third baseman Graig Nettles. The combination of New York's lefty-heavy staff and Los Angeles's abundance of pull hitters made third base one of the most tested positions on the field. Time and again LA batters yanked shots down the line that appeared ticketed for extra bases, and time and again Nettles — who played deeper than any third baseman in the American League — dove, made an impossible play, and threw them out. The strategy Lasorda would employ in 1981, the manager joked, was based around the simple premise that "we just won't hit it at him."

So what happened? The first batter of the first game, Davey Lopes, smashed the fourth pitch of the World Series straight down the line, a surefire double against any team but this one. Nettles knocked the ball down with a requisite dive, gathered it in, and rifled a throw to first to beat the flying base runner by an eyelash. It was as if no time had passed since '78. "I deflated ten pounds," said Lasorda afterward.

Guidry allowed only one ball past the infield — a harmless Garvey single* — through the first three innings, while at one point striking out four consecutive hitters. Dodgers starter Jerry Reuss, making his first-ever start at Yankee Stadium, was far less sharp, getting into an early hole when first baseman Bob Watson took him deep for a three-run homer in the first inning. Watson was 35 years old and batted

---

* When a leaping Nettles failed to come down with Garvey's hit, which bounced about four feet over his head, somebody in the press box commented facetiously that the 37-year-old was "obviously losing it."

just .212 on the season, but his homer couldn't have come as too much of a surprise given that he'd gone 10-for-21, a .476 average, against Reuss when he played in the National League.* Watson's firepower meant that nobody even missed Reggie Jackson, who sat out the game with a sore left calf muscle.

"Yankee Stadium was historic," said Reuss, looking back on his start. "Everywhere you walked, something historical had happened. I think that got to me." The Dodgers might not have wanted to admit it, but home-field advantage was a tangible asset for the Yankees. In 1978, Bill Russell complained about New York fans making it difficult to concentrate on the game, a sentiment that sat just fine with the Yankees. "I hope they react the same way [now]," said Nettles of his opponents before the Series began. "I don't ever want to see rowdy fans, but if the Dodgers are intimidated by the noise, the city and the stadium, that's one more thing in our favor."† The stadium's history might have been impactful for Reuss, but so too was the fact that, starting his third game in 10 days, his usually dominant sinker was nowhere to be found.

---

* When Watson was a high school senior, despite his Fremont High baseball team winning the 1963 Los Angeles city championship, the Dodgers' area scout opted against signing him, a slight that Watson never forgot. That scout: Tommy Lasorda.

† Lasorda offered his own take on the historic stadium: "I pitched in this park once in the old City Series, in 1955," he recalled. "It was what I had dreamed about ever since I was 10 years old, and there I was — the big crowds, the stadium, two on, two out, and the batter was Yogi Berra." When pressed for details about what happened, the manager demurred. "Aw, I don't want to tell you that I got Yogi Berra out," he said. "A great hitter like that, a Hall of Famer. That would demean him if I told you that a Humpty Dumpty like me got him out. I don't want people to hear about that." Except that, yes, he did want people to hear about that. And now that he'd told them, they had. (Lasorda also failed to note that the first time he faced Berra at Yankee Stadium, the Hall of Famer hit an RBI double. To the pitcher's credit, he did retire Berra the other three times they met there, even though none of the four at-bats came with two on and two out. Lasorda's career ERA in the Bronx sat at a cool 18.00.)

From that point on, it was simply a matter of New York's defense, which turned out to be more than just Nettles. In the fifth inning, second baseman Willie Randolph made a backhanded snare of Rick Monday's one-hop screamer up the middle and threw the runner out, a play that took on added weight when the next batter, Yeager, connected for a solo homer, giving Los Angeles its first run. By that point, however, the Yankees had scored twice more — once off Reuss, who was pulled in the third, and once off reliever Bobby Castillo, who issued four walks in the fourth — to make it a 5–1 game.

New York's defensive effort continued with an outstanding play by Randolph to retire Lopes in the sixth and a perfectly played carom off the left-center-field fence by Dave Winfield in the seventh, which allowed him to throw out a stunned Ron Cey at second base. The efforts stood in stark contrast to the Dodgers, for whom defense was a primary weakness. Between 1972 and 1980, the up-the-middle guys, Lopes and Russell, each led the NL in errors at their position twice, and collectively boasted 14 top-five finishes in the category. Russell averaged 32 errors per year in his seven full seasons prior to 1981, the most in the majors for that period at any position, many of the miscues coming on routine throws. Once, after the shortstop collected four such errors during a spring training contest, Jay Johnstone roped off the seats behind first base prior to the next game and posted a sign reading, ENTER AT YOUR OWN RISK. BILL RUSSELL IS PLAYING SHORTSTOP TODAY. ALL SEATS 25¢.

"I get tired of talking about the same stuff — the errors, the criticism," Russell said in 1981. "People are tired of hearing about it and I'm tired of talking about it." One didn't have to mention the errors, of course, to note their impact on the scoreboard.

Game 1 was actually the only game in the Series in which the Dodgers *didn't* make an error (they'd end up out-erroring New York, 9–4), but that didn't much help. Yeager's homer was all the Dodgers got off of Guidry, and they went into the eighth trailing by four. Improbably, it was against the Yankees bullpen that they found their best shot.

Setup man Ron Davis started the frame by walking Darrel Thomas and Lopes, at which point Yankees manager Bob Lemon dropped the hammer. Goose Gossage had cumulatively saved more games than any American Leaguer since 1975 (even counting a 1976 season in which, while used as a starter by the Chicago White Sox, he pitched 224 innings with 15 complete games) and was coming off a campaign in which he'd finish fifth in Cy Young voting and ninth in the MVP race. Now, with a potential Dodgers rally brewing, Lemon went to his closer to obliterate any chance Los Angeles might have. Gossage, however, had not seen action since Game 3 of the ALCS five days earlier and had to warm up hurriedly given Davis's unexpected wildness. He promptly allowed an RBI single to Jay Johnstone and a run-scoring sacrifice fly to Dusty Baker. Now it was 5–3, with Steve Garvey coming to the plate as the tying run. Garvey was just the man the Dodgers wanted in this spot, a proven postseason monster who'd batted .335 with 10 homers across LA's five playoff tilts and three World Series since 1974.

It was the Series' first epic late-game showdown, and Garvey more than held his own, tattooing a 3-1 pitch toward the left-field corner for certain extra bases . . . until Nettles, playing well off the line, dove back and to his right to snare the ball on the fly, at full extension, with a perfect backhand at the apex of his leap, executed more quickly than could be believed. He'd done it again. "I've never seen such a burglar!" enthused Keith Jackson on the ABC telecast. Garvey, who could not have hit the ball harder, was cooked. The Dodgers were cooked. Gossage set down the next four men in order, game over, New York's fifth straight postseason victory — and fifth straight World Series win over the Dodgers — intact. "When they decide to put up the Graig Nettles monument at Yankee Stadium," wrote Mike Littwin in the *Los Angeles Times*, "some Dodger will hit a line shot right into the statue's glove."

Afterward, Lasorda said that New York's infield defense made him "sick to my stomach," and that Nettles "must go to bed hoping and praying he can kill us with his glove." Nettles himself low-keyed it, saying only that such plays "take a little steam out of them." Lasorda agreed with the point.

The game's other story line involved Yankee Stadium itself, in particular the patrons therein. Russell's previous comments about being distracted by grandstand rowdiness suggested that churlish fandom might be an asset for the Yankees, but Game 1 saw a new low for a group already considered to be among the most obnoxious in American sportsdom. In the third inning, as Dusty Baker lined up a fly ball off the bat of Dave Winfield near the wall in left field, a glass bottle flew out of the bleachers and landed about 15 feet away from him. Baker, focused on the ball, didn't even notice, but left-field umpire Rich Garcia did. So did Lasorda, who raced from the dugout to confer with plate ump Larry Barnett. Steve Garvey later called the moment "ugly, inhumane and dangerous."*

Then something remarkable happened, at least from the standpoint of the Dodgers: nearby fans pointed out the perpetrator, who was arrested and spent the night in jail. Maybe it was a new era after all.

That said, the Dodgers were again down in a series, just like they had been against the Expos and the Astros, not to mention their previous two meetings with the Yankees. Forget the enormous roster turnover in LA since '78; the more things changed, it seemed, the more they stayed the same.

In 1978, Tommy John was one of the National League's best pitchers, a mainstay on the Dodgers' World Series staff against the Yankees. Three years later, he was one of the American League's best pitchers, a mainstay on the Yankees' World Series staff against the Dodg-

---

* A bottle wasn't the only thing Baker collected. During the course of the game, he also scooped up four quarters, each hurled at him from the grandstand. "I've heard that Reggie Jackson has got $82 this year," Baker joked after the game. "I've got $81 to go."

ers. The process of John's free-agent transition to New York wasn't exactly smooth, with the pitcher insisting on a three-year deal from LA, and the Dodgers unwilling to surpass two. "We begged them to sign Tommy John," said Dusty Baker. "We *begged* them. The Dodgers' theory was that it was better to get rid of a guy a year too early than a year too late, so we said, hell, pay him for two years, we'll win, and then that third year we won't give a shit. *Please* sign Tommy John." It didn't work. The Yankees, more than happy to meet the right-hander's terms, presented a three-year pact for nearly $600,000 per season. In Game 2, John wanted more than ever to make Los Angeles brass regret its decision.

So concerned were the Dodgers about the tailing sinker thrown by their former teammate — let alone John's propensity for illegally scuffing and loading the baseball, a detail about which they were all too aware given their proximity to him for seven years in Los Angeles* — that the team's eight right-handed hitters devoted batting practice to working the opposite field. Lasorda reinserted Landreaux, one of the team's best bunters, in the starting lineup, not only to affect Nettles's deep positioning but to perhaps exploit John's subpar fielding ability. None of it helped. John tossed a perfect game through four, then gave up lone singles in each of the fifth, sixth, and seventh innings. By that point the Yankees led 1–0 against Burt Hooton on a fifth-inning RBI double by Larry Milbourne, a career backup filling in

---

* John himself admitted as much. "I have four basic pitches — fastball, curve, slider and changeup — plus eight illegal ones," he said. On ABC's pregame show prior to Game 2, Howard Cosell asked Jim Palmer, "Would you say that Tommy John is a clever pitcher?" Palmer's response: "Well, he cheats." The Dodgers, of course, never called John on it publicly, given that members of their own staff — of nearly every staff — undertook similar pursuits to varying degrees. Even years later, John's former catcher refused to indict him. "He had a sinkerball," insisted Steve Yeager. "Sinker, sinker, sinker." When asked about John's reputation as a scuff artist, the catcher said only, "He never got caught, did he? He never got thrown out of a game, so what else can I say?"

for Dent since the shortstop tore a ligament in his hand in August. It was all the Yankees would get against Hooton — and it was unearned at that, the runner, Willie Randolph, having reached on a Davey Lopes error — but it was enough.

Hooton departed in the seventh, and the Yankees immediately took advantage of LA's bullpen. Steve Howe opened the frame by giving up one-out singles to Lou Piniella and Graig Nettles, and Lasorda called on Dave Stewart to clean things up. The right-hander had seen the field only once since his back-to-back collapses against Houston in the division series (he'd pitched one uneventful inning a night earlier), and Lasorda, all but desperate for a trustworthy power arm out of the bullpen, hoped that Stewart could regain solid footing.

He could not. Stewart gave up an RBI single to Bob Watson, then, trying to pick Nettles off of second, threw the ball into center field, putting runners at second and third and setting up an intentional walk to Rick Cerone. Willie Randolph hit a sacrifice fly, scoring Nettles, for the inning's second out. The only batter Stewart retired without damage to the box score was Goose Gossage, who'd come in a half-inning earlier. By the time Gossage struck out to end the inning, the score was 3–0, which was two more runs than the closer would need.

Gossage simply overwhelmed the Dodgers in the ninth, striking out the last two hitters, Ron Cey and Pedro Guerrero, looking. It was the closer's seventh appearance in New York's 10 postseason games, and he still had not yielded a run while striking out 15. "There's not a soft spot in my heart for any hitter," he snarled afterward.

For the third straight series, the Dodgers found themselves with a multigame postseason deficit. Then again, they'd already overcome similar odds twice, so why not again? "We've got them where we want them," joked Garvey, reprising the line he'd used on Frank Sinatra back in the Astros series. Things were actually a bit easier this time around, given that the World Series was best-of-seven, not best-of-five, and LA was not yet on the brink of elimination. That alone was worth something. Still, Dodgers hitters were a collective 9-for-

62 (.145) through two games (.109 with Garvey subtracted from the equation) and in their six postseason losses had scored a total of five runs. Minus Garvey's .340 batting average since the start of the play-offs, Los Angeles was batting just .185.*

After the game, media members stood outside the Dodgers' club-house, wondering why the doors were closed when they should have been open. As it turned out, Lasorda had some things to say to his team in private, and he didn't give a whit about newspaper deadlines. It was LA's sixth straight loss at Yankee Stadium, and 10th against the Yankees in their last 14 World Series contests. Apart from Rick Monday's dramatic homer in Montreal, the Dodgers had yet to come from behind to win a game all postseason. When reporters were finally admitted to the clubhouse, somebody asked Lasorda if he'd considered the possibility of a Yankees sweep. "Sweep?" he spat. "My rear end, that's what they'll sweep."†

Were there a mitigating factor, it was that the Series was return-ing to California, where the Dodgers were 4-1 in the playoffs thus far. There was also the not-inconsequential detail that, whether or not they enjoyed the process, LA seemed to play well from behind. "You'll

---

* Things grew so dire that Reggie Smith, who had not played in the outfield since July 1980, went so far as to suggest that October might be a good time to make a full comeback from shoulder surgery. He figured that with two left-handed out-fielders, Ken Landreaux and Rick Monday, going 0-for-8 against Yankees south-paws over the first two games, he himself might be the answer against the next New York lefty, Dave Righetti. Smith could not get his shoulder loose during an off-day workout, however, and reluctantly rescinded the proposition.

† Most of the questions from reporters had to do with the team facing yet an-other deficit, and players found themselves delivering by-then-familiar mono-logues about perseverance and staying within themselves. Davey Lopes was in the middle of one such exchange when somebody shouted a question from the rear of the media scrum: "Do you think you can come back after losing the first two games and win the Series the way the Yankees did in '78?" The second base-man was about to answer before pausing to consider the question. "Johnstone, is that you?" he asked. From the back of the crowd, Jay Johnstone giggled.

see a different team in Los Angeles," promised Garvey. Maybe it was all he could say, but maybe also it was true.

Five times in World Series history a team had come back from losses in the first two games. The Dodgers were involved in four of those decisions, turning the trick twice (in 1955 against the Yankees, and in 1965 against the Twins) and having it twice turned on them (in 1956 and 1978, both by the Yankees). Each time the team on the winning end had dropped the first two on the road—just like the Dodgers. "We just couldn't believe that that they could beat us three times in a row," reflected Dusty Baker. "We refused to believe that."

As the teams jetted west, LA had a number of reasons for optimism. One was that Valenzuela would take the mound in Game 3 after surrendering only two runs over 17 innings in two starts against Houston, plus his masterpiece three-hitter in Montreal. He was, wrote *Sports Illustrated*, "a legend at age 20."

Another factor was far less expected. In the sixth inning of Game 2, Nettles jammed his thumb diving toward the line for a Bill Russell single. At first, it did not seem serious. The third baseman remained in the game, flawlessly fielding a grounder from the very next batter, Dusty Baker. In the bottom half of the frame, he flied out to right, then singled in the eighth.

After the game, however, Bob Lemon made a shocking announcement: Nettles, his thumb grotesquely swollen, would be out indefinitely. The third baseman claimed optimism even while being fit for a plastic splint, then went to St. Vincent Medical Center for X-rays once the team reached Los Angeles. The exam found no break, which was good news, but there was no way Nettles could play in Game 3. Taking his place would be Aurelio Rodríguez, a 14-year veteran with a .237 lifetime batting average, mostly with the Tigers.* Rodríguez

---

* Nettles joined Reggie Jackson, still missing from the Yankees lineup, and Bucky Dent among the ranks of New York's injured. On the Dodgers' end, rookie re-

had hit .346 in 27 games with New York in 1981, but that barely registered with the Dodgers. The guy could have hit like Babe Ruth — as long as he didn't field like Nettles, it'd be all right by them.

As it turned out, Valenzuela wasn't the only rookie sensation in the World Series. Starting for the Yankees was 22-year-old Dave Righetti, whose 8-4 record and league-best 2.05 ERA would earn him the American League Rookie of the Year Award.* (The lefty would likely have won several more games had he not received six runs of support, total, in his four losses.) It would be the first time since Yankees great Whitey Ford beat Philadelphia's Bob Miller in 1950 that first-year players squared off in the Fall Classic.

Righetti hailed from San Jose — he'd grown up a Giants fan, loathing the Dodgers — and this was a big deal for his family, especially his father, Leo, who was himself a former minor leaguer. (Leo Righetti spent a dozen seasons in the bushes, seven of them in Triple-A, quitting when his wife was eight months pregnant with Dave.) The rookie wrangled 20 tickets to the game for family members; unfortunately, 21 showed up. Leo volunteered to hang back, "knowing he could get in somehow, if he needed to," said his son later. Enter Tommy Lasorda.

The Dodgers skipper had played against the elder Righetti in the Sally League in 1949, Lasorda with the Greenville Spinners and Righetti with the Augusta Tigers.† As Leo Righetti tried to sort things out at will-call, he was spotted by Tom Nettles, a Bay Area sports-

---

liever Alejandro Peña was out after collapsing in the clubhouse shower following Game 1 with what was later determined to be a bleeding ulcer. Teammates had to carry him, still soapy, into the trainer's room for treatment.

* The Dodgers nearly traded for Righetti, then a minor leaguer, in 1980, offering impending free agent Don Sutton in exchange. Only after ex-Dodger Tommy John weighed in on the potential downside of integrating a curmudgeon like Sutton into New York's clubhouse did the Yankees reduce their offer from Righetti to borderline big leaguer Mike Griffin. The Dodgers were not interested.

† Greenville was where Lasorda first laid eyes on his wife, Jo, spying her in the grandstand during a game.

caster and the cousin of Yankees third baseman Graig. Upon hearing Leo's story, Nettles found Dodgers coach Monty Basgall (Leo Righetti's teammate on the 1955 Seattle Rainiers), who filled in Lasorda, who pulled some quick strings to get Dave's dad into the stadium just before the game began.

When Graig Nettles heard about the situation from his cousin, he weighed his options. He didn't want to distract his teammate from the biggest start of his young career, but there was a chance that Dave might somehow have forgotten to include an extra ticket in his will-call envelope and could offer an easy fix. Ignorant of Lasorda's machinations to get Leo Righetti into the ballpark, Graig took a chance and raced to the bullpen to inform the pitcher that his father was stuck outside the gates. Powerless, Dave Righetti spent the rest of his warm-up session distracted by details, wondering just what the heck was going on. "That's what was on my mind just before I went out to pitch," he said later.

Across the field, Sandy Koufax — working for the Dodgers as a roving pitching instructor and in town to throw out the ceremonial first pitch — was recruited to toss batting practice. The Hall of Famer delivered 24 pitches to a succession of batters — Garvey, Baker, Cey, rotating after several hacks each — most of which thundered, untouched, to the rear of the cage. Nobody could so much as connect for a loud foul. Koufax, the least hittable pitcher on the planet when he was 29, still had it at 45. Finally, Garvey stepped in and flipped his wrist to request a curveball. From Koufax. The guy with the most devastating bender in history. Obligingly, the left-hander snapped off a hook that dropped almost two feet through the strike zone, so filthy that it buckled the world-class hitter who was expecting it. Garvey could do nothing but watch it tumble past.

By that point people were paying attention to the display, including members of the Dodgers coaching staff, who were aghast at what they saw. Someone raced to the mound and quietly suggested to the Hall of Famer that it might not be the best idea to further dishearten the best hitters on a team that was already struggling at the plate. With a nod, Koufax decamped for the dugout, ceding his duties to somebody less governed by primal competitive instincts.

Despite their inadvertent humbling, the Dodgers were an upbeat bunch for a club that couldn't afford to lose. As the teams were being introduced, Jerry Reuss and Steve Howe — part of the first group to leave the dugout, made up of coaches, bench players, and pitchers — were supposed to wait down the left-field line, leaving space for the starters alongside Lasorda, who stood near home plate. Instead, the duo subverted the system and headed directly toward the bewildered manager. As Lasorda did his best to ignore them — exploding wasn't an option, given the live broadcast — the duo took positions alongside him, blowing bubble-gum bubbles. "We were just a couple of excitable boys," Howe said later.

Once things got under way, the game seemed just as backward as the pitchers standing at the wrong end of the line. Valenzuela, LA's playoff savior, opened the action by walking New York's first hitter, second baseman Willie Randolph, to culminate a 10-pitch at-bat. After a fielder's choice, Fernando also walked Dave Winfield, on four pitches no less. This was nuts. Valenzuela had averaged just over two walks per start during the regular season, yet somehow managed to match that within the span of the game's first three batters. Before alarms began to ring too vigorously in the Dodgers' dugout, the left-hander induced an inning-ending double-play grounder from Lou Piniella. Maybe, hoped the brain trust, this would be the extent of the pitcher's troubles.

It would not. The next inning, New York's first batter, Bob Watson, demolished the second pitch he saw, a hanging screwball, powering it directly over the center-field fence. It was only one run, but it felt entirely a part of Valenzuela's early-game struggles. So did the double pulled to left by the next hitter, catcher Rick Cerone, which bounced off the top of the low outfield fence, millimeters from being New York's second straight homer. After a sacrifice fly advanced

Cerone to third, Larry Milbourne brought him home with an RBI single, shot through the hole between first and second. Now it was 2–0, and with Valenzuela having retired only three of the eight men he'd faced, Lasorda reluctantly called the bullpen with instructions to get Goltz loose. The manager was known for an early post-season hook when it came to struggling pitchers, and with no team having ever come back from a three-game World Series deficit, the Dodgers were hardly inclined to break new ground. Two things prevented Lasorda from removing his best pitcher in the second inning of the biggest start of his young career. Both had to do with Righetti.

The first was that, with runners on first and second, New York's rookie pitcher — who hadn't batted since turning pro in 1977 — was coming to the plate.

The other was that, after seven days off, Righetti had shown even less on the mound than Fernando. It was entirely out of character: the guy had been indomitable to that point in the playoffs, going 3-0 while allowing only one run over 17 innings — or 31 innings, counting his 14 shutout frames at the end of the regular season — and striking out a hitter per. None of it mattered, though, when Lopes led off for the Dodgers with an opposite-field double down the line, then went to third on Russell's bunt single.* Ron Cey brought them both home with a three-run homer — only the second off of Righetti all season — hit some 400 feet into the left-field pavilion. It gave the Dodgers their first lead of the Series, 3–0. It also provided Lasorda all the justification he would need to keep Fernando in the game.

Righetti might not have been able to swing a bat, but he proved to be a capable bunter, sacrificing Milbourne to second with a well-

---

* With Righetti's follow-through pulling him toward the third-base side of the mound, second baseman Willie Randolph was the only player with a chance at a play. Instead, he raced to cover first — from which Bob Watson never departed — and left his position unmanned.

placed ball down the first-base line. Valenzuela then put *another* runner aboard by walking Randolph for the second time. The lefty was not yet out of the second inning and already at 44 pitches. Two were out, however, and Lasorda gave his star the last inch of rope at his disposal. It took six pitches for Fernando to utilize it — bringing his pitch count to an even 50 — but he rewarded his skipper by getting Jerry Mumphrey to tap an easy, inning-ending comebacker.

Lasorda rationalized his decision by noting that Valenzuela had overcome a number of shaky starts over the course of the season to settle into middle-innings grooves, but the southpaw did him no favors by falling into further trouble straightaway in the third. With one out, Piniella stroked a line single. With two outs, Cerone blasted a two-run homer to left-center, just to the right of, and a bit farther than, his earlier double. (The catcher had homered only twice in 234 at-bats all season, and Valenzuela had yielded one long ball over his last 13 starts. What other way could it have gone?) Now it was 4–3 Yankees, Valenzuela was on the ropes again, and again Lasorda had to figure out if and when to pull his pitcher.

The next batter, Aurelio Rodríguez, Nettles's replacement, hit a ball up the middle, past Valenzuela, that Lopes fielded cleanly, then threw past Garvey into the photographers' well alongside the Yankees dugout, allowing Rodríguez to advance to second.* Once more Lasorda found himself at the boundaries of his tolerance. Once more, Valenzuela's salvation arrived in the person of Righetti. Following an intentional walk to Milbourne,† Fernando got his counterpart to swing fruitlessly at a fastball to end the frame.

---

* Rodríguez's at-bat in the second inning marked the first time that two Mexico-born players squared off in the World Series. Prior to 1981, Bobby Avila had been the only Mexican national to have played in the Fall Classic, with Cleveland in 1954.

† Two innings earlier, the shortstop came up with a base open and Righetti to follow. Lasorda had Valenzuela pitch to him, and Milbourne responded with an RBI single. That mistake would not be made again.

Over three innings, Fernando had given up a total of four runs, six hits (two of them homers), and four walks. It took him 72 pitches to do so, not to mention the 31⅔ innings he'd already thrown over the first two playoff rounds (the most on either team)* and the 192⅓ he'd accrued over the truncated regular season (the most in the National League). Maybe the guy was just gassed.

To the benefit of Valenzuela and the Dodgers, Righetti never got right. After giving up four hits, one walk, one hit batter, and three runs over the first two innings, the left-hander started the third by ceding a sharp single to Garvey and walking Cey. Yankees manager Bob Lemon reluctantly faced the same decision Lasorda had been contemplating since the top of the second: whether to pull his pitcher early. Unlike Lasorda, Lemon did it.

In came right-hander George Frazier, who had been all but unhittable after being acquired from St. Louis (where he was pitching in the minors) just before the strike, his 1.63 ERA in 16 games across August and September serving as the final ingredient in the American League's best relief corps. The move paid immediate dividends, Frazier striking out Pedro Guerrero (after two failed bunt attempts) and inducing Monday into an easy fly ball to left field. With two on and two out, however, the unintended consequences of Lemon's decision would be inexorably felt.

Lasorda had maintained his season-long catcher platoon through the playoffs, with Mike Scioscia playing against right-handers and Steve Yeager against lefties. One attendant downside of the scheme was that, with the Dodgers facing only 14 left-handed starters all season, Valenzuela had pitched to Yeager only twice, accounting for 19 of his 225 combined innings on the year, regular season and playoffs combined. Add to that the fact that Scioscia spoke some Spanish and

---

* By comparison, Righetti led New York with 15.

it should come as little surprise that Fernando felt viscerally more comfortable throwing to him.*

It did not help the pitcher when, upon seeing a parade of Yankees right-handers leaning over the plate to reach Valenzuela's screwball, Yeager pressed him to bust his fastball inside. The strategy did not sit well with Fernando, who spent the early innings repeatedly shaking off signs. With Righetti replaced by a right-hander, however, Lasorda was able, by sticking with his established order, to give Valenzuela his preferred target. With two on and two outs, Scioscia batted for Yeager. That he grounded out to end the inning hardly mattered. His influence would be felt elsewhere.

With Scioscia calling pitches, Valenzuela immediately improved, breezing through the fourth. In the fifth, he allowed a bloop double to Watson and intentionally walked Milbourne for the second time in the game, but emerged unscathed. Still, the Dodgers trailed, 4–3, and Fernando, 101 pitches in, was scheduled to bat sixth in the bottom of the fifth inning. If his spot in the order came up, a pinch-hitter was a near-certainty.

Garvey led off the frame with a high chopper down the third-base line that Rodríguez gloved on one hop without trouble, but because the enormous bounce had backed him up to the lip of the outfield grass, his throw had no chance to beat the runner. Frazier then walked Cey, bringing up Pedro Guerrero, who two innings earlier had come up in exactly the same situation — runners at first and second, nobody out — and fouled off two bunt attempts before striking out. Lemon put his infielders on alert. Now, again in a bunt situation, Lasorda was caught by TV cameras saying, "He can't bunt." Maybe it was for the

* When Yeager first caught Valenzuela in spring training, he called a quick time-out to discuss things, which drew Lasorda from the dugout. "What are you trying to tell him?" the manager asked.
"How to pitch to this hitter," Yeager responded.
Lasorda couldn't believe it. "This guy doesn't understand English!" he yelped.
"How do I know?" Yeager said. "He keeps nodding his head to everything I say."

best. Allowed to swing away, Guerrero rewarded his skipper with a chopper down the third-base line that bounced, barely, over the outstretched glove of Rodríguez, who'd been playing in.* Garvey scored, Cey went to third, and Guerrero, eyeing Dave Winfield take his time corralling the ball in left field, motored into second with a double. Tie game.

Still, there was nobody out. Lemon had Monday intentionally walked to load the bases, then replaced Frazier with lefty Rudy May to face Scioscia. Lemon, assessing his team's chances against a vulnerable Dodgers bullpen, kept his infield back, which allowed Cey to score when Scioscia topped a ball to Randolph at second to begin a double-play. Now the Dodgers led, 5–4.

Lasorda had some serious thinking to do. Valenzuela had turned in one of the worst starts of his career, had thrown a ton of pitches, and was now due to bat with two outs and a runner at third. Reggie Smith was already in the on-deck circle, loosening up. There was, however, a wrinkle. For the first time all game, the Dodgers led. Lasorda would have liked another run, certainly, but now he didn't *need* it. The manager wondered just how angry people back home would be if his move backfired, then opted to stay with his horse. Smith was recalled, and Valenzuela grabbed a bat.† That he grounded out to end the inning represented the least of Lasorda's gamble. What really mattered was to come.

Fernando opened the sixth by walking Randolph — his seventh free pass of the game, drawing Lasorda from the dugout. Goltz had long since gotten loose, and Valenzuela figured that he was done for. Why else would Lasorda come out for a visit rather than pitching coach

---

* Afterward, Lemon joked that the proper defensive strategy in that situation would have been to bring in the six-foot-six Winfield from left field to man third base.

† Valenzuela was capable at the plate, his .250 average on the season ranking higher than Smith's . . . or anybody else on the LA bench save for Steve Sax. It was also, remarkably, 45 points better than hitters batted against *him*.

Ron Perranoski? The answer was that the manager wanted to see for himself what his pitcher had left. Lasorda sought assurance, and as he began talking to Fernando, he got it — not from anything the pitcher said so much as his general demeanor. As always, the lefty appeared entirely unfazed by the pressure of the situation. So instead of yanking Fernando, Lasorda opted for a pep talk. "If you don't give up another run," he said in Spanish, "we're going to win this ballgame." *Si no te rindes otra carrera, vamos a ganar este juego.*

Valenzuela stared at his manager, then responded quizzically, in English: "Are you sure?"

Lasorda was not sure, but he understood the importance of convincing the pitcher of his certainty. Leaving him in went a long way toward that end.

"Everybody thought I was going to take him out," the manager said. "A lot of people wanted me to take him out, but I knew him. He loved to pitch out of jams. He used to pitch like he didn't know we had a bullpen. He didn't like to come out of games. A lot of guys, when they get in trouble, they're looking down there for help. But not him."

On the telecast, Howard Cosell offered another perspective, calling it "a silent memorandum on what [Lasorda] thinks of his bullpen."

Valenzuela gained a reprieve when Scioscia threw out Randolph trying to steal. Suitably settled, the pitcher struck out Mumphrey looking and got Winfield to ground out to Cey. Three outs, three innings to go.

The Dodgers were unable to touch New York's next two relievers, Rudy May and Ron Davis, but with Fernando beginning to deal like he had early in the season, it didn't matter. Valenzuela got three outs on 10 pitches in the seventh and needed only nine pitches to get through the eighth thanks to a providence-borne double-play after a hard-charging Cey, forearm brace and all, snagged pinch-hitter Bobby Murcer's popped-up bunt attempt with a dive into foul territory, then doubled Milbourne off of first. Three up, three down in the ninth, capped by Lou Piniella flailing at a fastball, ended it. Somehow, after being on the ropes for most of the first five innings, Valenzuela had thrown a complete-game victory while allowing 16 base runners and four runs. It took him 146 pitches.

Afterward, opinion was divided on how El Toro managed to persevere. Yeager said that Fernando "was all over the place" and "didn't have good stuff at all." Scioscia said that when he was watching from the bullpen, Valenzuela's pitches appeared to be consistently high, but that by the time he entered the game the pitcher was already making adjustments. Fernando, said Lasorda in the postgame clubhouse, "was like a championship poker player, bluffing his way through a hand."

"I don't play boker," responded the pitcher. "I play beisbol."

Valenzuela himself shied from remarking on his own doggedness, instead couching his postgame assessment in terms of the small earthquake that had shaken Southern California overnight: "I thought the earthquake was tonight, they were hitting the ball so hard."*

Not everyone shared that opinion. Down the hallway, one pitcher in particular was agog over Fernando's performance. "In my opinion, Valenzuela should be the National League's MVP," said Dave Righetti. "Mike Schmidt had an awesome year, but Valenzuela filled parks. No one player did more for his league or team. I watched him as often as I could on TV, and was impressed with the way his confidence just oozes out. His poise stems from his confidence in the same way that mine does. It's not a matter of being cocky or arrogant. It's just knowing you can do the job."

The good news for the Dodgers was that they finally had a victory, and two more games at home. The bad news was that they still trailed in the Series, two games to one, and it was unlikely that Valenzuela would throw another baseball for them before March.

---

* The line of the day came from Yankees coach Yogi Berra, who said, "I didn't feel it. It must have bypassed me."

There was life anyway. It was a bargain they were only too happy to accept.

The Dodgers had finally beaten the Yankees for the first time in seven tries, but all was not well in LA's camp. After hurting his wrist while fighting in Montreal, Dusty Baker had struggled to make contact at the plate, garnering only a soft single in 15 World Series at-bats. All four of his Game 3 turns came with runners on base, two of them with men in scoring position, and Baker failed to advance any of them. In the postgame clubhouse, the man was borderline miserable. "I've hit bottom," he said morosely. It seemed to be the only thing he *could* hit.

More problematic for the Dodgers was that their offensive woes were hardly limited to Baker. Even counting their five-run outburst in Game 3, Los Angeles was batting just .191 against the Yankees, averaging fewer than three runs per game. For the playoffs as a whole, the Dodgers were hitting .210 and averaging 2.77 runs. Unless something changed, LA pitchers needed to make peace with the necessity of throwing shutouts.

It didn't take long for Bob Welch to serve notice as to which option would be necessary in Game 4. The right-hander, stuck in the bullpen since the end of the regular season, was forced to take the start because the rainout in Montreal had eaten the schedule's off-day, compressing LA's rotation to the point of cracking. Welch had been a World Series hero for the Dodgers back in 1978, when he came into Game 2 with two on and one out in the ninth inning to protect a 4–3 lead and retired Thurman Munson and Reggie Jackson — the latter on an epic, nine-pitch strikeout — to end it. Now, however, Welch had pitched only two and two-thirds innings over the previous three weeks. The effects of his layoff were impossible to miss.

New York's leadoff hitter, Willie Randolph, laced a ball into the right-field corner that Rick Monday overran by several feet, turning a bounding double in front of him into an easy triple behind him. The next batter, Larry Milbourne, laced a double to nearly the same spot, plating Randolph. Welch then walked Winfield — to that point 0-for-10 in the World Series, not to mention in possession of the biggest strike zone on either team — on four pitches. Reggie Jackson, playing in his first game since injuring his calf in Game 2 of the ALCS against Oakland, singled to left to load the bases.* Only one run had scored, but Welch was already 16 pitches in — only six of which were strikes, and three of those had been blasted all over the yard — and all four New York batters had reached base. With the game on the precipice of spiraling out of control, Lasorda staggeringly found himself tromping to the mound and, with nobody out in the first inning, signaling to the bullpen. With that, Welch became the first pitcher in 17 years to be yanked from a World Series start so early. Fernando-level leeway would not be in the offing. In jogged Dave Goltz.

On paper, the big righty didn't provide much of an upgrade. During the season, the free-agent bust had been the only National League pitcher to lose twice each to the worst team in each division, the Cubs and the Padres. He'd gone 9-18 over two lackluster years in Los Angeles, with a 4.24 ERA in a league where the average was 3.50. He hadn't been used at all in the first two rounds of the playoffs. Still, Goltz did his job in Game 4, getting three straight outs, with only Bob Watson's sacrifice fly costing Los Angeles on the scoreboard. After all of that offense, the Yankees' lead was somehow only 2–0.

Successful as it was, Goltz's effort exposed the pitcher's propensity for giving up flyballs — a dangerous trait against a power-hitting team. Sure enough, after the Dodgers went down quietly in the first against veteran right-hander Rick Reuschel, Willie Randolph, hitter of two long balls all season, pounded a Goltz fastball deep into the

---

* Jackson later insisted that he'd been ready for Game 3 a day earlier, but with free agency awaiting the superstar at year's end, George Steinbrenner wanted to prove that the Yankees could win without him and ordered Lemon to sit Reggie an extra day.

right-center-field bleachers for his second homer of the World Series. Now it was 3–0.

In the third inning, Rick Cerone singled home Jackson. Now it was 4–0.

With the ninth spot due up for LA in the bottom half of the frame, the Dodgers were in a precarious position, having already burned through two pitchers while trying to chase an incrementally increasing deficit. Dave Stewart had been all kinds of shaky throughout the entire postseason, so he was out. Castillo had walked five in his lone inning of work in Game 1, so he was out too. That left Terry Forster, Tom Niedenfuer, and Steve Howe to handle the final six innings. Lasorda would need them all.

Giving the Dodgers hope was that Reuschel was experiencing his own struggles. While holding LA scoreless through the first two innings, the right-hander allowed six straight hard-hit balls — four line-drive outs buffeting two well-struck singles. In the third, leadoff hitter Ken Landreaux, batting for Goltz, continued the streak with a double down the first-base line. Lopes brought him home with a sharp single, stole second, took third on Garvey's one-out infield hit, and scored on Cey's grounder to shortstop. Now it was 4–2 New York.

From that point forward, sloppy play came to dominate the action on both sides. It soon became clear that whichever team was better able to minimize mistakes while capitalizing on those of the opposition would have a clear advantage. It was a battle of attrition.*

This was never more obvious than in the top of the fourth, when Randolph led off with a full-count walk against LA's third pitcher of the game, Forster, and was sacrificed to second by Milbourne. The

---

* At a press conference after the game, a reporter mentioned that a radio broadcaster had called the last two games at Dodger Stadium "clinics for Little Leaguers on how not to play baseball." Lasorda was incredulous. "Who said that?" he snapped. It was Vin Scully, he was told. "Oh," said Lasorda, "the guy obviously knows his baseball."

Yankees appeared primed to score for the fourth straight inning . . . until Dave Winfield hit a grounder to Russell. Before the shortstop could throw to first, however, he noticed that Randolph had more or less wandered away from the bag. Russell held the ball as Randolph took off for third, his throw easily beating the runner, Cey applying the tag after a truncated rundown. It was a gift out for the Dodgers.

Forster almost gave it all back without missing a beat. Winfield, who'd reached on Randolph's miscue, promptly stole second as Scioscia nearly threw the ball away, saved only by an acrobatic play by Russell. Reggie Jackson walked. Oscar Gamble then topped an easy grounder up the middle to Lopes's side of the bag, custom-delivered for an easy force at second and the inning's third out . . . had Russell not also tried to chase down the ball, leaving nobody to cover the bag when Lopes came up with it. Now the bases were loaded. With the power-hitting Bob Watson one swing away from busting the game apart, Forster buckled down, inducing a grounder to shortstop which Russell underhanded to Lopes for a play that should have happened one batter earlier. LA's deficit held at two for at least an inning more.

Reuschel opened the bottom of the fourth by walking Monday, then giving up a single to Guerrero. Bye-bye, Rick. Left-hander Rudy May came on and neutralized the threat, not allowing a ball out of the infield for the rest of the inning and stranding both runners. Going to the bullpen when he did, however, set up Yankees manager Bob Lemon to contribute to the game's list of mental errors. A half-inning later, in the top of the fifth, Lemon let May hit for himself with two outs and nobody on, a move keyed toward keeping the left-hander in the game as long as possible. May fouled out against LA's fourth pitcher, Tom Niedenfuer, to end the inning, then had to be yanked anyway only minutes later after giving up a one-out double to Garvey and a run-scoring single to Cey. New pitcher Ron Davis got two quick strikeouts to end the frame, but now the Dodgers trailed by only one, 4–3. The game was only four and a half innings in and had already seen seven pitchers.

In the top of the sixth, New York's first batter, Willie Randolph, reached when Bill Russell threw the ball up the first-base line, forcing Steve Garvey to use all of his five feet, 10 inches to grab it with a leap as the runner slid past, directly underneath him. Garvey stabbed downward with a desperation tag, which appeared on replay to have touched Randolph in time, but first-base ump Rich Garcia ruled that it had been applied too late. It was that kind of game. After Milbourne popped out to left, Winfield put a scare into the fans at Chavez Ravine when he pulled a Niedenfuer fastball deep down the left-field line, a would-be homer that Dusty Baker tracked down with his right hand atop the low fence. It was by that point standard fare for Winfield, who had hit the ball consistently hard but was 0-for-13 in the Series. Still, it allowed Randolph to advance to second. With two outs, Lasorda had Niedenfuer intentionally walk Reggie Jackson, a move that at first looked good when the right-hander put Oscar Gamble into an 0-2 hole, and then looked terrible when he surrendered a single that brought home Randolph and sent Jackson to third. Five-three, Yankees. The next hitter, Bob Watson, culminated an eight-pitch at-bat by roping a sinking liner to left field that Baker caught for what would have been the inning's third out had umpire Nick Colosi not ruled it a trap, allowing Jackson to score. Baker vociferously argued the call, and so, after racing from the dugout, did Lasorda. "I had it," insisted the left fielder after the game. "There's no way to short-hop it with your glove hand pointing to the sky. When he said I trapped the ball, I thought *Jeez, what else can go wrong?*" (It was, of course, subterfuge. Decades later, Baker finally came clean. "I trapped it," he admitted. "There wasn't any replay on the field, so you trap it and you hold the glove up." *But you were so insistent that you made the catch.* "Yeah, well, what else am I supposed to say? Sometimes you have to go for an Academy Award.")

Now it was 6–3. Niedenfuer induced a fly ball from Cerone to end the rally, but the damage was done. All the work of whittling New York's four-run lead down to one had been undone. Worse yet, it was now the sixth inning, a point at which the New York's best relievers could make their presence felt.

It started with Ron Davis. The All-Star right-hander was the most trusted member of New York's bullpen save for Gossage, a guy who, apart from one horrid inning in September, had posted a 0.66 ERA since August 29, a span that included 10 postseason frames.

It would not be his day.

With one out in the sixth, Davis walked Mike Scioscia, at which point Lasorda sent up Jay Johnstone to pinch-hit for Niedenfuer. Johnstone was 35 years old and over the course of his career had been sold once, released twice, and traded three times. He was a 16-year vet but had collected as many as 500 at-bats in a season only once. By the time he reached Los Angeles as a free agent in 1980 — he accepted a $20,000 pay cut to move closer to his hometown of West Covina, about 20 miles from Chavez Ravine, the first free agent ever, it was said, to lose money on his new deal — he'd settled into something of a Svengali-like pinch-hitter role. ("Svengali" in this instance being defined as "crazy person put on the planet to drive Tommy Lasorda batty.") The guy was an inveterate prankster, unable to stop himself when it came to stirring the Dodgers' pot.

Johnstone once enlisted Jerry Reuss and Don Stanhouse to help him replace the desk in Lasorda's office with a makeup mirror ringed by white lightbulbs, to better suit the TV-friendly manager. In another prank, he removed every one of the dozens of photos from the wood-paneled walls of Lasorda's office — even those of Sinatra — and replaced them with publicity shots of himself, Reuss, and Stanhouse. At Vero Beach one year, Johnstone broke into Lasorda's room while the skipper was out and removed the mouthpiece receivers from the telephones. Later that night, when everyone was asleep, he and Yeager cinched a rope as tightly as possible between Lasorda's doorknob and a nearby palm tree, preventing the manager from pulling his door open. Unable to escape or call for help, things truly hit home for Lasorda when he realized that he might have to miss breakfast. The manager knew exactly who to blame. During that day's game in Orlando he stole Johnstone's street clothes and forced him to ride home in his underwear.*

The prank for which Johnstone is best known occurred in September 1981, a month before the World Series. Back in 1979, Reuss and then-Dodgers pitcher Ken Brett donned groundskeeper outfits and helped drag the infield during a game. Ever since, Johnstone had desperately wanted some of that action for himself. So before a game against the Pirates at Dodger Stadium — Los Angeles had clinched a playoff spot months earlier — he convinced Reuss to revisit the stunt. The players copped some coveralls and proceeded to serve as members of the four-man infield crew that went to work in the fifth inning. Because it was Reuss's off-day and Johnstone rarely started, nobody missed them.

That's not the same as going undetected, of course. Rick Monday made sure that scoreboard cameras were trained upon the duo so that everybody in the stadium could see what was happening. Upon finishing their dragging, the ballplayers received a full ovation. The only man in the building who didn't seem to appreciate the gesture was Tommy Lasorda, who issued $250 fines before the players had even returned to the dugout. Johnstone was still in a side room, pulling on his uniform pants, when he heard the manager bellow, "Where the fuck is Johnstone?" As comeuppance for his childish behavior, Lasorda wanted him to pinch-hit for pitcher Terry Forster, posthaste. Johnstone was still buckling his belt as he made his way to the plate — and proceeded to bash a home run.

---

* Johnstone's shenanigans were prolific. He went into the Dodger Stadium stands in full uniform to wait in line for a Dodger Dog. He put pine tar in Al Campanis's shoes. Before a game in 1980, Johnstone and Stanhouse tied up Reuss in the outfield and left him there, giggling, as the game was about to begin. He once terrorized a Dodgertown nurse by putting apple juice in his urine-sample jar and saying, upon her proclamation that it looked cloudy, "Let me run it through again." Then, to her horror, he guzzled it.

By the time Lasorda called upon him to bat for Niedenfuer in Game 4 of the World Series, Johnstone was in the throes of a deep tailspin, having hit .095 over the last three weeks of the regular season and .205 overall. He'd collected only three at-bats through LA's first two playoff series and was still looking for his first postseason hit. That pinch homer against the Pirates had been his only long ball since May.

Facing Davis with one out and one on and his team trailing by three, Johnstone — whose entire persona seemed to revolve around doing the unexpected — pulled his grandest trick to date: he homered.* The Dodgers' bench, which had to that point resembled the LA County morgue†, came suddenly to life. "Here we are," thought Johnstone as he rounded the bases. "That changes the whole game." The two-run blast pulled the Dodgers to within one, at 6–5.

New York's woes continued with the very next batter. Reggie Jackson, battling the sun on a Davey Lopes pop fly, took a circuitous route to the ball, then let it bounce off his left bicep, allowing Lopes to streak into second (and spurring a sarcastic chant of "Reg-gie, Reg-gie" from the fans at Dodger Stadium). Lopes had stolen 20 bases on only 44 hits during the regular season, plus another one earlier in Game 4, showing basepath acumen that left him increasingly frustrated with steady public messaging from the Dodgers front office that suggested his best days were behind him. "They say I can't run anymore," he muttered before Game 3. "If I can't, who on this club can? Who in this whole organization can? It's a ridiculous statement. If you want to get rid of me, just get rid of me, but don't say I can't run." Then he set about proving his point.

----

* Asked afterward if he'd hit a fastball, Johnstone answered: "Does [Davis] throw anything else?" Responded a reporter who covered him regularly: "Can you hit anything else?" Wrote Jim Murray in the next day's *Los Angeles Times*: "Jay Johnstone is not supposed to be winning World Series games, he's supposed to be pouring cayenne pepper in the coffee."

† Jack Klugman was currently starring in the NBC drama *Quincy M.E.*, about the Los Angeles County coroner. He was also a friend of Tommy Lasorda.

Unchecked by Davis, Lopes took a walking lead and made it to third, his second steal of the game, almost before catcher Rick Cerone had received the ball. The veteran could still run. A moment later he scored on Bill Russell's single over a drawn-in infield, tying the score at six. With that, Lemon called upon his fourth pitcher of the game, right-hander George Frazier, who ended the inning without further damage. But the Yankees' slipshod implosion was not yet complete.

With Steve Howe on the mound for Los Angeles in the top of the seventh, Rodríguez smacked a leadoff single to center, then was thrown out by Guerrero at second trying to stretch it into a double. (That he hesitated slightly while rounding first, then failed to dive toward the inner half of the base, away from the tag, did him no favors.) In a game in which it was becoming clear that every base runner would matter, this was a precipitous turn. Howe retired the next two hitters without incident.

The Dodgers answered in the bottom half of the frame, when Dusty Baker led off with a high chopper to shortstop. It was standard soft contact for him by that point, given his damaged wrist. Baker was so down about his lack of production, in fact, that Johnstone and Reggie Smith had pulled him aside for a pep talk before the inning. *Stop thinking so much*, they said. *Do what you do best. Swing the bat.* Baker only half-listened, given that he had not yet told them (or any teammate) about his injury. Still, he ran like hell and beat out the bounder. "I guess it's that easy," he said after the game. For the Yankees, it was another hit enabled by the infield dirt of Dodger Stadium. "I've seen more high chops in two games here than I've seen in my whole life," groused Rodríguez afterward. "I'm tired of it. This field is worse than Astroturf."

Dodgers players didn't necessarily disagree. The infield dirt, made of crushed brick, was unique to Chavez Ravine. Its orange hue was beautiful on TV but could turn ground balls into adventures. "When you watered it, it would sit in the sun and bake, and then you'd come out and run on it and it would crack up," said Garvey, looking back.

"It would be in chunks. They could drag it, but there would still be enough to alter the ball when it hit them. It looked great, but boy was it tough to play on."

"The Yankees might not have liked it," added Cey, "but we weren't so happy with it either."

George Steinbrenner went so far as to compare the infield to a ping-pong table, referring to LA's high bouncers off of it as "chicken-shit hits." Baker didn't care what anybody called it — he was standing safely on first.

The next batter, Rick Monday, hit a sinking liner up the middle. Jerry Mumphrey, New York's regular center fielder, had started more than three times as many games there during the regular season than any other Yankee. For reasons never fully explained, however, Mumphrey had been ordered to the bench for Game 4, replaced by Oscar Gamble. "I just wanted to shake it up," said Lemon afterward, noting that Mumphrey had gone hitless in two straight games. Even by that logic, though, Gamble had already been removed for a pinch-hitter, and it wasn't Mumphrey who replaced him in the field but the far less defensively capable Bobby Brown. Lemon explained later that he wanted Mumphrey available to pinch-hit, but one further possibility remained: the outfielder would be a free agent at season's end and had already talked about a multiple-year contract at nearly a million dollars per. Some theorized that George Steinbrenner ordered him benched to knock down his asking price. Or maybe the Boss was just angry at recent developments that had little to do with Mumphrey. "Steinbrenner was predictably enraged after the Yankees' narrow loss of the previous evening," reported *Sports Illustrated*, "and when he's in that humor, the bodies fall."

"That's a good question," said Reggie Jackson when asked about the possibility of Steinbrenner's meddling, "but I won't answer it."*

---

* "Did you in any way order the manager not to use Mumphrey under any circumstances?" Howard Cosell asked Steinbrenner in an interview aired on ABC

So it was Brown, not Mumphrey, trying to field Monday's hit, and it didn't go well. He started by getting a bad read on the ball, then took an awkward route to reach it. Finally, with a fruitless dive, Brown let the ball bounce past him for a double, allowing Baker to race to third.

With two runners in scoring position and nobody out in a tie game, Lemon had Pedro Guerrero intentionally walked to load the bases. Nine outs to go was too early for Gossage, no matter how dire the circumstance, and New York's skipper had already burned through his two other trusted relievers. This is how he came to turn to an unlikely source, somebody he was confident could at least keep the ball over the plate: Game 2 starter Tommy John.

John, of course, was slated to start Game 6 three days hence, but that was a concern for another day. The left-hander walked fewer batters per nine innings than any of New York's regular relievers, and his sinker was perfect for inducing ground balls — an especially prevalent detail given the slow-footed Steve Yeager, pinch-hitting for Scioscia with a southpaw on the mound, at the plate.

The X-factor, of course, was that Yeager had caught thousands of John's sinkers during the pitcher's years in Los Angeles and knew just what to look for. He hit John's second pitch in the air to right field, plenty deep enough to score Baker from third and give the Dodgers their first lead of the game, 7–6. Steve Howe bunted Monday and Guerrero over for the inning's second out. Lopes then topped a grounder toward third, another high hop off the hard Dodger Stadium dirt that was driving Steinbrenner so nuts. By the time the ball came down, Rodríguez had no play — everybody was safe, including Monday, at home. LA's eighth run of the game was as many as the Dodgers had scored over the first three contests combined. It also gave them a two-run lead.

John retired Russell to end the inning, but the damage was done.

---

prior to Game 5. Steinbrenner answered, "Absolutely not . . . There was never any order from me not to play Mumphrey."

Howe closed out the Yankees over the final two frames, ceding only an eighth-inning homer to Reggie Jackson (his third hit of the night in addition to two walks, leading to further questions about why he hadn't been utilized in Game 3). It was a solo shot, however, and the Yankees needed two.

The top of the ninth was typically painful for such a slovenly game. With two outs and a runner on first, Tommy John's spot in the Yankees' order came up, but instead of tabbing the switch-hitting Mumphrey and his .307 batting average to pinch-hit, Lemon inexplicably sent up the left-handed Bobby Murcer to face the southpaw Howe. It was a particularly egregious decision given that Lemon's stated reason for not starting Mumphrey in the first place was that he wanted him available late, to pinch-hit. Howe induced what should have been a game-ending bouncer to first, but Garvey bobbled it, recovering with barely enough time to shovel the ball to Howe covering . . . except that the pitcher pulled his foot off the bag a moment before receiving it. Reported *Sports Illustrated*: "It was as if all the locked-in tensions suddenly burst through the barriers of traditional postseason restraint and both teams abandoned themselves to simply winging it."

"It's mad," said Garvey afterward. "You can get caught up in the chaos of a game like this one."

Howe finally got the next batter, Willie Randolph, to fly out to deep center for the game's final out. Somehow — after their starting pitcher failed to record an out; after burning through four relievers, three of whom pitched multiple innings; after allowing the Yankees to bat .333 with two homers on the day; after committing two errors, one of which nearly gave the game away in the ninth — the Dodgers emerged victorious. The combined box score recorded 36 players who totaled 27 hits. Twenty-two runners were stranded. Of the 318 pitches thrown on the day, 114 missed the strike zone. The side wasn't retired in order until the fifth, and despite the tight score, Lemon didn't find an opening for Gossage, the game's most dominant closer, who hadn't pitched in three days. "This game wasn't your basic Picasso," sighed

Monday in the postgame clubhouse. Somehow, some way, the World Series was tied at two games apiece.

After being left for dead in New York, momentum had undisputedly shifted to Los Angeles's corner. "What a game! Wasn't it? What a game! Oh, boy! Oh, boy!" cried Lasorda, the back of his jersey stained with tobacco juice inadvertently spit there by Howe when the manager hugged him a bit too vigorously after the final out. Adrenaline was everywhere, fueled by equal parts success and relief. Russell probably wouldn't have admitted as much had the Yankees won, but he confessed that "I didn't know if we had it in us."

"It was like a tug-of-war, a teeter-totter of emotions," reflected Monday. "When it was over, both teams were absolutely worn out both physically and mentally."

In the postgame interview room, as Garvey answered questions, Johnstone raced the length of the aisle and, vaulting a table with the cry of "Our favorite hitter!" tackled the first baseman to the floor. Garvey, unperturbable as ever, even with his teammate maintaining a lock on one of his thighs, deadpanned, "As you can see, I'm used to this. He'll be back in the home in two hours."

Before his thumb injury, Graig Nettles might have been the key to New York's World Series success, but in his absence Ron Guidry provided an excellent backup option. The diminutive left-hander with the all-world slider had been tormenting the Dodgers for years, right up through his Game 1 win over Jerry Reuss at Yankee Stadium.

Now it was rematch time, Guidry versus Reuss in Game 5. Apart from Bob Welch's abbreviated tilt in Game 3, it was the first start by a fully rested Dodgers pitcher since rain allowed Fernando Valenzuela to take the hill against the Expos in the final game of the NLCS. This was by design, with Tommy Lasorda making short rest an institutional priority so as to lean on his top three starters while riding a string of elimination games. "The pitchers can rest all winter," he reasoned. "Koufax, Drysdale and them, they worked on three days' rest all summer long." (When somebody brought this up to Reuss later, his response was irrefutable: "Koufax was 31 years old when he retired."*)

Reuss was all too aware of what kind of performance would be necessary to finally best his opponent, but come game time he didn't pitch like it. Not even close. From the very beginning, the left-hander couldn't hit Yeager's target, his ball flying all over the strike zone. Early on, the pitcher's primary hope was that the Yankees would go up hacking.

They did, but it didn't much help. In the second inning, Reggie Jackson stroked a leadoff double down the left-field line, his 11th straight World Series game with a hit—during which time he'd batted .500 with eight home runs, every stitch of that damage coming against the Dodgers. With the leadoff runner in scoring position, Reuss induced the next batter, Bob Watson, to top a grounder to the right of second base—a productive out, something to advance Jackson to third. Then Lopes dropped the ball as he transitioned it to his throwing hand, allowing Watson to reach safely.

The next batter, Lou Piniella, hit a ball into the hole at shortstop, just out of Russell's range, for a single that brought home a clapping Reggie with the game's first run—the fourth time in five games that New York scored first.

Reuss managed to escape without further damage, but found himself back in the muck in the fourth. It began with a leadoff walk to Watson, which appeared to be mitigated when the next man up, Piniella, hit a custom-made double-play grounder to second base. For the second time in the game, however, Lopes lost the handle, bobbling the ball, then bobbling it again, and finally firing it into the Yankees' dugout for his second and third errors of the day, and fourth and fifth

---

* That Koufax was actually 30 made Reuss's comment even more potent. Drysdale hung 'em up at 32.

of the Series. Watson advanced to third, Piniella to second.* With no-body out, Russell kept looking into the dugout for the order to play in, but it never came, and he ended up holding his position. With that kind of depth, Rick Cerone's ensuing grounder to shortstop should have easily scored Watson from third, but for reasons never explained, the base runner didn't budge, allowing Russell to complete the relay to Garvey at first without repercussions. That set up an intentional walk to eighth-place hitter Aurelio Rodríguez, loading the bases with one out and the pitcher coming up.

No squeeze play was ordered, but Guidry, who hadn't picked up a bat since the 1977 World Series, nonetheless laid down a bunt. The ball bounced directly to Reuss, who made an easy throw to Yeager to force Watson at the plate. New York couldn't believe the rate at which its rally was withering. When Randolph followed with a soft tapper to Garvey, it was snuffed entirely. Thanks to the ongoing series of mental errors by the Yankees, LA's deficit remained 1–0.

Lopes was beside himself about his slipshod fielding. Upon reach-ing the dugout, he dropped his glove on the steps and, without break-ing stride, raced directly into the clubhouse. The guy who made two errors all year had become one of the biggest defensive liabilities — statistically anyway — in World Series history and needed a moment of solitary reflection. "You can't hide out there," he explained later. "If you start thinking that way, nine times out of ten the ball comes right to you."

Sure enough, the very next inning a ball did come to him. After Guidry struck out the side in the fourth, Dave Winfield connected

---

* After the World Series, Larry Eldridge of the *Christian Science Monitor* was sufficiently inspired to write a counter to the famous ode to the Cubs infield, "Tinker to Evers to Chance": "The bases are loaded, one out in the ninth / When a grounder lifts Dodger fans' hopes / Just once might they hear those rarest of words: Garvey, from Russell and Lopes? / But no, there's the ball in the outfield grass / While the tying and winning runs score / And up in the press box, his voice filled with gloom / The announcer intones: 'Error-4.'"

for a one-out single — his first hit of the Series — against Reuss in the top of the fifth.* The next hitter, Reggie Jackson, bounded a high two-hopper to second that Lopes, looking up at the bounce, momentarily lost in the daytime glare. Still, he managed to corral the ball near the bag, which he touched for a force-out before completing the relay to first, just in time. "Somebody would have written that it was the first ground ball lost in the sun," he said after the game. "I know if I didn't field that damn ball I would have run straight off the damn field and never come back."

The effort kept the Dodgers close, which was all they needed. Guidry shut LA down on two hits through six innings (none after the second) while striking out eight, by which point he'd retired 14 of the last 15 men he faced. "It looks to me like he's got his best slider in the last month," marveled Jim Palmer on the telecast. In the dugout, Lasorda, watching the left-hander blow away a succession of hitters, recalibrated his strategy. Knowing that the shimmer of day games at Dodger Stadium made pitches difficult to pick up, the manager sidled over to Pedro Guerrero, set to bat second in the seventh inning, for some quick scheming. Slide toward the back end of the batter's box, he told the slugger, to get a better bead on the ball. Like many of his teammates, Guerrero had spent the day swinging at sliders in the dirt, and Lasorda figured that the positioning would help him resist the temptation to swing early at balls that were dropping away from his bat. Swing easy, Lasorda said — go with the pitch instead of against it.

Guerrero had already adjusted his approach once on the day, after spending 15 minutes talking to coach Manny Mota before the game. Mota suggested that he was standing too tall in his stance, rather than utilizing the crouch that had served him so well throughout the sea-

---

* Before he even reached first base, Winfield — 0-for-16 before that point — smilingly signaled that he wanted the ball as a memento. Reuss, who had surrendered Winfield's first-ever hit as a big leaguer back in 1973, was confused, but handed it over nonetheless.

son, so after Dusty Baker struck out to lead off the seventh (Guidry's ninth whiff of the day), Guerrero crept into the rear of the batter's box, crouched low, and waited.

At the far end of the bench, Reuss sat alone, staring at the field. He'd done his best with subpar stuff and pitched his heart out, but he also knew that if his team was unable to do anything offensively, he'd be removed for a pinch-hitter when his spot in the order came up four batters hence. "Goddamn it, just give me a run," he said out loud, to no one in particular. "Tie this up. Keep me in the game."

Guerrero obliged him. He was in many ways the ideal guy to be hitting in this situation, having finished second among Dodgers regulars in batting average, home runs, on-base percentage, and slugging average on the season. It was a breakout campaign for the 25-year-old, but a long time coming for a guy who'd been knocking around the minor leagues since 1973.

Guerrero hailed from sugarcane country in the Dominican Republic, living with his mother, three brothers, and six others in his grandfather's house in San Pedro de Macorís after his father abandoned the family when the lad was eight years old. They had indoor plumbing, but no hot water. Pedro's diet consisted primarily of rice, beans, and bananas that grew on the property. He made it through the eighth grade before joining the workforce, at which point he helped transport giant sacks of sugar for $2.60 per day.

Sugar, of course, is only one of the industries for which San Pedro de Macorís is known. The other is baseball, with stars like Juan Marichal, Rico Carty, and the Alou brothers setting an example around local ballfields about what could happen for those with talent. Manny Mota, another of the ballplaying forebears from Guerrero's hometown, would become a major influence on his career.

In January 1973, when he was 17, Guerrero signed with Cleveland for a $2,500 bonus, but things did not look immediately promising. Assigned to the team's rookie-level Gulf Coast League franchise in Sarasota, Florida, he found himself living in a motel, unable to speak the language. None of his teammates were from Latin America. Depressed and slumping, the only reason he didn't pack it in, he said, was because he "had nothing to go home to."

And then: providence. The man who scouted Guerrero for the Indians, Reggie Otero, was hired away by the Dodgers and urged Al Campanis to acquire the kid. Soon thereafter, Los Angeles sent minor league pitcher Bruce Ellingsen to Cleveland in a one-for-one swap. It was one of the best trades Campanis ever made.

Guerrero ended up in the minors for seven years—the last two shuttling back and forth between Albuquerque and Los Angeles—and hit .300 or better six times. Frustration at his lack of major league opportunities grew so pronounced that he began to alternate threats to quit with demands to be traded. It was Mota—who, like Guerrero, spent the better part of seven seasons in the minors before getting an opportunity—who most frequently talked him down from the ledge. He knew whereof he counseled.

It was only after Guerrero ran out of minor league options in 1980 that the 24-year-old found himself in Los Angeles to stay. He collected 199 plate appearances that season, batting .322 with seven homers while filling in at first, second, third, and all three outfield positions. In 1981 he was an All-Star. And now he was coming to bat with one out in the seventh inning of Game 5, his team trailing, 1–0, on the wrong end of a two-hitter. Guerrero positioned himself as Lasorda suggested. He crouched low, like Mota had said. He looked for something up in the zone.

With Guidry's second pitch, he got it: an 86-mile-per-hour slider that didn't do quite enough sliding. Guerrero pounced, sending the ball on a line deep into the left-field bleachers.* Just like that, the

* The on-deck hitter, Steve Yeager, didn't even see it happen. The weighted bat he'd been swinging near the dugout fell apart at the worst possible moment, its end disengaging and rolling toward the grandstand just before Guerrero's blast. "[Commissioner Bowie Kuhn] was watching the bat fall apart, and I was watch-

game was tied, 1–1, on only the third hit Guidry had given up. "Wow," thought Reuss on the bench. "Maybe I should've asked for a tie game sooner."

The next hitter, Steve Yeager, had already taken Guidry deep once, in Game 1 at Yankee Stadium. Then, he'd taken advantage of a fastball to his liking, a detail about which the pitcher was obviously paying attention. This time around Yeager saw a steady stream of sliders. The catcher watched the first two sail past, one for a strike, one for a ball, and missed badly with a swing at the third. Despite having hit only five homers in the previous two seasons combined, Yeager was considered to be the best batting-practice power hitter on the team, mainly because he would ask for nothing but waist-high fastballs, then murder them into the bleachers. Such success rarely followed him into games, given that he rarely saw such pitches when opponents were actually trying to get him out. Down in the count, however, Yeager knew what he wanted. He adjusted his helmet and set his sights on a fastball.

Guidry delivered as hoped, which is how a backup catcher who'd batted .209 on the season and barely played over the first two rounds of the playoffs connected for his third hit of the Series — and his second homer — against one of the best pitchers in the sport, planting the pitch for which he'd been so impatiently waiting very near to where Guerrero's had only recently landed. In the span of two hitters, the Dodgers went from hopeless to ahead, 2–1. "If he had thrown another slider, I was history," admitted Yeager — whose World Series batting average sat at .349 — after the game.

Guidry retired the next two hitters without incident and retreated to the dugout with hopes that his teammates could find a way over the final two innings to mitigate his brief bout of ineffectiveness. On LA's side of the field, Reuss went into the routine he employed when the

---

ing him watch me," said Yeager after the game. "I didn't see Pete until he was rounding second base. I guess the Commissioner missed it too."

Dodgers led late, starting a process he called The Countdown, where he would meticulously consider every possibility for each upcoming hitter — how he would pitch to them in different counts, with various permutations of base runners. "I redid the whole scouting report, because now I'm pitching with a lead as opposed to trying to maintain," the left-hander explained later. "When you're pitching from behind, you just try to keep things close. But when you're pitching with the mentality of holding the score, you've got to take charge of it. It was up to me to control the game."* Reuss was alert in ways both familiar and new. Time slowed. He took note of the hitter's feet, the way Yeager flashed his signs, how plate umpire Rich Garcia set up behind the catcher. He knew what he wanted to do.

The Los Angeles scouting report, put together by lead scout Charlie Metro, urged an abundance of breaking balls against New York hitters, but in Game 1 Reuss had surrendered four runs over two and a third innings using that approach. So he audibled. "I decided that if I was going to win, I was going to win with what made me successful, and that's the fastball," the left-hander admitted in the postgame clubhouse.† Hurling heater after heater — "I don't think he threw more

---

* It was Reuss's first lead since the fourth inning of Game 3 against the Expos — a game the Dodgers lost — and taking charge helped him remain grounded. "I'm fighting the adrenaline, 56,000 on their feet, and considering the boyhood dream," Reuss said. "There's a lot going on in your head."

† Afterword, Metro was heated, not only at Reuss's blatant disregard of the coach's pregame preparation, but at his public discussion of it. After the pitcher's comments were published, Metro lit into him. "Why did you rip us because of your misgivings in Game 1?" he asked. "You blamed us and our scouting reports for throwing all those curveballs that you couldn't get over!" In an effort to diffuse a potentially explosive situation, Reuss demurred. "Charlie, it wasn't you at all, it was the Yankees hitters that got me," he said. "It was my location. I saw that I couldn't get them out with breaking balls, even though you suggested it, and so I went with what I could do." Metro grudgingly accepted the explanation, but after accepting a position with Billy Martin's Oakland A's the following season, he never spoke to Reuss again.

than two or three curveballs," Yeager said afterward—Reuss retired 12 of the final 13 Yankees he faced, 17 total on grounders, while striking out six. "The pressure increased, hitter by hitter," he reflected. "I could sense it in the crowd, I could sense it on the field. There's an electricity, and everybody feels it. I was thriving off of their electricity. What a great place to be, mentally: *I am what's happening in the world of baseball at this moment.*"

With two outs in the ninth, Reuss struck out Rodríguez on three pitches to make it official: the 2–1 victory gave Los Angeles a three-games-to-two lead and put the Dodgers on the cusp of a championship.

After the Dodgers lost the first two games at Yankee Stadium, it was impossible to ignore that it had been New York in such a position back in '78, dropping a pair in LA before sweeping four straight for the title. Further bolstering the Dodgers' hopes was that Hooton and Valenzuela were primed for action as the Series headed back to the Bronx. It would have been a storybook ending but for one detail. With two outs in the eighth inning of Game 5, Goose Gossage sent a 94-mile-per-hour fastball directly into the side of Ron Cey's head.

Cey had been determined to stand strong against Gossage's heat, no matter what, and dug accordingly into the box. By the time he was able to recognize where the pitch was headed—at first it looked to him like a backdoor slider with late break—it was too late to bail. "The ball just followed me, like a magnet," he said later. Helmets with earflaps had been mandatory in Little League since 1958 and used regularly in the majors since Phillies outfielder Tony González first wore one in 1964. Cey, however, used an old-style flapless bowl, and the ball connected close to the brimline, knocking the helmet backward as the ball ricocheted past the visitors' dugout and into the first-base field boxes.* As Cey crumpled, the Dodger Stadium crowd of 56,115 fell im-

---

* Cey's explanation for why he liked the flap-free helmet: "There's a different sound the ball makes coming off the bat when you have an ear flap. It doesn't

mediately into silence. Gossage later described the sound of the impact as being "very loud . . . like it had hit a hollow log." Dusty Baker, on deck, compared it to a cannon shot. Rick Monday could hear it clearly from the bullpen. Plate umpire Rich Garcia frantically waved to the Dodgers' dugout for help.

"[Cey] was conscious the whole time," reported Yankees catcher Rick Cerone, the first man on the scene. "He didn't say a whole lot, but I heard him say, 'It feels numb over here,' pointing to the left side of his head. And then I heard some of the Dodgers saying, 'Thank God for helmets.'"

As Cey lay on his back, team trainers Bill Buhler and Paul Padilla spoke quietly to him, trying to assess the extent of the damage. "His eyes were making circles," recalled Padilla. "There was a fear about what was going on within him, confusion. It was a concussion for sure." The first goal of the medical staff was to make sure that Cey didn't pass out. They asked him questions — Where are you? What day is it? — that he had trouble answering. "What do I look like?" the player asked. "Am I all right?" Cey didn't move for four long minutes, after which Buhler and Padilla helped him to his feet and led him through the dugout and down the tunnel to the clubhouse. There, Cey's wife, Fran, who'd been near hysterics after watching the incident from the loge seats behind home plate, was rushed to his side. "I thought you were dead," she cried. Cey's response — "I'm okay" — was true inasmuch as he was not dead. How he would be for the rest of the Series, however, remained to be seen. The Penguin, wearing a turban of bandages to hold a bag of ice in place atop his skull, momentarily lost his balance as he was getting dressed. About an hour after the game — the wait designed to avoid traffic should an unexpected devel-

---

sound as if you're hitting the ball as well as you should be, and for some people it can be a psychological factor."

opment occur — he was taken to Centinela Hospital Medical Center for testing.*

Throughout both clubhouses, Cey's beaning merited nearly as much conversation as the game's outcome. "Imagine what it would be without that helmet," said Gossage, still in shock, as he emphatically denied intention behind the placement of the pitch. Said Davey Lopes: "Anybody who throws that hard would have to be nuts to throw at someone." Gossage's teammate Rudy May put it in starker terms, saying, "Nobody digs in against Goose. They know that if his fastball gets away from him they're DOA with a tag on their toe."

When hospital reports came back clean, Cey was sent home for the night, his wife under orders to wake him every two hours to test his alertness. A visit to the neurologist was scheduled for the morning, with hopes that the third baseman would receive permission to catch up with the rest of the Dodgers, who had already boarded the team jet for Game 6 at Yankee Stadium.

"He'll play in New York if he can remember his name," Fran Cey told reporters in the hallway outside the clubhouse just before departing with her husband for the hospital. It sounded good in the moment anyway. Putting it into action would be a battle for another day.

Somehow, despite the abundance of compelling story lines from Game 5 — Cey's beaning, the pitchers' duel, the astonishing back-to-back homers, LA's rousing comeback to take a three-games-to-two lead as the Series headed back to New York — the focus ended up on

---

* The doctor unexpectedly stopped the CAT scan machine during Cey's second pass. "I instantly changed my mind about whether things were okay," the third baseman reflected. "They pulled me out, and were not putting me back in. I'm saying to myself, 'Oh my God, what in the world did they find?' I saw my life in front of me, ending up in a wheelchair, crazy thoughts." Finally, the doctor emerged and informed the ballplayer that they were simply double-checking the results, and that everything looked good. There's value in bedside manner, as it turns out.

George Steinbrenner. Some people have a way of making that kind of thing happen.

After the game, it was reported that the 51-year-old Yankees owner got into a physical altercation with a pair of Dodgers fans in Los Angeles. The evidence was borne across his face and beyond: a cut lip, a lump on his head, a variety of bruises, and a plaster cast on his left hand.

As Steinbrenner told it, he was riding an elevator to the lobby of the Hyatt Wilshire Hotel when he was joined by a 20-something male sporting a Dodgers cap, who held the door for a friend down the hallway. When the fan made an unkind comment about the Yankees — "You're going back to the animals in New York now, and you're taking your choked-up team with you," Steinbrenner recalled him saying — the owner responded by taking a swing at the guy. The fan reportedly responded by hitting him in the side of the head with a beer bottle, which Steinbrenner countered with a straight right hand that felled his assailant. When the guy's friend swooped in, the Boss offered up a left hook — a blow "that felt like it loosened a couple of his teeth and knocked him off the elevator," the owner told reporters. When it was over, Steinbrenner said later, one of the guys was sitting and the other was on his back. "It's not like an old man like me to do this," the owner shrugged. With his attackers disabled, Steinbrenner arranged his jacket, smoothed his hair, and decamped for the ground floor, to meet executives Cedric Tallis and Bill Bergesch for dinner.*

---

* The *Los Angeles Times* did a thorough investigation, detailing the number of elevators in the bank (three), their size (six-by-six), and their interior design (a combination of mirrored paneling and upholstery). Among the key conclusions: it took about 14 seconds for an elevator to travel from the seventh floor, where Steinbrenner said he was accosted, to the lobby — not a lot of time for an argument and a fight. Various people — a cab driver outside the hotel who picked up some drunken Dodgers partisans at about that time, some Yankees fans who later called in to sports-radio talk shows — stepped forward over coming days to offer shaky accounts of the aftermath. The most believable tale had Steinbrenner being verbally accosted on the elevator as previously described, but punching

The problem with Steinbrenner's story, apart from the notion that an out-of-shape, middle-aged man — even one who had boxed some as a youth at Culver Military Academy in Indiana — could take down two young antagonists in an enclosed space, let alone after being clocked by a bottle, was that nobody saw it happen. Not before the fight. Not during the fight. Not after the fight. Steinbrenner never filed a police report, and his assailants were never identified.* "We're still looking for those two guys," said Monday dismissively, decades later.

"I knew what Steinbrenner was doing," said Reuss, looking back. "He did what Donald Trump did in the election. He was working people. He wanted the attention on him, and he would do things that made people hate him, which didn't matter because they were *aware* of him. He kept people on their toes, and he got the results he wanted."†

Steinbrenner's true motivation may have been on display during the 11:00 p.m. press conference he called in New York following his team's flight east. That's where, determined not to let the details of his team's collapse dominate media coverage, he spilled the beans on the entire affair. On Monday, the *New York Post* blared a headline reading "Yank Boss Brawls with LA Fans." Mission accomplished.

On Monday and Tuesday, it rained. Game 6 was called before the teams even reached Yankee Stadium.

---

a wall, not a Dodger fan, in frustration. Another theory held that Steinbrenner busted himself up intentionally, to bolster a story he hoped might motivate his players.

* Reported *Sports Illustrated*: "If nothing else, Steinbrenner should be credited with selecting the most original venue for fisticuffs in baseball history. George may very well be the first brawler to ask his antagonists to step *inside*. Knocked down going up? Floored between floors? Out, please." The *Toronto Globe and Mail* saw fit to mention that "the injury is not expected to hamper his managing."

† Reuss wasn't the only Dodger to compare Steinbrenner to the 45th president while looking back at the '81 season. "There's a lot of George in Trump, and a lot of Trump in George," said Steve Garvey.

With no ball to be played in the Big Apple, the Dodgers had time for some sightseeing, and reporters had time to catch up with the minutiae of the series, starting with the ballpark. With the left-field fence at Yankee Stadium stretching as far as 430 feet from the plate, home runs were much harder to come by for right-handed hitters than in Los Angeles — and the Dodgers were stacked with right-handed power. Yeager said that the homer he hit to win Game 5 would have amounted to "a can of outs" had it been struck in New York.

Cey, meanwhile, traveled to Manhattan a day later than his teammates, and though he was still struggling to recover from concussion symptoms, he was buoyed by the fact that the abundant autumn rain increased his chances of a timely return. Every day delayed was another day closer. Cey awoke Tuesday with thoughts of availability, but while resting in his hotel room he rolled across the bed to answer the phone and was stunned when he was barely able to make it. "I was literally within a second of picking it up and saying, 'Get me a doctor,'" he recalled. "Just rolling over made me so dizzy that it shocked me." The feeling quickly subsided, but it was clear that had baseball been played that evening, Cey would not have been able to participate.

With no other place to be, the third baseman ended up explaining his situation to reporters in the coffee shop at the New York Sheraton. "It's strange what turns your life can take," he said, edging toward the philosophical. "Sunday, the only thing that mattered was playing that game. Today, the only thing that matters is that I'm sitting here, no blood clot, no fractured skull. Your priorities change. You realize how your whole world can change in one instant." Cey would dress for the following day's game, he said, only if he felt marked improvement. "I'm not going to endanger myself," he proclaimed, "no matter how much I want to play."

He also added that he'd be wearing an earflapped helmet from that point forward, even if he had to get one from "a local sporting goods store."

• • •

Wednesday was dry. There would be baseball.

Ron Cey had plenty to consider. The off-day had done him well. He was feeling good. Maybe even good enough to play. He left the Sheraton early and flagged down a cab, not to the ballpark but to Central Park. Back home, the Penguin used his commute as thinking time, silent travel during which he'd consider the game ahead. "Getting into my frame of mind," is how he put it. Without a car of his own in New York, Cey told the cabbie to drive around the park for a bit. He wanted to figure out with certainty not only whether he'd be going to the stadium later that day with the intention of playing, but to make sure that if he did — *when* he did — he went about it the right way. "I didn't want to leave anything uncovered until I was comfortable with it," he said later. The moment he reached that point, he was ready. "Take me to Yankee Stadium," he told the driver.

Cey arrived at about 1:30 p.m., well ahead of his teammates, and began to assess. He did some light jogging, tossed a ball around. His head felt okay. When Lasorda arrived, the Penguin had yet to hit or take infield, two vital tests, and the manager wasted no time informing him that he'd leave the fourth spot in the lineup open, just in case. Which didn't mean that he was in any way willing to be patient about it. "How are you feeling now?" Lasorda asked when Cey took the field, only minutes after the manager had lodged an identical query in the clubhouse. "I'm *fine*," Cey told him. "Just leave me alone." The Penguin began running bases two at a time, pushing game pace to make sure that his head could withstand the strain. When he picked up a bat, along with a new earflapped helmet, Lasorda sidled up to the cage (like a "shadow dog," Cey said later) and watched his putative cleanup hitter foul a pitch back, take one, foul another, and then hit a shot into deep left-center field. "How's it going?" Lasorda pleaded like a kid in the backseat, asking his parents how much longer until they arrived. "How do you feel? What do you think?" Cey appreciated his manager's fervor, but not its overtness. He had not yet reached a decision. "When we're done," he said firmly, "I'll come and see you." Lasorda nodded glumly and retreated to his office.

Ten minutes later, the Penguin walked through the door and held his hand, palm out, above his head for a high-five. He was in.

By that point, the rest of the Dodgers had arrived and were taking the field for warm-ups.* As they did, the PA system at Yankee Stadium blared "The Way We Were," a seemingly innocuous Barbra Streisand song from the 1973 movie of the same name. It would have gone completely unnoticed (and almost certainly unplayed) had the Dodgers — well, one Dodger anyway — not carried an inadvertent and entirely uncomfortable connection to the song. It was in rotation under direct orders from George Steinbrenner, who wanted to emphasize the wife-sized hole that had recently appeared in Steve Garvey's all-American veneer. The song was cowritten by Marvin Hamlisch, who, notably, was dating the first baseman's soon-to-be-ex, Cyndy, and would shortly share an apartment with her on the Upper East Side, not far from the ballpark. As far as the Yankees were concerned, any opportunity to get Garvey off his game was worth a shot. The first baseman was hitting .429 in the Series, his nine hits more than double every player save for Bob Watson. He did this despite constant public reminders about how his family — Cyndy, along with his two young daughters — were making new lives for themselves just south of where the Dodgers were, at that moment, warming up.

From the very beginning, the Garveys' marriage was storybook

---

* Those Dodgers who weren't around for the 1977 and 1978 World Series were stunned by the batting practice display put on by Reggie Jackson. Not the balls he was hitting, but the timing of when he hit them. The slugger reserved the final BP slot for himself, the better to put on a show for his adoring fans, going so far as to call his extended session "Reggie Time." LA players who weren't aware of this thought that he was simply trying to psyche them out, and laughed at the audacity.

stuff. Cyndy embodied the SoCal ideal — pretty, trim, blond, and perpetually smiling, a model who hosted a local TV talk show with Regis Philbin. They were college sweethearts, Steve and Cyndy, looking, wrote *Playboy* in 1981, "frighteningly like human versions of the Ken and Barbie dolls." With the birth of their children, they evolved from the perfect American couple into the perfect American family.

That changed in 1980, when *Inside Sports* ran a cover story that the couple had been led to believe would be a typically flattering portrait of their idealized life together. Instead, it exposed — and occasionally inflated — cracks in their facade. Titled "Trouble in Paradise," the piece was 12,000 words' worth of muckraking sensationalism by journalist and former minor leaguer Pat Jordan. It dished on their decor ("Everything in this house looked the same . . . Disposable. Objects with no real past"), Cyndy's looks ("Pretty in the manner of a Miss America contestant. Undistinguished. Lacquered"), Cyndy's attitude toward her looks ("'I don't try to look this way. I just always was glamorous'"), and even the couple's amiability ("Nice in that bland, middle American conception of niceness").

The story painted an unnecessarily mean — though not necessarily inaccurate — picture of a troubled marriage that, until the magazine came out, few people knew was troubled. Rather than using Steve and Cyndy's names, Jordan referred to them as "the wife" and "the husband," even in contexts that had nothing to do with their relationship. But what really set the rumor mills aflame was the overwhelming discontent that poured from Cyndy Garvey onto the page, some of it under a banner reading: *The Problem*. "Go try to sleep with it," she said, bemoaning the gilded trappings of her life with an absentee husband. "There's always a dark moment when you want to make love to someone and there's no one there."

Cyndy maintained that she was "much more sexual" than Steve, claimed that her husband was "like a brother to me," said "I want a man when I want one," and talked about getting involved "with a lover somewhere."* She wondered about cashing in on their marriage "in order to find something more fulfilling." The story was serialized in the *Los Angeles Herald Examiner* and quoted in the *Los Angeles Times*. There was no escaping it.

Its publication may have brought the rapid dissolution of the Garveys' marriage into the public light, but it did manage to unite Steve and Cyndy in at least one respect: they both disputed the details therein and used them to at least partially explain why their relationship didn't last. That September, just as the Dodgers were preparing for the playoffs, the couple announced Cyndy's move to New York and Steve's decision to remain alone in Los Angeles to focus on baseball, the thing he was best at anyway.

The Garveys ended up suing *Newsweek*, the publisher of *Inside Sports*, for $11.2 million, citing invasion of privacy and breach of contract, but upon recognizing their long chances of success, settled for what Steve Garvey described as "pretty much [breaking] even on expenses and legal fees." *Newsweek* claimed to have paid out $112,000, or one penny on the dollar.

Beset by the swirling drama of his private life, Garvey batted .283 in 1981, his lowest mark since becoming a regular by almost 15 points. His teammates couldn't help but notice. "He was lost," noted Dusty Baker the following spring. "He looked lost at the plate. He didn't know a fastball from a curveball. I asked him, 'Hey, Garv, what's wrong?' He said, 'I'll tell you.' But he never did. There is no one he can release to. That's one of the problems."

---

* Perhaps in response, Steve Garvey discussed the idea of having an affair in a Q&A with *Playboy* the following June, several months before the couple's split was announced: "It's a feeling I've had for, gosh, a couple of years now. Anything is possible. But given the relationship I have with my wife and the feelings we have for each other, the odds against it are lopsided. Of course, I've had thoughts about having an affair, but, in essence, the actuality has never happened. I'm still basically a romantic."

That Garvey had nobody to release to *was* a problem. His allies in the clubhouse insisted that the guy was genuine, that his perpetually smiling, noncursing, sign-every-autograph, kiss-all-the-nuns-and-babies style wasn't some public front but buried within his DNA. "Garvey is the same everywhere," insisted Jay Johnstone. "The butter melting out of his mouth, the apple pie hanging out of his back pocket, the flag on his car."

Garvey's detractors rarely argued in the opposite direction so much as they pointed out that, despite any authentic motivation behind Garvey's actions, their execution frequently came off as contrived. Take the first baseman's approach toward children. Calling them "the real backbone of this country," he said in 1980 that "making a child smile is the key to life." Garvey harkened back to his own childhood and being in awe when Gil Hodges took the time to play catch with the batboy son of the team bus driver. "That behavior — the kindness, the responsiveness to the fans — said all the more to me when contrasted with the actions of those players who didn't sign autographs, who had no time for the people," wrote Garvey in his 1986 autobiography, *Garvey*. Which itself was part of the puzzle. It was less Garvey's willingness to play catch with a youngster that rankled teammates than his need to grandstand about it. It was image cultivation in its most blatant form, an affront that no amount of genuine goodwill on Garvey's part seemed able to mitigate.

"Garvey was very careful in what he said," said Mark Heisler, who covered the team for the *Los Angeles Times*. "You just never got a lot that was human. You didn't get despair, you didn't get ecstasy — you got a programmed version of reactions. This is the way I handle good news, this is the way I handle bad news."

"Garvey's image was real," posited Chris Mortensen, "but it felt like he had written his own script for himself."

Once, said Cyndy, she caught her husband practicing a variety of facial expressions in front of their bedroom mirror. "Practicing being an All-American, Steve?" she asked. The media lapped it up. In 1976,

Garvey appeared on the cover of *Sport* magazine eating an apple pie decorated with American flags, with the associated story headlined: "Steve Garvey Can't Help It if He's Perfect." "With his boyish brush cut and his square-jawed handsomeness," the magazine reported, "Steve would be ideal for any number of products." A year earlier the *San Bernardino County Sun* wrote: "If Steve Garvey ever grew out of his Dodger uniform, he could always be fitted for vestments."*

Making time for such reportage was one thing, but asking whether the story would be on the cover struck teammates as too much. Doing a TV interview with Howard Cosell over the objections of Tommy Lasorda, and then referring to teammates' negative reactions to it as "jealousy" further eroded goodwill.† Taken as a whole, it was clear that those Dodgers who cared most about their own images — who thirsted for their due as successful ballplayers — were the ones who held firmest to this particular grudge. "Sometimes you feel they get caught up more with selling the product than with playing it," reflected Don Sutton in 1984. "There's a tendency within the organization to want players to be extroverted salesmen."

Things reached an almost unbelievable crescendo in 1978, when Lindsay, California, a citrus farming community about 170 miles north of Los Angeles, named its junior high school after Garvey. The rundown building housed a troubled brew of townies and farmworkers' children, and the administration wanted a fresh start. "Steve Garvey

---

* In a 1982 cover story titled "As Always, a Man of Principle," *Sports Illustrated* described Garvey's clean-cut profile with an example of his humor. "His idea of a risqué joke is right out of Tampa, 1956," wrote William Knack. "*What do you do with an elephant with three balls?* 'What?' you ask. *You walk him and then pitch to the giraffe.*"

† Jealousy was an ongoing topic for Garvey. In the 1981 *Playboy* interview, he recalled failing in his efforts to run for school office. "I was a perennial vice president," he said. "A lot of the times I ran for office, kids said, 'Hey, Steve's involved in a lot of things. I'll vote for the other guy.' I remember there was a certain amount of jealousy — *always*. I could feel that even then."

Junior High" had a nice ring to it, and who was the humble first baseman to refuse such a request? The fact that the school had previously
been named for Abraham Lincoln was, scoffed numerous teammates,
fitting. All hail the new American hero.*

Some of the laudatory comments from a fawning press hurt Garvey's standing for reasons entirely beyond his own control. In a
reverential profile in 1980, for example, the *Saturday Evening Post*
contrasted Garvey ("the noblest example of all") with the boorish behavior of other Dodgers, providing comparisons that the rest of the
team couldn't help but resent:

> How, indeed, could a wide-eyed youngster idolize shortstop Bill
> Russell after listening to him obscenely jeer a Dodgertown em-
> ployee through an open bus window in the presence of several
> cringing women? Would he watch himself in a mirror to emulate
> the sullen demeanor of Davey Lopes, the perennial All-Star sec-
> ond baseman who demonstrated his dissatisfaction by resigning
> the Dodger captaincy last year? Or would he appreciate the sight
> of sneaker-clad manager Tom Lasorda telling long-winded, ego-
> tistical tales aboard the Dodger plane and at the Dodgertown bar,
> while his passing players openly mock his spreading paunch and
> gluttonous eating habits? The team's lack of class spreads all the
> way to the front office, as even publicity department flack Steve
> Brener proves arrogant and uncommunicative to visiting jour-
> nalists.

LA's clubhouse dynamic was fully exposed in 1975, when the *San
Bernardino County Sun* ran a feature containing numerous quotes
about Garvey from teammates — Cey and Lopes allowed their names
to be used; others did not — about just how fractured the first baseman's relationship with much of the roster actually was. Lopes said
that eight men in the starting lineup approached baseball as a game,
while Garvey saw it "more as a business."† Cey added that "basically

---

* The school shut down in 2011.

† Garvey himself admitted to at least partial motivation along such lines, saying

everyone knows he's a public-relations man." It wasn't that Garvey didn't drink much—it was his judgmental looks toward those who did. It wasn't that he refused to curse, but that he made known his disapproval of the practice.* He couldn't even carpool to the stadium with teammates from his neighborhood, less because of personality conflicts than the fact that none of them were willing to wait out the requisite postgame media sessions that Garvey held long after everybody else had wrapped up. When the team traveled, Garvey frequently rode in the bus used by coaches and the press, steering far away from the rest of the players. On airplanes, he sat up front, alone, going through fan mail, doing paperwork, and reading magazines. He was spotted in bars on the road, briefcase in hand, a stack of eight-by-ten photos of himself at the ready to pass out to whichever members of his adoring public might want one. This approach may have worked for the care and maintenance of Garvey's image, but it did increasingly little to endear him to teammates. Players threw parties to which he was not invited. Garvey admitted to being spurned after home runs, to feeling ostracized and alone on the bench. Some players went so far as to applaud when he was thrown out trying to bunt for a hit. "It was really a hallmark of that team how much Garvey was resented by his teammates," said Heisler.

"He knows he's not really understood enough to let his hair down in public," said Yeager. "I've been with him when I know he wanted to have a few more cocktails, and he couldn't. He knows that instead of being X-rated, his jokes have to be PG. The Steve Garvey I see occasionally is the one who tries to be funny and can't. Who tries to mingle with the guys, and, because of his own feelings, can't."

---

in 1980 that "the more exposure you get, the more popular you are and the more people will pay to see you and the more money you'll make. That's just good business sense."

* Once leading Steve Yeager, out at a restaurant while the two were playing in the Dominican Winter League, to charge at him headlong.

"He wants to be one of the guys," added Reggie Smith, "but his personality won't let him."

This all came as a shock to a viewing public who to that point had been fed a vision of harmony among the Dodgers — and to Garvey himself, who, while understanding that he'd be hard-pressed to win a clubhouse popularity contest, at least figured that his teammates respected his good-guy image. He was wrong. Even his response to the story — calling a team meeting to address the issue — fell flat. Instead of explaining his behavior and opening a dialogue to help him understand how he came off to the rest of the Dodgers, Garvey delivered what one player described as a "Boy Scout speech on unity."

Even the first baseman's approach on the field rankled, as his embrace of 300-200-100 — his annual target of a .300 batting average, 200 hits, and 100 RBIs — painted him in some teammates' eyes as putting his own success above that of the group. Garvey's response that such a stat line would invariably help the Dodgers win games gained little traction. The fact that he relentlessly chased RBIs — frequently swinging at pitches out of the strike zone with runners on base in an effort to drive in runs, rather than taking a walk and leaving it to the next guy in the order — earned additional antipathy, especially from those batting behind him.* "Steve didn't have any malice in him," said Peter Schmuck of the *Orange County Register*. "He wasn't going around behind people's backs and undercutting them. But he had these little things he did, like always flipping the ball to the pitcher on ground balls to first, even if he could run them there himself. People suspected that he did that so he would have a high assist total, which would give the impression that he had a good arm. That was the suspicion anyway."

Garvey openly theorized that he'd be better suited for an individual sport, like tennis. In 1978, the *Los Angeles Times* reinforced the sen-

---

* Garvey averaged 33 bases on balls per 162 games over the course of his career.

timent with an expansive feature headlined "The Isolation of Steve Garvey, Mr. Clean."

Garvey took to hanging out with the team's flakier members, like Reuss and Johnstone, or kids, like Sax. Lasorda loved him.* Dusty Baker, whose affection for Garvey helped perhaps more than anything to prop up the first baseman's clubhouse standing, said: "The number one question is, 'Is he for real? Is he really that nice? That straight?' People either love him or don't believe him." The players to whom Garvey was close shared a common trait: none had risen through the minor leagues with him, and thus did not carry long-term resentments.

Garvey sought to dispel increasing awareness of this discord by sitting down for an interview with *Playboy*, published in June 1981, the motivation for which he explained within the interview itself: "The reason I'm doing the *Playboy* interview is so people will get a better idea of Steve Garvey's thoughts and opinions, and know that I am sincere in my feelings about myself and my family and the people that I associate with and how much I truly respect and enjoy being an American in this country."† As far as many of the Dodgers were concerned, it was just more of the same.

The nadir of Garvey's relationship with teammates offered a direct connection to his 1981 troubles. In 1978, with the team in New York, the first baseman got into a physical confrontation with Don Sutton,

---

* Let this quote from Lasorda, delivered during the 1981 World Series, suffice: "I've known Steve Garvey since 1968, and I can say this about him: The only time anybody has ever disliked him is because they were jealous of him. They call Steve Garvey the All-American boy. They say he's too perfect to be true, that nobody can be that perfect. Well, let me tell you, it's not a front. If you were around him every day you would know that he's real. This is one hell of a man, and one hell of a ballplayer."

† He also mentioned that his greatest moment was telling a quadriplegic girl, just moments before game time, that he'd try to get a hit for her — on Nuns' Day at Dodger Stadium, no less — and then went 5-for-5.

spurred by a *Washington Post* report in which the pitcher said, "All you ever hear on our team is Steve Garvey, the All-American boy. Well, the best player on this team for the last two years — and we all know it — is Reggie Smith. As Reggie Smith goes, so goes us. Reggie doesn't go out and publicize himself. He doesn't smile at the right people or say the right things. He tells the truth, even if it sometimes alienates people. Reggie is not a facade, or a Madison Avenue image. He is a real person."

When Garvey confronted Sutton about it in the visitors' clubhouse at Shea Stadium the following day, the pitcher brought up Cyndy's name among his list of grievances, along with alleged inflammatory statements about her fidelity. At that point, Garvey, who'd made a career out of avoiding confrontation, had no choice. If he didn't stand up to this, he wouldn't stand up to anything. Soon, the pair were wrestling each other to the floor, fists swinging wildly until they were separated. Garvey emerged with a bloodshot eye and scratches on his face. "I'm human," he explained to the press afterward. "I can only take so much. I can take a lot of things, but when my family is mentioned, that's going too far."*

Which is part of what made the revelations several years later about the dissolution of Garvey's marriage so startling. Steve had long lauded Cyndy as his bedrock, their relationship a foundation for his life and career. So when reports emerged about Captain America's habit of bedding women who were not his wife, an obvious response followed. This was the guy who in 1975 had proclaimed that "self-control is the biggest thing I have going for me," and that "somebody who

---

* Sutton eventually issued a public apology, not for what he said, but for "the tone in which it came out." The Dodgers went 22-11 in the aftermath, increasing their lead in the National League West from one game to eight and a half games, during which Garvey hit safely in 20 straight, eclipsing the 200-hit plateau for the fourth straight season.

concentrates and is under control can therefore control himself and also the situation."

Self-control? Concentration? If Garvey couldn't even control his marriage, why was he still being held up as a public paragon? During the World Series, there would be no avoiding it. Instead of concentrating strictly on the Yankees, the first baseman found himself forced into steady public discourse about familial loss. He lamented that he was "no longer married to a wonderful wife and mother." In trying to explain how he continued to perform amid such personal mayhem, he compared his separation to that of church and state, saying, "State is my profession; church is my private life." He noted that he'd always had the ability to minimize distractions, even while admitting that the current development in his life was next-level stuff. "There's no way that you block it all off," admitted the king of compartmentalization. "There is no privacy for me now."

Never mind their three-game winning streak, or the fact that they were, for the first time, up in the Series—the Dodgers wanted every edge they could get. This is why Davey Lopes and Steve Yeager showed up shaggy for Game 6, having vowed not to shave following the team's two opening losses. Yeager described it as wanting to be "scruffy-looking, dog-eating guys," a plan limited in scope by the fact that nobody else saw fit to join them. If totems were what it took to shake a string of World Series failures running four deep—losses to the Orioles in 1966, the A's in 1974, and the Yankees in 1977 and 1978—then totems it would be.

Somehow, in 32 trips to the Fall Classic, the Yankees had never lost in six games.* Extending that streak to 33 would set up a Game 7 rematch of Valenzuela versus Righetti, but the Dodgers did not want to let things get that far. For that they had Burt Hooton, the last LA pitcher to win in the Bronx—in Game 2 of the 1977 Series—on the

---

* They'd won six times in six.

mound. The right-hander sought to avenge an undeserved loss in Game 2, when his six innings of three-hit, one-unearned-run ball were outshone by Tommy John's seven shutout frames. Now Hooton and John, the former teammates, were at it again.

The first time around, Hooton was removed with nobody out in the seventh after precisely 100 pitches. He spent the ensuing days talking about the importance of efficiency, and how dominant pitchers worked deep into games. Then he went out and walked the leadoff hitter in Game 6, Willie Randolph, on a full count. It wasn't exactly the start he'd pictured, especially after Randolph stole second. With the Dodgers on the cusp of a championship, however, the Texan was not much for bending. Pitching out of the stretch, he retired Jerry Mumphrey on a fly ball to center field, then got Winfield to line out to Baker in left. Even Reggie Jackson, with four hits in seven World Series at-bats since returning from his leg injury, was no match for the right-hander's sudden fire, striking out swinging to end the inning. Early threat over.

Still, it was quickly clear that Hooton was without his best stuff. The right-hander found trouble again in the third, again at the hands of Randolph, who this time sent a low fastball just beyond the wall in left for a two-out homer, his second of the Series — not bad output for a guy who hit two or fewer homers in 10 of what would eventually be 18 big league seasons. It gave the Yankees an early lead, and they weren't finished. The next hitter, Mumphrey, singled to right. That brought up Winfield — not a good development on the surface, given that the slugger had made five straight All-Star teams and was batting third in New York's lineup. Then again, Winfield was 1-for-19 to that point in the Series and looking increasingly lost at the plate. In that regard, there was nobody Hooton wanted to face more.

He walked Winfield on four pitches.

Suddenly, the guy striding toward the plate for the Yankees was the guy the Dodgers *least* wanted to see, Reggie Jackson, who was hitting .500 with a double and a homer in two-plus games. It was the second time in the game that Mr. October had come up with runners on base, and Hooton made sure it was the second time that Mr. October failed to deliver, inducing an easy fly ball to center field to end the inning and hold the deficit at 1–0.

Despite having given up only one run, it was a troubling inning for the right-hander, especially since the lone run he allowed in Game 2 had been enough to tag him with the loss. The last time around, however, Tommy John was pitching like a world-beater. This time John — working on just two days' rest after closing out the final two frames of Game 4 — looked far shakier. He allowed base runners in each of the first three innings, including back-to-back two-out singles to Garvey and Cey in the second, but managed to wriggle out of trouble each time. Still, the Dodgers had never — never, *ever* — scored a run against Tommy John, and with every failed rally it seemed more likely that Hooton would again be the victim of an impotent offense.

That mind-set lasted until the fourth. Baker started things off with a one-out bloop single and one out later advanced to second on Monday's one-hop smash to first baseman Bob Watson, who managed to knock the ball down but could not corral it. That brought to the plate the man on the Dodgers' roster best equipped to hit John, the guy who, having caught him for six seasons in Los Angeles, knew every one of the left-hander's tricks. Steve Yeager came to the plate expecting something down — sinker or scuffball, no matter — but when he unexpectedly caught one up in the zone, he pounced hard, driving the ball on a hop toward the hole at short, between Milbourne and a diving Nettles, who'd only just returned from his thumb injury.* The ball skipped into left field for a single, allowing Baker to race home and tie the score, 1–1. The hit was especially important given Yeager's eighth-

---

* Before the game, Mike Scioscia was asked how the catcher platoon sat with him given that he'd be on the bench. His response: "Yeager has started against lefthanders all year. That's what the Yankees are throwing, and if I were the manager, I'd do the same thing. Did I say that okay, Tommy?"

place spot in the batting order; John struck out Hooton in short order to end the threat.

The bottom half of the inning was where everything changed.

The drama started with Nettles, because with New York's biggest Dodger-killer back in the lineup, how else could things go? With one out, the third baseman, wincing with every swing he took, laced a double down the first-base line, Lasorda's mind racing with possibilities as the ball bounced around in the right-field corner. The scenario that most excited the manager could be enacted only if the next hitter, Rick Cerone, was held off base. If Cerone failed to advance the runner, that'd be even better.

Hooton, his knuckle-curve beginning to dive like it had in Game 2, struck out Cerone on three pitches.

With that, Lasorda leapt into action, ordering the right-hander to intentionally walk New York's number-eight hitter, Larry Milbourne. That set up a force at any base and, more importantly, brought up the pitcher's spot with two outs. Tommy John had given up six hits to that point, but only one run, and Lasorda was hoping that that would be all Bob Lemon allowed.* Twice before in the Series, Lasorda had walked Milbourne to face the pitcher, and both times Lemon responded with a pinch-hitter. It was only the fourth inning, unreasonably early in the game, but if there was the slightest chance that Lasorda could bait his counterpart into relegating one of his best pitchers to the bench, he was willing to give it a try.

To the Gamble in his dugout Lemon added a gamble on his score-card. To Lasorda's delight, he recalled John, who'd thrown only 45 pitches, from the on-deck circle and sent up Bobby Murcer to hit.

---

* John started the first regular-season game Garvey ever attended in person, back in 1966 at Comiskey Park in Chicago, when John was 23 and pitching for the White Sox and Garvey was a freshman at Michigan State University. Improbably, John's career would outlast Garvey's, the former retiring in 1989 at age 46, the latter in 1987 at age 38.

On the mound, Hooton stared in disbelief. He'd roomed with John shortly after the left-hander underwent his soon-to-be-famous elbow ligament surgery, and understood better than most what kind of battle his former teammate could force upon LA. *If I get Murcer out*, Hooton thought as the pinch-hitter settled in, *we're going to win the World Series.*

It was not a ludicrous move for Lemon. Twice in New York's Game 3 loss a Yankees pitcher had come up with two on, two out, and a one-run lead — first Dave Righetti, then George Frazier — and the manager hadn't pinch-hit for either of them. Both times the pitcher struck out.* Even more tellingly, neither pitcher retired a single hitter the following inning. Lemon was determined to not make that mistake again.

Further bolstering the decision was Murcer's .394 career batting average against Hooton, built during stints with the Giants and Cubs. Sure enough, when the count reached 1-1, Hooton threw a changeup that didn't fool the slugger a bit. Murcer's swing was perfectly timed, the ball flying off the end of the bat toward the bleachers in right field. Hearts in the visitors' dugout momentarily skipped a beat at visions of a 4–1 Yankees lead, but the drive lost momentum amid the swirling winds above the stadium and dropped into Rick Monday's glove at the warning track for the inning's final out. All at once the Yankees did not get their run and lost the services of their starting pitcher, who pulled on a warm-up jacket and retreated in disgust to the far end of the dugout. "I can't believe that," he said to himself with a dismissive wave. Hooton saw it. *I agree with you, Tommy — I can't believe it either*, he thought as he returned to his own bench. His best chance dashed, Lemon hoped that his bullpen would hold.

His bullpen would not hold. New York's relievers were among baseball's finest during the regular season, but the Dodgers had scored against them in three of the five games so far, to the tune of

---

* Helping New York strand a World Series–record 55 base runners by the time things wrapped up.

a 5.06 ERA. The man to whom Lemon first turned, George Frazier, was having an especially rough go of it, taking losses in his only two appearances, in the process becoming the first pitcher in 40 years to lose back-to-back Series games. After Dave Stewart lost two straight against Houston in the NLDS, Lasorda effectively banished him. To judge by Lemon's actions, the Yankees' skipper was far more forgiving. It would cost him dearly.

Lopes led off with a single and was sacrificed to second by Russell. Frazier managed to handle LA's biggest threat, retiring Garvey on a fly ball to left field for the second out, and should have been out of the inning when he got Cey to top a high hopper directly up the middle. The Penguin was not fast on his best day let alone in the aftermath of a concussion, and Willie Randolph was among the American League's quickest second basemen, in possession of a powerful arm. The play should not have been close. Randolph raced so quickly to his spot, however, that he had to slow to a stop behind the bag to wait for the ball, which kicked up at the edge of the grass and slipped under his glove. Shortstop Larry Milbourne had ranged over in plenty of time for backup, but overran the play. The ball rolled behind him too, into center field, Lopes flying home to give the Dodgers a 2–1 lead.

Dusty Baker, up next, tapped a looper just a bit deeper than where Cey's hit ended up, the ball landing just beyond the reach of a desperately retreating Milbourne and allowing Cey to motor into third. Five batters into the inning, Frazier had given up three hits. None of them were struck particularly well, though, so Lemon left him in to face Pedro Guerrero.

It took only one pitch for New York's manager to regret the decision. Guerrero tattooed Frazier's first offering toward left-center field, where it rocketed over Mumphrey's outstretched glove and rolled to the wall, everybody running like mad around the bases. Cey and Baker scored easily, and Guerrero pulled into third with a stand-up triple that made the score 4–1. Frazier struck out Monday to end the inning, but for the Dodgers, it was now a matter of simply hanging on.

Hooton did his part in the fifth, limiting the Yankees to a harmless Randolph double. In the sixth, Lemon turned to Ron Davis, the only setup man in either league to make the All-Star team. As with Frazier, the World Series had not been kind to the right-hander, who'd surrendered three hits, four walks, and five runs (four earned) over two innings pitched across three appearances. In Game 6, things got even worse.

Davis struck out Yeager to open the frame, but then, unforgivably, walked Hooton. Almost as unforgivably, the guy who'd allowed fewer than one base runner per inning during the regular season also walked Lopes. In the dugout, a visibly uneasy Lemon began to relax when Davis put the next batter, Russell, into a 1-2 hole, but he tensed right back up when the shortstop slapped a single to left, scoring the jacket-clad Hooton. Now the Dodgers led 5–1, and Lemon's ploy to remove Tommy John in search of offense was backfiring loudly. The manager didn't yet know it, but the wrongness of his decision hadn't even fully played out.

With Lemon's relievers failing to do the job, he called for his Game 4 starter, Rick Reuschel, who'd been hammered two days earlier. The Dodgers greeted the right-hander with a double steal, Lopes taking third, Russell second, at which point Lemon went into full prevent mode, walking Garvey to load the bases with one out. It seemed like a perfect opportunity for LA's king of the returned, Ron Cey — back first from a broken arm and now from a beaning — to inflict further damage. The Penguin was already 2-for-2 with an RBI and a run scored in the game, but had grown lightheaded while running the bases an inning earlier. When the dizziness persisted into the bottom of the frame — while tracking Jerry Mumphrey's humpback liner, Cey had the queasy feeling that the ball was fuzzy, more suited for tennis than baseball — the Penguin removed himself from the lineup. "I would not be able to live with it," he said later, "if I messed up a play that involved [the Yankees] getting back into the game."

Lasorda sent up Derrel Thomas to pinch-hit and was rewarded

with a ground ball to third that Nettles took to the bag himself for the putout, Lopes scoring on the play. The Dodgers led 6–1.

The next batter, Baker, hit another grounder to third, just in time for Nettles's defensive magic to run out. The Gold Glover fumbled the play, possibly while favoring his injured thumb, to load the bases again. Pedro Guerrero promptly unloaded a couple of them, his bloop single to center scoring Garvey and Thomas. Eight to one, and Yankee Stadium seemed to deflate all at once. Reuschel ended it by getting Yeager, in his second at-bat of the inning, to ground out to shortstop, but by that point everybody in pinstripes seemed resigned to an inevitable fate. On the telecast, Howard Cosell said, "[The Yankees] are flat, listless, and have looked all evening like a team that came to be beaten."

When Hooton allowed a single and two walks to load the bases with one out in the sixth, Lasorda couldn't yank him quickly enough, bypassing his middle-innings options and turning directly to closer Steve Howe. The left-hander ceded an RBI single to the first hitter he faced, Lou Piniella, which made the score 8–2, but that was effectively that. From that point forward, Howe cruised to the finish line, allowing one more hit and a walk over three and two-thirds innings.*

As the game wound down, Lasorda grew so amped up that he began looking for ways to actively manage, trying to keep himself busy when no action on his part was remotely necessary. With Howe preparing to bat with the bases empty and one out in the ninth, Lasorda

---

* The Yankees would likely have scored at least one more had third-base coach Joe Altobelli not repeatedly held Rick Cerone at third base, first after Piniella's single (Cerone was running from second), then on a Willie Randolph fly ball that was plenty deep enough to score the runner. This is noteworthy less for its functionality (down by so many runs, Altobelli had every reason to play it conservatively) than for its motivation: the previous time a Yankees third-base coach waved a runner into a postseason out — Mike Ferraro, in 1980 — Steinbrenner publicly ripped him, fired the manager, then demoted the coach to the first-base side of the field. Of this, Altobelli was all too aware.

called across the dugout: "Hey, Reggie, Reggie! Grab a bat!" By that point the Dodgers had extended their lead to 9–2, thanks to a Pedro Guerrero homer in the eighth, and Smith was cool in his response. "Tommy," he said calmly, "you don't need a pinch-hitter right now." Lasorda paused. "Okay!" he yelped. "Sit down!"

For Howe, the primary moment of drama came when he faced Reggie Jackson with one out and nobody on in the seventh inning. Jackson had taken Howe deep in Game 4, after which he crowed to reporters, "Ask Steve Howe if I can still hit a fastball." The pitcher stewed, less because of Reggie's braggadocio than the fact that it wasn't a fastball Jackson had pummeled but a hanging slider.

This time around Howe was determined to beat him with nothing *but* fastballs. Four pitches later he did just that, Jackson swinging through high heat for strike three. As the closer walked back to the dugout, he turned toward Reggie and yelled, "*That's* a fastball. That was *three* fastballs."

Reggie would face the closer once more, with two outs in the ninth, as the last Yankee standing between the Dodgers and the title. It was a position in which Jackson, a guy known for ending games with homers, not outs, decidedly did not want to be. He battled Howe through nine pitches, fouling off ball after ball before finally tapping a full-count fastball toward second base. His fate as the final batter of the World Series was spared only by Lopes, who kicked the ball for his record sixth error in six games. Upon reaching first, Jackson had plenty of time to contemplate the situation, as the second baseman, having stirred up a plume of dirt, ended up with some of it in his eye and had to spend three long minutes in the clubhouse clearing his cornea before play was resumed. Garvey used the time to chat up the base runner. "You really didn't want to make the last out, did you?" he asked. Reggie shook his head vigorously. "You know how it is," he replied. Given a moment to take in the setting, Jackson made sure to offer congratulations to an opponent he'd vanquished three times in World Series play, once with Oakland and twice with the Yankees.

"Well, Garv, it's your turn," he said, patting the first baseman on the rear. "You deserve it." On the next pitch, Bob Watson tapped the ball softly to center field. The clock on the scoreboard in right read 11:59.

Defensive replacement Ken Landreaux blinked away light raindrops to put the ball away, and the Dodgers exploded. "All I could think about," Landreaux said later, "was being in elementary school, listening to the Dodgers in the World Series on the radio, and now realizing that I'd won a championship with the team I grew up with." As players charged the infield to celebrate, Yeager grabbed Howe near the mound and swung him joyously, the reliever's elbow inadvertently connecting hard with Garvey's chin, knocking the first baseman's cap off his head, where it was nabbed by an encroaching fan. "Gimme that hat!" Garvey commanded, and was surprised when the fan did as instructed. Lasorda sprinted from the dugout as fast as a fat man could run, screaming, "You gotta believe! You gotta believe!" Half of the Yankee Stadium crowd had already departed.*

As the Dodgers retreated to their clubhouse — greeted at the door by Hooton, who had long since decamped to ice his arm — the celebration was subsumed, perhaps, by recognition that the team's greatest moment would also likely be its last, at least in current form. "They can do anything they want with us now," shouted Lopes, the most certain among them to depart, as champagne corks popped around him. "I've got the ring. They can't take that away from me." Garvey called it "the end of a very sentimental journey," adding that "the infield may not be all together another year." It was enough, he admitted afterward, to bring him to tears as the game ended.

"It was a silent feeling that this might be our last chance," reflected

---

* The only players not to join the scrum were the relievers, who opted against traversing a fan-laden field, instead taking backdoor tunnels to the clubhouse. Because both teams utilized the same route through the stadium bowels, it made for an extremely awkward trip, Yankees pitchers leading the way and Dodgers pitchers trying to maintain polite decorum until they reached their celebration.

Russell in the immediate aftermath. "We didn't mention it, but it was there."

They were correct, all of them. The six games of the 1981 World Series were the final ones the storied infield would play together. In the last three, Games 4, 5, and 6, it was only appropriate that the quartet maintained the first four spots in the batting order: Lopes, Russell, Garvey, Cey.* It was enough to overwhelm Cey, who, as the Dodgers began to break out the bubbly, retreated to his locker to ponder the implications of not only what had just happened but what was about to happen. After a while, Steve Sax wandered over to check on him. "Are you okay?" he asked. "Why aren't you out there jumping up and down?" Cey looked up at his enthusiastic young teammate, fully recognizing the unbridled joy that a rookie could hold, which for the third baseman was jumbled up amid years of frustration and colored by what he viewed as a legitimate near-death experience. Call it veteran's ennui. "I'm jumping up and down inside," he told Sax softly, "but I need a couple of minutes to regroup."† The rookie bounced away, and Cey joined the party soon enough.

By way of celebration, players ended up drinking more champagne than they sprayed, with Reuss going so far as to issue an order to not waste bubbly by spraying it on him. Those players who doused Lasorda, Campanis, and O'Malley on the TV interview stand did so in measured doses. Cey looked at the bottle of champagne he was about to consume and, considering his head trauma, reasoned, "If I pass out, there are lots of doctors nearby."

Even as outsiders were noting that the clubhouse carpet was aw-

---

* This had become clear during the NLCS in Montreal when Lopes, Johnstone, Smith, Yeager, and Russell were together in a sauna. "We ought to get one of these in LA," said Johnstone, impressed. Lopes looked at him with incredulousness. "Look who's in here with you," he said. "There's a good possibility that none of us will be here next year."

† "We all know about death," Cey told a reporter minutes later. "Some play with it, laugh at it. But when he decides to play with you, it's a bit scary."

fully dry for a team purporting to celebrate, Scioscia unexpectedly emerged from the shower room with a garden hose and sprayed down the landscape. Leave it to the kids. Maybe there was some life to this bunch after all.

It was a spark. Freshly soaked, Reuss decided to take things to another level and screamed two words that quickly changed the nature of the celebration: "Food fight!" Soon, Scioscia, Forster, Niedenfuer, Smith, and Johnstone were tossing every item on the postgame spread, from slices of deli meat to handfuls of ketchup, mustard, and mayonnaise. Dave Goltz, late to the party because he'd been delivering a bottle of champagne outside to players' wives, was ambushed by Reuss as he returned to his locker, getting a face full of potato salad for his troubles. ("It wasn't that tasty either," he said later.) "It became like *Animal House*," said Scioscia, referencing the iconic John Belushi–led cafeteria scene from the 1978 film.

Poking his head out of his office door, Lasorda surveyed the tableau and cried, "I thought I'd apologized for my sins, but I guess the Lord is paying me back. He gave me Johnstone and Reuss." The pair descended, and soon the manager resembled the interior of a Canter's Deli sandwich. "It was," proclaimed Reuss later with no small amount of pride, "the best food fight in the history of baseball."*

"To have a little spread thrown on you is more a baptism than anything," noted Garvey, looking back. "A baptism of accomplishment, of achievement." A baptism of mayonnaise.

Between salvos, discussion hovered about who might win the Series MVP Award. Yeager and Guerrero led the team with two hom-

---

* When asked for his recollections from the celebration, Monday offered a bullet-point list:
- *"It's amazing the colors that you can get from mustard, ketchup, mayonnaise.*
- *How much it takes of any one of those three items to stick lettuce onto somebody's back.*
- *How long you have to stay in a hot shower to get that stuff off.*
- *How good it feels to have your eyes burned with champagne."*

ers apiece, with Guerrero's seven RBIs — five of them in the decisive Game 6, capping a remarkable streak during which he went 7-for-13 after opening the Series 0-for-8 — setting the pace. Cey batted .350 with six RBIs, with his return from Gossage's beaning being nothing short of heroic. Garvey led all Dodgers with a .417 average.

Ultimately, the decision-makers opted to split the difference. Unable to reconcile a four-part division, perhaps, the award was split between Yeager, Guerrero, and Cey — the first time the honor had been shared at all, let alone three ways — with Garvey omitted based largely on the fact that he had not driven in any runs. There was some confusion at first, when Dodgers publicist Steve Brener told Garvey, in the tunnel immediately after the game ended, that he'd won MVP. As it turned out, Brener had heard somebody say "Steve" and jumped to conclusions. The PR man subsequently had to track down Garvey in the clubhouse and awkwardly inform him that it was actually Yeager that the voters selected.* Things grew further complicated when ABC's Bob Uecker called the MVP trio up to be interviewed and also claimed the wrong Steve. Garvey — wearing a Brooklyn Dodgers T-shirt given to him by a fan — went up as instructed, wondering if Brener might have been wrong. No such luck.

"I'm glad [the award] didn't come posthumously," said Cey, who described himself as "tired, dizzy and absolutely terrific."

In the game's aftermath, the primary conversation concerned Lemon's decision to yank Tommy John in the fourth inning of a 1–1 game, thus opening the floodgates for LA. Postgame comments from the pitcher himself were particularly telling. "I definitely didn't agree with the move," John said. "I didn't try to talk [Lemon] out of it because I never argue with the manager. I am only paid to pitch. It just

---

* "If we would have had our normal offense, I'd probably have been right there for the MVP," said Garvey later, referencing his dearth of opportunities with men on base. "If I had that one, I would have won all four MVPs — regular season, playoffs, World Series, and All-Star."

seems highly unlikely that you would take out your best pitcher — at least I assume that your starting pitcher that night is your best pitcher — that early in a tie game. I mean, I was throwing well. I wasn't getting cuffed around. I just completed thirteen innings against a club of that caliber, and held it to one run. I wanted to keep pitching, and thought I would. But what I think doesn't really matter. We hadn't been scoring runs, and Lem had a move to make. He thought it would work out, but it didn't."

It was one of a litany of complaints to be lodged against the manager. Lemon was also questioned about why he'd held Reggie Jackson out of the first three games and then kept him in Game 4 with a three-run lead, after which the outfielder's key error helped the Dodgers tie the score. In that same game, Lemon's decision to tab Bobby Brown as a defensive replacement in center field instead of the far more accomplished Jerry Mumphrey led to another run. With the tying run on base in the ninth inning of Game 4, why had Lemon used backup catcher Barry Foote — who'd batted .208 in 40 games with New York — as a pinch-hitter rather than the .307-hitting Mumphrey? (Foote whiffed for the second out of the inning.) There were questions about why Gossage, the game's most dominant closer, had appeared in only three games, despite high-leverage situations in every one — especially in light of the meltdown staged by the rest of New York's relief corps, particularly Davis (23.14 ERA over four games) and Frazier (17.18 ERA, tagged with the loss in all three of the games in which he appeared). Steinbrenner himself fanned the flames of discontent by issuing a public apology for his team's performance almost as soon as the game was over, which smacked of nothing so much as a slap at certain employees, particularly the manager. So burdened, Lemon made it 14 games into the 1982 season before Steinbrenner finally canned him. He would never manage in the big leagues again.

By contrast, every one of Lasorda's moves seemed to work out. He'd left Valenzuela in to pitch in Game 3 despite marked struggles and was rewarded with a complete-game victory. ("I'm not blowing my own horn," the manager said later, "but that took a lot of guts. If it hadn't worked out and Fernando hadn't lasted to beat the Yankees, they'd have chopped off my head and rolled it down Wilshire Boulevard. I'd have heard about it all winter long.") That decision allowed Lasorda to save Bob Welch for the Game 4 start, and even though it didn't work as planned, the skipper was decisive in yanking the right-hander with no outs in the first, minimizing the damage and allowing the Dodgers to come back. Starting Welch also allowed Lasorda to pitch both Reuss — who'd lobbied strongly for the Game 4 start — and Hooton on full rest in the Series' final two games, and lined up Valenzuela for a potential Game 7.

Now the manager, who had shouted himself silly through the duration of a frantic postseason, sought mostly to soak it all in quietly and get some rest — not necessarily in that order. "I just want to put my head down on the pillow for once," he said, "knowing that we're the world champions."

12

Aftermath

THE FLIGHT HOME from New York offered a potent concoction of celebration and relief. Champagne continued to flow, but the energy of the clubhouse festivities quickly dissipated in the wake of two weeks' worth of on-edge, verge-of-elimination baseball. Garvey held an ice pack to his aching jaw, which had grown increasingly sore after Howe elbowed him in the celebratory scrum. Before long, many of the players were passed out in their seats. "I swear, within an hour almost everybody was asleep," said Reuss.

"We were worn out, physically and mentally," recalled Monday. "It was a quiet flight from the Mississippi River to Los Angeles."

"It's pretty amazing," said Garvey. "Losing isn't nearly as exhausting as winning."

Players awoke to 10,000 fans awaiting them at the airport, where they decamped the Kay-O II at 6:05 a.m. to a raucous chorus. Police barricades restrained the masses — barely — as players staggered down the line toward waiting limousines. The victory celebration the next day included a parade through downtown — the first such event for the Dodgers since the one welcoming the team to Los Angeles in 1958 — starting on Broadway at Seventh Street and ending at City Hall. Every player attended save the guy people wanted most to see. As the throng, 80,000 strong — small by some standards, but remarkable for a city with a long history of eschewing public celebration — chanted,

"We want Fernando," Lasorda had to take the dais at the parade terminus and announce that the pitcher was too ill to attend.*

In reality, Valenzuela simply didn't want to be there, his absence driven by an underestimation of the importance of these kinds of events to the cities that host them — a wild miscalculation given the preponderance of Latinos in LA — and fear of what brushing shoulders with the violently adoring masses might actually look like. Instead, the crowd-shy pitcher went out to dinner with some friends at a Mexican restaurant, but even that was cut short when a TV camera crew barged in. Soon, *La Opinion*, a local Spanish-language daily, ran an editorial bashing Fernando's parade absence and claiming that with his "special popularity" came special responsibility, given the abundance of cross-cultural appeal. "I'm very, very sorry," the pitcher said when reached for comment. "I did not know I would hurt people that much. I really didn't know all the details of the occasion." People came to forgive him, of course. The Cy Young Award, which Valenzuela won weeks later, boasts significant restorative power.†

It didn't take long for various Dodgers to leverage their newfound success. Utilizing music industry connections, Johnstone, Monday, Reuss, and Yeager cut a record — "We Are the Champions," backed by "New York, New York" — under the name Big Blue Wrecking Crew. The quartet actually had to audition for it, which seemed odd given its vanity-project nature and the fact that the producers were banking on the players' marketability, not their musical ability. (The audition took place on a parking-lot pay phone near an appearance the players were making, each man singing in turn into the receiver.) "Turns out

---

* Technically, Alejandro Peña was also absent, though unlike Fernando he was actually ill, still recovering from the bleeding ulcer that felled him during the World Series.

† Valenzuela received eight first-place votes and 70 points from the 12 voting members of the Baseball Writers' Association of America, beating out Tom Seaver by just three points, the equivalent of a single second-place vote.

that Yeag can sing a little bit," said Monday, "but I can't sing. Jerry told Jay that he, Jerry, could sing, but Jay doesn't realize that Jay can't sing." A couple days later the quartet was in the studio, warbling over backing tracks that had already been laid down. "There were some notes that I just backed out on," recalled Monday. "Jay thinks he hit all of them. He didn't."*

The very next day the record was off to be pressed, 50,000 copies' worth, with proceeds going to the Children's Hospital of Orange County. The foursome was booked to perform live on *The Tonight Show*, complete with choreography. During rehearsals, bandleader Doc Severinsen sidled up to ask, incredulously, "So you guys are actually going to go out and do this thing?" As the players took their marks behind the curtain and Johnny Carson began his introduction, Monday turned to Reuss and asked, "What's your pucker factor?" Reuss, laughing, replied, "You couldn't drive a greased needle up my ass with a sledgehammer." Once things were under way, each of the performers actually managed to remember the words, which itself exceeded many expectations. The act concluded with the players removing suit jackets and ripping off dress shirts to reveal blue T-shirts with bedazzled Dodgers logos. After they'd finished, Carson said simply, "I think people thought you were going to be bad."

More appearances—on *The Mike Douglas Show*, *The Merv Griffin Show*, and *Solid Gold*—followed. It is safe to say that the previous year's champion Philadelphia Phillies were not offered these types of opportunities.

The feel-good vibe would not last long. In February, the Dodgers bought out Lopes's no-trade clause for $150,000, then shipped him to Oakland for an inconsequential minor leaguer, kicking in a considerable sum to help cover the $1.3 million remaining on his contract.†

---

* "I'm the singer of the group," said Yeager. "The other guys are all wacko, just screaming a lot."

† "I always thought that *I* was going to be the first one traded," said Cey later.

The second baseman's departure had long been seen as inevitable, but this made it concrete: LA was willing to take a financial hit in order to clear out the veterans. Lopes provided the perfect combination: a player clearly past his peak, whose defensive liabilities in the World Series nearly cost the team a championship, was butting up against the brightest second base prospect in baseball. And now that the thread had begun to unravel, the Dodgers saw little reason to prevent more of the same.

They let free agent Reggie Smith walk to the Giants and tried in earnest to replace Russell at shortstop with Ozzie Smith of the San Diego Padres, going so far as to offer Pedro Guerrero in trade. When San Diego wouldn't bite, LA dangled Landreaux, Perconte, and either Stewart or Sutcliffe to the Cubs for Iván de Jesús, whom they themselves had sent to Chicago in the Rick Monday deal five years earlier. Again, no dice.

"It was almost as if management was doing them a favor, letting them win the World Series before they got rid of them," said journalist Mark Heisler.

The following winter the Dodgers sent Cey to the Cubs for two low-ceiling minor leaguers. Even more shocking was the decision to allow Garvey to depart for San Diego as a free agent following the 1982 campaign. It wasn't just that the first baseman had been the face of the franchise since 1974, or that he remained one of the most marketable figures in all of baseball, or that he had done as much as anybody to advance the Dodgers brand. Lord knows, his production hadn't slipped. For Garvey, it was a matter of equity. Before the 1977 season, he'd signed a six-year, $2 million contract, which at the dawn of free agency seemed like a lucrative deal. It very quickly became a bargain for Los Angeles, however, a detail that Garvey never held against the team by trying to renegotiate. He repeatedly and publicly proclaimed that he would honor the arrangement because he was certain that the Dodgers would make things right once the deal expired. "Garvey is to the Dodgers what Gehrig once was to the Yankees — their pride," reported *Sports Illustrated* after the 1981 season. Yet for reasons beyond the first baseman's comprehension, with his pact set to expire at the end of 1982, the Dodgers refused to extend him prior to opening day and only reluctantly began talks in midsummer.* Although the team insisted that its doors were open, for the first baseman the season felt like a conclusion, a point driven home when numerous teammates stopped by his locker after the finale to say good-bye.

The sides finally sat down in earnest that autumn, at which point Garvey requested a five-year deal, through his age-38 season. The club countered with four years and $5 million, which the slugger would have taken as a starting point six months earlier, but which by October he viewed as a flashing neon sign pointing toward the exit. The two sides bargained until the midnight deadline on November 15, with the team refusing to budge. "My baseball life started at Al Lang Field in St. Petersburg, being a batboy for the Brooklyn Dodgers, growing up with my idols, and then becoming a Dodger myself," said Garvey, looking back. "All of a sudden I'm in a consecutive-games streak, and we win the world championship, and now they're playing hardball. We were very creative, came up with a lot of different options, after-career addendums to make up what we thought was parity, and they were just rigid. And that was it. We all got up and walked out of the room, and I saw the TV: 'Dodgers and Garvey fail to come to an agreement.' I was a free agent."

The Dodgers did not even select Garvey in the reentry draft, a necessary step toward reaching a new agreement once the old one expired. That December he signed a five-year deal with San Diego for $6.6 million, plus assorted bonuses. "The Dodgers think they're living

---

* Garvey's contract uncertainty ate at him to the point that it affected his performance. Over the first two months of 1982, he batted just .246 with four homers, his play suffering so profoundly that speculation placed the team's primary motive in opening negotiations as an effort to get the first baseman out of his funk. Garvey hit .298 from that point forward, but still ended up at .282 on the season, his lowest mark since becoming a regular.

in Camelot," he said sadly, "but they're letting the knights get away." Branch Rickey had lived by the principle of getting rid of a player a year too early rather than a year too late, and now his disciple, Al Campanis, was putting theory to test.

Each of the departed players went on to success elsewhere. With Oakland, Lopes led American League second basemen with 17 homers in 1983, stole 47 bases for the Cubs in 1985, and held a big league job until 1987, when he was 42 years old.

Cey averaged 24 homers a year for the Cubs over the next three seasons, teaming with Lopes, Jay Johnstone, and Rick Sutcliffe to lead Chicago to a National League East title in 1984. Garvey made two All-Star teams over his first three years in San Diego and slugged 21 homers in his fourth. It was his Padres team that beat Cey's Cubs in the '84 playoffs to reach the World Series.

The Dodgers ditched Baker after the 1983 season, releasing him with two years and $1.6 million remaining on his contract only two months after he'd batted cleanup in the NLCS. (He ended up signing a two-year deal with the Giants.) After the 1985 season, an aging Yeager was sent to Seattle for a second-line reliever, leaving Bill Russell as the only remaining player who had been incubated by Lasorda in the minor leagues. Six years after winning the World Series, only six players remained from 1981's opening day roster — Guerrero, Landreaux, Niedenfuer, Scioscia, Valenzuela, and Welch — and questions began to arise about how effective Lasorda might be with a new generation of players unaccustomed to his particular brand of motivation.

"I was just sad on how it ended for damn near all of us," said Baker, looking back. "We got broken up too soon."

"Probably four or five years sooner than they had to," added Garvey. Said Yeager: "I could never figure it out. Why do you win the World Series and then disassemble your champions?"

At least they kept Fernando, though even that wasn't easy. The pitcher demanded $750,000 for the 1982 season — a considerable raise over the $42,500 he'd been making — and refused to report to spring training when the Dodgers wouldn't give it to him. He eventually settled for $360,000, won 19 games, finished third in the National League's Cy Young voting, then earned a $1 million pact via arbitration in 1983, in the process becoming LA's first-ever seven-figure-per-year player.

The 1982 season went down to the final day, when, needing a win in San Francisco to pull into a divisional tie with the Braves, Lasorda opted to pinch-hit for Valenzuela in the seventh inning of a 2–2 game. The bases were loaded with two outs, and like Bob Lemon in the 1981 World Series, the skipper felt that the trade-off was worth it. The guy he chose to hit, Jorge Orta, grounded out to end the inning, and in the very next frame Giants second baseman Joe Morgan hit a three-run homer off of Terry Forster that effectively ended LA's season.

In 1983, the Dodgers were steamrolled by Philadelphia in the playoffs. In three of the four years thereafter, they didn't even post a winning record, the exception being 1985, which is remembered primarily for Lasorda's decision to pitch to St. Louis slugger Jack Clark with two outs, two on, and first base open in the ninth inning of the NLCS's decisive Game 6. Clark's homer off of Tom Niedenfuer turned a 5–4 deficit into a 7–5 win for the Cardinals, and Lasorda's reputation as a game manager, shaky to begin with, was further tarnished.

Through it all, unsettling allegations continually seemed to surface around players on their way out the door. When Valenzuela held out of spring training in 1982, scuttlebutt appeared in the local media that the pitcher's early success had turned him greedy and that his agent's lust for the dollar was preventing Fernando from negotiating with the team in good faith. "We have been treated like children," Valenzuela said. "I am only 21, but I am a man to be considered with dignity."

Before Lopes left, there was amplification of long-standing rumors about how he could no longer run, which the player knew were hogwash and felt certain had originated with the front office. As the team was preparing to dump Baker, stories cropped up about his friendship with Steve Howe — who was in the midst of protracted, cocaine-induced drama for which the team cut ties with him in 1985 — and other associations with a variety of unsavory characters. The Dodgers, undergoing a youth movement, had been desperate to unload Baker, but when the outfielder cited unfavorable terms in vetoing a trade to the A's, he effectively forced the team to waive him. Many saw the ensuing rumors as an effort to soften public perception about the move.

"Obviously, someone was angry at Dusty," reflected Garvey. "Someone wanted to punish him with the only tool available, by blackballing him from baseball." When Baker became available prior to the 1984 season, Garvey tried like mad to get San Diego to snap him up, but the Padres wanted nothing to do with the outfielder's tainted reputation.

"The Dodger image," said Steve Howe later, "was makeup that concealed a lot of blemishes."

Baker, who ended up signing a two-year deal with San Francisco, was himself incredulous. "I was a good friend of Bob Welch back when he was having troubles with alcohol, but nobody ever accused me of being an alcoholic," he said. "But now that I was a good friend of Steve Howe, and since he has a drug problem, somebody decided I must have a drug problem, too. And it isn't true."

"They can make you uncomfortable," reflected Cey years later. "We saw enough of it happen before us to understand that no one is going to escape it."

One guy to whom nothing of the sort happened was Tommy Lasorda, who hung around until midway through the 1996 season, when he stepped down at age 68 amid health concerns, handing the team over to his handpicked successor, Bill Russell. Lasorda had managed more years in a Dodgers uniform, 21, than anyone in franchise history save for Alston, and in 1983 he became the team's first skipper to receive anything more than a one-year contract.

Lasorda guided the franchise to another championship in 1988, which, given that the Dodgers finished below the league average in hits, doubles, triples, home runs, RBIs, walks, stolen bases, batting average, on-base percentage, slugging percentage, and OPS, was saying something. Facing the heavily favored Oakland A's in the World Series, the manager trotted out an injury-riddled roster filled with cast-offs and the one guy who mattered — Cy Young winner Orel Hershiser, who dominated Oakland over both his starts to carry the team to a five-game victory. Kirk Gibson's ninth-inning, two-out, two-strike, gimp-kneed, pinch-hit, two-run, game-winning homer against A's closer Dennis Eckersley in the opener helped cement that team into SoCal memory banks. The lasting renown came largely at the expense of the '81 club, whose victory in a tainted strike year could never measure up to the underdog achievement of their successors.

Lasorda led Los Angeles to only one more playoff berth after that, a surprise National League West title in 1995, whereupon LA was promptly swept by the Reds in the divisional round. Over his final five seasons, including that one, the Dodgers went 321-337, hardly the type of success that, thanks in part to the manager's own efforts, the franchise had come to expect. Unlike many of his players, though, Lasorda wasn't forced out. When he left, it was his body that did him in, a heart attack sneaking up in June 1996. Five days later, he announced his retirement. In short order, Lasorda was named a Dodgers vice president, and in 1998 served as interim general manager. In 2000, he managed the United States Olympic team to a gold medal in Sydney. He survived the sale of the Dodgers to Rupert Murdoch's News Corp in 1998, and again when Frank McCourt bought the club in 2004 (not to mention when he sold it in 2012). In so doing, Lasorda was the last man standing from the family ownership of Walter O'Malley, the lone survivor with memory of the team as something other than a corporate entity.

It was more than that, though. Lasorda preceded Los Angeles itself. Other Brooklyn Dodgers were still around, Don Newcombe continuing to be a regular at Dodger Stadium into his nineties, and Sandy Koufax making sporadic appearances at Chavez Ravine. Wouldn't you know it, though, it was the guy who was cut so that Koufax might stick around — more so than the living legend himself, or any of the guys from '81 — who made the biggest impression on the franchise. When Tommy Lasorda took over as manager of the Dodgers and said that he was less worried about replacing Walter Alston than he was for whoever had to follow him someplace down the line, he couldn't have known that the date in question would be more than two decades off.

One time, way back in March 1968, when Lasorda was managing in Ogden, Walter O'Malley called him into the press room at Dodgertown during spring training and, before an assembled crowd, presented him with a gift. It was a tombstone, made of marble and inscribed: TOMMY LASORDA, A DODGER. Below that, it read, DODGER STADIUM WAS HIS ADDRESS, BUT EVERY BALLPARK WAS HIS HOME. There was a red heart, bleeding a drop of Dodger blue. Talk about a performance bonus.

It was perfect. Before long the manager had worked it into his routine, telling the same story about the headstone year after year when addressing an audience. "Once I told Mr. O'Malley I hoped to continue working for the Dodgers after I die," the story goes. *How will you do that?*, O'Malley asks. "I'll have the Dodgers schedule engraved on my tombstone," Lasorda tells him. "Then, when people come out to my grave, they'll say, 'Hey, the Dodgers are in town today. Let's go to the stadium.'"

Tommy Lasorda always did pledge perpetual loyalty to the team that ended up giving the same to him. It's been easy for critics to dismiss the manager's fervor, decades' worth of it, as so much bluster, but in the end maybe there was something to it after all.

Let's go to the stadium. A perfect ending.

Conclusion

I don't want players who are pussycats. I want tigers.

— AL CAMPANIS, 1977

ONE OF THE most beloved players in LA history spent only three injury-riddled seasons in Chavez Ravine, during which he batted .264 while averaging 14 homers and 47 RBIs. In the lone World Series the Dodgers reached during his short tenure with them, he collected a single, lonely at-bat.

What he did with it, though, was the stuff of legend.

So serious were the injuries to Kirk Gibson's legs — a torn left hamstring tendon and a swollen right knee, the former hurt in Game 5 of the 1988 NLCS against the Mets, the latter the result of a slide gone wrong two days later in Game 7 — that he didn't even come out for introductions before the opener of the ensuing World Series. The Dodgers were up against the highly favored Oakland A's, who'd won 10 more games during the regular season (104 to 94) and boasted five All-Stars (including three starters) to the Dodgers' one. LA's home run leader since 1981, Pedro Guerrero, spent much of the season's first half on the disabled list, and the entirety of the second half in St. Louis after being traded for pitcher John Tudor in response to injuries and ineffectiveness up and down the rotation. With the hobbled Gibson replaced in the lineup by utilityman Mickey Hatcher (who'd collected fewer home runs over his 12-year career than Oakland masher José Canseco hit in '88 alone), the Dodgers' Game 1 lineup averaged fewer than seven homers apiece on the season. This in contrast to the Bash Brothers A's of Canseco and Mark McGwire, who finished first and third in the American League in that category, respectively.

The discrepancy in firepower made Gibson's absence even starker. While his teammates were warming up before the game, the slugger received injections, then spent the early and middle innings wearing shorts and a T-shirt in the clubhouse, icing both legs at once. So certain was he about his inability to participate that he sent his wife, JoAnn, home to take care of their two-year-old son. He wasn't going to do anything worth watching, he told her.

As the game progressed, Tommy Lasorda raced back and forth to the trainer's room to lodge intermittent inquiries about the health of his best hitter, hoping against the evidence before him that Gibson might suddenly feel well enough to participate. The outfielder's most frequent response was simply a downward-pointed thumb.

This is where things stood heading into the bottom of the ninth. The A's led, 4–3, behind a stout performance from their ace, former Dodger Dave Stewart. Nineteen-eighty-eight, however, was the season in which Oakland's final inning became the purview of reliever Dennis Eckersley, who in his first full year as closer posted a league-leading 45 saves with such ruthless efficiency that he not only finished second in the Cy Young voting and fifth in the MVP race but would come to define the role for a generation of ballplayers to come. To face him, the Dodgers had the bottom of their order — Mike Scioscia, Jeff Hamilton, and Alfredo Griffin — and then the pitcher's spot, if things lasted that long.

Lasorda was trying to figure out his strategy for the inning when his concentration was interrupted by a voice from inside the stadium tunnel. It was clubhouse attendant Mitch Poole, who, as non-uniformed personnel was not allowed in the dugout while the game was under way. So he stood near the doorway and yelled, with increasing urgency: "Tommy, come here! Come here!"

Lasorda wanted no part of it. "I'm trying to manage a game, kid," the skipper muttered from down the bench. "Leave me alone."

Poole persisted, though, until the manager finally sidled over to find out just what was so goddamn important. "Gibby says he can hit," the clubbie breathlessly exuded. Now Lasorda was interested. He raced up the hallway, and there he was, his slugger, a snarl on his lips. Gibson had been watching the game on TV when Vin Scully announced his unavailability for the late innings over the air, saying, "He will not see any action tonight, for sure." Injuries to Gibson's legs were one thing, but blows to his pride would not be tolerated. "My ass!" the outfielder shouted into the ether. He pulled on his uniform and hobbled down to the batting cage to loosen up. With the team's coaches all in the dugout, Poole stepped in to help. Alternating tee work and soft toss, the outfielder audibly grimaced with each hack. Somehow, though, it was working. His legs held up. "Mitch," he said, "this could be the script."

Even then, Gibson didn't want to go directly to the dugout for fear that the A's would note his presence and prepare accordingly. This is why he had Lasorda meet him under the grandstand. The manager had planned to save slugger Mike Davis for pinch-hitting duty when the pitcher's spot came up later in the inning, but with Gibson suddenly available, everything changed. Before Lasorda could say anything, Gibson himself verbalized the strategy that was already forming in the skipper's head. "Hit Davis eighth, and I'll hit for the pitcher if you want me to," the outfielder said. That sounded just fine to Lasorda. To avoid detection, Gibson lurked in the tunnel until his time came to bat . . . if only somebody could get on base.

After Scioscia popped up to shortstop and Hamilton struck out, chances did not appear to be good. Sticking to plan, Lasorda sent up Davis to hit for Griffin. The outfielder had batted only .196 in his first season in Los Angeles but averaged 22 homers over the previous three years with the A's, and Lasorda knew that manager Tony La Russa and Eckersley had long memories. With no power behind Davis on the bench, Eckersley was determined to offer nothing that the hitter could square up, and ended up nibbling aggressively at the corners. The closer, who would issue only seven free passes over the next two seasons *combined*, walked Davis on five pitches. It was all the Dodgers could have asked: the game had been extended for the most dramatic appearance imaginable. As Gibson limped out of the dugout, Dodger Stadium erupted. "I've never heard anything like that," Lasorda said later. "I got goose bumps."

Eckersley wasted no time attacking the injured star, Gibson fouling off two quick fastballs to fall into an 0-2 hole. That was when the hitter switched strategies, employing something he called his "emergency stance," in which he spread his feet wide and swung short, for contact rather than power. Given his inability to generate strength with his lower half anyway, the adjustment suited him just fine. Gibson proceeded to hack at anything near the strike zone, fouling off pitch after pitch while holding up on offerings that weren't close. One of his fouls, a squib down the first-base line, looked for a moment as if it might stay fair, and the effort Gibson expended hobbling out of the box was excruciating to watch. *Someone should shoot this animal and take him out of his misery,* thought Steve Sax, watching from the on-deck circle. On the broadcast, Scully intoned that "it's one thing to favor one leg, but you can't favor two."

With the count at 2-2, Davis stole second. Now all Gibson had to do to tie the game was bloop a ball over the infield.

Eckersley hadn't given up a home run since August 24, and Gibson, all but throwing his bat at pitched balls, presented little danger in that regard. He was, however, steadily grinding the closer down. Tiring of watching Gibson foul off fastballs, Eckersley decided to mix things up. With his eighth pitch of the at-bat he went with a backdoor slider — a breaking pitch on the outside corner, designed to fool hitters into thinking that it possessed more movement than it actually showed, then unexpectedly hanging around the "backdoor," or outer edge of the strike zone.

Eckersley's slider was a useful pitch. Unfortunately for him, it was also the pitch for which Gibson was looking. The report given to Dodgers hitters by scout Mel Didier specifically mentioned that should a left-handed batter reach a full count against Eckersley with the tying or winning run in scoring position, that is precisely what he'd see.* Eckersley's previous pitch had run the count to 3-and-2, and Gibson was ready, his all-arms swing sending the closer's offering sailing toward the right-field bleachers. As Canseco took several defeated steps in half-hearted pursuit, the ball settled just beyond the fence. Dodger Stadium became a wall of noise.

As Gibson rounded first base he threw his right hand above his head. As he rounded second, he pumped his arm. As he rounded third, he slapped palms with coach Joey Amalfitano. Upon crossing the plate, Gibson was mobbed by his teammates, Lasorda in the middle of everything to plant a kiss upon his ear. "In a year that has been so improbable," intoned Scully on the broadcast, "the impossible has happened."

The 5–4 win set the stage for an unexpected five-game domination of the mighty A's, Los Angeles winning behind two complete-game victories from Hershiser and an out-of-his-mind series from Hatcher, who, starting in place of Gibson, led all starters with a .368 batting average, two home runs, and five RBIs.

So compelling was Gibson's moment that it obscured to a nearly complete degree the details not only of the other games in the Series but of the Dodgers' own bookend championship from the beginning of the decade, in 1981. There's an easy test for this. Bring up the '81

---

* Never mind that Eckersley never went 3-2 on a left-handed hitter during the entirety of the 1988 season.

World Series team with any casual Dodgers fan, and you will more likely than not hear reference to the glory of Kirk Gibson.*

It was only seven years later, but LA's 1988 championship squad featured only two holdovers from the opening day roster in 1981. Most prominent was Fernando Valenzuela, who — as he'd done seven years earlier — started the season's first game for the Dodgers. With a salary in excess of $2 million, the left-hander was by that point baseball's best-paid pitcher, but '88 would be the worst season of his career. In the middle of June, Valenzuela's record sat at 5-8 and his ERA at 4.39, and he'd walked more hitters (76) than he'd struck out (64). He was shelved with a shoulder injury for all but seven innings of the season's final three months and was left off the team's postseason roster entirely. After two more middling campaigns, the Dodgers let Fernando walk as a free agent.

The other relic from 1981 was Mike Scioscia, who over the ensuing seasons had grinded his way into a well-earned reputation as one of the best defenders — and unequivocally the toughest catcher — in baseball. In 1989, his 10th major league season, Scioscia would make his first All-Star Game. In 1990, he did it again. The following year, however, he was platooned with Gary Carter. In 1992, at age 33, he split time with Carlos Hernández and a rookie named Mike Piazza. The end comes for everybody sooner or later, but what made Scioscia's departure so representative of his 1981 teammates was less that the Dodgers let him walk as a free agent following the '92 season† than the way his managerial career began eight years later.

Scioscia had been eyed as manager material almost since his arrival in Los Angeles, so it seemed only natural for the team to tab him as

---

* We're talking about water-cooler warriors here, plumbing the depths of their baseball knowledge in pursuit of small talk. This proposition excludes serious fans of both the Dodgers and baseball in general.

† Scioscia ended up signing with San Diego and, later, Texas, but never played in the big leagues again.

bench coach once Bill Russell took over for Tommy Lasorda in 1996. Three years later, however, Russell was fired, and the new regime — Peter O'Malley had sold the team to Rupert Murdoch's News Corp — bypassed Scioscia in favor of an outsider, Davey Johnson, late of the Mets, Reds, and Orioles.* So Scioscia took over at Triple-A Albuquerque and then, in 2000, accepted a job across town as manager of the Anaheim Angels. Even as the ex-catcher set club records for managerial longevity — he helmed the Angels for 19 years, through the 2018 season, ending up with more wins and a higher winning percentage than Lasorda — and led his team to a championship in 2002, the Dodgers employed six managers, none of whom won them a World Series.

It was a retro move, this premature spurning of a longtime loyalist, even in the face of evidence that he might be the best man for the job. Scioscia was iced out, like Garvey, Lopes, Cey, and Baker before him, for a shinier and less effective version of himself. It was attrition, pure and simple, roster turnover as agenda item, pushed mostly because it could be. Dating back to Walter O'Malley, the Dodgers were fond of intoning their institutional stability and familylike atmosphere, but there was no mistaking that the team was geared, above all, toward winning and its associated profits. "The Dodgers are a very generous organization," reported *Sports Illustrated* in 1983, "but they don't let sentiment interfere with important business decisions."

"The Dodgers had a peculiar idea of what a family organization was," said reporter Mark Heisler. "The family was upstairs [management], not downstairs [players]. It was, truly, what have you done for me lately?"†

. . .

---

* Johnson lasted two years in Los Angeles.
† This sentiment was espoused by Cubs manager Herman Franks in 1977, after Tommy Lasorda called the recently traded Bill Buckner "my son." "All I can say is that Buckner was Lasorda's son when he was healthy," Franks responded. "As soon as he hurt his leg, Lasorda kicked him out of the house."

Peter O'Malley, son and scion, a Wharton graduate groomed into his post, was in every way a businessman. In 1981, he was in his 10th year as president of the Dodgers, his team a perpetual-motion machine that, largely through the bounty of its legendary 1968 draft, had enjoyed remarkable continuity even as the free-agency era settled upon baseball's landscape. Those '81 Dodgers, without a single Hall of Famer on the roster, were a collective effort in every way. "There's no magic to a team, but there are some ingredients that are really strong," reflected Rick Monday. "When you ask who brought it up for us in 1981, it could have been all the guys. Every one of them had something to offer."

The 1981 Dodgers clubhouse didn't much break down along racial or social lines, or even between pitchers and position players, so much as according to where everybody began. The primary group — Garvey, Lopes, Russell, Cey, Yeager — came up with Tommy Lasorda and participated together in four World Series. Bob Welch, who arrived in 1978, is also included on the homegrown list.

There was a group of outsiders who ended up sticking around, guys like Dusty Baker, Reggie Smith, Rick Monday, and Burt Hooton, veterans of the 1977 and '78 Series.

There were more recent additions, like Jerry Reuss, Ken Landreaux, Derrel Thomas, and Jay Johnstone.

And there were those for whom the 1981 veterans would slowly be sold off, the core of a youth movement that carried the team through the ensuing decade — guys like Fernando Valenzuela, Mike Scioscia, Steve Sax, Pedro Guerrero, and Steve Howe.

Tommy Lasorda may have been a master motivator, but in '81 his players needed little in the way of incentive. They held each other to a level of accountability that no amount of pleading from the manager's office could replicate. "We had very big egos at every position," reflected Burt Hooton. "Everybody wanted to be the guy. If Don Sutton pitches a shutout, I want to pitch a shutout the next night. And if I pitch a shutout, then the guy after me wants to pitch a shutout too.

When we needed a big hit, when we needed a big game pitched, everybody wanted to be that guy. Everybody. We had people who didn't like each other, but when you put the uniform on, everybody wanted to shine."

There might have been no magic to it, but in a room without a clear-cut leader, there were plenty of magicians. If nobody's a leader, after all, then everybody's a leader. Ask players from the team about who drove direction in that clubhouse, and you'll receive a diversity of answers. Let Dave Stewart's response stand as representative:

> Reggie Smith was a strong force in our clubhouse. So was Dusty Baker. So was Davey Lopes. Terry Forster was great in our bullpen, because we were a young group of kids and Terry did a great job with us. At the same time, Jay Johnstone was a part of that club, and leadership comes in a lot of ways. He and Jerry Reuss, Steve Howe — those guys kept the clubhouse loose, made it fun. There was leadership from Garvey. Ron Cey had a strong personality too. All of those guys, Steve Yeager and Mike Scioscia . . . I can't just finger one person as the key.

For an example of how that looked, stick with Stewart, and go back to spring training 1978. The pitcher was 21 years old and ticketed for Double-A San Antonio, but found himself pitching against the team's big leaguers during a practice session in Vero Beach. The nervous right-hander began by drilling Davey Lopes in the ribs. Then he threw a fastball at Ron Cey's head, forcing the hitter to dive out of the way. Thoroughly rattled, Stewart bounced a fastball off of Steve Garvey's shoulder, and another off of Reggie Smith's knee. By that point he had Tommy Lasorda's full attention, and not in the way he'd hoped for when the drill began. "Get off the mound before you take out my entire lineup!" the manager screamed. Stewart slunk into the clubhouse, ashamed.

The pitcher sat, spinning. Given the chance to prove his ability amid the guys he wanted so desperately to impress, he had failed, abjectly. The feeling stuck with him through game's end and into the evening. It continued to dominate his thoughts as he walked the Dod-gertown hallways after dinner, lost in a fog. His reverie was snapped suddenly by an order shouted through an open doorway: "Hey, Stew-art — get in here!"

It was Reggie Smith. He'd seen the young pitcher pass by and wanted to give him a piece of his mind. *I'm really going to hear it now*, Stewart thought.

Stewart did hear it, but not in the way he expected. "The only thing you did wrong out there today was come off the field with your head down," Smith said sternly. "You don't *ever* leave the field hanging your head. If you did the best you could, you hold it high."

Hold it high. That stuck with Stewart. It could have served as a rallying cry for those 1981 Dodgers.

For all the diversity in the clubhouse, for the veteran status and self-motivation and institutional pride and Fernando-freaking-ma-nia, one figure managed to tower over all of it — the guy who'd kept everybody tethered from the low minor leagues all the way through Game 6 at Yankee Stadium. As with the roster he so enduringly shep-herded, Tommy Lasorda's own longevity ended up as the mark of a bygone era, akin to some storybook tale. The sport's most boisterous, overt, and downright infectious manager was the perfect guy for the job he ended up with, providing an enviable blend of acumen, enthu-siasm, and unvarnished loyalty.

Because of that, Lasorda became the last active link to the most storied period in the team's history. When he joined the Dodgers as a 21-year-old minor leaguer, the roster was loaded with golden-era names in their primes: Jackie Robinson, Duke Snider, Pee Wee Reese, Roy Campanella, Gil Hodges, Don Newcombe, Carl Furillo. When he landed his first managerial gig, with Ogden in 1965, the major league Dodgers were about to win again, this time behind Sandy Koufax and Don Drysdale. By the time he finally quit in 1996, almost a half-cen-tury after first pulling on a Dodgers uniform, only 60 percent of the

Boys of Summer — the championship team of 1955 — were even alive. By sheer dint of longevity, Lasorda became the greatest spanner of generations not only in Dodgers history but damn near in the history of the sport. Hell, 27 members of that 1996 roster weren't yet born when he managed his first game back in '65.

There is nothing complex about how Lasorda so capably endured. He was competent. He was loyal. He followed orders. Praying to the Big Dodger in the Sky? Fine, but there was more to it than that.

"Anybody who ever thinks Tommy isn't real when it comes to Dodger blue and all that kind of stuff is so far off," said trainer Paul Padilla, looking back. "Tommy is so Dodger blue, so baseball. I can get emotional just talking about him because he's that kind of a great guy, you know? Nobody was more joyful and jubilant than Tommy Lasorda. When he'd scream and throw his arms into the air and jump up and down, the little roly-poly that he was, it was just so much fun to watch. He was the ballplayer who never had the opportunity. He was living his life through his players, and he made sure that he did it just as fully as he could."

How much did Lasorda care? "I don't think he'd ever admit it, but he felt like *he* let *us* down if we didn't play well," said Steve Yeager. "He wanted so badly for us to go out and do the best that we could do."

Shortly before the 1981 campaign kicked off, Lasorda addressed a Los Angeles Area Chamber of Commerce luncheon and vociferously guaranteed a championship. It was pure chutzpah and might have been seen as visionary had the manager not made similar promises every season to anyone who would listen. This time, he insisted, he meant it.

Lasorda leaned on veteran players to the point that he was accused of using them as a crutch, yet he nurtured young players successfully enough to produce nine Rookies of the Year. To those insisting that his brand of minor league motivation had no place in the majors, Lasorda arrived in Los Angeles and didn't change a thing. To those who swore that his outsized personality would quickly wear out its welcome, he stuck around the manager's office for 21 years and in the front office for decades thereafter. For those who said that Lasorda's way — less technically proficient than emotionally driven — was simply not how an evolving sport should look, the manager offered a final retort: from the ranks of that 1981 Dodgers team emerged four major league managers — Dusty Baker, Mike Scioscia, Davey Lopes, and Ron Roenicke — plus dozens of coaches at every level. In 2002, one of Lasorda's players, Scioscia, beat another, Baker, in the World Series. Talk about legacy.

"Tommy exemplifies what the Dodgers are about," said Dave Stewart. "He is the true tradition."

"In everything that he did, you always sensed it was important that when the day ended, you loved Tommy," said reporter Peter Schmuck. "And people did." So what if the manager was constantly working an agenda with that point in mind? He wanted to look good — to his players, to the public — and, ultimately, he did.

One time Lasorda went to the mound to remove Jerry Reuss, and the pitcher met him with a litany of reasons why he should remain in the game. He felt strong, the left-hander said. Those hits against him had all been bloops, none of them well struck. He'd been missing the strike zone almost intentionally, trying to lure hitters into unnecessary swings. Lasorda had no interest. Rather than getting upset over an argument that was beginning to turn into insubordination, however, he turned to the catcher, Steve Yeager. "Boomer," he said, "this is a democratic society. I want to take him out. He wants to stay in. You provide the deciding vote." Yeager looked at Reuss. He looked at Lasorda.

"You should have taken his ass out *last* inning," the catcher said.

That was the manager in a nutshell. He got what he wanted while empowering Yeager and letting Reuss know that there was more to him than crackpot opinions. At the very least, it was *two* crackpot opinions. And that had to count for something.

• • •

"When I came to the organization, I was surrounded by the nucleus of the next chapter in Dodgers history," said Ron Cey, looking back. "Tommy worked hard with us, spent countless hours nurturing us, fought for us. You have to make the guys at the top think that you're good enough — you have to sell them — and Tommy was the guy to do that, for all of us. He sold them on us, and he sold us on them."

Which cuts to the heart of the matter. Not every player loved Lasorda. Many didn't. Not every player loved each other. The clubhouse was noteworthy for an abundance of members who flat out didn't get along. Even the cornerstone infield — *especially* the cornerstone infield — spent so much time grousing about each other that it's difficult in retrospect to imagine how cohesively they actually played together. "It was good that [Cey and Garvey] were on the opposite ends of the infield," said Dave Goltz, reflecting on various personalities.

Forget the issues that various Dodgers took with Garvey's throwing. Or Lopes's throwing. Or Russell's throwing. Or Lopes's hands of stone. Or that Russell wouldn't dive. Or that Garvey was aloof and Cey was cranky. Somehow they not only stuck it out through nine seasons together, but went to four World Series, finally winning one just in the nick of time. To a man, the players insisted that they were better as a unit than they were individually, and the fact that their legacies are invariably tied to the collective bears this out. "I think Steve Garvey is synonymous with the Dodgers," Garvey said back in '81, a sentiment that could easily be taken as an effort to subvert the team to his personality and claim position as the high man on the totem. Instead, though, he was trying to illustrate just the opposite — that without his ballclub, Garvey's own brand would be measurably reduced. "They don't usually say Steve Garvey alone, but Steve Garvey of the Dodgers," he added. "The Dodgers, Steve Garvey — *that* goes hand in hand."

If it was true for Garvey, it was true for all of them, even Lasorda. They needed each other in ways that not all of them were eager to admit. They might not have been in thrall with their mutual codependence, but even the most reluctant among them had to admit that it worked.

Jay Johnstone tells a story about Garvey and Cey — who lived near each other but rarely carpooled to work together — sharing a rare ride one day with then-teammate Bill Buckner. "Buckner never talks in the mornings anyhow," recalled Johnstone, "and he and Garvey weren't exactly pals. So here were these three guys, all teammates, in a car together, and there is *no* conversation." For 45 minutes the trio drove silently, and upon arriving at the ballpark simply set to going about their business.

It didn't make a bit of difference. Whatever happened before those Dodgers took the field was strictly ancillary — it was what they did with cleats on that mattered. And in the end, despite age and injuries and an abundance of doubts from outside the clubhouse, they satisfied their end of the bargain, emerging, like a 21-year-old Dave Stewart in Vero Beach, with heads held high and rings on their fingers.

Acknowledgments

It might not benefit my credibility as the author of this book to admit that I am a lifelong Giants partisan, but it's true. Many highlights of my pre-teenage fandom are Dodgers-related, and not in a good way regarding the boys in blue: sitting a couple dozen rows up from where Reggie Smith charged into the Candlestick Park grandstand in 1981; cheering like mad from seats high up the third base side when Joe Morgan knocked the Dodgers out of contention in '82; gleefully booing Tommy Lasorda as he blew kisses to the crowd on his regular cross-field walk to the visitors' dugout in San Francisco.

There is a reason why so many of my baseball memories have to do with beating LA: in the late 1970s and early '80s, Giants fans had little else to root for. With winning the division all but out of the question, we mostly settled for hoping that our team could prevent the Dodgers from doing the same. Sometimes that was enough. Usually it wasn't. For years I had an annual $5 bet with a Dodgers-fan cousin about which team would finish higher in the standings. This rarely worked out in my favor. Even when the Dodgers sank to fourth place in 1984, the Giants finished dead last; when the Dodgers rebounded to win the NL West in '85, the Giants finished last again.

When I was eleven or twelve, I rode my bike to downtown Palo Alto to be one of the first in line at a Steve Garvey appearance at Rapp's Shoes. Meeting a genuine big leaguer was worth it to me, and

Garvey did not disappoint, but once I brought home the signed give-away poster — featuring the first baseman, forearms bulging, standing on the moon next to the phrase "The harder you hit it, the further it goes" — I couldn't bear to hang it on my wall. It was just too Dodgery. It now resides in another cousin's LA-area home.

Over the years I've even named two dogs after Dodgers-turned-Giants (or, as I referred to them, "reformed Dodgers"): Reggie (after Smith) and Dusty (after Baker).

All of which is prelude to saying that when I started this project, I figured to gain a new appreciation of the franchise upon which I expended so much negative childhood energy. What I learned is that every detail I needed to respect this team, I already knew. The Dodgers were a model franchise, helmed by an earnest and enduring spokesperson in Tommy Lasorda. They featured a cast of ballplayers who were utterly serious about winning, leaning on excellent veterans while breaking in an almost unbelievable string of four straight Rookies of the Year. They knew how to ride a hot hand and, while doing an awful lot of bending, refused to break. It's a pretty good model for any team with title hopes. Heck, it's the kind of model I spent my youth wishing my hometown team might one day develop.

There is a tale in this book about Houston's Enos Cabell carpooling to Dodger Stadium with Rick Monday and Jerry Reuss. The two Dodgers told it to me independently, in the same way: Cabell, whose off-season residence was close to Reuss's home in Los Angeles, thumbed a ride to Chavez Ravine in advance of the first two games played there in the 1981 NLDS. Each player offered charming details for what turned out to be a fun little ditty.

There was only one problem: Cabell played for the Giants in 1981.

When someone like me sets out to tell a decades-old tale — especially a tale about which one has no firsthand knowledge — the insights and recollections of those who were there make all the difference. The trouble with interviewing people about long-ago events, however, is that the events happened long ago. Memories fade and jumble, details from one episode get transposed onto another or fade away altogether.

The Cabell car rides, it turned out, occurred in 1980, when the Astros traveled to Los Angeles for their pivotal, season-closing series. Because the 1981 playoffs also involved Houston and are much more prominent to the careers of both Reuss and Monday — the ensuing championship was the only one either player would win — that's how they remember it. The story still appears in the book, but it took some tweaking to make it fit appropriately.

For an even better example of how memories work, take this snippet from my interview with Steve Garvey, wherein he described the celebration on the mound at Yankee Stadium following the clinching Game 6 of the World Series:

> GARVEY: "There's a great shot of Steve Yeager picking up Steve Howe, and I'm way up high, the highest I've ever leaped, I think. I think it was a full page, or double-page spread in *Sports Illustrated*. We all come down, and Yeager spins Howe around, Howe clocks me with his elbow, knocks my hat off, and I'm seeing stars. But it's New York, and people are rushing, and I see my hat, and I think, *I better grab it*. I grab it, and I run off the field . . ."
>
> ME: "I'm going off memory here, but someone in that scrum told me that you actually had to yell, 'Hey, give me my hat!' to a guy who grabbed it before you."
>
> GARVEY: "I don't have a license on this one, but I'm quite sure I grabbed it. Believe me, I would have had to tackle the guy, a New Yorker, yeah. There would've been a scrum going on."

I checked my files when I returned home, and sure enough I found the reference confirming that a fan had indeed snatched the first baseman's hat away. I even got Garvey's quote right upon recollection, almost to the word: *"Gimme that hat!"*

The source: Garvey's own autobiography.

This is not to suggest that Garvey, Reuss, or Monday were anything less than terrific interview subjects. To the contrary, they were all gracious and accommodating. Heck, Garvey spent five hours with me and an enormous, friendly, drooling Rottweiler named Spartacus on his back patio in Palm Desert, for which I offer nothing but gratitude . . . and a slobber-induced dry-cleaning bill. Monday met me twice, first at the Dodgers spring training facility in Arizona and later at his hotel when the team was in San Francisco. Reuss was the first Dodger I interviewed for this book, in a Las Vegas restaurant, and set the bar very high, very early. (In a career spent sitting down with athletes, my conversation with Jerry ranks among the absolute best.) Like everybody, their memories are subject to the vagaries of time. In telling this tale I did my best to verify everything verifiable, and omitted an awful lot that wasn't.

I would like to thank the players and other key characters who took time to go over, in granular detail, the makeup and accounts of this team, many of them in person — at their homes and offices (Garvey, Dusty Baker, Fred Claire), at restaurants and cafes throughout California and Nevada (Reuss, Jay Johnstone, Derrel Thomas, Steve Sax), at Dodger Stadium (Ron Cey, Steve Yeager, Mike Brito, Jaime Jarin, Mark Langill), and at ballparks around the country (Monday in Glendale, Arizona; Mike Scioscia in Oakland; Burt Hooton in Phoenix; and Ken Landreaux at the MLB Youth Academy in Compton). Those who I reached on the phone, particularly players (Dave Stewart, Dave Goltz, Dave Righetti . . . a regular Dave Patrol), trainers (Paul Padilla and Herb Vike), and reporters (Mark Heisler, Chris Mortensen, Peter Schmuck, and Lyle Spencer) helped make this tale what it is. Special thanks to the big man himself, Peter O'Malley, for taking the time to speak with me, and to *Split Season* author Jeff Katz, who made the research draft of his book available for me to peruse themes and sources. Additional thanks to Joe Jareck and Daisuke Sugiura of the Dodgers PR department for their help on the ground in Los Angeles.

Appreciation, as usual, goes to the team at HMH, particularly my editor, Susan Canavan; editorial assistant Jenny Xu, who expertly kept everything on schedule; and copyedit whiz Cindy Buck. Also and always, huge thanks to my agent extraordinaire, Jud Laghi, for not only helping me get this project where it needed to be before HMH came on board, but who may even have come up with the idea in the first place. His is a percentage well earned.

Finally, my gratitude to my wife, Laura, is abiding. Her support and confidence make all the difference in my line of work. She is the ultimate cheerleader, and has even begun to care (ever so slightly) about baseball . . . which has far more to do with the fact that my son is now of playing age than with the fact that I write about it for a living. My parents have offered unwavering support through every step of my career, and now, in addition to being exemplary role models as father and mother, have stepped up their game as grandma and grandpa. Way to stay involved. My children got enough of a kick out of seeing their names in print the last time around that I'd be derelict to deny them a repeat performance: Hi, Mozi. Hi, Reuben. I love you all.

Notes

Prologue

page

xi *"one of the shrewdest and most significant plays"*: The Sporting News, November 4, 1978.

xii *"The problem is that we had an afternoon start the next day"*: Ron Cey interview.
"We made one mistake": The Sporting News, November 4, 1978.
"Unfortunately, we'll be remembered for the last six games": Ibid.

1. The Manager

1 *"When not pitching, Lasorda does the coaching at first base"*: The Sporting News, June 18, 1958.

2 *"Son, you've been here one day"*: Tommy Lasorda and Bill Plaschke, *I Live for This! Baseball's Last True Believer* (New York: Houghton Mifflin, 2007).

3 *"I knew I couldn't throw him three straight strikes"*: Tommy Lasorda and David Fisher, *The Artful Dodger* (New York: Arbor House, 1985).
"What inning?": Ibid.

4 *"Dear Tom, the exhibition you put on last night"*: Ibid.
"I'd fight just for the fun of it": The Sporting News, May 6, 1978.
"If I was in charge": Tommy Lasorda and David Fisher, *The Artful Dodger*.

7 *"Greenville ballclub"*: Lasorda and Fisher, *The Artful Dodger*.
"Tommy believed. He believed all the time": Herb Vike interview.

8 *"Lasorda's [Ogden] Dodgers are the talk of the league"*: The Sporting News, September 9, 1967.
"a walking pledge of allegiance": The Sporting News, April 9, 1977.
"Dodger blue monologues": Thomas Boswell, *Why Time Begins on Opening Day* (New York: Doubleday, 1984).

"You've heard about the 'Blue Fever'": *The Sporting News*, April 1, 1978.

9   "This must be the Garv!": Steve Garvey interview.

"It was all about dreaming big": Lasorda and Plaschke, *I Live for This!*

"Listen. guys, my wife hates the fact that I cuss": Peter Schmuck interview.

10   "I'd never heard anybody cuss and scream that way": Lou Sahadi, *The LA Dodgers: The World Champions of Baseball* (New York: Quill, 1982).

"Oh, he tells us to stop": *New York Times*, October 31, 1981.

11   "Usually, when a baseball player leaves for the ballpark": Lasorda and Fisher, *The Artful Dodger*.

"That's fine. I want the chance": Sahadi, *The LA Dodgers*.

"just for the fun of it": *The Sporting News*, May 6, 1978.

12   "Tommy Lasorda is the most publicized third base coach in baseball": *The Sporting News*, January 31, 1976.

13   "heir apparent": *Los Angeles Times*, August 23, 1976.

14   "This is the greatest day of my life": *Los Angeles Times*, September 30, 1976.

"No, I'm worried about the guy who is going to replace me": Lasorda and Plaschke, *I Live for This!*

"I just couldn't see myself telling people": Lasorda and Fisher, *The Artful Dodger*.

15   "Lasorda was the biggest bullshitter in the world": Mike Brito interview.

16   "When Tommy held his first clubhouse meeting": *The Sporting News*, October 29, 1977.

"It reminded me of my Italian grandmother, Nonna": Steve Sax interview.

"Everybody was a Dodger fan": Jerry Reuss interview.

"It can be agonizing going into his office": *Orange Coast Magazine*, April 1992.

17   "When I said I bled Dodger blue, a lot of cynics": *The Sporting News*, March 11, 1978.

"I thought he was crazy at the time": Herb Vike interview.

2. Snatched

18   "You move players from one position to another to fill your needs": Al Campanis, *The Dodgers' Way to Play Baseball* (New York: E. P. Dutton & Co., 1954).

19   "I'm still rough around the edges": *Los Angeles Times*, June 24, 1981.

"wouldn't be all-streetcorner in LA": Ibid.

"the usual ghetto thing, the typical environment": *Los Angeles Times*, September 1, 1974.

20   "Maybe they'll let you play outfield on the thread factory team": Ibid.

"Davey had terrible hands — terrible — and he couldn't make the double play": *Sport*, August 1977.

"He had literally run into my life": Lasorda and Fisher, *The Artful Dodger*.

21   "One hundred [Dodgers minor leaguers] were sleeping": *Los Angeles Times*, September 1, 1974

"They're doing me a favor": *The Sporting News*, August 30, 1975.

"psychological warfare": The Sporting News, July 8, 1978.

"Davey Lopes was the most serious player": Chris Mortensen interview.

"With a righthanded pitcher, the shoulder is open": Sport, August 1977.

23 *"I'm walking back to my position"*: Los Angeles Times, June 23, 2013.

"a dumpy little fellow": Los Angeles Times, June 24, 1981.

"I don't even know his first name": The Sporting News, May 28, 1977.

"Walks like a duck, hits like a truck": Lyle Spencer interview.

24 *"I motherfucked him all the time"*: Ron Cey interview.

"Penguin was a little bit of a grouchy Penguin": Chris Mortensen interview.

"Charm": Steve Yeager interview.

27 *"You can't mention anyone from that infield"*: Baseball Digest, June 2009.

"That infield was tight on the field, but not anywhere else": Peter Schmuck interview.

28 *"Dodger Blue Is Turning Gray"*: Sports Illustrated, July 2, 1979.

"I've never had this kind of year": Ibid.

29 *"He didn't like being second-guessed"*: Chris Mortensen interview.

"He started teeing off on me": Lyle Spencer interview.

30 *"I had to pitch a shutout in every game"*: 1981 Los Angeles Dodgers yearbook.

31 *"With that extra day of rest I was way too strong"*: Dave Goltz interview.

32 *"We begged Lasorda to go with Fernando"*: Dusty Baker interview.

3. Eighty-One

34 *"What would [Lasorda] say?"*: Los Angeles Times, March 12, 1981.

"I keep telling you guys, I don't use sandpaper": Los Angeles Times, April 9, 1981.

"It's not here, but you're getting warm": Los Angeles Times, April 12, 1981.

35 *"I just don't believe that I could play for a manager"*: Los Angeles Times, September 28, 1976.

"one of [Lasorda's] bobos": Los Angeles Times, March 12, 1981.

"You know what you can do with those notes you're making?": The Sporting News, April 1, 1978.

"Aw, c'mon, Tommy": Orange Coast Magazine, May 1986.

37 *"I'm not in the habit of stealing boats"*: Los Angeles Times, February 25, 1981.

38 *"I'd ask [Ferguson], 'What is it today'"*: Los Angeles Times, March 9, 1981.

"the little fat kid from Delco": Los Angeles Times, October 18, 2002.

"I was taught that it was a badge of honor": Mike Scioscia interview.

39 *"I really believe Mike could have been a lifetime .300 hitter"*: Los Angeles Times, April 6, 2003.

"After the workout I probably would have paid them to sign me": Colin Gunderson, Tommy Lasorda: My Way (Chicago: Triumph Books, 2015).

"Blocking the plate is when you're standing on it": Los Angeles Times, May 16, 1981.

40 *"People say I like him because he's Italian"*: Sports Illustrated, May 12, 1980.

"The way you give yourself up at the plate": The Sporting News, November 14, 1981.

41 "LA is probably the greatest place to play": Los Angeles Times, March 9, 1981.

42 "They hire two guys just to pick up the balls": The Sporting News, March 25, 1978.

43 "What're you doing?": Sports Illustrated, April 12, 1982.

44 "We don't know how much longer we'll all be together": Sahadi, The LA Dodgers.
"Even the team's hometown newspaper": Los Angeles Times, June 24, 1981.
"for sentimental reasons": New York Times, October 17, 1981.

46 "Man, I'm not that old": Ken Landreaux interview.
"There were times that we'd be low on bats": Ken Landreaux interview.
"If you'd stayed in Minnesota": Los Angeles Times, March 29, 1981.

47 "When it comes to Reggie Smith": Ibid.

48 "You guys let me know what your plan is": Dave Stewart interview.

49 "Sometimes there's no justice, Stew": The Sporting News, June 13, 1981.
"He tried to make it seem special": Dave Stewart interview.

50 "complete puzzlement": New York Times, April 27, 1981.

4. Mania

52 "He is, how shall we say it — he is — well, he's fat": Los Angeles Times, April 10, 1981.

53 "We don't know what's going on inside him": Ibid.
"He wasn't one bit nervous": Ibid.
"All I'm worried about": Los Angeles Times, March 4, 1981.

54 Pedazo de pastel: "Dodgers: Brotherhood of the Game," Japanese American National Museum, Los Angeles.
"if he had been 100 years old and in the majors for 90 of them": Los Angeles Times, April 10, 1981.
"When I get on the mound I don't know what afraid is": Ibid.
"Hell, you've got to break him in somewhere": Jay Johnstone interview.
"Fernando threw the best BP": Derrel Thomas interview.

55 "The cold weather, it made me a little stiff": San Francisco Chronicle, April 15, 1981.

56 "catching hell for not bringing him up earlier": Los Angeles Times, April 19, 1981.

57 "There was no one moment when I realized he was for real": Dave Stewart interview.
"After his first single, he got a standing ovation": Los Angeles Times, April 28, 1981.
"He seems to think there's a better league somewhere else": Los Angeles Times, April 29, 1981.

58 "I was too young": Los Angeles Times, April 24, 1981.

60 "I remember waiting at the bus station": Sahadi, The LA Dodgers.
"Castro signed Tony Oliva, Camilo Pascual": Mike Brito interview.

61 "Cabron, a screwball?": Ibid.

62 "Twice, the other team had the bases loaded": Inside Sports, June 30, 1981.
"Seguro": Fernando Nation, ESPN.
"I said, 'I'm Mike Brito from the Los Angeles Dodgers'": Mike Brito interview.
"a chance": New York Times, October 24, 1981.

63 "Mike, you're right": Ibid.

64 "Mike, it's not the money, it's the honor": Ibid.
"We're not going to lose this guy": Ibid.

65 "If that foul ball I hit had landed fair": Ibid.

66 "It has different spin that'll stay down": Mike Scioscia interview.

67 "it was like watching a great horse": Sports Illustrated, March 23, 1981.
"Nature never intended a man to turn his hand": Los Angeles Times, April 30, 1981.

68 "the only Dodger performance worth noting": Los Angeles Times, September 16, 1980.
"No, I want to finish here": 2015 Los Angeles Dodgers yearbook.

69 "The only words with which I'm able to communicate with him": Los Angeles Times, July 9, 1990.
"He has the right formula exactly": Los Angeles Times, April 30, 1981.

70 "I've never seen anything like it": Sports Illustrated, March 23, 1981.

5. Buried

71 "They never told you about the conflict": Fernando Nation, ESPN.

72 "the worst slum in the city": John H. M. Laslett, Shameful Victory: The Los Angeles Dodgers, the Red Scare, and the Hidden History of Chavez Ravine (Tucson: University of Arizona Press, 2015).

73 "creeping cancer": Ibid.

77 "Our base scale for endorsements is $50,000": Associated Press, October 27, 1981.
"At Dodger Stadium, Monday nights are filled": Steve Garvey interview.

78 "The fan demographics of Dodger Stadium changed in a month": Peter Schmuck interview.
"The best part about it is that it was completely spontaneous": Lyle Spencer interview.

79 "He looked like a man, but he acted like a kid": Dusty Baker interview.

80 "We scored a run off him": Los Angeles Times, May 3, 1981.
"New York writers are so mean": Jaime Jarrín interview.

81 "I felt like I was following the heavyweight champion": Chris Mortensen interview.
"Es my difícil": Los Angeles Times, May 8, 1981.

82 "His father didn't talk too much": Mike Brito interview.

83 "Fernando liked his privacy": Ibid.

84   *"Obviously, I didn't get through"*: Los Angeles Times, May 25, 1981.

85   *"It just kind of makes me wonder"*: Los Angeles Times, May 14, 1981.

6. Struck

87   *"time bomb"*: John Helyar, *Lords of the Realm: The Real History of Baseball* (New York: Villard, 1994).

88   *"many millions of dollars"*: New York Times, July 13, 1981.

"Bowie, they'll get compensation over my dead body": Helyar, *Lords of the Realm.*

90   *"They started out giving us Rod Carew and Vida Blue as examples"*: Ibid.

"They're trying to ram it down our throats": Boston Globe, February 20, 1981.

91   *"Marvin had a saying"*: Rick Monday interview.

92   *"You could feel the tenseness in the air"*: Dave Goltz interview.

93   *"Maybe age had started to show"*: Ibid.

"We've got some key guys not hitting": Los Angeles Times, May 16, 1981.

94   *"I hear you're a great ballplayer"*: Los Angeles Times, June 9, 1981.

"The most powerful people in the country": Jaime Jarrín interview.

"He didn't give a shit": Mike Brito interview.

95   *"Things got very quiet in that clubhouse"*: Rick Monday interview.

"You got anything else to do tonight, Jerry?": Los Angeles Times, June 11, 1981.

96   *"For whoever cares, I'll be in Las Vegas"*: The Sporting News, June 27, 1981.

"There is no strike": Los Angeles Times, June 11, 1981.

"canceled until further notice": Los Angeles Times, June 13, 1981.

97   *"[Refusing entry onto the plane] is not a punitive action"*: Los Angeles Times, June 12, 1981.

99   *"another macho test of wills"*: Helyar, *Lords of the Realm.*

"normal, family-oriented programming": Los Angeles Times, June 13, 1981.

100 *"The worst part is the realization that there is nothing else"*: The Sporting News, August 15, 1981.

101 *"Somehow bats and balls mysteriously appeared"*: Rick Monday interview.

"I don't care if we've got to sell our homes": Los Angeles Times, June 19, 1981.

"We were just taking ground balls and fly balls": Ron Cey interview.

102 *"We thought at first it would only be a week or two"*: Rick Monday interview.

"I told you to work out": Dusty Baker interview.

"He killed me at first": Ibid.

"My dad's garage was bigger than mine": Jay Johnstone interview.

103 *"I actually played in a couple of games"*: Mike Scioscia interview.

"getting anxious": Los Angeles Times, June 29, 1981.

"Eventually I realized that if something doesn't get better": Steve Garvey interview.

"He didn't want us to use power tools": Steve Yeager interview.

104 *"I play an LA-based detective working with David"*: Associated Press, July 22, 1981.

105 *"I just knew how the strike was going"*: Jo Wetton interview.

"I certainly got name recognition out of it": Brad Jenkins interview.

"We don't have people in socially anymore": Christian Science Monitor, July 10, 1981.

106 *"Man, we didn't have this kind of problem at Albuquerque"*: The Sporting News, July 4, 1981.

"nobody has a clause that says they'd get paid": Los Angeles Times, July 18, 1981.

"The contract guaranteed payment except in cases": Steve Greenberg interview.

"everybody had an opportunity to negotiate their contract": Los Angeles Times, July 18, 1981.

107 *"We all voted to strike, and now what does his vote mean"*: Los Angeles Times, July 23, 1981.

"I just try to control the things I can control": Steve Garvey interview.

108 *"My intentions were good"*: New York Daily News, June 27, 1981.

"I was warming up and there was a buzz": Mike Witt interview.

"I just can't believe it happened": Orange County Register, June 24, 1981.

109 *"Al Campanis was like a father to me"*: Mike Brito interview.

"The Dodgers insisted that it didn't happen": Peter Schmuck interview.

"Solomon the Wise was lenient": Los Angeles Times, June 26, 1981.

"I'm so angry I'd sell everything I have": Los Angeles Times, June 19, 1981.

110 *"The gap between us is so great"*: Los Angeles Times, July 2, 1981.

"One guy might say the locker room in St. Louis": The Sporting News, August 15, 1981.

111 *"Many of us felt this should have been resolved"*: Los Angeles Times, July 4, 1981.

112 *"He kept needling me"*: Sport, August 1977.

"Do Doug DeCinces and Bob Boone have legal backgrounds?": Los Angeles Times, July 23, 1981.

113 *"The last thing I want to do is pick up a paper"*: Ibid.

"It's impossible to make 25 telephone calls a day": Ibid.

"This forget-the-season attitude really eats at me": Ibid.

"worse than ever": Los Angeles Times, July 24, 1981.

114 *"They still think they can bring the union to its knees"*: Los Angeles Times, July 24, 1981.

"I don't want to be a martyr": Helyar, Lords of the Realm.

115 *"If it's information he wants"*: Los Angeles Times, July 28, 1981.

116 *"I don't know where my players stand on the issues"*: Jerry Reuss, Bring in the Right-Hander: My Twenty-Two Years in the Major Leagues (Lincoln: University of Nebraska Press, 2014).

"About half the players here tonight didn't have the facts": Los Angeles Times, July 28, 1981.

"to see what the hell was going on": Los Angeles Times, July 30, 1981.

"If someone has an objection, dammit, say something": Helyar, Lords of the Realm.

"Who in this room isn't with the Association?": Jeff Katz, *Split Season: Fernandomania, the Bronx Zoo, and the Strike That Saved Baseball* (New York: Thomas Dunne Books, 2015).

117   *"That was like a civil war"*: Dusty Baker interview.

"upset and emotional": *The Sporting News*, August 15, 1981.

"If that's what it takes, yes sir": *Los Angeles Times*, July 30, 1981.

119   *"a victory for the spirit of the players"*: *Los Angeles Times*, August 1, 1981.

"You're a liar": Helyar, *Lords of the Realm*.

"a paid commercial for the players": *Los Angeles Times*, August 2, 1981.

"You don't see any of us jumping for joy": *Los Angeles Times*, August 1, 1981.

7. La-La

121   *"runs approximately parallel with the third base line"*: *Los Angeles Times*, October 17, 1978.

122   *"As a Dodger, the scene opens up for you"*: Ken Landreaux interview.

"The dancers weren't our concern": Ibid.

123   *"Tommy [Sr.] was obsessed with the word* faggot*"*: *OUT: The Glenn Burke Story* (film), (NBC Universal/Comcast SportsNet, 2010).

"I like all people": *No Mag*, 1981.

"I guess you mean to a woman": *The Week*, September 2, 2011.

124   *"really loved his son and was always there for him"*: *GQ*, October 1992.

"It's hard not to like him": *No Mag*, 1981.

125   *"He basically turned the clubhouse into the Friars Club"*: Mark Langill interview.

"Only in LA": Burt Hooton interview.

126   *"To me this was like meeting Babe Ruth"*: Lasorda and Plaschke, *I Live for This!*

"should be the next manager of the Dodgers": *Saturday Evening Post*, July/August 1981.

"The town mayor is willing to rip": Society for American Baseball Research, *The National Pastime: Endless Seasons, 2011: Baseball in Southern California* (Phoenix, AZ: ABR, 2011).

127   *"I really think that Tommy's life thrilled him"*: Mark Heisler interview.

"these big sons of bitches in three-piece suits": Jerry Reuss interview.

128   *"Where have you been?"*: Steve Garvey interview.

"Somebody finally introduced us": Peter Schmuck interview.

129   *"Tommy said, 'Go take him out, Don'"*: *Variety*, June 19, 2008.

"Peter [O'Malley] is Mr. Conservative": Mark Langill interview.

130   *"O'Malley . . . would just as soon have his manager managing"*: *The Sporting News*, May 24, 1980.

"Tommy fetishized celebrity to a notable degree": Mark Heisler interview.

"Look at that stomach": Michael Fallon, *Dodgerland: Decadent Los Angeles and the 1977–78 Dodgers* (Lincoln: University of Nebraska Press, 2016).

"How long are you going to make [your wife] clean hotel rooms?": "Don Rick-

les Insults the Dodgers," 1986, posted on YouTube December 26, 2010, https://www.youtube.com/watch?v=Nxipk-Oaufo.

131 *"Drugs are used openly [in Los Angeles]"*: New York Times, October 31, 1982.
   "A lot of people began using amphetamines": Washington Post, October 27, 1981.
   "The 'All-American drug' has hit like a blizzard": Time, July 6, 1981.
   "It seemed like everyone in Los Angeles was snorting the stuff": Steve Howe with Jim Greenfield, *Between the Lines: One Athlete's Struggle to Escape the Nightmare of Addiction* (New York: Masters Press, 1989).

132 *"Drug dealers, some of them riding in chauffeured limousines"*: New York Times, October 31, 1982.
   "There were a lot of busts back in those days": Dave Stewart interview.
   "I only know a few people that didn't try something": Dusty Baker interview.
   at which time Mets first baseman Keith Hernandez: Time, June 24, 2001.
   "I knew Curtis Strong, but he wasn't my kind of cat": Ibid.
   "I'm a pretty good judge of character": Ibid.

133 *"The kid has ice water in his veins"*: Sports Illustrated, May 12, 1980.

134 *"I was used to talking with small knots of reporters in the clubhouse"*: Howe and Greenfield, *Between the Lines*.
   "to the point of total preoccupation": Ibid.
   "was borderline insanity": Chris Mortensen interview.

135 *"All right, Howzer, give me some of that stuff"*: Howe and Greenfield, *Between the Lines*.
   "the list of non-partiers on the 1980 Dodgers": Ibid.
   "between 70 and 80 percent of professional ballplayers": The Sporting News, July 12, 1982.
   "If there were any heavy users": Ibid.
   "Any time you see a correlation": Dusty Baker interview.

136 *"Nobody on the Dodgers pressured me to do drugs"*: Howe and Greenfield, *Between the Lines*.
   "Why do you hang around the blacks": Ibid.
   "Al Campanis was one of the more fair ones": Dusty Baker interview.
   "I truly believe [that African American players] may not have some of the necessities": Nightline, ABC-TV, April 6, 1987.

137 *"We had our own little clique of guys"*: Derrel Thomas interview.
   "It was an experimental time in our country": Dusty Baker interview.

8. Second Act

138 *"Me not putting on a baseball uniform"*: Los Angeles Times, July 31, 1981.

139 *"That's the mark of a true professional"*: Los Angeles Times, August 1, 1981.
   "There were lights and cameras involved": Rick Monday interview.
   "You know how many Cadillacs that man owes us?": Steve Yeager interview.
   "It's like, okay, we're back": Rick Monday interview.

140 *"Neither did I"*: Howe and Greenfield, *Between the Lines*.

I *told* you to turn the damn lights on: Ibid.

"The players expected it": Los Angeles Times, August 7, 1981.

141 *"I know I don't deserve to be here"*: Los Angeles Times, August 5, 1981.

"It's been the kid's year": Los Angeles Times, August 9, 1981.

144 *"I suppose it means that every time we play Seattle or Toronto"*: Toronto Globe and Mail, August 8, 1981.

"If our own fall season wasn't in such a state of flux": Los Angeles Times, August 17, 1981.

145 *"My job is to get the Cardinals into the playoffs"*: Los Angeles Times, August 17, 1981.

"solely to eradicate any possible question of integrity": Los Angeles Times, August 21, 1981.

"Apparently, other considerations are more important than integrity": Ibid.

"There is no ideal solution": Los Angeles Times, August 16, 1981.

"Five extra days' pay": Los Angeles Times, August 7, 1981.

146 *"Give me my money"*: Ibid.

"Every club is going to try and maintain as much momentum as it can": Los Angeles Times, August 10, 1981.

"I got to work on pitches like a cutter": Dave Goltz interview.

147 *"I want out of the Dodgers right now"*: Los Angeles Times, August 21, 1981.

148 *"Howser nicknamed us 'Canned Heat'"*: Dave Stewart interview.

"Talk about a Kiddie Corps": The Sporting News, September 5, 1981.

"When I was 10 years old, I was on the Giants": Steve Sax interview.

149 *"He was like the Energizer Bunny"*: Derrel Thomas interview.

"Davey took someone's job": Los Angeles Times, September 4, 1981.

150 *"He's hanging his pitches a lot more"*: Los Angeles Times, August 16, 1981.

"Mexico is baseball crazy now": Los Angeles Times, August 12, 1981.

152 *"I'll see you after the game"*: Pittsburgh Post-Gazette, August 26, 1981.

"Reggie had that voice that carried": Jerry Reuss interview.

"Bottles were thrown at my house": Sports Illustrated, October 2, 1978.

153 *"Reggie was a proud man"*: Chris Mortensen interview.

"took my aggressiveness as being mean": Los Angeles Times, January 22, 1981.

"can go off the deep end real quick": Dave Goltz interview.

"If you have a Reggie bar in New York": Los Angeles Times, September 17, 1981.

154 *"Lasorda came to me and said, 'I need you'"*: Steve Delsohn, True Blue: The Dramatic History of the Los Angeles Dodgers, Told by the Men Who Lived It (New York: William Morrow, 2001).

"the difference between first and second place for us": Sports Illustrated, October 2, 1978.

"the second-best player I ever played with": Dusty Baker interview.

"I can't seem to find the concentration this year": The Sporting News, May 26, 1979.

"Reggie was a force in every way": Lyle Spencer interview.

155 *"It wasn't our nature to be low-key"*: Jerry Reuss interview.

156 *"like a wild buffalo"*: *Pittsburgh Press*, August 26, 1981.

"It was like, push the elevator button": Peter Schmuck interview.

"Pops, this has nothing to do with me and you": Ken Landreaux interview.

157 *"a bunch of little guys trying to look over a fence"*: Dave Stewart interview.

"It was like a scene from Braveheart*"*: Steve Garvey interview.

"All the years we'd been in that stadium": Rick Monday interview.

"Let's put it this way": *Los Angeles Times*, August 26, 1981.

158 *"Love Baseball, Hate the Giants"*: *The Sporting News*, July 24, 1971.

"a medical first": Ron Cey interview.

160 *"D, what are you trying to do to me?"*: Dusty Baker interview.

"Shit, we don't need no fucking signs": Ibid.

"Of course not": Ibid.

161 *"I can't come up"*: Nick Peters with Stuart Shea, *Tales from the San Francisco Giants Dugout* (New York: Sports Publishing, 2003).

"What will it take to get you up here?": Jay Johnstone with Rick Talley, *Temporary Insanity: The Uncensored Adventures of Baseball's Craziest Player* (Chicago: Contemporary Books, 1985).

"You can't possibly be that stupid": Rick Monday interview.

"like he was Bruce Lee": Dusty Baker interview.

162 *"Oh shit"*: Johnstone and Talley, *Temporary Insanity*.

"Oh shit": Rick Monday interview.

"a big black guy with glasses": Johnstone and Talley, *Temporary Insanity*.

"You do that in Philadelphia or New York or San Francisco": Steve Garvey interview.

163 *"That's the guy"*: Ibid.

"If Lasorda would keep his club in the dugout": *Associated Press*, September 25, 1981.

164 *"I did not acknowledge Giants fans"*: Jerry Reuss interview.

165 *"That's it. He's our second baseman"*: *Los Angeles Times*, September 8, 1981.

"Who was the second baseman before Sax?": *The Sporting News*, September 26, 1981.

"I'm not going to let people bury me": Ibid.

166 *"Some things were said at the meeting"*: *The Sporting News*, August 4, 1979.

167 *"If you don't mention anything about it"*: Steve Sax interview.

168 *"If you've got the talent"*: *Los Angeles Times*, September 15, 1981.

"It was like taking candy from a baby": Ibid.

"The Old Goats beat their ass every day": Steve Yeager interview.

"What was really funny": Steve Sax interview.

169 *"Oh my God, you had Reggie Smith"*: Mike Scioscia interview.

"They were very competitive": Ibid.

"There's something to be said for old goats": Steve Yeager interview.

170 *"Maybe it was too heavy"*: *Los Angeles Times*, September 28, 1981.

171 *"Sunday, the ushers confiscated the baseball"*: *Los Angeles Times*, October 5, 1981.

"We've won one game [at Dodger Stadium]": Los Angeles Times, October 4, 1981.
172 "Hell, I knew he was apprehensive about bunting": Jerry Reuss interview.
173 "Hey man, you're already in trouble": Dusty Baker interview.
"I will never play again for Tommy Lasorda": Los Angeles Times, October 4, 1981.

9. Houston-Ho!

176 "What you should be asking is, are we picking up any Spanish?": Los Angeles Times, October 6, 1981.
177 "What the hell you gonna do?": Los Angeles Times, October 7, 1981.
178 "They couldn't contain me": Sports Illustrated, October 5, 1987.
"The only way you can get by with nothing but a fastball": Ibid.
179 "You need to raise that goddamn cap up": Dave Stewart interview.
"The key to getting a hitter out": Ibid.
"[The Astros are] not a home-run hitting team": Orange County Register, October 7, 1981.
181 "criminal": Los Angeles Times, October 8, 1981.
182 "I haven't done anything good in this series": Ibid.
"We did what we do best": Ibid.
183 "No team has ever come from 0-2 down": Ibid.
"You guys aren't going to lose this next one": Steve Garvey interview.
184 "All we have to win is three games in a row": Los Angeles Times, October 10, 1981.
185 "nothing we hadn't heard before": Ibid.
"I thought it went over pretty well": Steve Garvey interview.
186 "I imagine somebody must have had a pitch like this": Sports Illustrated, May 15, 1972.
"Three and a half years after I got there": Burt Hooton interview.
187 "the best young pitcher I've ever seen": Los Angeles Times, September 23, 1975.
"I'm thinking, there ain't no way I'm playing for this guy": Burt Hooton interview.
"a big blob": The Sporting News, April 17, 1982.
188 "If you ain't shot for a while": The Sporting News, May 24, 1975.
"Look at him": Los Angeles Times, October 14, 1981.
"[Lasorda's] vision pierced Hooton's blubber": 1981 Los Angeles Dodgers yearbook.
189 "Happy's idea of a high-five": Rick Monday with Ken Gurnick, Tales from the Los Angeles Dodgers Dugout: A Collection of the Greatest Dodgers Stories Ever Told (New York: Sports Publishing, 2013).
"What happened to their bats": Burt Hooton interview.
"Maybe there is a psychological factor": Sahadi, The LA Dodgers.
"was when the Astros plane landed": Orange County Register, October 10, 1981.
"You played like a Trojan!": Los Angeles Times, October 10, 1981.

190 *"Thanks, Jerry"*: *Orange County Register*, October 12, 1981.
   "My son is tough to hit in twilight": *Los Angeles Times*, October 10, 1981.
191 *"I wish I'd had that kind of poise"*: *Los Angeles Times*, October 11, 1981.
   "that ball would not have gone out of the Astrodome": *Orange County Register*,
   October 10, 1981.
   "I'm sure if you ask them": *Los Angeles Times*, October 10, 1981.
192 *"trying to throw the ball through the backstop"*: *Los Angeles Times*, October 12,
   1981.
   "He throws it and you can't see it": Sahadi, *The LA Dodgers*.
193 *"I felt like calling the National Guard for help"*: *Los Angeles Times*, October 12,
   1981.
   "Something changed with Nolan": Jerry Reuss interview.
194 *"I was thinking shades of Mickey Owen"*: *Los Angeles Times*, October 12, 1981.
   "Fernando Valenzuela, who led the team": *Ibid*.
195 *"I believe in something called the last breath"*: *The Sporting News*, October 24,
   1981.

10. Tundra

197 *"He is so fast"*: *Los Angeles Times*, October 15, 1981.
   "Raines signed with Montreal four years ago": *Ibid*.
198 *"Anyone can go out with good stuff and win"*: *Los Angeles Times*, October 14,
   1981.
   "Are your pitchers at their peak?": *Ibid*.
   "I've done my work": *New York Times*, October 13, 1981.
199 *"When you get a player back"*: Steve Yeager interview.
   "There's no question we're a better club": *New York Times*, October 13, 1981.
   "I was ready to play": Ron Cey interview.
   "He's amazing": *Christian Science Monitor*, October 22, 1981.
201 *"Ray Burris . . . Can you believe that?"*: Ken Landreaux interview.
   "You can't pitch undernourished": *Los Angeles Times*, October 14, 1981.
202 *"Gentlemen, bring your long underwear"*: *Los Angeles Times*, October 16, 1981.
   "The best way for me to describe the weather in Montréal": *Ibid*.
203 *"From Burris to B-r-r-r."*: *Los Angeles Examiner*, cited in *The Sporting News*, Oc-
   tober 31, 1981.
   The *Boston Globe* mentioned: *Boston Globe*, October 16, 1981.
   "The less you talk about it, the better": *New York Times*, October 16, 1981.
   "We just have to put it out of our minds": *Ibid*.
   "at least we have a Penguin on our team": Lasorda and Fisher, *The Artful Dodger*.
205 *"This is our weather!"*: *Los Angeles Times*, October 17, 1981.
   "This is not a good decision": Ron Cey interview.
   "We're out there freezing our asses off": Steve Yeager interview.
   "Whatever you do, don't shiver": Lasorda and Fisher, *The Artful Dodger*.

"Center field in Montreal is the closest position": Lasorda and Fisher, *The Artful Dodger*.

"where I was ahead when it started snowing": *Toronto Globe and Mail*, October 13, 1981.

"Coming from Minnesota": Dave Goltz interview.

"I just missed a few no-hitters": Ibid.

"It worked for me freezing my ass off": Ken Landreaux interview.

207 "the asshole of all time": Leo Durocher with Ed Linn, *Nice Guys Finish Last* (New York: Simon & Schuster, 1975).

"It wasn't like, 'Oh, we got Jerry Reuss'": Mark Langill interview.

"like a kid with a new toy": Ibid.

"That's a fine!": Reuss, *Bring in the Right-Hander*.

208 "I'm stronger": *The Sporting News*, July 12, 1980.

"It doesn't take a Rhodes scholar": *Sports Illustrated*, August 25, 1980.

209 "If you'd have given me a look at the lineup": *Los Angeles Times*, October 17, 1981.

"I never heard of a team holding a damn celebration": *Los Angeles Times*, October 17, 1981.

"Best dresser in the league": *Sports Illustrated*, October 26, 1981.

211 "a Loretta Young–type moment": Monday and Gurnick, *Tales from the Los Angeles Dodgers Dugout*.

"Since all of you have opinions to express": Reuss, *Bring in the Right-Hander*.

"All bags in the lobby by 10 a.m.": *Boston Globe*, October 18, 1981.

"I'm going to New York either way": Dusty Baker interview.

212 "Hey, Dusty gave me this parable to read": Ibid.

"That means that we all got to go out there": Sahadi, *The LA Dodgers*.

"Go get 'em": Ibid.

"I know my Bible pretty good": Dusty Baker interview.

214 "I wish somebody would get me some runs": Ken Landreaux interview.

"If he throws me a slider on the first pitch": *Gannett News Service*, October 18, 1981.

"Oh man, I'd have been screaming": *Los Angeles Times*, October 18, 1981.

215 "I like going out and beating the Montreal Expos": Ibid.

"The true essence of a competitor": Ken Landreaux interview.

216 "The roof was supposed to be on five, six years ago": *Los Angeles Times*, October 19, 1981.

218 "a number that my mom": Rick Monday interview.

220 "Rick Monday was an underrated tough guy": Lyle Spencer interview.

"When I was 17": Rick Monday interview.

221 "I saw Dawson looking up": *Los Angeles Times*, September 9, 1983.

"A lot of things go through your mind": *Orange County Register*, October 20, 1981.

"I didn't think that it was possible": Ron Cey interview.

222 "putting a little bit extra on my pitches": *Orange County Register*, October 20, 1981.

"It's time for a fresh horse": *Los Angeles Times*, October 21, 1981.

223 *"180-mile-per-hour fastball"*: *Orange County Register*, October 20, 1981.
"I feel very glad": *Toronto Globe and Mail*, October 20, 1981.
"That was a contract swing": *Orange County Register*, October 20, 1981.
"Go get 'em, you fuck": *Los Angeles Times*, October 24, 1981.

224 "I don't want any fights here": insidesocal.com, October 19, 2012.

225 "I had enough of that kind of thing": Ken Landreaux interview.
"It didn't last very long": *Akron Beacon Journal*, October 26, 1981.
"Uppercuts — I threw a lot of uppercuts": Ibid.
"We ain't the same if you ain't out there": Dusty Baker interview.
"There were a lot of baths": *Los Angeles Times*, October 18, 2002.

226 "My dad saw my friends as free labor": *Sports Illustrated*, August 23, 1999.
"I asked my brother Victor": *Sacramento Bee*, February 15, 2016.

227 "Son, a black man who hates white people": *Sports Illustrated*, August 23, 1999.

228 "I liked to talk a lot": Sahadi, *The LA Dodgers*.
"I heard the Dodgers had the best athletes": *Los Angeles Times*, October 5, 2016.
"Did your dog get an assist on the play?": Dusty Baker interview.
"Tommy [Lasorda] didn't really tamper": Dusty Baker interview.

229 "From the dugout to home plate": Ibid.
"Lasorda kept telling me, 'Dusty'": *The Sporting News*, March 18, 1978.

230 "Everybody probably had a complaint about somebody": Chris Mortensen interview.
"Dusty was the unifier": Lyle Spencer interview.

231 "This is going to cost you something": Dusty Baker interview.
"Six weeks?": Ibid.
"I learned to lock my wrist": Ibid.

11. Doodle Dandy

232 "That flight coming home from New York": Ibid.
"Because God delays does not mean that God denies": Delsohn, *True Blue*.

233 "We knew that most of us were going to be gone": Steve Yeager interview.

234 "Just get me to the Series": *Los Angeles Times*, October 26, 1981.
"I had a good spring training": Steve Yeager, interview, ABC-TV, *1981*.

235 "the brightest catching prospect to come through the Dodgers' ranks: *The Sporting News*, July 1, 1972.
"No ballplayer ever led a more active social life": Jay Johnstone and Rick Talley, *Over the Edge: Baseball's Uncensored Exploits from Way Out in Left Field* (Chicago: Contemporary Books, 1987).
"I'm eating from the four food groups": Reuss, *Bring in the Right-Hander*.
"I've never seen a guy who could smoke and drink coffee": Dusty Baker interview.
"Unlikable? I'm not unlikable": *Los Angeles Times*, October 26, 1981.

237 "we just won't hit it at him": *Christian Science Monitor*, October 22, 1981.
"I deflated ten pounds": *New York Times*, October 21, 1981.
"obviously losing it": *Los Angeles Times*, October 21, 1981.

238   *"Yankee Stadium was historic"*: Jerry Reuss interview.
        "I hope they react the same way": Los Angeles Times, October 20, 1981.
        "I pitched in this park once in the old City Series": Christian Science Monitor, October 22, 1981.
239   *"Enter at your own risk"*: Johnstone and Talley, Temporary Insanity.
        "I get tired of talking about the same stuff": Los Angeles Times, June 24, 1981.
240   *"When they decide to put up the Graig Nettles monument"*: Los Angeles Times, October 21, 1981.
        "sick to my stomach": The Sporting News, November 7, 1981.
241   *"take a little steam out of them"*: Sports Illustrated, November 2, 1981.
        "ugly, inhumane and dangerous": Toronto Globe and Mail, October 22, 1981.
        "I've heard that Reggie Jackson has got $82 this year": Los Angeles Times, October 21, 1981.
242   *"We begged them"*: Dusty Baker interview.
        "I have four basic pitches": Thomas Boswell and Walter Iooss, Diamond Dreams: Thirty Years of Baseball Through the Lens of Walter Iooss (New York: Little, Brown, 1996).
        "He had a sinkerball": Steve Yeager interview.
243   *"There's not a soft spot in my heart"*: Sports Illustrated, November 2, 1981.
        "We've got them where we want them": Ibid.
244   *"Sweep? My rear end"*: Los Angeles Times, October 22, 1981.
        "Do you think you can come back": Sports Illustrated, November 2, 1981.
245   *"You'll see a different team in Los Angeles"*: Boston Globe, October 22, 1981.
        "We just couldn't believe that that they could beat us": Dusty Baker interview.
        "a legend at age 20": Sports Illustrated, November 2, 1981.
246   *"knowing he could get in somehow"*: Dave Righetti interview.
247   *"That's what was on my mind"*: Ibid.
248   *"We were just a couple of excitable boys"*: Howe and Greenfield, Between the Lines.
252   *"What are you trying to tell him?"*: UPI, February 10, 1981.
254   *"If you don't give up another run"*: ESPNLosAngeles, June 24, 2010.
255   *"was all over the place"*: Los Angeles Times, October 24, 1981.
        "was like a championship poker player": The Sporting News, November 7, 1981.
        "I thought the earthquake was tonight": Los Angeles Times, October 24, 1981.
        "In my opinion, Valenzuela should be the National League's MVP": Los Angeles Times, October 23, 1981.
        "I didn't feel it": The Sporting News, November 7, 1981.
256   *"I've hit bottom"*: Los Angeles Times, October 25, 1981.
258   *"clinics for Little Leaguers on how not to play baseball"*: Arizona Republic, October 27, 1981.
260   *"I had it"*: New York Times, October 25, 1981.
        "I trapped it": Dusty Baker interview.
262   *"Where the fuck is Johnstone?"*: Johnstone, Temporary Insanity.
263   *"Jay Johnstone is not supposed to be winning World Series games"*: Ibid.

"Here we are": *New York Times*, October 25, 1981.

"They say I can't run anymore": *Los Angeles Times*, October 23, 1981.

"Does [Davis] throw anything else?": *Los Angeles Times*, October 25, 1981.

264   *"I guess it's that easy"*: *New York Times*, October 25, 1981.

"When you watered it, it would sit in the sun and bake": Steve Garvey interview.

265   *"The Yankees might not have liked it"*: Ron Cey interview.

"chickenshit hits": *Los Angeles Times*, October 25, 1981.

"I just wanted to shake it up": *New York Times*, October 25, 1981.

"Steinbrenner was predictably enraged": *Sports Illustrated*, November 2, 1981.

"That's a good question": *New York Times*, October 25, 1981.

267   *"It was as if all the locked-in tensions"*: *Sports Illustrated*, November 2, 1981.

"It's mad": *New York Times*, October 25, 1981.

"This game wasn't your basic Picasso": *Sports Illustrated*, November 2, 1981.

268   *"What a game! Wasn't it?"*: *New York Times*, October 25, 1981.

"I didn't know if we had it in us": *Los Angeles Times*, October 27, 1981.

"It was like a tug-of-war": Rick Monday interview.

"Our favorite hitter!": *Los Angeles Times*, October 25, 1981.

"As you can see, I'm used to this": *Sports Illustrated*, November 2, 1981.

"The pitchers can rest all winter": *Los Angeles Times*, October 26, 1981.

270   *"You can't hide out there"*: *Los Angeles Times*, October 26, 1981.

"The bases are loaded, one out in the ninth": *Christian Science Monitor*, October 29, 1981.

271   *"Somebody would have written"*: *Ibid.*

272   *"Goddamn it, just give me a run"*: Jerry Reuss interview.

273   *"had nothing to go home to"*: *The Sporting News*, March 27, 1982.

"[Commissioner Bowie Kuhn] was watching the bat fall apart": *Los Angeles Times*, October 26, 1981.

274   *"Wow. Maybe I should've asked for a tie game sooner"*: Jerry Reuss interview.

"If he had thrown another slider": *Los Angeles Times*, October 26, 1981.

275   *"I'm fighting the adrenaline, 56,000 on their feet"*: Jerry Reuss interview.

"Why did you rip us because of your misgivings in Game 1?": *Ibid.*

276   *"The pressure increased, hitter by hitter"*: *Ibid.*

"There's a different sound the ball makes": *Los Angeles Times*, November 29, 1981.

277   *"very loud . . . like it had hit a hollow log"*: *Los Angeles Times*, October 26, 1981.

"[Cey] was conscious the whole time": *New York Times*, October 26, 1981.

"His eyes were making circles": Paul Padilla interview.

"What do I look like?": *Associated Press*, October 27, 1981.

"I thought you were dead": *Sports Illustrated*, November 2, 1981.

278   *"Imagine what it would be without that helmet"*: *Akron Beacon Journal*, October 26, 1981.

"Anybody who throws that hard would have to be nuts to throw at someone": *Los Angeles Times*, October 26, 1981.

"Nobody digs in against Goose": *New York Times*, October 26, 1981.

"He'll play in New York if he can remember his name": Los Angeles Times, October 26, 1981.

"I instantly changed my mind": Ron Cey interview.

279   *"You're going back to the animals in New York now"*: Los Angeles Times, October 27, 1981.

280   *"We're still looking for those two guys"*: Rick Monday interview.

"I knew what Steinbrenner was doing": Jerry Reuss interview.

"Yank Boss Brawls with LA Fans": New York Post, cited in Sports Illustrated, November 9, 1981.

"If nothing else, Steinbrenner should be credited": Sports Illustrated, November 9, 1981.

"the injury is not expected to hamper his managing": Toronto Globe and Mail, October 28, 1981.

"There's a lot of George in Trump": Steve Garvey interview.

281   *"I was literally within a second of picking it up"*: Ron Cey interview.

"It's strange what turns your life can take": New York Times, October 28, 1981.

"I'm not going to endanger myself": Boston Globe, October 28, 1981.

"a local sporting goods store": Toronto Globe and Mail, October 28, 1981.

282   *"Getting into my frame of mind"*: Ron Cey interview.

"I didn't want to leave anything uncovered": Ibid.

"shadow dog": Ibid.

"How's it going?": Monday and Gurnick, *Tales from the Los Angeles Dodgers Dugout*.

284   *"frighteningly like human versions of the Ken and Barbie dolls"*: Playboy, June 1981.

"Everything in this house looked the same": Inside Sports, August 31, 1980.

285   *"pretty much [breaking] even"*: Steve Garvey with Skip Rozin, *Garvey* (New York: Times Books, 1986).

"He was lost": Sports Illustrated, April 12, 1982.

"It's a feeling I've had for, gosh, a couple of years now": Playboy, June 1981.

286   *"Garvey is the same everywhere"*: Orange County Register, September 30, 1981.

"the real backbone of this country": Saturday Evening Post, July/August 1980.

"That behavior — the kindness, the responsiveness": Garvey and Rozin, *Garvey*.

"Garvey was very careful in what he said": Mark Heisler interview.

"Garvey's image was real": Chris Mortensen interview.

"Practicing being an All-American": Cynthia Garvey and Andy Meisler, *The Secret Life of Cyndy Garvey* (New York: Doubleday, 1989).

287   *"with his boyish brush cut"*: Sport, April 1976.

"If Steve Garvey ever grew out of his Dodger uniform": San Bernardino County Sun, June 15, 1975.

"jealousy": The Sporting News, September 9, 1978.

"His idea of a risqué joke is right out of Tampa, 1956": Sports Illustrated, April 12, 1982.

"I was a perennial vice president": Playboy, June 1981.

"Sometimes you feel they get caught up": Orange Coast Magazine, April 1984.

288   "How, indeed, could a wide-eyed youngster": Saturday Evening Post, July/August 1980.

"basically everyone knows he's a public-relations man": Sports Illustrated, April 12, 1982.

289   "It was really a hallmark of that team": Mark Heisler interview.

"He knows he's not really understood enough": Los Angeles Times, March 29, 1978.

"the more exposure you get": Los Angeles Times, November 5, 1980.

290   "He wants to be one of the guys": Ibid.

"Boy Scout speech on unity": Los Angeles Times, November 5, 1980.

"Steve didn't have any malice in him": Peter Schmuck interview.

291   "The Isolation of Steve Garvey, Mr. Clean": Los Angeles Times, March 29, 1978.

"The number one question is, 'Is he for real?'": Sports Illustrated, April 12, 1982.

"The reason I'm doing the Playboy interview": Playboy, June 1981.

"I've known Steve Garvey since 1968": Arizona Republic, October 27, 1981.

292   "All you ever hear on our team is Steve Garvey": Washington Post, August 16, 1978.

"I'm human": The Sporting News, September 9, 1978.

"self-control is the biggest thing I have going for me": San Bernardino County Sun, June 15, 1975.

"the tone in which it came out": The Sporting News, September 9, 1978.

293   "no longer married to a wonderful wife and mother": Boston Globe, October 31, 1981.

"scruffy-looking, dog-eating guys": Steve Yeager interview.

295   "Yeager has started against lefthanders all year": Sahadi, The LA Dodgers.

297   If I get Murcer out: Burt Hooton interview.

I agree with you, Tommy: Ibid.

299   "I would not be able to live with it": Ron Cey interview.

301   "Tommy, you don't need a pinch-hitter": Paul Padilla interview.

"Ask Steve Howe if I can still hit a fastball": Howe and Greenfield, Between the Lines.

"That's a fastball": Ibid.

"You really didn't want to make the last out": Garvey and Rozin, Garvey.

302   "Well, Garv, it's your turn": Ibid.

"All I could think about": Ken Landreaux interview.

"You gotta believe!": Garvey and Rozin, Garvey.

"I've got the ring": Los Angeles Times, October 29, 1981.

"the end of a very sentimental journey": New York Times, October 30, 1981.

"It was a silent feeling": Sports Illustrated, November 9, 1981.

303   "I'm jumping up and down inside": Ron Cey interview.

"If I pass out, there are lots of doctors nearby": Los Angeles Times, October 29, 1981.

"We ought to get one of these in LA": *Washington Post*, October 27, 1981.

"We all know about death": *Washington Post*, October 30, 1981.

304   "Food fight!": *Los Angeles Times*, November 2, 1981.

"It wasn't that tasty either": Dave Goltz interview.

"It became like Animal House": *Mike Scioscia interview.*

"I thought I'd apologized for my sins": *Sports Illustrated*, November 9, 1981.

"It was the best food fight in the history of baseball": Jerry Reuss interview.

"A baptism of accomplishment": Steve Garvey interview.

"It's amazing the colors that you can get": Rick Monday interview.

305   "I'm glad [the award] didn't come posthumously": *Washington Post*, October 30, 1981.

"I definitely didn't agree with the move": *Los Angeles Times*, October 29, 1981.

"If we would have had our normal offense": Steve Garvey interview.

"I'm not blowing my own horn": *Toronto Globe and Mail*, October 29, 1981.

307   "I just want to put my head down on the pillow": *New York Times*, October 29, 1981.

12. Aftermath

308   "I swear, within an hour almost everybody was asleep": Jerry Reuss interview.

"We were worn out, physically and mentally": Rick Monday interview.

"It's pretty amazing": Steve Garvey interview.

309   "special popularity": La Opinion, cited in *Los Angeles Times*, November 8, 1981.

"I did not know I would hurt people that much": *Newsday*, November 4, 1981.

"Turns out that Yeag can sing a little bit": Rick Monday interview.

310   "There were some notes": Ibid.

"So you guys are actually going to go out and do this thing?": Ibid.

"What's your pucker factor?": Reuss, *Bring in the Right-Hander.*

"I'm the singer of the group": *Los Angeles Times*, November 5, 1981.

"I always thought that I was going to be the first one traded": Ron Cey interview.

311   "It was almost as if management": Mark Heisler interview.

"Garvey is to the Dodgers": *Sports Illustrated*, November 9, 1981.

312   "My baseball life started at Al Lang Field": Steve Garvey interview.

"The Dodgers think they're living in Camelot": *Sports Illustrated*, April 25, 1983.

313   "I was just sad on how it ended": Dusty Baker interview.

"Probably four or five years sooner than they had to": Delsohn, *True Blue.*

"I could never figure it out": Ibid.

314   "We have been treated like children": *Sports Illustrated*, April 5, 1982.

315   "Obviously, someone was angry at Dusty": Garvey and Rozin, *Garvey.*

"The Dodger image": Howe and Greenfield, *Between the Lines.*

"I was a good friend of Bob Welch": *The Sporting News*, March 5, 1984.

"They can make you uncomfortable": Ron Cey interview.

317   *"Once I told Mr. O'Malley I hoped to continue working"*: *Los Angeles Times*, December 8, 1978.

Conclusion

318   I don't want players who are pussycats: *Los Angeles Times*, April 3, 1977.
320   *"Tommy, come here!"*: *Grantland*, April 5, 2013.
       "I'm trying to manage a game, kid": *Los Angeles Times*, October 21, 2017.
       "Gibby says he can hit": *Sports Illustrated*, October 15, 2013.
       "Mitch, this could be the script": *Los Angeles Times*, October 21, 2017.
       "Hit Davis eighth": *Sports Illustrated*, October 15, 2013.
321   *"I've never heard anything like that"*: *Grantland*, April 5, 2013.
       "Someone should shoot this animal": *Sports Illustrated*, October 15, 2013.
324   *"The Dodgers are a very generous organization"*: *Sports Illustrated*, April 25, 1983.
       "The Dodgers had a peculiar idea": Mark Heisler interview.
       "All I can say is that Buckner was Lasorda's son": *The Sporting News*, June 25, 1977.
325   *"There's no magic to a team"*: Rick Monday interview.
       "We had very big egos at every position": Burt Hooton interview.
326   *"Reggie Smith was a strong force in our clubhouse"*: Dave Stewart interview.
       "Get off the mound": *MLB.com*, December 21, 2014.
327   *"The only thing you did wrong out there today"*: Ibid.
328   *"Anybody who ever thinks Tommy isn't real"*: Paul Padilla interview.
       "I don't think he'd ever admit it": Steve Yeager interview.
329   *"Tommy exemplifies what the Dodgers are about"*: Dave Stewart interview.
       "In everything that he did": Peter Schmuck interview.
       "Boomer, this is a democratic society": Steve Yeager interview.
330   *"When I came to the organization"*: Ron Cey interview.
       "It was good that [Cey and Garvey] were on the opposite ends of the infield": Dave Goltz interview.
       "I think Steve Garvey is synonymous with the Dodgers": *Playboy*, June 1981.
331   *"Buckner never talks in the mornings anyhow"*: Johnstone and Talley, *Temporary Insanity*.

Index